The New Promise
of
American Life

The New Promise of American Life

edited by
Lamar Alexander
Chester E. Finn, Jr.

Contributing Authors:

David M. Abshire
Howard H. Baker, Jr.
Philip Burgess
John J. DiIulio, Jr.
Francis Fukuyama
Michael S. Joyce
William Kristol
Frank I. Luntz
James Nuechterlein

Diane Ravitch
Carolynn Reid-Wallace
Alan Reynolds
William A. Schambra
William A. Schreyer
Robert A. Sirico
Abigail Thernstrom
Stephan Thernstrom
Paul Weyrich

Hudson Institute
Indianapolis, Indiana

ISBN 1-55813-053-5
© Copyright 1995 Hudson Institute, Inc.

Printed in the United States of America
This book may be ordered from:
Hudson Institute
Herman Kahn Center
P.O. Box 26-919
Indianapolis, Indiana 46226
(317) 545-1000 or 1-800-HUDSON-0

Contents

Part IV: Culture and Spirit

Part V: The Economy

Part VI: Domestic Concerns

Part VII: America in the World

Preface

Hudson Institute is pleased to publish this thoughtful set of essays by some of the nation's leading policy analysts, ably edited by Hudson senior fellows Lamar Alexander and Chester E. Finn, Jr. The volume is a major product of our two-year-old project on "The New Promise of American Life," chaired by Mr. Alexander and directed by Dr. Finn.

The project's intellectual foundation is a proposition that has attracted increasing attention across the political and intellectual spectrums: that the kinds of governmental and programmatic arrangements we have been accumulating in the United States since the Progressive Era have become ineffectual, even dysfunctional, and would benefit from fundamental rethinking.

That is why terms such as "devolution," "federalism," "delayering," "relimiting government," and "reinventing government" have entered our policy discourse, where they are uttered and written by individuals and organizations as varied as Bill Clinton, Al Gore, Alice Rivlin, Peter Drucker, Ross Perot, the Democratic Leadership Council, and the Cato Institute, to name only a few.

Part of what is distinctive about the Hudson project is that we have gone back to the dawn of the Progressive Era, to the ideas of Herbert Croly. It is no coincidence that Croly's best-known book, *The Promise of American Life,* first published in 1909, is again enjoying lively sales—though it has never been out of print—and has recently captured attention in the *New Republic* (which Croly founded) and the *New York Times.*

Croly envisioned—and recommended—a big, active central government as the surest way to realize the promise of American life. That's pretty much what we've erected in the decades since he wrote, and much of what that government has done was certainly worth doing. But today we find many Americans doubting that their children will participate in the American dream and skeptical of the national government's role in their lives and their communities.

This book examines those concerns with rigor, passion, and imagination. I am proud to have played a role in its initial conception by suggesting to Messrs. Alexander and Finn that they reacquaint themselves with Croly's treatise. They have done that and more with considerable distinction. And they are admirably qualified to engage Croly on the battlefield of ideas. Lamar Alexander, besides having been a two-term governor of Tennessee and U.S. secretary of education, is a former university president and the author of several books. Chester Finn is a tireless champion of education reform and a prolific writer, and has served in both federal and state government.

The New Promise of American Life also draws upon the insights of a number of the nation's foremost policy thinkers in fields such as economics, crime, religion, civil rights, education, and foreign policy. Its authors were charged with the task of envisioning an America that does not necessarily take for granted—Mr. Alexander's essay is clear about this—many of the assumptions about government we have absorbed in our classrooms, court-rooms, workplaces, and pocketbooks. It was not enough for these authors to explain, complain, or criticize. They have also taken the forward-looking step of imagining an alternative future.

Such visionary thinking is not new to Hudson Institute. Our founder, the late Herman Kahn, was known for his ability to step out of the limiting assumptions of his time in order to explore better ways of doing things. This book continues Hudson's long tradition of combining optimism about solving our nation's problems with healthy skepticism about the conventional wisdom. Renewing the promise of American life requires that we shape the future according to new ways of thinking. *The New Promise of American Life* offers an army of fresh and often provocative ideas.

I would like to join Messrs. Finn and Alexander in thanking their fellow authors, the Hudson staff who have served this project so well, and the donors who made it possible. This book is a collaboration between many individuals concerned about America's future, and Hudson gratefully acknowledges all their efforts.

Leslie Lenkowsky
President
Hudson Institute

Introduction

Lamar Alexander and Chester E. Finn, Jr.

Early in this century, at a time when many Americans were troubled by changes that were sweeping the land and unsure that old practices could meet the challenges of a new era, Herbert Croly, one of the leading intellectual lights of the Progressive Era and a founder of the *New Republic,* wrote an influential book called *The Promise of American Life.* In it, Croly supplied us with one of the clearest and most enduring descriptions we've ever had of the American dream or, as he termed it, the "promise of American life": an ever brighter future of opportunity and prosperity. This sense of possibility and progress drew immigrants to U.S. shores from around the world because they understood that all who came could share in its promise.

What made that promise distinctively American was that it was future oriented, limitless, and open to everyone who strove for it. Yet for many in 1909, he judged that the promise had not yet come true. Securing a brighter future for oneself and one's country was, in Croly's phrase, "an ideal to be fulfilled."

Croly had strong ideas about how that fulfillment could occur: primarily through enlargement of the role of government, especially the national government, in the lives and work of people and their communities.

The Progressive Era traces many of its intellectual and policy roots to Croly and his associates. They believed that the individual could not hold his own in a world of giant corporations and other large institutions. The village of yeoman farmers was not a suitable civic structure for the industrial age. Jefferson's ideas about democracy they judged to be out-of-date. The aggregation of individuals' self-interest did not yield a reasonable facsimile of the public interest. The pursuit of one's own ends did not necessarily benefit the society in which one lived, or so Croly and his contemporaries concluded.

What they prescribed for these ills was a much more vigorous government, a powerful, activist state that would play a far larger role in American life, setting directions, shaping behavior, harnessing resources, regulating the institutions of the private sector, defining the common good, and securing the general welfare.

As a country, we have followed Croly's advice for most of the ensuing eight and one-half decades. During that period, the United States experienced a dramatic expansion of the scale, role, and power of government, particularly the government in Washington, D.C. Government (at all levels) now consumes a whopping *42 percent* of our GNP. Along with expansion of government has come a commensurate increase in its interference in our lives, accompanied by parallel declines in self-reliance, individual responsibility, and private forms of common provision; government expansion has also eroded such traditional nongovernmental entities as family, church, and neighborhood.

As we enter the next millennium and exit what historians have sometimes termed the "American Century," we would be wise to evaluate the prospects for the American dream. Today, many Americans, especially the young, believe that the dream Croly hoped to make real has instead dimmed. The U.S. seems to have become a more cynical land, the promise of American life to have withered, and yesterday's sense of individual possibility and intergenerational improvement to have been overtaken by anxiety that one's children will fare less well than oneself.

We could be fatalistic about this, agreeing that our country's best days are behind her and there is nothing much to be done about it. But that would not be the American way. Croly had this one right: what's distinctive about our land is its unyielding belief in an unlimited future, the unquenchable conviction that tomorrow can be better than today. If we are discontented with the way things are going, we have the capacity—and the obligation—to do something to change them.

A "progressive" follower of Croly—today we're more apt to say a "liberal"—can be expected to recommend more of the same as the cure for what ails us: more government programs, more regulations, more activity in Washington, more taxes, more meddling, and more national preoccupation with White House pronouncements, congressional actions, and bureaucratic machinations.

The authors of this book think otherwise. We believe that Croly's prescription is now making us sicker. Big government has itself become a sizable part of the problem and a major impediment to realizing the American dream. We are not alone in thinking this. It's difficult to read the 1994 election results as anything but a vast repudiation by the American people of policies, practices, and public officials that have turned our government into a powerful brake on our future.

Why We Wrote This Book

The purpose of this book is to help blaze a new trail to the promise of American life. We seek to inject a healthy dose of practical thinking into American discourse and to outline a policy agenda for the years ahead. Only a few of the chapters that follow are retrospective. Most point to the future, combining restatement of a noble dream with pragmatic steps for realizing it.

Part I, "The Promise," serves as an extended introduction to the book. Lamar Alexander sets forth in broad strokes what it would be like to live in a country that reversed key assumptions of progressivism and organized itself around very different principles. Chester E. Finn, Jr., looks more closely at Croly's ideas, both the durable elements of the promise of American life and the cult of "governmentalism" that dominates our public affairs today. Frank Luntz insightfully interprets recent survey research data on how Americans see the American dream today—and what needs to change if they are to regain a sense of confidence in its fulfillment.

The authors of Part II, "What Sort of Nation?", examine tensions between pluralism and unity, between black and white, and between native-born and immigrant. Diane Ravitch discusses the civic culture that binds us together—and helps maintain our freedom to differ—at a time of widespread concern with ethnic and cultural diversity. Abigail and Stephan Thernstrom review indicators of equality and progress that bear on the oldest American dilemma, the relationship of white and black. Francis Fukuyama sheds light on more recent but equally vexing concerns about immigrants and immigration.

In the book's third section, "Government and Civic Institutions," we turn to government itself: what ends it should pursue, what is to be done about its scale, and what we might do instead if we had less of it. William Kristol argues that reducing government is an insufficient remedy and that we need a "sociology of virtue" at the heart of our public policies as well as a "politics of freedom." Philip Burgess scrutinizes the culture of Washington, D.C., and offers, as illustration of the bold steps that would alter that culture, a provocative plan for physically decentralizing the government itself. Michael S. Joyce and William Schambra go further still, asserting that America needs nothing less than a new civic life in which individuals, families, and nongovernmental institutions shoulder primary responsibility for the well-being of people and communities.

In Part IV, "Culture and Spirit," Paul Weyrich offers the bracing proposition that America does not need to develop a new or different culture but, rather, to recover core elements of the one we had in the 1950s. James Nuechterlein reflects on the role of religion in Croly's thought and in that of more recent Progressive writers (notably Reinhold Niebuhr), and cogently analyzes today's controversies about the place of religion in American life and politics.

In Part V, "The Economy," Alan Reynolds and William A. Schreyer examine the U.S. economy from two perspectives. Reynolds debunks claims that the distribution of income and wealth became less fair during the 1980s, discusses the growth of government itself as a barrier to prosperity, and examines the nature of today's jobs and job-creation efforts. Schreyer draws on a lifetime of experience in the world of business to offer some pointed conclusions about entrepreneurship, today's savings crisis, and government-induced economic problems that call for strong solutions.

The volume's sixth section, "Domestic Concerns," takes up a trio of key policy issues and sketches post-Croly alternatives to the ways they have been handled in recent decades. Father Robert Sirico weaves a social safety net that does not rely on government to handle such needs as welfare and health care—and will not produce the damage that too often accompanies government programs. John DiIulio, Jr., turns a powerful spotlight on crime, specifically the failure of our public policies to respond to the public's central concerns, and alternatives that would make our streets and persons safer. Carolynn Reid-Wallace argues that young Americans can gain access to a high-quality education if we muster the resolve (and political force) to overturn tired practices and dysfunctional policies.

Part VII, "America in the World," concludes the book by placing America in its international context and asking what policies are needed for the post–cold war world we now inhabit. Foreign policy, national defense, and America's global responsibilities are among the issues raised by Howard Baker, who discusses the interests and principles that should guide our dealings with other nations, and by David M. Abshire, who sets forth the essential elements of an "agile strategy" for handling power and achieving peace.

Why Keep Reading?

Herbert Croly wrote *The Promise of American Life* in response to troubling changes that the twentieth century had ushered in. Now, as we prepare to enter the twenty-first century, Americans are again troubled by changes sweeping the land and are as unsure as Croly and his associates were that old assumptions and traditional arrangements can meet the challenges of a new era. Croly sought to help the country think afresh and manage the turmoil of his day by writing a book that called for a national community, bureaucratic machinery, expert planning, and large-scale government provision of services.

Today, we are grappling with our own transition, but our program—and our book—involve dismantling many of Croly's governmental constructions and replacing their intellectual and policy foundations. We believe, as Croly did, that the previous arrangements are not working. In fact, they are contributing to our present woes. Our aim in this book is to do for our time what Croly did for his.

It is not enough to disassemble failed elements of the old system. America needs a new system to replace it. We need a sweeping overhaul of our assumptions, our priorities, and our structures if we are to address the gaping discontinuity between today's givens and the needs of tomorrow. As we search for ways to replace the outdated arrangements of the Progressive Era, we naturally begin to visualize alternatives, some of them as bold as Croly's were in his day.

A hundred years from now, another round of changes may demand that another book be written to renew the American dream once more. We welcome that possibility and suspect that those future authors will improve upon our ideas. Meanwhile, however, we hope to stimulate a useful public dialogue and perhaps a policy revolution. A century hence, we hope our book will be judged by the same standards as Croly's is today.

The chapters that follow contain a plethora of sound ideas and a generous measure of imagination. We urged their authors not to be constrained by current realities or old assumptions. We asked them not to get so immersed in the details of particular programs or policies that they obscured their larger vision. And we encouraged a sense of optimism, both because that attitude is itself part of the promise of American life and because we felt that little would be gained by a morose, vengeful, or backward-looking volume.

For every problem the nation faces, a variety of solutions waits to be discovered and carried out. Some are elaborate, some remarkably simple. Some depend on such old-fashioned virtues as common sense and hard work. Many hinge on our ability to recall the values that made sense yesterday and would make as much sense tomorrow—provided we can distance ourselves from the nihilism, relativism, and "politically correct" thought of today.

Lots of Americans are able to recall those values. Right now, in every corner of the land, people already know what we need to do and are getting on with it in their own lives and communities.

Lamar Alexander drove nine thousand miles across the United States and talked to such people about what the dream means to them and about their own efforts to renew it. He visited with dozens of men and women whose daily work attests to their faith in the American dream—and who do not conceal their exasperation with the big-government foolishness that makes it more difficult for them to pursue that dream for themselves, their families, and their communities.

To them, and to the millions like them, this book is dedicated, with the hope that it will help clear some of the obstacles they face and light a path to the future they seek.

Acknowledgments

We join the book's eighteen authors in thanking the many individuals and organizations whose efforts made possible both the volume you hold in your hands and Hudson Institute's project, "The New Promise of American Life," out of which this volume grew. Hudson's president, Leslie Lenkowsky, did much to launch the entire project when he recalled Croly's book to our minds and suggested it as a possible framework for an undertaking that then took shape around it. He has subsequently helped in a thousand ways with the project's evolution.

As the essays included in this book moved from concepts to drafts, Hudson hosted a spirited conference in December 1994, in which many people gathered to consider early versions of the ideas set forth in them. A number of authors participated in conference panels, as did Morton Kondracke (executive editor, *Roll Call*), William J. Bennett (codirector, Empower America), Robert Grady (principal, Robertson-Stephens Company), Sister Jennie Lechtenberg (executive director, PUENTE Learning Center, Los Angeles), Sarah Vandenbraak (assistant district attorney, Philadelphia), Rev. Dr. William Carl (senior pastor, First Presbyterian Church, Dallas), and Robert Rauh (principal, Urban Day School, Milwaukee). The audience asked good questions, the atmosphere was lively, and the essays in this book have been improved as a result.

Others at Hudson Institute who made extraordinary contributions to the evolution of the project and the development of this volume include Neil Pickett, Hilda Maness, Pat Hasselblad, Peter Pitts, Sam Karnick, Deborah Hansen, Denise Braye, Hazel Mayo, and Clay Sasse.

Within Hudson's "New Promise" project itself, deepest thanks are due to Scott W. Hamilton, Bruno V. Manno, Mary McCullough, Dylan Amo, and especially to Gregg Vanourek, who joined us after this book was half-done but more than made up for lost time, and who deserves considerable credit for its strengths (and bears only a little responsibility for its weaknesses).

Besides his essay in this volume, the survey research undertaken for this project by Frank Luntz yielded two earlier Hudson reports on how Americans view the American dream today. In combination, these comprise what is probably the most comprehensive body of data ever assembled on this topic, and constitute a baseline against which changes can be tracked in the future. We're grateful to Dr. Luntz and the Luntz Research Companies for a job well done.

The project is also indebted to—and Lamar Alexander would like personally to thank—the many people who invited him into their homes during his drive across America in the summer of 1994, and who took the time to talk with him about the promise of American life.

None of these activities and publications would have been possible without generous financial support for Hudson Institute and for the "New Promise" project from a number of donors, particularly Lewis Eisenberg; Dee Kelly; the Lynde and Harry Bradley Foundation; the John M. Olin Foundation, Inc.; JM Foundation; Winthrop, Inc.; Procter and Gamble; the John W. Pope Foundation; and the Fares Foundation.

Part I

The Promise

Chapter One

The New Promise
of
American Life

Lamar Alexander

This is a book about large ideas. What could be more important as we enter a new century than restoring the promise of American life and reviving our national dream? In this book, we dare to imagine a future that discards many of the assumptions that ordered our lives in the twentieth century and replaces them with convictions grounded in the best of our traditions and suited to our highest aspirations for tomorrow. These beliefs include:

- That the "American dream" is not rhetoric but, rather, what makes us climb out of bed in the morning and set off to accomplish something for our families and communities.
- That this dream can and indeed must be revived for millions of Americans, and that reviving it entails marking pathways toward it down which people can imagine themselves moving.
- That government in general and the national government in particular now place more obstacles along those pathways than they clear away.

- That the main engine by which the American dream can be realized is not government at any level but opportunity, initiative, and personal responsibility. The surest path to the promise of American life leads through ourselves, our families, and our communities. It does not pass through distant bureaucracies, experts, or policymakers.
- That a revival of our spirit, character, and sense of responsibility will go hand in hand with diminished reliance on government.

Most of the essays in this volume cut new paths toward the American dream or restore old ones that have become cluttered and worn. This opening chapter provides me with an opportunity to frame these essays with a few ideas—and some true stories. In such a discussion, stories can help. They're more vivid than abstractions. Sometimes they stick with us longer. They also grow naturally from my own preferred form of research, which is undertaken not in lab or library but in the kitchens, front porches, and backyards of ordinary Americans.

To be sure, solemn conferences of experts have their value. (We held one in connection with this book, and I learned a good deal from it.) But spending the night and staying up late talking with folks in places like Jennings, Louisiana, or Fair Lawn, New Jersey, can be as illuminating—and often more memorable. I did quite a bit of that in connection with this project.

Let me begin with a story about growing up in America. When I became education secretary in 1991, one of the major newspapers felt obliged to write that "Mr. Alexander grew up in a lower middle class family in the mountains of eastern Tennessee." That was all right with me but not, I discovered when I called home the next week, all right with my mother. She was literally reading Thessalonians to gather strength for how to deal with this slur on the family. And she said the following—which many American mothers might have said to their children in similar circumstances: "We never thought of ourselves that way. You had a library card from the day you were three, you had music lessons from the day you were four, you had everything you needed that was important."

Everything I needed that was important. That included a grandfather who ran away from home when he was eight, made his way somehow to the West, became a railroad engineer, and got back to the mountains in time to instruct all of us growing up in Maryville, Tennessee, that we should "Aim for the top. There's more room there." So all of us thought exactly that. We believed we could be a railroad engineer or the high school principal or the president of the Kiwanis Club or the president of the United States.

My experiences growing up in Maryville—not so different, I think, from those of millions of other Americans—illustrate what Herbert Croly called "the promise of American life." What is special about this country, what is unique, what no other country has in quite the same way, he wrote in 1909, is an almost irrational belief in our unlimited future and the certainty that all Americans—no matter what their station—have a chance for a part of that future. That is the promise of American life.

The first chapter of Croly's book is as brilliant a statement as I can imagine of the promise of American life. I wish every schoolchild in the country would read it (though, unlike the 103d Congress, I don't think the federal government should mandate that sort of thing!). But the first chapter is only part of what made Croly and his book famous. More important—and powerfully influential in this century—were his next twelve chapters, setting forth how he thought the promise should be realized. For Croly had concluded that opportunity itself was not enough, that individuals beset by large corporations and rapid industrialization needed help, and that that help ought to come in a big way from the central government in Washington, D.C.

And that's pretty much what happened. Herbert Croly went on to found the *New Republic*, now eighty years old and still influential (if a bit more skeptical about big government these days). His book and his ideas shaped many of the programs and actions of liberal progressives during this century as the New Deal was fashioned, the New Frontier was explored, and the Great Society was constructed. Many people still believe Herbert Croly was right. A lot of those people live in Washington, D.C. The 103d Congress, for example, was full of them. So is the Clinton White House.

The authors of this book think otherwise. We have undertaken to help ourselves and our readers imagine what America would be like if those twelve chapters were wrong, certainly wrong for our time if not necessarily for Croly's. We endeavor here to visualize an America in which "the promise" depends more on rolling government back than on reinventing it, a land where realizing "the dream" depends more upon the greatness of communities and individuals, families and schools, neighborhoods and civic organizations, than on authority wielded by the central government in every aspect of our lives.

The 1994 election reminded us that most Americans believe their government has grown too big, too meddlesome, too greedy, too controlling. But this was not the first election in which the issue was the arrogance of Washington, D.C. That issue has loomed large for at least three decades.

The Arrogant Empire

In October 1994, I was invited to California to help observe the thirtieth anniversary of the address that Ronald Reagan delivered in the closing days of Barry Goldwater's presidential campaign. That was in 1964, of course, two years before Reagan served in any public office. His speech—"A Time for Choosing"—became a landmark for conservatives. It deserved to.

I had been a student at New York University at the time, not paying too much attention to such matters. So in 1994 I went back and read the speech. In essence, Reagan said that freedom was our central value and that there were two great menaces to our freedom. One was communism abroad. The other was big government at home.

Reflecting on what has happened over the thirty years since he spoke, I think it's evident that communism abroad—what President Reagan later called "the evil empire"—has collapsed, and that freedom has spread all around the world. But big government at home, the other menace that he saw three decades ago, has grown into a sort of "arrogant empire" that now involves itself in practically every aspect of our lives. One down, we might say, and one to go.

Reagan observed in 1964 that, in twenty-eight of the previous thirty-four years, we had not had a balanced federal budget. Making a similar calculation today, we find that this is true of fifty-seven of the past sixty-four years.

Reagan complained in 1964 that the government in Washington was spending $17 million more a day than it took in. Well, today, every day, the government spends $643 million more than it takes in. In fact, *each day's* federal deficit is now almost equal to the entire federal budget at the time that Croly wrote his book.

But none of us really needs statistics to prove that the federal government has grown bigger than most Americans think it should be. Consider a couple of real-life examples from the two-month drive I took across the country in the summer of 1994.

Father Jerry Hill, who runs a homeless shelter in Dallas—and has been on the streets of Chicago and Dallas for twenty-two years helping homeless men—won't take a federal grant anymore. He said he is tired of spending his Fridays filling out forms to justify what he did Monday through Thursday. "I throw up my hands," he also said, when drug addicts walk in with a $446 monthly Social Security disability payment. "How can I help them if they have that kind of support?"

The former Cherokee chief told me that he could have eliminated poverty in the Cherokee nation if he had been allowed to take the money the federal government was sending for dozens of different programs and make his own decisions about what to do with it.

Henry Delaney, a minister on 32d Street in Savannah, Georgia, got rid of crack houses in the neighborhood by increasing his church membership, buying the buildings, and putting preachers in them instead of drug dealers. He wondered why someone didn't ask him what to do about welfare, because he knew the people who needed help, he knew what kind of help they needed, and he knew how to provide it. But bureaucracies don't ask. They only tell.

All around us, people are having similar experiences. College presidents receive thick, plastic-wrapped packets from their associations interpreting the newest regulations from Washington. Classroom teachers and principals struggle to make decisions about what is best for children in the face of hundreds of federal constraints. Congress passes hundreds of laws and rules about one's workplace and home that serve mainly to boost our cost of living and enrich plaintiff lawyers. The nation has had it with the meddlesomeness of government. People are tired of the arrogant empire. That was *the* issue of the 1994 election.

It was only a few weeks before the election, after all, that Congress—while reauthorizing the Elementary and Secondary Education Act—said, in effect, that Americans are too stupid to set a weapons policy for their neighborhood schools. So in fifteen thousand school districts, we now have, by edict of the Congress, a federally mandated weapons policy that every school must follow. If I am in the third grade and I bring a scout knife into school, my teacher and principal won't be allowed to decide what to do about it. A federal regulation will tell them what they must do. The message is that my teacher, my principal, my parents, my school board, my neighborhood, and my community are not nearly so smart—or trustworthy—as the United States Congress or the bureaucrats at the federal Department of Education.

Most people don't buy that. They didn't in November. That's one reason we have a different crowd in charge on Capitol Hill today.

The 103d Congress also told us what to talk about at parent-teacher conferences. It defined what a family is (and not the way most Americans would have defined it). It promulgated rules for "gender equity" in the curriculum and created the position of "special assistant for gender equity" so that Washington can help second-grade teachers teach little boys and girls how to deal with the differences between them.

The arrogant empire does not confine itself to education, of course. Consider length of sentences for criminals. The district attorney in Baton Rouge really doesn't want members of Congress, no matter how much he might respect them, saying what sentences ought to be handed down in Louisiana. He agrees with me that convicted criminals should serve much longer sentences than most of them do today. Except in the case of a handful of bona fide federal crimes, however, these are not decisions to be made in Washington.

Yet how to educate our children and punish criminals are exactly the sorts of things that senators and representatives and bureaucrats have felt compelled to tell us. The question the country has been asking is, as well intentioned as those people in Washington might be, as good persons as they might be, *who needs their help?* Can we not make these kinds of decisions for ourselves? Shouldn't we expect to?

A few months ago, we read reports that one of the government's myriad "civil rights" agencies was even thinking about making rules about what people could wear to work. We have a hundred million people working in this country, and there was about to be a new government rule about whether you could wear a cross or a Star of David to work. Washington seems to have become a city that thinks the rest of America is too stupid to get up in the morning and make good decisions about what to do the rest of the day.

The Roots of Centralization

How could this have happened in the great, big, magnificent, diverse, and decentralized America that Tocqueville described in the nineteenth century? Where did we get this impulse to centralize? To standardize? It has several sources. The industrial age is one. The belief that big is beautiful and uniform is efficient encourages centralism, as does reliance on assembly lines, simplification, and repetition.

Wars have also played a role. This has been a violent century from beginning to end, and we have naturally relied upon our central government to conduct those wars. That pulled a lot of power toward Washington. Toward the end of World War II, 90 percent of the gross national product was being directed toward the war effort. That meant, of course, that all that economic activity was largely managed by the federal government.

The media, too, have a huge centralizing effect. Most of our news—and the day's conventional wisdom—is issued through just a few television networks, a few magazines, a few radio networks. This tends to give us all the same information base and to establish a correct sort of thinking.

Television deserves special mention. Perhaps none of us yet understands its impact. But think of this. We were thrilled by the fall of communism, and we stayed up late watching as Boris Yeltsin, standing on a tank outside the Moscow White House, confronted tyranny and groped his way toward democracy for the people of Russia. What kind of country will this be? he was asking. What are our principles? What do we have to contribute to one another, to our communities, to our country, perhaps to the world? We Americans were riveted to our screens and simply sat there watching. We should have been—and should today be—asking those same questions of ourselves. Instead, we sat and watched.

We seem to be a nation that would rather sit and watch Michael Jordan shoot three-pointers than get out and try shooting a few ourselves. A certain passivity has been introduced into America by our television habit. After all, our five or six hours a day of TV viewing occupies time that could be spent on other things. And because we're watching more-or-less the same shows, seeing more-or-less the same commercials, listening to more-or-less the same commentators, and talking with each other about what we're seeing and hearing rather than what we're doing, our passivity is accompanied by a kind of group-think.

Experts contribute to that tendency. Experts seem to have become more important to us. As the world grows more complex, experts keep arriving on television to explain to us that what we think is right is actually wrong, what we believe to be true is doubtful, and what we doubt is in fact what we ought to think. No wonder we are confused and go back to watching someone sink three-pointers for five or six hours a day.

And—let's acknowledge it—one source of the impulse to centralize has been tough problems that demanded "central" solutions. The federal government has become more involved in our lives at times when it seemed that nobody else would or could, such as the Great Depression and during wartime. And anyone sensitive to the history of civil rights in this country knows that without the federal government we wouldn't have made the remarkable progress in combating discrimination that we have made over the last four decades.

I drove across the country once before, when I was a student in 1964. In that year, black Americans driving the same route couldn't have gone to the same hospitals as I when they were sick, couldn't have stayed in the same motels when they were sleepy, couldn't have eaten at many of the same restaurants when they were hungry. The federal government made a huge difference in that state of affairs. Put off as we are by some of that government's more bizarre "civil rights" policies today—college scholarships, say, that *only* minority students may receive—there was a time when Washington was a force for good in this domain.

The final large source of today's hypercentralism, I think, is the breakdown of key civic institutions: the family, the church, the school, the neighborhood. Today there are many things wrong with these essential institutions. Some of their problems were caused or inflamed by well-meaning actions by the government. But it doesn't take much to throw these institutions out of kilter. And when they malfunction, there is nothing—least of all the government—that can really take their place.

What Has Changed

The expansion of the federal government and its growing arrogance have been going on for quite a while. The early signs were evident to Ronald Reagan in 1964, even before the period in the late 1960s and early 1970s when so much fell apart so visibly. But Americans are not so stupid as the experts like to think. They sensed that all was not well, that centralization and big government were no longer good for us, and that the world that had summoned them forth was itself changing in fundamental ways. That Washington was not attuned to those concerns is now evident. The electoral jolt of November 1994 made that plain. It was like a major earthquake that happens when the pressure between the plates has built up over a long time and hasn't been able to release itself in smaller movements.

That pressure had been building for years. Father Jerry Hill told me in Dallas that his world changed around 1980, about the time Lone Star Steel downsized. He could see it as the people coming to his shelter changed. Instead of alcoholic white men in their fifties, they began to be unemployed men of all races in their thirties.

I saw the world changing at about the same time Father Hill did, when I was governor of Tennessee. People found themselves changing jobs every five years, and the new jobs they were taking were not much like those they had had before. Employees at the Saturn plant in Tennessee, for instance, now have to know statistics and estimation.

Jobs were just the beginning. Here came divorces and unformed families by the tens of thousands. Here came AIDS. Here came kids selling crack. Here came the kind of crime that caused elderly people not to venture out after dusk.

Here came the telecommunications age, with computers and satellite dishes and, suddenly, dozens of choices, options, and confusing possibilities. Here came schools that were not teaching our children and university professors who no longer believed that there was such a thing as truth to search for.

For at least the last dozen years, this has been a country in the midst of profound turbulence. Through the 1980s, we paid very little attention to that as a nation, but it was going on in the lives of every family. According to Dr. David Birch, during George Bush's presidency, 33 percent of Americans lost their jobs.[1] They almost all got new ones, to be sure, and many got better ones. But it's hard to say to a nation caught in that sort of turbulence that "the economy is getting better."

Turbulence is unsettling. It makes us worry about the future and our children. The promise of American life is harder to understand amid tumult in our households and communities.

Millions of Americans felt this turbulence but the government in Washington seemed oblivious to it—or paid it lip service, or made matters worse. Washington functioned in a time warp and, for a while, could get away with it. For so long we were absorbed by the machinations of the evil empire abroad that we forgot to cultivate the promise of American life at home. We defined ourselves by our international stand for democracy and freedom, and when that stand was vindicated we were caught off guard. We knew it was time to turn most of our attention to home, but we did not yet have a good understanding of what had happened there or a clear alternative in sight.

What we knew for sure was that enough was enough, that things we did not like or want had just piled up too high. The camel's back finally had too many straws on it, and it was aching. When we looked to see where those straws had come from, we found that most of them had been placed on us by the government in Washington. We concluded that that government does too many things we know perfectly well it shouldn't be doing. Instead of a source of energy to propel us toward the American dream, it has become a burden on our lives and a drag on our future. It is on a collision course with the American people, and the time has come to stop it. That's what the voters said last November.

Fading Dreams

Putting a bridle on an ornery government is only part of what we sense is needed. On my drive, I asked this question of many of the families I stayed with: "Looking ahead twenty years, do you think your children and grand-children will have more opportunity growing up in this country than you have had?" Most of the people I talked with were afraid to say yes. Some said no. And I thought what a change from the past this represented and how worri-some it was for the country. I thought about my own college-age children whose friends say they don't believe there is any longer such a thing as the American dream. I thought of children whose schools I visited as education secretary, children who gave me a book of their poems entitled "Farewell to the Morning." That's how they looked at their future.

And then I thought about "the promise of American life" described by Herbert Croly. In 1909, Croly correctly identified that promise, that spirit of optimism about our future, as what's special about our country. What troubles our country most today is that we're losing some of that spirit.

It won't be easy to revive. I see three big impediments. First, we may have become addicted to government, and addictions are hard (but not impos-sible) to overcome. Observe what President Clinton and many members of Congress thought of as "health care reform." Observe the welfare debate. What we *should* be doing is ending welfare in Washington and sending it back home to states and communities, to Reverend Delaney and Father Hill. But what many are talking about doing instead is "fixing" welfare in Washington once again. Even some of my fellow Republicans want to hold on to the apparatus of big government now that they have a chance to control it. We could make no larger error than to try to replace *their* arrogant empire with our own.

Second, there is enormous resistance to any effort to roll back the central government. We can already see this. A great many people and organizations, careers and reputations, jobs and habits, now depend on keeping the central government intact and spewing money, programs, and regulations. They must be expected to engage in what, during the days of the cold war, we called "disinformation." That was a subtle but relentless form of propaganda by Soviet agents that sought to change our actions and our views by getting us to believe things that weren't true. The "big lie," some called it. The evil empire was good at spreading disinformation. The arrogant empire has learned how to do it, too. Look at the stories and reports already circulating about children and adults who will, we're solemnly warned, be harmed by any significant change in the practices of the welfare state. (Look, too, at the arrogant empire's insistent denial that any harm results *from* those practices. Beware the double standard. It's part of disinformation.)

The third reason we won't have an easy time reviving the American dream—perhaps the most important reason—is because it's so hard to imagine things that are very different from what we've grown up with. We often wear blinders constructed from our own experience. This was apparent to me when we were designing the "America 2000" education reform strategy several years ago. We had the idea of establishing "new American schools," of actually throwing out all our old assumptions about how a school works, starting afresh, and breaking the mold. We asked people to look anew at children and try to envision what they might need, and then to create whatever would help them most. Many people responded by asking, "Well, what do you want us to do?" And we would say, "That's up to you to imagine." But this was hard for most people to do. It was harder still to imagine schools that would not necessarily operate 180 days a year, that might not consist of separate rooms, each with 27 children and one teacher, or that could regularly use something more technologically advanced than an overhead projector.

Similarly, it's hard to imagine what America would be like if, after a century of rolling the central government forward, we were actually to begin rolling it back and out of our lives. This book addresses the problem of our timid reliance on the status quo. It seeks to serve as a kind of aid to our imagination. We need to start thinking "outside the box"—boldly and creatively. What would life in America be like if it were really different from anything we have known? If the arrogant empire were actually to go the way of the evil empire? And if the promise of American life were to be revived?

Imagining the Alternative

As we try to visualize what the new promise of American life might look like in a land where the central government plays far less of a role, let's first identify some general characteristics of life as it has developed under the arrogant empire, features so ubiquitous that we tend to take them, like the 180-day school year, for granted.

The five defining characteristics of the present arrangement are these: it's *centralized, uniform, governmental, monopolistic,* and *no-fault.* Let's consider each of these in turn.

Centralized. We have what Phil Burgess in his essay calls a "mainframe government in a PC world." No, not "politically correct" (though that's a concern, too.) Personal computers. There are millions of them, networked every way you can imagine. Their ability to access vast troves of information and provide communications links with others enables us to work at home, decide things for ourselves, get answers to our questions from far away. Yet our "mainframe" government does not give individuals such power and opportunities. The arrogant empire still believes in centralizing because it believes that people cannot be trusted to do what's right and to make decisions for themselves. That's what brought us Clinton-style national health care, national welfare reform, a federal Department of Education charged with approving or disapproving state plans for school reform, and an Environmental Protection Agency that prescribes not only the standards of clean air and water that communities and manufacturers need to meet but also the technologies they must use to meet them.

Uniform. The arrogant empire believes that identical, standardized, and uniform are best. It has concluded that in all matters large and small, "equal" or "fair" must mean uniform. One size must fit everyone. There are national policies for students who bring weapons to school, for sex education, for gender equity, even for praying. There are national rules for how many months a person gets welfare benefits, national rules for how long criminals serve in prison, and national regulations for how every college must make its buildings "accessible" to the handicapped and every town must treat its sewage. Standards that say what *result* should be achieved are sometimes desirable. But the arrogant empire favors regulations prescribing exactly *how* all of us must get there.

Governmental. An ever larger portion of our gross national product goes to government. Today, William Schreyer tells us in his essay, it's up to 42 percent. That's why, despite recent indicators of prosperity, so many Americans don't see any more disposable income in their take-home pay. Look at how much government costs. Look at how much we've turned over to government: it runs the post office, the public schools, the trains. Government gives money to arts and humanities (inevitably politicizing these important parts of our culture). Government builds and operates public housing. Government sets milk prices and grazing fees. Government seizes our property, with little or no compensation, whenever it thinks it knows better than we do what should happen on a particular piece of land. Government tells us how to avoid falling off ladders at work. Government pays off our college loans if we don't feel like paying them ourselves.

There are, to be sure, some things the government *should* do: regulate the securities industry, make sure the food we eat isn't contaminated, operate the air force. But most things it does inefficiently and ineptly. Some days it looks as if even President Clinton has figured this out—though most of his efforts to "reinvent" government involve reviving it, or creating quasi–governmental corporations that solve few of its underlying problems. I cannot imagine why they suppose that the kind of structure that continues to bungle the delivery of mail will do a better job of air traffic control.

Monopolistic. Government is inherently coercive and monopolistic. It does not give people many choices. (The wealthy can sometimes escape from its clutches and buy what they want directly.) It discourages competition. It shuns incentives and accountability. Look at our public schools. You have to attend school, and unless you're well-to-do, you have to attend a specific government-run school—the one you're assigned to. You can appeal to the bureaucracy for an alternative but more often than not you will be turned down. Monopolies run for their own convenience. They do not respond to their clients. They do not need to. And when they're government monopolies, they're even less responsive. They use enormous political energy to fend off competition and close escape routes. Thus the 103d Congress enacted a fake school choice program. They claimed that federal funds could henceforth be used in connection with state or local choice programs. But when you read the fine print, you saw that these programs were restricted to government-run schools, and—incredibly—that both the receiving and the sending schools had the right to veto each child's decision. Question: What kind of choice is it if the place you're trying to escape has the power to bar the door? Answer: It's a government monopoly playing games with you.

Education is a particular hot button with me, but it's not by any means the only example of a government monopoly. We have no options about how our Social Security funds will be invested or the terms on which they'll be made available to us. We can use our IRA and Keogh savings only for things the government approves, and only when we reach ages that the government decides are appropriate. We have only one post office for our letters and parcels—unless, of course, we can afford Federal Express. The federal minimum wage is the same everywhere, even though living costs vary enormously. And so forth.

No-fault. The nanny state we've created, especially in Washington, D.C., frees people from responsibility for the consequences of their own actions, whether a woman giving birth out of wedlock; a criminal who knows that, even if caught and convicted, he'll be released from prison in a few months;

or the principal of a bad school who knows there will be no consequences for educational malpractice. Sometimes the nanny state even creates incentives for behavior that goes against the common morality. That's how we find ourselves with welfare programs that give more aid for additional illegitimate births and no real incentives to get off the dole, NEA grants for "art" that many find obscene, and "affirmative action" programs that confer and deny benefits on the basis of race or gender.

Centralized. Uniform. Governmental. Monopolistic. No-fault. That's the way of the arrogant empire.

Now let's try to imagine the opposite of each of these characteristics. That does not mean thinking as the arrogant empire does, devising more short-term "programs" to combat turbulence, enhance our self-esteem, or make us feel more "secure" (and less responsible!). It means visualizing strong and durable alternatives to the maxims by which the arrogant empire operates.

Decentralized, not centralized. We could organize our civic lives much as we organize our personal lives with the help of our PCs. States, communities, families, and individuals would work things out for themselves. They'd be free to do so. Washington wouldn't get in the way. In the information age, Americans in all walks of life would then have the tools *and* the flexibility to make their own decisions, share ideas, and develop their own ways of responding to problems.

The clear message that the governors have been sending is that states can make most important decisions for themselves—and would prefer to do so. That's why block grants and other forms of resource transfers should replace hundreds of federal "categorical" programs. That's why warehouses of federal regulations should be torched.

But devolution of many decisions to the states is a beginning, not an end. State bureaucracies can be overly centralizing and regimented, too. We need to get most of these decisions down to families, neighborhoods, and civic institutions. Today, the flow of information is such that people can decide a lot of things for themselves. Isn't that what freedom means?

Diverse, not uniform. The word *diversity* has become harder to use lately because of its embrace by the political correctness crowd. But America remains a big and varied country, full of people who agree about some things but not others. One size rarely fits all of us. To be sure, standardization is necessary in a few areas (for example, tariffs and air traffic control), but we end up fighting endless battles with each other when we try to make other things exactly the same for everyone everywhere. Instead of relying on a single national welfare system, each state or community should work out decisions about welfare for itself. The same is true of education; we don't need a single, federally enforced model of school reform. Each community and family should figure out for itself what reforms to make. Things work better when a diversity of choices can flourish. People like the results better, too, because they had something to say about how to achieve those results in their particular corner of America.

Reuben Greenberg, the police chief in Charleston, South Carolina, persuaded HUD to let him kick crooks out of the housing projects. He made those two thousand housing units as safe as any part of town. But he had to have Washington's permission first!

In Tulsa, the district attorney will put parents in jail if their kids don't go to school. This policy has had a dramatic effect on school attendance. In Henning, Tennessee, they'd like to have a code of parental responsibility and a curfew at nine o'clock at night for children under eighteen. That appeals to me as well, but it shouldn't be a national rule, applicable, for example, in Houston or Chicago. Neither should there be a national rule about school prayer or sex education or condom distribution.

Diversity doesn't mean flying apart in a spasm of pluralism where every segment of the society looks out only for itself and denies that it has anything in common with the rest of us. Our shared civic culture helps hold us together. But one of the central tenets of that culture is the freedom to be different—and the obligation to tolerate differences.

Private, not governmental. Much of what today is governmental could be handled by private organizations that are more efficient, more varied, less bureaucratic, more responsive. I'm not suggesting the creation of quasi–governmental corporations such as the postal service, Amtrak, or President Clinton's air traffic control scheme. Those are still essentially creatures of government with nearly all its shortcomings. Instead, I'm advocating real privatization, including churches, community groups, entrepreneurial firms, and the myriad civic institutions, small platoons, and associations that every perceptive visitor to America has noted for two centuries. Those are durable institutions that the arrogant empire, despite huge effort, has failed to stamp out. But it has weakened them. And its monopolies have kept others from starting up.

Instead of channeling our funds for cultural activities and for welfare and human services through Washington, for example, why not leave them with citizens to deploy directly? The tax code, of course, has a lot to say about this. What about a credit for contributions to organizations that meet certain criteria, such as helping to feed, shelter, and find jobs for poor people? What about insisting that government agencies compete with private providers for the public's business—and its tax dollars? Others have proposed that the arts and humanities might best be supported by providing individual donors with tax credits to encourage philanthropy, rather than channeling funds through federal bureaucracies. Similar reasoning might apply to parkland acquisition, wetlands preservation, and so forth.

There is also ample scope for government to charter or contract with private organizations to provide services that need not be delivered directly by public agencies. This is already visible in the schools of Baltimore and Hartford. Dan Biederman is showing with remarkable success how quasi–municipal services can be privately delivered in some of the most congested areas of New York City.[2] He is transforming several blocks of Manhattan, making them safe, clean, and relatively free of homelessness, by using a private corporation created by property owners. (This is in addition to what the city does.) And Biederman uses very "sophisticated" ideas. For example, the way he makes those blocks clean is by picking up the trash. He makes the city safer by stationing (unarmed) patrolmen on the streets. He helps the homeless by hiring former homeless people to wake them early and to offer them five dollars in cash, a hot breakfast, and a place to go to find out how to get a job. Sometimes private means commonsensical.

Private is not the same as panacea, but it's got a lot going for it. Ownership brings a sense of responsibility that government rarely feels. The profit motive brings a potent form of accountability for results. (Dissatisfied clients will take their business elsewhere.) The absence of cumbersome bureaucracies allows for flexibility and adaptability. Private enterprise is why the U.S. economy is so strong. We need to bring that strength to many of the domains that government has usurped for itself.

Competitive and free, not monopolistic and restrictive. In an America that allowed competition and celebrated freedom, families would pick the school that meets their child's needs—and schools that attracted no students would go out of business. Firms would compete with each other to provide the most efficient trash collection system for a community. People would make their own decisions about what to do with the funds in their IRA accounts, perhaps even in their Social Security accounts. There would not be just one "welfare office." Here, too, competition would foster effectiveness and efficiency.

There are a few things the national government should monopolize— defense, foreign policy, the currency, and the like. But we can count them on our fingers. All the rest would benefit from competition and freedom, which would also give us greater confidence in them. Contributor Frank Luntz's survey data—as well as the words of dozens of people I've spoken with directly—make clear that most Americans don't trust the central government nearly so much as their local governments and private (nongovernmental) institutions.

Moral instead of irresponsible. We need to rekindle personal responsibility and morality if we are to transform today's "no-fault" society into a society that fulfills the promise of American life. Sometimes that means encouraging good behavior, sometimes withdrawing incentives for bad.

Curbing government in favor of freedom is only part of the new promise. Just as necessary is what Bill Kristol in his essay calls a "sociology of virtue."

Communities can figure this out for themselves. I'll never forget going to Orrville, Ohio, as education secretary to talk about character education. I had not paid much attention to my schedule before I got there, so I was surprised to find myself in a room full of four hundred people wanting to talk about character education. I could just imagine what we would get into. But it proved to be a very interesting discussion. First, we spent a few minutes deciding whether we should have values in school. None of the four hundred people thought we shouldn't. It was just a question of what should they be.

Then the discussion leader said, "Imagine that there is a sign over the door to your neighborhood school and you only have room on the sign for a few words. What would those words be?" Out of the audience came all sorts of words. Then we began to narrow down the list. And those four hundred people, a broadly diverse group, were able to do that fairly easily in three or four hours for their community and their school. That, I believe, is the way to deal with these difficult questions of values and morality.

We don't need government "programs" to do this for us, or even to help us do it for ourselves. Michael Joyce and William Schambra point out in their essay that communities can heal themselves when given the right incentives. As they observe, "The inevitable tendency of neighborhood groups is to incorporate ever more activities into their ambit, until they have grown into genuine communities, within which civic order has been restored, the humble bourgeois virtues reign once again, and the residents once again feel that they control their own lives, and are fully self-governing citizens."

Those five adjectives—*decentralized, diverse, private, competitive,* and *moral*—strike terror into the heart of the arrogant empire. They are, for it, what the bucket of water was for the wicked witch in *The Wizard of Oz:* they actually have the potential to dissolve it. But they ought to be the watchwords of our effort to achieve the *new* promise of American life.

An American Dreamer

On my drive last summer, I stopped by Mount Rushmore. It's hard to think about driving across America for an extended period and not doing that. There were the familiar faces in granite: Washington imagining a country, Jefferson imagining what it could be, Lincoln imagining that it was worth saving, and Teddy Roosevelt just up there imagining. But Bill Janklow, the governor of South Dakota, said to me, "Go over and see Crazy Horse. It's even better."

I'd never heard of the Crazy Horse monument, but when I went there, this is what I discovered. While they were sculpting Mount Rushmore, Chief

Henry Standing Bear wrote to a young sculptor in Boston and said, "Come carve a mountain for us. We have heroes, too." And so after World War II, Korczak Ziolkowski began to do exactly that. And he continued doing it until he died in 1982.

It's a mountain so big that all four faces of Rushmore will fit on the face of Crazy Horse. Today, Korczak's widow and seven of his ten children are still sculpting away. And they're doing it without the government.

Korczak, I learned, began alone, building a ladder with five or six hundred steps that he would climb every day with a case of dynamite on one shoulder and a drill on the other. The compressor at the bottom of the mountain would break down several times a day, and down Korczak would come and then back up again to keep drilling. Twice he was offered $10 million of government money to finish the project. Twice he said no. He explained, "I have a dream of an Indian hospital, of an Indian college, of just how I want this monument to Crazy Horse to be, and if the government becomes involved, they'll have their own ideas. They'll step on my dream."

On my drive, I met plenty of Americans who, in their different ways, are as bold as Korczak. They, too, are imagining how their lives and their communities ought to be. They are working together to realize the promise of American life. And they're struggling with rules that, as former governor of New Jersey Tom Kean said, "make our country seem like Gulliver all tied up in our own regulations."

The people I met in the small towns and big cities of America are not winners of special merit badges or exceptions to the rule. They're more than points of light. They *are* the American way of life. They're working every day to recover and strengthen that irrational belief in our unlimited future that Croly said was unique about this country.

Reviving the American dream is a constant endeavor that mostly takes place at home, in church, in the neighborhood. It relies on the unwavering determination of ordinary people to do the best they can for their families, their communities, and themselves. The new promise of American life gleams today from the eyes of Father Hill and Reuben Greenberg, Reverend Delaney and Dan Biederman, the widow and children of Korczak Ziolkowski, and countless more of our fellow citizens whose lives attest to their belief that tomorrow can be made better than today for every participant in the American experiment.

Notes

1. David Birch is president of Cognetics.
2. Dan Biederman is president of the Grand Central and 34th Street Partnerships in New York.

Chapter Two

Herbert Croly and the Cult of Governmentalism

Chester E. Finn, Jr.

An August 1994 speech by Al Gore illustrates the degree to which government has become its own end within a certain political subculture. Addressing the American Federation of Government Employees, the vice president asserted that "If . . . many Americans continue to believe that no matter what the problem is, you cannot rely on any solution that involves the federal government and hope to solve it . . . that will erode our self-confidence to the point where the whole future of self-government is eroded."[1] He pledged himself and the Clinton administration to keep that fate from coming to pass.

Of course the assembled delegates cheered. The second highest official in the land had just tied the future of democracy itself to Uncle Sam's credibility as a problem solver. It was music to their ears. And the 1994 election was still several months in the future.

To his credit, Gore also said that government should become more efficient and responsive. Yet like the "reinventing government" movement he spearheads for the administration, the vice president's true goal seemed to be a more aggressive, vigorous, and enveloping federal government whose savings from efficiencies in one domain would pay for expansion into another and whose heightened credibility would induce the citizenry to want it to do more and more.

It is likely that Gore and Clinton, not to mention the former's rapt audience of public employees, could not readily imagine the alternative scenario: that *less* government might be a form of progress, that widespread dismay about Washington may attest to its overreaching rather than underperforming, that new efficiencies in the delivery of public services will yield savings that ought to be returned to taxpayers rather than channeled into still more services, or that the rationale for government's responsiveness to citizens' concerns has more to do with its role as servant of the people than with a need to burnish its image.

Yet such an alternative scenario seemed easy for the majority of 1994 voters to embrace. And by January, some of the White House rhetoric had begun to change. Clinton and HUD Secretary Henry Cisneros murmured the word *vouchers* (though not, it must be noted, for elementary and secondary schooling). There was talk of consolidating programs and shrinking agencies (though the administration pulled back from actual abolition). Gore even vowed to try to "find and eliminate things that don't need to be done by the federal government."[2]

But one does not have to be a cynic—or a Republican—to sense that the White House is swaying with the political winds rather than altering its fundamental course, a course so familiar that Washington follows it on *autopilot*. It is, indeed, the only course that comes naturally to minds such as Clinton's and Gore's. That is because they and their aides, advisers, and pals—and thousands of other policymakers and wannabees—came of age within a belief structure that might be termed "governmentalism." Today they not only lead the executive branch of the national government; their minds, their careers, and their political fortunes belong to the governmentalist cult.

Like members of most cults, those belonging to this one rigidly adhere to a few simple beliefs. They believe that Uncle Sam is the problem solver of first resort, that a federal program is the *natural* response to a need, a hurt, or a pressure, that a federal law or regulation is ordinarily the best way to cause something good to happen or something bad to cease, and that the nation's wealth belongs to Washington except insofar as the wise decisionmakers who reside there permit people to keep some.

The Roots of Governmentalism

Where did this cult originate? Its belief structure is rooted in history and theory as well as in habit. Alexander Hamilton anchors one strand, believing as he did in the virtues of a strong national government and vigorous executive as a means of safeguarding liberty and advancing the common good. Another root stretches to Lincoln, who in time of great peril for the nation argued persuasively (and acted decisively on the belief) that the federal government had both authority and obligation to do all within its power to solve that problem.

Seminal as their ideas and actions are, Hamilton and Lincoln were men of the eighteenth and nineteenth centuries. Closer at hand, both in time and in the character of the problems to which it sought solutions, is the third great tributary of today's cult of governmentalism. I refer, of course, to the period that Richard Hofstadter termed the "age of reform" and, in particular, to the ideas and policies we associate with the "Progressive" movement.

Weakly schooled Americans may suppose that this began with FDR and the New Deal. In reality, its origins are several decades older. One of the most eloquent and perceptive (if idiosyncratic) expressions of its ideas is found in Herbert Croly's celebrated 1909 book, *The Promise of American Life.* Here one encounters the way of thinking—stated with unfailing passion if not always with clarity—that has since manifested itself in Wilsonian progressivism, the New Deal, and the Great Society, as well as in today's impulses to "reinvent" government, transform the health care delivery system, and combat crime, ignorance, and solid waste through new federal programs. Progressivism, in several manifestations and with only a few short detours, has been the dominant political ethos of twentieth-century America.

Croly's great work contains all three of the reformer's essential elements: an articulate critique of the society he inhabited, a large vision of what that society should instead be like, and a plan for realizing his vision by setting right those things that he judged to have gone wrong. Best of all—and, as it turns out, most enduring—he had a general framework within which to place both diagnosis and prescription.

Defining the Promise

That framework bears attention today, even by those who have scant use for what Croly placed inside. It remains an uplifting rendition of "the promise of American life" and an insightful discussion of the role that promise has played in our national psyche, indeed in our very sense of nationhood.

"The American system," Croly wrote, "stands for the highest hope of an excellent worldly life that mankind has yet ventured—the hope that men can be improved without being fettered, that they can be saved without even vicariously being nailed to the cross."[3]

Implied in that sentence and spelled out in his lengthier exegesis of "the promise of American life" are five key elements:

First, the idea of progress. As Croly saw it, one is better off in America than in the distant land from which one came—no matter where that was. Thus the journey to U.S. shores is itself a form of progress. But it is only the beginning. Each tomorrow can be an improvement upon every today. One's children can reasonably be expected to lead a better life than oneself. "[I]n spite of . . . obstacles and pitfalls," Croly wrote, "our country is still figured in the imagination of its citizens as the Land of Promise. They still believe that somehow and sometime something better will happen to good Americans than has happened to men in any other country; and this belief, vague, inno-cent, and uninformed though it be, is the expression of an essential con-stituent of our national ideal. . . . From the beginning Americans have been anticipating and projecting a better future."

Second, economic opportunity. Croly was convinced that through hard work one can become prosperous here, with no real limit to what one can accomplish for oneself and one's family. Unshakable confidence in the attain-ability of prosperity is the keystone of the American dream. But he did not see that prosperity as something that would land unbidden on one's doorstep, while one reclines on the sofa.

Third, political liberty. "[T]his economic independence and prosperity," Croly wrote, "has always been absolutely associated in the American mind with free political institutions." At their core, of course, were freedom from oppression and persecution; the right to speak, worship, and associate as one wished; and the ability to choose those who do the governing and to insist that they remain servants of the people, not its masters.

Fourth, goodness or virtue, arising from a "greater faith in the excellence of human nature." As Croly saw it, the American dream is not wholly materi-alistic, much less hedonistic. It has a large moral and ethical component: "The implication was, and still is, that by virtue of the more comfortable and less trammeled lives which Americans were enabled to lead, they would con-stitute a better society and would become in general a worthier set of men."

Fifth, what Croly termed "individual and social amelioration." The "bet-ter society" of America was, he judged, perforce a more equal and just soci-ety than others on the planet, one that afforded opportunities to all and enslaved none, that eased suffering while conferring freedom and prosperity upon everyone. Yet this "ameliorating" element of the American dream was not entirely materialistic, either. All who lived amid freedom and opportuni-ty would, Croly trusted, become better people, no matter how they began. Here, virtue could thrive. "The more consciously democratic Americans become, . . . the less they [are] satisfied with a conception of the Promised Land, which went no farther than a pervasive economic prosperity guaranteed by free institutions. The amelioration promised to aliens and to future Americans was to possess its moral and social aspects."

Not a bad quintet, that, perhaps as full and compelling a statement of the American dream as we have ever had, albeit more complex than a slogan or sound bite. Nor was it a static vision. Its enduring relevance derives in large measure from its dynamic character. Croly's was no one-night dream, confined to a point in time or to particular circumstances. As political scientist Everett C. Ladd puts it, "Croly saw the promise as a restless, never-ending search," different for each generation in part because each would necessarily build on (or seek to alter) the works of its predecessors, in part because the obstacles and challenges to realization of the promise were not the same from one period to the next.[4]

Indeed, the bulk of Croly's book consists of a valiant if occasionally tortuous effort to chart a new path toward that promise through the wilderness of changes in American society that he observed in the post–Civil War era. Much had changed since the Founders' time, and it appeared to Croly that many assumptions, institutional arrangements, and practices needed to be altered and modernized if Americans were to continue making their way toward the promise.

Problems in Search of Solutions

Though not all of his fellow Progressives agreed with his specific nostrums, they shared Croly's alarm over the problems the society faced. With few exceptions, those were problems that have continued to engage the attention of reform-minded Americans for the eighty-five years since *The Promise of American Life* was first published. The list is daunting:

- Economic and social dislocations came in the wake of industrialization. Huge corporations, matched by giant trade unions, were becoming the dominant source of economic activity. The yeoman farmer and village artisan were vanishing. Rail lines (and rapacious railroad companies) were forever changing transport and residential patterns. Vast concentrations of power and wealth, great factories (and sweatshops), hourly (and piecework) wages, child labor, titans of industry, tense relations between employer and workers—these were transforming workplace, economy, and society.
- Urbanization, much of it connected with industrialization, was changing how and where Americans lived. From the stable town with its extended family structure and sense of safety, people were flooding into the metropolis. There they found opportunities unavailable back home, but they also found anonymity, temptation, danger, and the sense of being completely on their own with no support system.

- Social hardships, many of them also concentrated in cities, included miserable living conditions, poor sanitation, exploitation of women and children, destitution of various kinds, juvenile delinquency, and gross discrepancies in economic well-being.
- Sinfulness—drunkenness, prostitution, gambling, criminality, irresponsible childbearing, and other forms of misbehavior—was also much on the minds of Progressives, who may fairly be thought of as the moral watchdogs of their day.
- Environmental outrages were manifold: the filthy meat packing practices chronicled by Upton Sinclair, rats and bad hygiene in the cities, the threats to great natural resources that led Theodore Roosevelt to put Yellowstone under federal protection as the first national park, and so forth.
- Immigration was changing the nation's demography, rendering it considerably more diverse and, particularly as people flooded in from the less familiar latitudes, raising questions about how the newcomers could be assimilated, what their peculiar ways would do to the American culture (and "racial stock"), and how the social problems they brought with them—or fell prey to upon arrival—might be solved.
- Older race issues had also taken a different twist. The Civil War was not long over, Reconstruction was even closer in memory, and America's black population, while legally free and officially equal, was still much affected by the legacy of slavery. The Supreme Court had decided *Plessy v. Ferguson,* and separate-but-(seldom)-equal was the rule. As for women, female suffrage was not a new idea, but ratification of the Nineteenth Amendment was still eleven years in the future.
- Political corruption, bossism, and rampant patronage were widespread, as was a sense that popular government was vanishing.

Any one of these could have been judged a vexing problem. Put them together, as the Progressives tended to do, and it is understandable why many judged the "system" itself to be in need of a top-to-bottom overhaul.

The Progressive Schism

It was, of course, the tension between such worrying developments and the lofty "promise of American life" that animated Croly and his associates to press for reforms. After all, it is the perception of a bridgeable gap between what exists and what could be that stirs the reform spirit. More is required than the presence of distress. Also vital is the belief that something can be done about it.

In many lands, harsh circumstances coexist with an attitude of fatalism or determinism: that what is was meant to be and there is nothing to be done about it. (India is a compelling example.) In America, by contrast, the belief in progress was endemic, the spirit of reform its boon companion. Here, from the beginning, we have trusted that things need not forever be as they are today. Men and women have been free to imagine what a different arrangement might be like for themselves and their society, and to act on the assumption that purposeful human effort could make that dream come true.

As to what should be done to right the wrongs sketched above, the Progressives split into two camps. Both believed that a more active and interventionist government was needed. In that fundamental respect they differed from conservatives of their day, people who generally felt that all was well, or that whatever was wrong would rectify itself so long as government did not interfere, or that tolerating the problems of the moment was a price worth paying for the extraordinary gains the society (and especially the vibrant U.S. economy) was also making.

Within progressivism, however, there was a schism of no small significance (one that interestingly parallels today's main fault line within conservatism). One major faction sought a renaissance of individualism, of Jeffersonianism, of individual rights and small-scale enterprise, of trust-busting, trade unions, and "fair" competition, of direct democracy, clean government, and popular participation in important decisions. True, government would have to intervene to bring all this about, but this faction did not particularly want government itself to take on a lasting role as the eight-hundred-pound gorilla at the garden party.

Brandeis, the early Wilson, and—sometimes—Theodore Roosevelt embodied this strand of progressivism. Government, they believed, needed to be strong enough to break up the trusts and keep anybody from gaining too much economic or political power, but it was not to take sides or tell people how to live. As Hofstadter puts it:

> If the power of the state had to be built up, it would be more important than it had ever been that the state be a neutral state which would realize as fully as possible the preference of the middle-class public for moderation, impartiality, and "law." If big business sought favoritism and privilege, then the state must be powerful enough to be more than a match for business. But the state must not be anti-business . . . ; it must be severely neutral among all the special interests in society, subordinating each to the common interest and dealing out even-handed justice to all.[5]

Herbert Croly thought otherwise. He had little use for Jefferson, whom he accused of "intellectual superficiality and insincerity," even—amazingly—of "pervert[ing] the American democratic idea." Nor did he think much of "equal rights" as a remedy for what ailed the nation. Because some people were naturally stronger and more capable, Croly reasoned, they would inevitably take advantage of more open competition to advance themselves, consolidate their gains, and thereby foster inequality and discrimination. Neither was he disposed to the trustbusters' strategy of leveling the playing field by barring large concentrations of economic might. He saw big corporations as an inevitable consequence of industrialization and as sources of efficiency that he prized. Rather than restore competition by busting them up or stamping them out, Croly proposed that they be allowed to grow—but that the federal government also be made to grow apace, equipped with whatever powers it needed to harness the corporations to the national interest, even the power to nationalize them.

Like other Progressives, Croly despised special interests, but he did not think that a neutral government that allowed them to duke it out with one another would lead to an acceptable version of the national interest. (He did not find labor unions, for example, any more selfless than corporations, and he fretted that the allegiance they commanded was distracting their members from pursuit of "the American ideal.")

Nor had Croly much use for the mechanisms of direct democracy, believing that, in addition to being costly, cumbersome, and inefficient, they would confer greater power on political bosses. "The way to make votes important and effective," he wrote, "is not to increase but to diminish their number. A democracy has no interest in making good government complicated, difficult, and costly. It has, on the contrary, every interest in so simplifying its machinery that only decisive decisions and choices are submitted to the voter. . . . The cost of government in time, ability, training, and energy should fall not upon the followers but upon the leaders...."

Those "leaders" were hugely important to Croly: the embodiment of wisdom, virtue, and clear-eyed pursuit of the "national interest." He had immense admiration for elites and experts who, he assumed, would be selfless, public-spirited, and forceful. (Croly himself was pale, mild, and timid. Eric Goldman describes him as a "waterish little man.") His reverence for Lincoln knew no bounds. The job of leaders, as he saw it, was to be visionary, vigorous, and decisive. He had no great faith in legislatures. A strong and largely unfettered (though ultimately accountable) executive was his preference. This was not antidemocratic, at least as Croly construed democracy, which had less to do with rights and freedoms and more to do with the universal fulfillment of national aspirations.

His approach to realizing "the promise" via national leadership was in important respects the forerunner of what came to be known in the Thatcher years as the "nanny state": minding people's business, deciding what was right, and employing the instrumentalities of a powerful central government to make that happen. In Croly's pages we can also find the seeds of what today is called "industrial policy." And it is not far-fetched to see in his book a more benign version of ideas that a quarter century after him would be labeled "national socialism." Strip away the wrapper of democracy and popular accountability and one finds something menacing, as when Croly wrote approvingly of "the American state," that is, the federal government, "becoming responsible for the subordination of the individual to the demand of a dominant and constructive national purpose."

"Advanced Progressivism" Prevails

The two strands of progressivism—we can think of them as Jeffersonian and Hamiltonian, though Croly's era dubbed them the "New Freedom" and "New Nationalism"—coexisted for a decade or two, jockeying for position, vying for dominance in people's minds, and coming before the voters in their cleanest alternatives in the four-way election of 1912. Wilson then embodied the Jeffersonian version, Roosevelt the Hamiltonian, while Republican William Howard Taft was not any kind of Progressive. Socialist candidate Eugene V. Debs, on the other hand, was well to the left of both Progressives.

Wilson won, of course, but within a few years the Wilson of the New Freedom began to be overwhelmed by what historian Arthur Link terms "advanced progressivism"—a program of comprehensive federal regulation of the nation's social and economic life that was virtually indistinguishable from the "New Nationalism" favored by Croly. "Although adopting advanced progressive concepts and legislation required abandoning some of the ideological foundations upon which the New Freedom rested," Link writes, "Wilson did not shrink from the necessity."[6]

The distinction can be glimpsed by contrasting the Federal Reserve Act of 1913 with the Federal Trade Commission Act a year later. The former measure, characteristic of the "New Freedom," contemplated a "banking and currency system in which the private interest would predominate and the public interest would enjoy only a supervisory function," while the latter "committed the federal government to a policy of vigorous regulation of all business activities," a strategy typical of the "New Nationalism."[7]

By the time of the 1916 election, Wilson and the Democratic party had embraced the key tenets of "advanced progressivism." Many socialists now joined the ranks of Wilson supporters. Though GOP candidate Charles Evans Hughes equivocated on the domestic controversies of the day—America's stance toward the war in Europe was, in any case, the main issue—the present ideological configuration of the two parties was beginning to take shape. By 1920, when Harding won on a platform dedicated to the repeal of Wilsonian progressivism, the lines were etched.

Though Herbert Croly thereupon pronounced progressivism dead (and turned his own energies and pen to a quixotic quest for "the redemption of the individual"),[8] in point of fact not too much repealing occurred, and the onset of the Great Depression brought such efforts to a decisive end. The New Deal soon followed, as did another world war that galvanized yet more national— and governmental—activity. After the war there was Europe to rebuild, jobs to create, and veterans to educate. Perhaps it is not surprising that "advanced progressivism" and governmentalism remained dominant in our political culture, both in Washington and in many state capitals, with the partial exception of the Reagan years and pending whatever changes may follow the 1994 election.

Conservatives Join the Cult

Today's cult of governmentalism is generally associated with the left, and for the most part that is a valid linkage. "Progressives" or, as we are apt to say nowadays, "liberals" are the most frequent seekers of government programs, regulations, mandates, and incentives designed to produce individual and societal changes they think desirable.

But that is not the whole story. So pervasive is the cult of governmentalism in contemporary society that it has also begun to draw followers from conservative precincts. Today a number of influential figures on the right have concluded that government—even the federal government—should strive purposefully to shape people's behavior, attitudes, and values. Such an attitude permeates the Republican "Contract with America" as promulgated in late 1994, with its provisions to require work for welfare, enforce child support, and enhance parents' roles in educating their children. This is quite different from an older strand of conservatism—little changed since 1912—that tries to get government, especially the government in Washington, to interfere as little as possible with people's lives, families, businesses, and communities. (Within the Republican Party, that strand was embodied in Robert Taft and Barry Goldwater.) Today one sees conservative efforts to use government to transform aspects of the larger society that are not going according to their liking. Like their liberal mirror images, these are activists whose goal is not that government leave people alone but that it retool the society (and, especially, the behavior of others) in ways they favor.

This tendency is most visible in the field of welfare policy, where using government incentives and disincentives to alter patterns of "dependent" behavior is practically a conservative mantra. It looms large in strategies for reducing the crime rate by creating deterrents and punishments that will—it is believed—change the behavior patterns of those disposed to criminal acts. And it can be glimpsed in education policy, where a number of exasperated reformers concluded that student achievement will not increase until students alter their study habits and priorities, and that *this* is not apt to happen until public and private policies are reshaped to induce more studious forms of behavior. (For example: tougher graduation and admissions standards.)

Some thoughtful conservatives note that it is impossible to combat something with nothing and that if, as they believe, government programs and policies have become wellsprings of social catastrophe, it is naive to say that government should simply desist. Too many pressures will keep government engaged in the domains it has entered; hence the "realistic" course of change is to press for *different* government policies, based on one's own sense of what Croly termed the "national interest."

William Kristol, for example, contends that the "erosion of virtue's moral capital" has gone too far to afford the option of a "merely conservative" reform strategy, that is, a withdrawal by government from domains it should never have entered. Conservatives instead need to devise and press for what Kristol (borrowing from Robert Nisbet) terms a "sociology of virtue," defined as "a thinking through of the way in which social institutions can be reinvented, restructured, or reformed to promote virtue and to foster sound character."[9]

Not all conservatives agree. Some find the "sociology of virtue" an escape from the arduous project of shrinking government. In *Dead Right,* for example, David Frum argues that "Conservatives have lost their zeal for advocating minimal government not because they have decided that big government is desirable, but because they have wearily concluded that trying to reduce it is hopeless, and that even the task of preventing its further growth will probably exceed their strength."[10]

Perhaps that is accurate. If so, it is the clearest evidence yet of the irresistible tug of the governmentalist cult. Note, though, how Kristol advances (and Frum recognizes) a Crolyesque explanation for governmentalism among conservatives: the impulse to use government to narrow the gap between today's reality and *their* conception of the promise of American life. For today's social conservatives, that promise entails restoring the family, cutting the crime rate, ending the cycle of dependency, rekindling personal morality, sharply decreasing abortion, and reviving religion. In their minds, of course, governmentalism itself is only part of the problem; the depredations of modernism (described later in this chapter) are at least as worrisome. To fend off that assault, minimize the damage, and try to make their own version of "the promise" come true, they will do whatever they must, including capturing the instrumentalities of government and mustering its powers to work for, rather than against, what they believe in.

This convergence of liberal and conservative is less than total. A durable distinction between the two kinds of governmentalists is that those on the left are more apt to see the *national* government as the preferred agent of change, while those on the right often look to state or local governments (and to welcome greater diversity in how these tackle problems). That is a non-trivial distinction in a country organized along federal lines. Yet one must ask whether the difference trumps the similarities: the Crolyesque tendency, shared by many on the political left and now by some on the right, to perceive government as the primary engine of change and progress—and to construe that progress in terms of their own vision of the good society.

Ill Effects of Governmentalism

If, like Rip Van Winkle, Herbert Croly were to awaken in today's America, he would see us wrestling with a number of familiar problems: vast private institutions (multinational corporations, labor unions, media combines, and the like) that wield immense power; worrisome breakdowns in values and behavior; race and class conflict, stemming in part from unequal distribution of wealth and opportunity; sundry troubles brought on by excessive emphasis on individual rights; proliferating special interests; and a tendency to emphasize group interests at the expense of the larger public interest.

But Croly would also find other matters vexing us today, issues that were not so troublesome in his day but that have become sizable problems in no small part because we followed his prescriptions (and those of other "advanced progressives") for what to do about the first set. These newer—one might say "induced"—problems include vast government bureaucracies that brim with delay, red tape, frustration, and constraint; widespread dependency—both material and behavioral—on government for the wherewithal of daily life; and a concomitant erosion of individual, family, and community responsibility.

Progressivism must bear considerable accountability for today's cult of governmentalism and its legacy. Croly and his peers wrote a seductive prescription that, for the most part, the country has followed. Presidents from Theodore Roosevelt to Bill Clinton have swallowed vast quantities of the drugs they bottled. It avails us little to second-guess the suitability of those medications to the ills of the early twentieth century. But it is clear that few heeded the warning labels about contra-indications and side effects. As the century nears its finale, the patient is again ill, arguably sicker than before; and his current malady, like a grave infection one acquires in the hospital to which one came for a simple tonsillectomy, was caused in no small part by the earlier treatments.

Two symptoms are especially visible: fading of the moral side of the American dream, and erosion of the principle of subsidiarity.

Morality and Modernism

It is not surprising that, in turning to government to do more, manage more, control more, and solve more problems, we weakened the cables that connect us to spiritual anchors. Cults, after all, tend to displace religion in the hearts and minds of their members.

Americans remain deeply religious people in their personal and family lives, in their living arrangements and neighborhoods. Eighty percent of us say that we are "religious," and even more of us—eighty-four percent—feel that "a belief in God is an important part of the American dream."[11] But we don't bring that conviction very far into the domain of governmental activity. There, with a handful of exceptions (like "In God We Trust" on the currency), we find unbridled secularism. We have worked ourselves into such a tizzy over the so-called wall of separation between church and state that, in building up the state, it was inevitable that we would diminish the church. When it comes to public policy, we tend to enshrine secularism, even irreligion, in our institutions and practices. Though distinguished constitutional scholars say that the Supreme Court has distorted what the Founding Fathers intended when they wrote the First Amendment's religion clauses, so intricate are the Court's guidelines and so heated are disputes in this domain—consider the endless furor over prayer in public schools—that many Americans have resigned themselves to supposing that, if it has anything to do with government, it can have nothing to do with religion. Hence the cult of governmentalism (at least on the left) is wholly secular, and the growth of government has been matched by shrinkage of the spiritual dimension of our public affairs.

But governmentalism is not the whole story here. Advanced modernism (some call it postmodernism) is at least as important—and even more destructive of ethics and good behavior. For even a tautly secular government can be neutral in matters of values and character. Almost any kind of government makes and enforces laws, regulations, and procedures that foster order and regularity, if not virtue and responsibility. Had governmentalism been the only dynamic force in American society during the twentieth century, we would be a bit less worried about the moral collapse of that society today.

Modernism, carried to excess, is more pernicious than governmentalism. In its milder forms, to be sure, modernism brought us much of value, including science, rationality, and the principles enshrined in the Declaration of Independence, the Constitution, and the Bill of Rights. But like a benevolent bacterium that mutates into a deadly disease, today's advanced modernism undermines authority itself (that of policeman and tax collector along with parent, teacher, and preacher). It encourages self-expression and pleasure seeking without regard for consequences, blurs the line between right and wrong, and disavows rules of all kinds. If advanced modernism were in charge of traffic, people would drive on whichever side of the road they felt like, there would be no speed limits, and red lights would sometimes mean "go."

Modernism is a potion compounded from many other "isms": Marxism, Freudianism, relativism, pragmatism, scientific rationalism, agnosticism, poststructuralism, multiculturalism, impressionism, existentialism, and more. It is not about to go away, and few Americans want to return to the kind of society that was typical of premodern times (though some orthodox sects reject most of modernism's features—and are free to do so because of the democratic rules it gave rise to!). But advanced modernism has become a major problem in its own right. Some of its features—erosion of the distinction between good and evil, excesses of hedonism and irresponsibility, contempt for religion (and those who take it seriously), deterioration of traditional institutions and their authority, chilling of honest discourse in the name of political correctness—have damaged the social order. They have contributed to the problems we face. And they have made it far more difficult to devise workable solutions.

Croly and Modernism

Croly would probably be dismayed by these developments of the late twentieth century. He was only partly a "modern" man. He was, to be sure, a positivist, a rationalist, and an agnostic. His parents were ardent followers of Auguste Comte. Baby Herbert, reports Eric Goldman, was "certainly the first, and perhaps the last, American infant to go through the Positivist 'Ceremony of Presentation' into the 'Religion of Humanity.'"[12] But with that kind of humanism, at least for Croly, also came a profound moralism. He possessed a keen sense of the virtues, and urgently wanted these to dominate both private lives and public policies. (Recall his emphasis on "becoming worthier.") In this important respect Croly resembled some of today's social conservatives—and in this respect he also differed both from today's advanced modernists and from the "advanced progressives" of his own day. The latter were pragmatists who subjected ideas to tests of reality rather than morality. They cared more, for example, about whose economic interests were served by such-and-such a measure than about whether it was the right thing to do.

Over time, the pragmatists prevailed and Croly's moralism lost. Though perhaps less visible than the contest between Jeffersonians and Hamiltonians, the outcome of this tussle within progressivism was at least as momentous. We wound up with the worst of both worlds: the all-encompassing governmentalism of the "New Nationalism" *without* the moral foundation that Croly would have placed under it. Instead of being grounded in virtue, the governmentalist cult rests on pragmatic relativism and has absorbed the values (or lack thereof) of advanced modernism. And it is there, as Eric Goldman writes, that the "troubles come":

> Relativism encourages the most blatant kind of self-aggrandizing politics; if all ideas reflect economic interests, why not advocate the program that most directly serves yourself or your group? . . . Relativism easily turns into a doctrine of expediency. Asserting the impossibility of absolute standards removes any very compelling check on the choice of means to an end, thus encouraging a practice that usually needs little encouraging anyhow—justifying the means by the end. But justifying means by the end brings a difficulty which has been emphasized as long as men have taken thought about their mental processes. Means not only lead to an end; they can change the end; they can even, as John Dewey himself has pointed out, "become the end."[13]

Thus Croly's "religion of humanity" turned out to have little lasting influence on the Progressive movement. It went the way of other absolutes grounded in faith, virtue, and strict morality. Modernism won the public policy battle of the day. Governmentalism would henceforth be shaped by pragmatics rather than principles.

Meanwhile, modernism was winning an even larger victory: it was prevailing in the cultural tug-of-war. This took a while, but few will deny that its triumph is nearly complete with respect to the media, entertainment, the arts, school (and university) curricula, clothing, social relationships, family structure, sexual mores, much of our commerce, and even our courtrooms. In time, movies about vampires would be box office hits while few watched *The Greatest Story Ever Told.* Popular television programs would feature adultery. And murderers would be set free on grounds that *they* were the true victims.

Combine modernism in the culture with pragmatism as the foundation of an ever growing government and we find ourselves with a powerful but pernicious brew. Having now consumed vast draughts of it over many decades, is it any wonder that we find ourselves with a bad hangover?

Subsidiarity

Most Americans instinctively subscribe to the principle of subsidiarity, even if they have never heard the word, which is a fancy term for a doctrine akin to federalism. Bruno V. Manno explains it well:

Subsidiarity refers to a way of organizing and ordering groups to pursue common purposes and objectives. . . . There are two principal parts to the general theory of subsidiarity. First, it is against social justice for a higher organization in the structure of the common good to claim for itself functions which a lower organization can perform adequately. Second, it is against social justice for a lower organization to try to capture and claim for its own goals any organization that is higher than it in the care of the common good.

The doctrine of subsidiarity values both individual liberty and community. It is skeptical about the ability of large bureaucracies and corporate structures to centrally plan solutions to social ills. It believes the growth and development of human identity and community is best fostered when groups are free of incessant invasion, domination, compulsion, and intrusion by large outside forces.[14]

In laymen's terms, subsidiarity holds that problems should be solved as close to home as possible; that few issues should be escalated up the ladder from individual to family to neighborhood to municipality to state to nation; and that, when escalation is necessary, it should go no higher on that ladder than is necessary to get the job done.

Americans resonate to this way of organizing things. Most of us have greater faith in close-at-hand institutions than in those larger and more distant. We believe that people should look after themselves and their families, that localities should control their schools, that states rather than federal officials should make decisions about welfare policy, and so forth. A survey by Frank Luntz found that 47 and 52 percent, respectively, of the American population judge local government best suited to solve crime and education problems, whereas just 26 and 14 percent would entrust those matters to Washington.

Subsidiarity in operation is also evident in Americans' proclivity to engage in volunteer service, to join civic organizations, and to support private charities. We have scant confidence in Uncle Sam to meet our needs or solve our problems. We have middling trust in state-level action. Yet we have warm feelings about what we can do for ourselves, our neighborhoods, our communities, and our fellow parishioners. And we prize local decisionmaking, the nearer home and more participatory the better.

Herbert Croly thought otherwise. He did not believe in subsidiarity. Neither did the other advanced progressives of his day. Nor, of course, do today's governmentalists. It is not surprising, then, that the history of twentieth-century America can be seen as the tale of efforts to weaken and repeal the doctrine of subsidiarity by boosting as many social functions and responsibilities as far up the ladder as possible.

What happens in a society that, over a long period of time, plays fast and loose with subsidiarity, that elevates more and more issues to the national (of late even the international) level, and that relies less on the closer-at-hand levels to get things done? The underutilized parts atrophy, like muscles that get no exercise. Private institutions wither. The family weakens. Neighborhood and community organizations are marginalized. Local and state governments make fewer decisions of their own and come to function more as branches of the national government.

But atrophy is not the whole story. As Manno says, it goes "against social justice" when a "higher organization in the structure of the common good" takes upon itself functions that "a lower organization can perform adequately." In other words, the social order is disrupted.

The Opportunity at Hand

For a very long time the United States has been buffeted by both the governmentalist challenge to subsidiarity and the cultural challenge to traditional virtues. Though Croly himself can only be charged with the former offense, his fellow Progressives bear responsibility for both. So, of course, does advanced modernism.

This has wrought havoc in every direction. It is all the more remarkable, then, to note how resilient, even stubborn, Americans have turned out to be with respect to their own understanding of how things ought to be. Most of us continue to believe in subsidiarity and to affirm the traditional virtues. Granted, we do not always live by the latter, and—perhaps it is human nature—we are usually glad to have government shoulder some burden we might otherwise have hoisted. But deep down we do not believe that is how things *ought* to be. We believe that people should behave themselves and that any problems they cannot handle for themselves ought to be solved as close to home as possible. One plausible interpretation of the 1994 election results is that a majority of Americans decided that the time has finally come to act on the basis of those underlying beliefs.

If so, most Americans are right. It is well past time to do something decisive to curb the excesses of modernism and governmentalism. Modernism has brought freedom and pleasure, to be sure, but it has also undermined values we hold dear and institutions whose importance grows clearer as they crumble. Governmentalism sometimes protects us from harm, but it has also made us lazy and dependent while taking vast sums out of our pockets, curbing our freedom through regulation, eroding our sense of opportunity, and causing at least as many problems as it solves.

The good news is that this gap between what is and what we know should be creates, once again, an environment in which the reform impulse can flourish. In that sense, the closing days of the twentieth century afford an opportunity for fundamental change that resembles the age of reform at the century's dawning.

Renewing the Promise

It is clear that we do not need any more advanced progressivism, surging governmentalism, or modernism-run-amok. Indeed, any serious strategy for renewal of the American dream must start by repairing the worst damage inflicted by those three "isms." Other essays in this volume provide specifics tailored to particular issues and policy domains. Let me here offer only a bit of general guidance.

First, we need to rebuild the sense of morality modernism has undermined. We need what Kristol calls a "sociology of virtue" to give renewed public legitimacy to the values most Americans hold dear. William J. Bennett's *Book of Virtues* is not a bad text to begin with—and its popularity attests to the widespread need it meets. Some may prefer to turn to the Ten Commandments and other religious guides.

This does not mean that we need government to make us behave properly, least of all the government in Washington. The best examples—William Kristol, Michael Joyce and William Schambra, and Robert Sirico enumerate specifics in chapters 7, 9, and 14—are often to be found in nongovernmental activity. But surely our public policies ought not encourage, subsidize, or turn a blind eye toward bad behavior. And our leaders—political, spiritual, educational—need to attend both to the values that undergird those policies and to the signals transmitted by the culture.

Second, we should dust off and give fresh life to the principle of subsidiarity. (Kristol's—and Nisbet's—more memorable phrase for this is the "politics of liberty.") That means entrusting responsibility for problem solving to the lowest levels that can satisfactorily shoulder it, beginning with the individual and the family. In this connection, one important asset Croly and his contemporaries lacked is ready access to information. Technology can be a huge aid to the practice of subsidiarity, freeing us from top-down decisions (where only the higher-ups have the requisite knowledge to make those decisions) and from bureaucratic management structures. The information highway is a place where people can steer their own vehicles. They do not need to be bused.

Third, we need systematically to undo or radically to alter the institutional arrangements that undermine the first two parts of the strategy. Whether this means term limits, a balanced budget, shrinking the bureaucracy, reviving the institution of "citizen legislators" (instead of career politicians), or a hundred other measures, we must transform our structures into servants of the

American dream. Croly's example should inspire and embolden us. Quarrel though one may with his recommendations, nobody could accuse him of lack of imagination or zeal when it comes to fundamental alterations in structures, roles, and processes.

None of this means that society should ignore its problems, both those that have hung on since Croly's day and those he never dreamed of (such as AIDS, nuclear weapons, assault rifles, and illegal immigration). It doesn't mean we have any less need for vigorous leadership. But it does mean we must take on the cult of governmentalism itself, not just one program at a time, but at the level of principle, moral philosophy, and basic institutional arrangements.

Cult members must, however, be expected to wage quite a battle to retain their control. Governmentalism is, by now, deeply entrenched. Its cult includes most of the media together with tens of thousands of people whose livelihoods and reputations hinge on its continuing vitality. It also benefits from the carnage wrought by modernism. If crime, for example, is a problem, and if people cannot be expected to behave virtuously, then why not create a bunch of new federal anticrime programs? The cult seldom thinks of a non-governmental alternative or imagines that virtue is chiefly the work of family, church, and association. And like any long-established regime, it will seek to impose far stricter "rules of evidence" on reform proposals than it will ever apply to the present arrangement. This double standard is one of the most potent weapons that protectors of the status quo possess.

But that weapon may prove less reliable in today's climate. As the 1994 election showed, Americans are mightily fed up with the status quo, particularly in Washington, D.C. They are more disposed to hold it accountable for its failures and less apt to believe assurances that the "hair of the dog" will cure our hangover. As the gap widens between the promise of American life and the circumstances in which we find ourselves living, an opportunity for change is again at hand.

Fortunately, that promise, the promise Croly described—all five elements of it—retains a strong hold on Americans, both those who have been here for generations and those who have just arrived. Indeed, it is the potency of that promise that causes so many more to seek to participate. That is why, when the State Department recently declared a lottery that would confer up to fifty-five thousand immigrant visas on people from countries "underrepresented" in the current U.S. population, *nine million* entries flooded in. Six-tenths of one percent of a chance of gaining legal entry to America was enough to fire their own dreams. As the *Washington Post* put it, those "millions of envelopes stacked to the ceiling . . . carry the hopes of families from Bangladesh to the Bahamas."[15]

The promise of American life was strong when Herbert Croly wrote. That it remains vibrant eighty-five years later may be especially clear to those outside our borders. I believe we can do much to refresh and burnish it at home, and enable millions more to make it real for themselves and their children. But we'll need to be as visionary and bold as Croly was—and to channel our boldness in a very different direction from where he pointed us.

Notes

1. Al Gore, speech before the American Federation of Government Employees, August 1994, quoted in Edward Walsh, "Government Threatened by Cynicism, Gore Says," *Washington Post,* August 16, 1994, A17.
2. Al Gore, quoted in Stephen Barr, "Gore Urges Rethinking for Reinvention," *Washington Post,* January 4, 1995, A13.
3. All citations of Herbert Croly are from *The Promise of American Life* (New York: The Macmillan Company, 1909), and later editions of this work. In an effort to keep notes in this volume to a minimum, the editors have chosen not to provide individual notes with page references for each quote of Croly.
4. Everett Carll Ladd, "The Promise of American Life," *Christian Science Monitor,* May 20, 1994, 10.
5. Richard Hofstadter, *The Age of Reform: From Bryan to FDR* (New York: Alfred A. Knopf, 1956), 232.
6. Arthur Link, *American Epoch: A History of the United States Since the 1890s* (New York: Alfred A. Knopf, 1966), 134.
7. Ibid., 130, 133.
8. Eric F. Goldman, *Rendezvous with Destiny: A History of Modern American Reform* (New York: Vintage Books, 1960), 223.
9. William Kristol, "The Future of Conservatism in the U.S.," *American Enterprise* 5 (July/August 1994): 35.
10. David Frum, *Dead Right* (New York: Basic Books, 1994), 3.
11. These data are from a study conducted by Frank I. Luntz for Hudson Institute, published in a Hudson Institute report entitled "The American Dream: Renewing the Promise," Indianapolis, Indiana, December 1994.
12. Goldman, 148.
13. Ibid., 155.
14. Bruno V. Manno, "Subsidiarity and Pluralism: A Social Philosophical Perspective," in *Toward Vatican III: The Work That Needs to Be Done,* ed. David Tracy, Hans Kung, and Johann B. Matz (New York: The Seabury Press, 1978), 320.
15. Thomas W. Lippman, "Avalanche of Mail for Trickle of Visas," *Washington Post,* October 27, 1994, A3.

Chapter Three

Americans Talk About the American Dream

Frank I. Luntz

How times have changed.

Throughout our history, we have been a people firmly committed to the concept of "American exceptionalism," the belief that our country has a unique place in history and offers a shared promise of a better life. From the Federalist Papers to the Gettysburg Address, from Manifest Destiny to the "Final Frontier," we have written, spoken, and thought in terms of great ideas and limitless boundaries. Until now.

In an age of instantaneous communication, volatility of opinion is to be expected. The national outlook that once changed as often as the seasons now changes as often as the temperature. Formerly, America's mood swings were confined to the short term—a year or so into the future—and were represented by the frequently asked survey question, "Is America heading in the right direction or are things pretty seriously off on the wrong track?" *Nothing* ever affected long-term or intergenerational optimism—not natural disasters, not economic crises, not political failures. The belief that the next generation could be worse off than the present one was foreign to America. Until now.

Everett Carll Ladd, a respected expert on public opinion, wrote in 1993 that "the froth and turbulence which dominate the way public life is now depicted and transmitted to the citizenry, while contributing to a more skeptical if not cynical national voice . . . [cut] only so deep."[1] Ladd argued that the "national self-image, expectations, norms, and values [of America] remain in place, largely undisturbed." My research suggests otherwise.

The American Century brought victory in two world wars, put a man on the moon, drove two cars into most garages, placed a computer in millions of homes, and witnessed the creation of the world's largest, most affluent middle class. Yet even those who were least well served by the American experience—the low income, the less educated, minorities, and younger adults—differed little in their attachment to the American creed from those who had tasted more abundantly that which Herbert Croly called "the promise of American life." No longer.

As a nation, we have begun to question our achievements, our future, and even the viability and relevance of the American dream. These doubts are new to us. They trigger worrying questions. Does the promise of American life still exist for most Americans? Are America's best days behind us? Can the American dream survive? Such questions laid the framework for a comprehensive mid-1994 public-opinion survey I conducted on the state of the American dream.[2] The results are disturbing. They suggest a nation struggling to maintain its optimism, plagued by growing insecurity, and dissatisfied with its once cherished governing institutions.

For decades, Americans have been raised to believe that we enjoyed the most enlightened government and highest standard of living in the world. Today, we stand alone as the most innovative nation, the most free nation, and the nation most capable of global and domestic leadership. The American dream stems from all of these facts. Embedded in the psyche of America is the pioneering spirit of cowboys and astronauts—from John Wayne to John Glenn—all pushing for a common purpose: to provide a better quality of life for ourselves and our children.

This dream has produced a nation unlike any other—one not founded upon a common religion, ethnicity, race, or culture. The face of America is as diverse as the world; what keeps us united is the common thread that brought us and our ancestors to America: the belief that America is "the land of opportunity." Today, however, when you ask people whether they believe that the country is headed in the right direction, a significant majority says no.

As Richard Nixon wrote in 1993, "A new negativism afflicts America today. A growing chorus of pundits, professors, and politicians speak of the decline of America." Talking to Americans reveals deep-seated disappointment. The well-off lament the disintegration of morality in society and the breakup of the family. The middle classes hope for opportunity and prosperity, but they are far from certain that they will experience it. For the poor, hope itself is beginning to fade. The cornerstones of the dream—democracy, opportunity, and individualism—not only are threatened, but are themselves threatening the American dream.

Defining the American Dream

Origins of the phrase *American dream* predate the nation's birth. Following the arrival of Columbus in 1492, Western literature began to refer to "the dream of opportunity" in the "New World." In 1885, the term "American way of life" was coined by General Hawley in an effort to describe the constitutional principles of freedom and democracy. It is unclear who was actually the first to use the phrase *American dream,* though President Warren Harding was reported to have said, "I don't know much about the American dream, but it's a damn good phrase with which to carry an election."

According to the *Oxford English Dictionary,* the American dream is the "ideal of a democratic and prosperous society which is the traditional aim of the American people, a catch phrase used to symbolize American social or material values in general." In the *Dictionary of Americanisms,* the American dream is defined as "the reasonable expectations of Americans which are, by tradition, that all men shall be created equal." Those may be dictionary definitions, but ask one hundred Americans to define the dream and you will receive one hundred different answers. It seems fitting that in a country as individualistic as the U.S., each and every person defines the term uniquely.

Indeed, a key element that makes Americans unique on this planet is their pervasive individualism—a view that gives unprecedented weight to each individual's own choices, interests, and beliefs. Americans still remain far more inclined than those in other industrial democracies to rely on individual responsibility rather than government involvement in economic and societal affairs. It is precisely this individualism which contributes to America's notion of a national creed.

Today, Americans remain firm in the priority they assign to individual freedom and choice, and are decidedly antistatist. For instance, Americans are more than three times as likely as Western Europeans to disagree with the statement "The state/government should guarantee every citizen food and basic shelter."[3] Similarly, Western Europeans are twice as likely as Americans to believe that "It is the responsibility of the state to take care of very poor people who can't take care of themselves."[4] It is not that Americans are less caring. Rather, the value of personal responsibility is more cherished here than elsewhere.

The protection of individual choice is also a sacred value of our polity. Even such contentious issues as a woman's right to an abortion and a patient's right to die are supported by the vast majority of Americans (67 percent and 62 percent, respectively).[5] The recent health care debate provided further evidence of the importance of individual choice in American society. When presented with an option of an "inexpensive health care program that does not allow you to choose your own doctor" or of an "expensive health care program that allows you to choose your own doctor," 58 percent pick the latter while only 32 percent choose the former.[6]

Another key aspect of the American dream is the primacy it assigns to opportunity. Opportunity is not simply tied to economic indicators. Rather, opportunity is a metaphor for attaining increasing levels of material well-being without limitations or restrictions. It is not just the chance for rapid social mobility, but has also to do with our entrenched belief in the concept of meritocracy. Americans are more likely than any other democracy to believe that people succeed because of actual individual talents, efforts, and accomplishments rather than the social class into which they were born.

But in the so-called land of opportunity there are warning signs that hope, responsibility, and opportunity are being replaced by fear, dependence, and entitlements. Every year, an increasing number of Americans would choose security over opportunity. Americans no longer feel they can trust the government, the media, or even our schools and religious institutions to perform their respective core functions. The public sees government as having the ability to effect only limited change, and sees Washington less as a partner—and more as an opponent—in the pursuit of the American dream.

Achieving the American Dream

Despite national reverence for this dream, and its past ability to weather even the most horrendous political and economic storms, there is fresh evidence today that the dream is in danger of dying. In 1986, 55 percent of America felt it would be more difficult for the next generation to attain the American dream. Today, 78 percent hold that view, and only 14 percent expect attaining the dream to get easier. This outlook is equally bleak across all age, income, education, and racial subgroups.

The generation now reaching adulthood is distinguished by two characteristics unique in our history: regression and pessimism. Eighteen-year olds may very well be the first generation to be worse off than the generation preceding them, and expectations of future growth and the role of America in the twenty-first century have become decidedly pessimistic. If the 1970s were the "me decade," and the 1980s the "decade of greed," unless there is a significant mood shift the 1990s may come to be known as the "decade of anger and dissappointment."

When asked how close they are to achieving their own American dream, 22 percent of Americans believe they have already achieved it, while nearly half (49 percent) say they are closing in on it. An alarming one-quarter (25 percent) say they are either "very far away" or will never achieve their American dream. Among the more important findings:

- Proximity to achieving the American dream is closely associated with age. While 60 percent of Generation Xers (those born between 1962 and 1982) are at least close to achieving their American dream, 82 percent of those over age sixty-five feel the same way. True, the longer people live, the more likely they are to achieve their dreams. Nevertheless, comparable data from the 1960s and 1970s suggest that the current crop of twenty- and thirty-year-olds are considerably more pessimistic than their parents were at that time in their lives.
- Expectations about the dream differ greatly by race and socioeconomic level. While 73 percent of white Americans believe they have already attained or are very close to attaining the American dream, only 56 percent of African Americans say the same. An even larger gap involves socioeconomic status: 61 percent of those in a low socioeconomic group felt in close proximity to the dream, compared to 87 percent at high socioeconomic levels.
- In fact, it is income that correlates most strongly with achieving the American dream. Just over half (55 percent) of all people earning under $20,000 per year feel close to achieving the American dream, in contrast to the 85 percent with annual salaries above $70,000 who said they felt the dream was easily within reach.

The perception of the American dream is as much about the work ethic, merit, and reward as it is about anything else. So often illustrated by the story of the mailroom clerk who rises through the ranks to become president of the company, the American dream is about the unlimited opportunity associated with employment. This hope still exists, as nearly three-quarters (74 percent) of Americans agree with the statement "In America, if you work hard you can be anything you want to be." This refutes the notion of a class-based society with limitations on those less fortunate. The "rags to riches" story continues to beckon immigrants from around the globe who come to our land to seek their fortune. Indeed, first-generation immigrants are among the most likely to believe in limitless opportunity.

But among the quarter of the population for whom opportunity feels restricted, cynicism is the prevailing mood. From scientifically structured conversations with these individuals (who participated in focus groups), it is clear that they do not believe they have the same chance as their fellow citizens to succeed in life. Consequently, they are less inclined to work hard and strive for the top—instead comforting themselves by asking, "Why shoot for the top if it's going to be closed to me when I get there?"

In what may come as a surprise to many observers, nearly two-thirds (63 percent) of Americans are satisfied with their current employment situation, including over one-third (34 percent) who claim they are "very satisfied." Only 21 percent say that they are unsatisfied with their jobs, including 11 percent who claim that they are very unsatisfied. Although the notion that "money can't buy happiness" has become a cliche in the antimaterialistic, postyuppie culture, the evidence generally refutes this platitude. The fact is, income directly correlates with job satisfaction: nearly all (89 percent) of those in the highest socioeconomic bracket are satisfied with their current job situation, compared to just half (50 percent) among those in the lowest bracket.

It follows that the American dream is a function of job satisfaction as well as material well-being. While 83 percent of those who are "very satisfied" with their employment say that they are close to or have already achieved their American dream, only 55 percent of those who are dissatisfied with their present jobs answer similarly. By the same token, those who are more likely to think that hard work determines success are far more likely than those who do not to say that they are close to achieving the American dream (80 percent and 52 percent, respectively).

Dream Escalation

If Americans think they are unable to achieve their dream, this is partly because their material definition of it keeps expanding. That is, more and more Americans are raising the requirements of their dream, and they consequently grow increasingly frustrated when their dream goes unfulfilled. Despite the current era of stagnant wages, Americans continue to raise their material expectations and demands—setting themselves up for disappointment and failure. Fully 35 percent of Americans say that they need more material things than their parents, and over one-half (52 percent) say they *want* more material things. Ironically, most Americans acknowledge that they *have* more things than their parents, but the more they have, the more they want. The greater the gap between one's perceived needs and wants, the more likely one is to perceive the failure of the American dream.

Americans' perceptions of the dream are also tightly linked to their outlook on America's future as a nation. Since 1776, we have had a positive outlook on the future. When we entered both world wars, we never doubted our eventual success. When a president told us the only thing we had to fear was fear itself, we believed him. When another president challenged us to put a man on the moon in less than a decade, we rose to the occasion. We have looked toward the future with confidence, determination, and an expectation of success. And these feelings have pervaded all levels of society.

Today, however, less than two-thirds (64 percent) of Americans agree with the statement "I am optimistic about America's future," and only one-quarter (26 percent) strongly agree. The fact that so many Americans concur with this statement is a positive sign of the dream's continued vitality, yet it suggests that something either real or perceived has already gone wrong for eighty-five million Americans.

Worse, a majority of Americans now believes that a country other than the United States will be the world's leading economic power in twenty years. True, more Americans pick America (44 percent) than any other country, with Japan second (28 percent) and China a distant third (8 percent), but that still indicates erosion in the perception of American exceptionalism.

The era of youthful optimism may be over. Generation Xers are especially dour in their prognosis: Japan is their favored bet to lead the world economically. More younger Americans (aged eighteen to twenty-nine) think Japan will surpass the United States in the next twenty years (38 percent) than believe the U.S. will maintain its leadership (33 percent). These findings are consistent with the results of an Ivy League student poll conducted after the 1992 presidential election, in which just 41 percent of Ivy Leaguers predicted that the United States would be the most powerful nation in the world in the year 2010.[7] This finding is the first sign of an impending crisis in confidence among the next generation of American leaders. In fact, the only age group among whom a majority expects the United States to remain dominant economically is that least likely to witness it, senior citizens.

Only among recent immigrants does belief in America's ability to remain the dominant economic power survive. Half of all first- and second-generation Americans think the U.S. will be number one in the future, while just 40 percent of those whose families have lived here for four generations or longer would agree.

Dream Decline

The American dream has survived over two hundred years because Americans have shared the belief, regardless of their socioeconomic status, that "My children will have a better life than I had," that each succeeding generation will be better off than the one preceding it. In nearly every other Western society, social status is determined at birth. Across generations, the emphasis is on continuity rather than advancement, and the belief is that "If it's good enough for me, it's good enough for my children." Not so in the United States.

The promise of American life is based on the premise that each generation will be better off than the one that came before it. Sadly, this belief is dissipating. While over two-thirds (66 percent) of Americans claim they enjoy a better standard of living/quality of life than their parents enjoyed at the same age, just under one-third (32 percent) think that future generations will be able to make the same claim. This is the lowest recorded reading for this statistic since scientific polling began in the 1930s.

These results empirically prove what others have observed and noted, that the American dream is dependent on perceived intergenerational improvement. Fully 75 percent of Americans who think "The American dream is very alive" believe that their standard of living is better than their parents', compared to just 47 percent among those who think "The American dream is dead." Similarly, two-thirds (66 percent) of those who think the American dream is dead expect the next generation to be worse off, while only 29 percent of those who think the dream is very alive hold such dour expectations. The conclusion is plain: failure to improve the quality of life from one generation to the next will gravely undermine the American dream.

It is interesting to note the difference between "standard of living" and "quality of life" results. To test a hypothesis, half of the respondents were asked the generational question using the phrase "standard of living," while the phrase "quality of life" was used with the other half. Americans are more likely to observe a deterioration in their quality of life than they are to witness deteriorating living standards. The reason? Standard of living is largely a barometer of economic well-being, while quality of life is affected by both materialistic and spiritual components (crime, morality, environment, and the like). The data suggest that roughly twenty million Americans believe that they are better off economically yet still believe that their quality of life is deteriorating.

It is therefore not surprising that those who anticipate improved living standards for the next generation of Americans are much more likely to say the American dream will be easier to attain than are those who think living standards will deteriorate or stagnate. In fact, of those who think that living standards are already deteriorating and will deteriorate further, almost no one thinks the American dream will be easier to attain in the future. Thus, as skepticism about future economic health rises, so does the threat to the American dream.

But beyond all the threats and widespread doubts—above the naysayers and defeatists—the simple question remains, "Is the American dream dead or alive?" Despite the pessimism and cynicism, hope springs forth. The vast majority of Americans (88 percent) continues to believe in the American dream; this group incorporates a majority from every demographic, geographic, and attitudinal subgroup—including racial minorities and the least educated and most economically deprived.

The American dream, the idea that everyone can make it, still exists, even among those who have not yet made it. But predictably, the American dream holds less promise to minorities and those at the lower socioeconomic level. In particular, blacks, individuals with incomes below $20,000, and 1992 Perot voters top the list of people who think the American dream is dead (22 percent, 20 percent, and 18 percent, respectively).

For Perot voters and the poor, this belief is consistent with their high level of discontent about current economic conditions and wage stagnation. For blacks, it is consistent with studies that have shown their perception of being shut out from economic opportunities. As Martin Luther King, Jr., noted three decades ago:

> When the architects of our republic wrote the magnificent words of the Constitution and the Declaration of Independence, they were signing a promissory note to which every American was to fall heir. . . . It is obvious today that America has defaulted on this promissory note in so far as her citizens of color are concerned. Instead of honoring this sacred obligation, America has given the Negro people a bad check—a check which has come back marked "insufficient funds."[8]

Institutions and the American Dream

James Bryce began his 1916 study of American life by observing that throughout his travels across the country, he was constantly greeted by the query, "What do you think of our institutions?" His explanation for why this question was raised so often was that American political ideas and institutions had been invented rather than grown.

> [American institutions] represent an experiment in the rule of the multitude, tried on a scale unprecedentedly vast, and the results of which everyone is concerned to watch. And yet they are something more than an experiment, for they are believed to disclose and display the type of institutions toward which, as by law of fate, the rest of civilized mankind are forced to move.[9]

It is precisely for this reason that political institutions in America are so much more important than they are in other nations. We simply do not have religious, ethnic, or cultural homogeneity to fall back on should the belief in our creed dissipate. Foreigners (and natives for that matter) who recognize this fact are apt to understand and appreciate America's special attachment to our national symbols, institutions, and government, which represent the shared vision of an otherwise diverse nation.

Because our commonalty is so limited, we have always looked to our institutions and governing creed to bind us together. When that binding frays, as it did first in the mid-1780s, again in the late 1850s, and more recently in the early 1930s and mid-1970s, so, too, does our unity. Today, the institutions of government which define America are under attack, this time from a more insidious source. The struggles against factionalism, slavery, economic depression, and the Soviet Union were battles with well-defined foes and discernible rewards. Through them all, Americans overwhelmingly held to the belief that, whatever its faults, the U.S. still had the best system of government in the world. But that was before the rise of overt cynicism among the populace.

Americans today believe that their institutions are in decay. In the years between 1966 and 1992, confidence in every American institution, from the military to the press, plummeted. During that quarter century, the percentage of those expressing a "great deal" of confidence in Congress decreased from 42 percent to 10 percent; in the executive branch, from 41 percent to 13 percent; in the military, from 61 percent to 50 percent; in the Supreme Court, from 50 percent to 30 percent; in the press, from 29 percent to 13 percent; and in educational institutions, from 61 percent in 1966 to a staggering 25 percent in 1992. Other examples of this slide in confidence abound.

Virtually each one of these institutions has been undermined still further in the last few years. Only the military's ability to defend the security of the nation engenders a significant degree of confidence, with 68 percent of respondents expressing "a lot of confidence" in that institution. This level of trust comes in stark contrast to the 38 percent who have faith in religious institutions to promote morals and values in society; 17 percent who feel the schools can adequately teach children what they need to know; 8 percent who feel the news media can provide full and unbiased truth; and a dismal 6 percent who have confidence in the government's ability to solve a problem. This evaluation should not really surprise anyone. From Iran-Contra to $1000 toilet seats, from the Clarence Thomas hearings to the O. J. Simpson trial, from *Heather Has Two Mommies* to sex education for eight-year-olds, from Gary Hart to Dan Rostenkowski, from *A Current Affair* to the *New York Post,* contemporary cultural influences have combined to erode the general confidence of Americans in their institutions.

Pundits and politicos wonder why so many Americans believe the country is headed down the wrong track. Short-term pessimism is nothing new, but today's pessimism has been compounded by a pervasive cynicism in the body politic. Americans simply do not trust government to do the right thing, and they have little confidence in the ability of our nation's institutions to address their fears, economic and spiritual. Hence, short-term pessimism is unmoved by even the most positive economic statistics. Simply put, faith in the survival of the American dream and faith in our government institutions go hand in hand. Today, there is little faith in either.

Nothing has undermined faith in the leading American institutions more than the news media, and few professions have received more public scorn than journalism. True, Americans have always had a healthy skepticism about the integrity of the press, but their skepticism now stands at historic proportions. Unlike Americans' attitude toward Congress (which directs anger less at individual members than at the institution overall), their evaluation of the press grows more negative as it focuses on the individual reporter. According to a 1992 *Times Mirror* poll, just 2 percent of Americans believe members of the news media *never* let their own political preferences influence the way they report the news, and only 12 percent believe that they *seldom* do.

Most damning is the fact that 59 percent of Americans believe "The news media has too much influence over what happens today," compared with the 5 percent who believe the media has "too little influence."[10] To cite Everett Ladd: "The more the press attacks, the more critical and demanding the public gets. The more vocal and strident the public gets, the more Congress evades and obfuscates. The more Congress tries to have it both ways, the more the press attacks."[11] Only pessimism, cynicism, and negativism can result from this cycle. The negative ramifications for American society are numerous. If the definers of history and arbiters of public opinion are viewed as biased, vicious, self-interested players in the events they are reporting, public cynicism will only deepen.

Similarly, in a republican form of government such as ours, it matters whether the people trust their elected representatives. The height of public trust in government came in 1964, a year after the assassination of President Kennedy, when 75 percent expressed confidence in the governing institutions that brought America through that tragedy. Yet the succeeding twelve months witnessed the first wave of urban violence and antiwar protests, and trust fell to 65 percent. Then followed the Vietnam War, the assassinations of Martin Luther King, Jr., and Bobby Kennedy, the Watergate scandal, and two Arab oil embargoes. By 1979, public confidence in government had plummeted to 25 percent.

There was a brief uptick caused by a rather unlikely character. Ronald Reagan may have been the most antigovernment president of recent times, yet the percentage of the public expressing confidence in the government rose to the mid-forties as his presidency helped restore faith in the national institutions. But this renewed faith did not last. Public confidence in government has since resumed its slide, reaching an all-time low of 16 percent in 1994. Today, when Americans are asked how much of the time they trust government to do what is right, only 2 percent say "all of the time" and just 14 percent answer "most of the time."

What makes these results so alarming is the consistency of intensely negative opinions across nearly all demographic cohorts, and the degree to which belief in the American dream is directly intertwined with confidence in our nation's institutions and with our expectations for the future. It is therefore not surprising that those who do not trust the government to do what is right are more than three times as likely to believe that the American dream is dead as those who have at least some faith in the government to do the right thing.

Low public confidence in government does not exist because people think government lacks the *ability* to address our nation's ills, but because people lack trust in government to do what is *right*. In fact, the results of this survey strongly suggest that American distrust of government is eroding confidence in other institutions, and is a primary force driving long-term pessimism.

Why the Discontent?

The genesis of this mistrust is uncertain—is it the system or the politicians who are to blame? A generic call for "change" was cited by voters more than anything else as the primary reason they voted for Bill Clinton in 1992. Change was one of the central themes of the Clinton campaign, and one that obviously helped him get elected. But what type of change do Americans really want? Do they wish simply to change the people in power in the hope that fresh faces will improve the institutions, or is the electorate clamoring for a wholesale reorganization of our system of government?

In April 1992, just as Ross Perot was becoming a household name, an ABC News poll found that 68 percent believed that it was the people running the government who needed changing, while 29 percent thought the government itself needed drastic change.[12] That sentiment has changed considerably in just two years. Today, when presented with a choice, a bare majority (51 percent) of Americans would choose to "change the people running things," while a sizable 39 percent think "We must fundamentally change our system of government," and a paltry 7 percent think that "No real change is needed."

The Perot phenomenon is partly responsible for the ensuing rise in hostility toward the system itself. When Ross Perot first announced his candidacy, people across the country saw him as someone who could march in and purge the system of its problems. He was an outsider, a nonpolitician, a troubleshooter uniquely qualified to fix what was broken. Perot appealed not to those who opted for systemic changes, but rather to those who preferred personnel changes. The failure of his candidacy, and to a great extent the candidate himself, reminded voters just how difficult and dangerous it was to rely upon an individual to bring about fundamental change for an entire nation.

The hope that a majority of Americans saw in Bill Clinton's election also contributed to the mounting desire for systemic change. With a new face at the White House and so many newly elected congressmen in 1992, the public expected a fundamental overhaul of the way things were run.

Instead they were treated to gridlock, partisan viciousness, and legislative inaction. The 1994 elections, sweeping Republicans into control of the House and Senate for the first time in forty years, were the second public outcry in as many years to end politics as usual. The Republican landslide was so overwhelming because a record number of self-described independents—those most supportive of systemic change—voted for the G.O.P. Moreover, roughly 20 percent of self-identified conservative and moderate-conservative Democrats also voted Republican, evidence that the clamor for fundamental systemic change within the Democratic Party comes from the party's center, not its left wing.

The 1994 elections aside, the American political arena still overflows with cynicism, and this poses the question, "What's wrong with our elected officials?" Perceptions of ethical shortcomings in Congress are not new. In 1986, Americans were far more likely to believe the overall level of ethics and honesty in politics had fallen than had risen over the past decade (fallen, 42 percent; risen, 17 percent). By 1992, the ratio had grown to more than six to one (fallen, 60 percent; risen, 9 percent),[13] thanks in part to the downfall of Speaker Jim Wright, and to the House banking and post office scandals. In August 1990, just 17 percent felt that "most" in the House and Senate were financially corrupt. By March 1992, this figure had increased to 30 percent.[14] In a profession that demands public accountability, members of Congress are deemed by just 2 percent of America to be "more honest than most people," while 33 percent believe they are less honest.[15]

When we asked Americans to choose among three very strong reasons for "throwing the bums out," 40 percent selected "too corrupt," 28 percent chose "too uncaring," and just 22 percent picked "incompetent." The fact that more people point to corruption, the result of deliberate behavior, than to lack of caring or incompetence, the result of negligence, illustrates the antipolitician mood that has swept the country. A long stage of unfulfilled expectations and dashed hopes has dampened Americans' enthusiasm toward their government. Many Americans can find little to celebrate in Washington, and the defeat of so many House incumbents in 1994 was the latest manifestation of this mood.

The expectation that Congress would perform to the liking of the American people plummeted to an all-time low in 1994. Approval of congressional job performance declined from 42 percent in 1990 to just 21 percent four years later. In 1937, 44 percent of Americans thought Congress was "as good a representative body as is possible for a large nation to have." In

1990, just 17 percent agreed, and subsequent surveys show the credibility of Congress continuing to deteriorate, even as its perceived power continues to grow.

Where Power Rests

When Americans are asked who they think has the most power in America today, a majority (55 percent) chooses Congress; the courts (18 percent) and the president (11 percent) finish a distant second and third. State government and local government combined are named by less than 10 percent. But when asked (before the 1994 election) who they think *should have* the most power in America today, a plurality (41 percent) chooses state and local governments, while Congress plummets to just 29 percent. The perception of too much power and too little accountability has destroyed the credibility of the greatest deliberative body in the world. To renew this credibility, a majority of Americans would strip Congress of most of its responsibilities and return power to the state and local governments.

While support for devolution—the transfer of government functions to state and local control—is currently popular, this represents a relatively new development. From the depression era through the early 1950s, a majority of Americans wanted power centralized in the federal government. But with the advent of the civil rights movement, the twin concepts of states' rights and local authority began to gain popularity. When President Reagan proposed the decentralization of government in the early 1980s under the rubric of the "new federalism," he met with significant resistance. Today, however, the possibility of transferring power back to the states and localities receives wide backing across the demographic and ideological spectrum. In fields ranging from education to welfare, from roads to housing, Americans want Washington to have less influence and their states and local communities to have more.

Those who would devolve power from the federal government to the states have the least trust in Washington to "do what is right" and the least confidence in our nation's institutions to solve the nation's problems; they also feel the government is hurting their ability to achieve their American dream. In a related finding, individuals who are the most pessimistic about the direction of the country are also the most likely to want to decentralize power. Fully 48 percent of those who think the country is on the "wrong track" prefer state and local power, whereas only 32 percent of those who think the country is going in the "right direction" agree. Similarly, 49 percent of Americans who have almost no trust in government favor state and local control, compared to just 25 percent among those who trust government all or most of the time.

In the current climate of intense voter cynicism, the devolution of power away from Washington may be the only way to restore the electorate's trust in government. At the very least, this will give the perception of more accountability and efficiency to a governing process that is seen by many Americans to have gone completely out of control.

Throughout the country, Americans are becoming less comfortable with the idea of sending their congressmen off to Washington, never to hear from them again except when election time approaches. To a growing number of Americans, it is not enough for their congressman to identify "home" as a place of residence. As November 8, 1994, demonstrates, the American electorate links its vote to the heartfelt demand: "Cut their pay and send them home."

This concept, first voiced by former governor of Tennessee Lamar Alexander, may face strong opposition from the Washington establishment because it is anti-Washington and populist, but it enjoys massive public support nationally. Nearly three-fourths (73 percent) support this proposal, including 45 percent who "strongly agree" with it. Less than one-quarter of Americans (24 percent) disagree with the concept. Voters have grown increasingly eager—and impatient—for their elected representatives to serve as Madisonian "citizen legislators" in a much more limited central government.

Yet for all their anger, frustration, and complaints, most Americans still think they can make a difference. Only 16 percent believe that "It is not worth taking the time to vote because all politicians are the same," most of this group being younger and less educated. Moreover, Americans still believe that government in general can make a difference. Even though Americans do not like or trust their government, 77 percent believe that government has the ability to change the general direction of the country, including 42 percent who believe that the government can effect "a lot" of change. On economic issues, this belief in government power is amplified: a full 80 percent think the government can affect economic change, including 46 percent who think it can effect "a lot" of change, while less than one in five (19 percent) say "minimal" or "no" change.

This query elicited sharp demographic breaks. African Americans, less educated Americans, and lower-income earners were more likely to say that the government has considerable impact on the state of economic affairs than their white, better-educated, high-income counterparts. It is an interesting paradox that those who think government has the greatest capacity to change the economic climate are also those most likely to suffer when the government fails to do so.

Survey participants were then asked how much influence the government has over "the moral behavior of the American people," an important inquiry at a time when public debate is focused on the decline of morality, the disintegration of the family, and the deteriorating quality of life. Nearly half (46 percent) of our citizenry think the government can do "little or nothing" to influence moral behavior, and only one-third (33 percent) think that the government has the ability "to make a lot of change" in this regard. Surprisingly, although the "religious right" has attracted considerable public attention in its efforts to promote a value-laden agenda, members of this group are actually less likely than the overall population to think that the government can influence moral behavior. (One might ask why Americans should be so wary of a group that is unlikely to think of the government as a vehicle to renew America's spirit and cure our social malaise.)

There is no doubt that the vitality of the American dream is being sapped by our mistrust and lack of confidence in government. As a summary question, we asked whether the government was "helping or hurting your ability to achieve the American dream." The result is as striking as any finding in the survey. Nearly three times as many citizens say that the government is hurting their American dream (44 percent) as say it is helping (16 percent). For just over one-third (36 percent), the government is not a factor. Moreover, those who are most negative about the current and future state of the American dream are also most likely to see government as a hindrance. Those who have less faith in government and less confidence in our institutions are more likely to believe the American dream is dead.

The conclusion is inescapable, and the policy implications are clear. Americans need to rethink how we govern ourselves in order to restore faith in the American dream. That means expecting less from the federal government and demanding more from ourselves. Washington can help more people achieve their American dream by leaving them alone—by doing less, but doing it well. Accordingly, the federal government must reexamine the functions it performs, and determine which level of government, if any, should carry them out. This change will involve significant devolution of power and may face stiff opposition from the entrenched elite, but the demand for it is unmistakable.

Religion and Family Values

Over three and one-half centuries ago, pilgrims suffering relentless persecution by their government came to these shores in search of religious freedom. From that landing at Plymouth Rock until today, religion has played a central role in our nation's development and has been an integral component of the American dream. Two hundred years ago, the Establishment and Free Exercise Clauses of our Constitution were written to protect religion from governmental intrusion and to allow religious diversity to flourish. Nurtured by this freedom, religious organizations have gone on to play decisive roles in our nation's most divisive struggles—from the abolition of slavery to Prohibition, from the civil rights struggle to the pro-life movement—and have often been in the vanguard of social change.

Today, America remains a nation united "under God." While our faith in religious institutions and their ability to promote morals and values may have fallen in recent years, it still remains relatively high, and Americans are still the most likely of all nationalities to believe in the existence of God. In recent years, however, the role of religion in American life, and in our political life in particular, has been a source of increasing controversy. The abortion and "alternative lifestyle" debates have pitted deeply held religious beliefs against the cherished American principles of individual sovereignty and self-determination. And the ascendance of the "religious right" and its entry into politics have raised concerns over the separation of church and state.

This clash plays against the backdrop of America's profound moral discomfort. Uncontrollable crime, widespread illegitimacy, and the disappearance of basic values have stoked concern about disintegrating families, declining morality, and deterioration in our quality of life. Public opinion tells the story: dissatisfaction with "the honesty and standards of behavior of people in the country today" went from 59 percent in 1963 to 72 percent in 1973, and to 78 percent in 1992.

Few changes have had a more profound effect on American society than the breakup of the nuclear family. For more than two decades, sociologists, demographers, and many in the religious and political communities have decried this development. In the 1950s, fueled in part by falling mortality rates and a high marriage rate, a greater proportion of children than ever before was raised in stable, two-parent families. Beginning in the 1960s, however, the rising divorce rate, the migration of women into the work force, and the explosion of illegitimate births all hit at once, provoking widespread debate about the decline of American society that grows more emotional every year.

It is not surprising that many Americans look back nostalgically at an earlier time when the key institutions of our society—government, churches, and schools—were perceived to be on the side of the family. Today, however, married parents face discrimination by the tax code, risk random violence in their own neighborhoods, oppose some of the "values" being taught to their kids in the public schools, and earn the scorn of intellectual elites for openly practicing religion.

Stephen Carter's best-selling book, *The Culture of Disbelief,* perceptively argues that our society has gone from being secular (not favoring one religion over another) to secularist (favoring nonreligion over religion). Some commentators, including the eminent writer Irving Kristol, see the country, and particularly our political system, becoming increasingly divided along religious and moral lines. The data from this survey seem to support this hypothesis.

Where will the new lines between government and religious values be drawn? How deep is America's commitment to religion? Have we become less religious than our parents? Do we believe in absolute rights and wrongs, or have our ethical values become situational? Is a nation based on Jefferson's "self-evident truths" now confusing pluralism with tolerance? Should we become a more religious society? A more tolerant society? Answers to these questions may very well point the way to a new era in American politics and a new approach to solving society's most pressing problems.

When explaining what has most detracted from the greatness of the United States, Americans often concentrate on household issues. Moral insecurity and family insecurity now top general economic insecurity in the minds of most Americans. When asked which of three specific problems scared them the most, a plurality of respondents (40 percent) chose "disintegration of the family," and an additional third (34 percent) selected "the decline of morality." Only one out of five Americans (20 percent) chose "a deteriorating quality of life."

Fear of the family's disintegration resonates across all income, education, and partisan groups. More surprisingly, the breakup of the family is the number-one concern of both religious populations on the right and secular populations on the left—a clear indication of widespread concern. Only among non-married Americans with children at home is the breakup of the family less of a concern than declining morality and quality of life. As is often the case, those at greatest risk tend to be least aware of the problem at hand.

With moral and ethical issues replacing economic concerns, it is not surprising that the topic of values has increasingly entered political forums—with very emotional and polarizing results. The United States may be the land of diverse opinions and open discussion, but a majority of Americans still embraces the fixedness of right and wrong. Finding or defining a consensus on a set of collective values—religious and moral—may be impossible, yet Americans are clear about what they believe. Although besieged by moral and cultural relativists, fully 70 percent of Americans say there is a definite right and wrong when it comes to values, while only one-fourth (26 percent) take a relativist position.

The preservation of diversity notwithstanding, many Americans also believe that U.S. society has grown too tolerant. Just as a significant majority of Americans believes in the certitude of their morality, a clear majority regards the country as having gone overboard in accommodating alternative values. A sizable three-fifths (60 percent) of Americans think our society is too tolerant, while just one-third (34 percent) think that America is not tolerant enough.

However, when asked whether we need to be more tolerant of people in our society who think and act differently from us, nearly 80 percent say yes. This discrepancy may result from the more personal nature of the second question, but it also suggests an inherent contradiction in attitudes. Americans believe that, as individuals, we all have an obligation to be (more) tolerant of our fellow man. But when asked generally about their society, a majority regards the country collectively as having erred on the side of permissiveness. The so-called silent majority deplores what it perceives as the prevalence of an "anything goes" mentality, even as members of that majority turn a blind eye to behavior they may not condone personally but refuse to condemn publicly.

Here we find a pronounced generational schism, with younger Americans far more likely than those over fifty years of age to say that America is "not tolerant enough." Among Americans aged eighteen to twenty-nine, half (51 percent) feel that the United States is not tolerant enough, compared to just 21 percent among people sixty-five and older. Younger Americans—less certain of the objectivity or universality of moral values—are also more comfortable with the diversity of a more "liberal" society. Similarly, nonwhites, in response to years of injustice and prejudice, are far more likely than their white counterparts to want a more tolerant society.

With Americans so concerned about the decline in moral standards, the next logical question is what role Americans expect the government to play in promoting values in our society. Consequently, we asked Americans whether the government should "promote traditional values in our society" or "not favor any particular set of values." A majority (54 percent) now thinks that the government should promote traditional values—twice as many as just two years ago. The conservative and Republican mantra of "getting government out of our lives" recedes when the matter turns to the advancement of traditional values.

Those who consider themselves conservative are much more likely to welcome government intervention where values are concerned (64 percent) than their liberal counterparts (40 percent). But religion appears to be the strongest determinant of opinion. Not surprisingly, the largest difference in attitudes exists between the "religious right" and the "secular left." A full 82 percent of the former think that government should promote traditional values, compared with just 30 percent of the latter.

There should no longer be any doubt about whether America is a religious country or whether religion plays an important role in who we are and how we define ourselves. Nearly 85 percent of Americans agree with the statement "A belief in God is an important part of the American dream," including two-thirds (64 percent) who strongly agree. This inseparable link between religion and the American dream may explain why political attacks on the so-called religious right have been met with a negative reaction from the general populace. Agreement with the statement crosses party lines; 90 percent of Republicans, 82 percent of Democrats, and 81 percent of independents consider belief in God an important part of the dream. Describing the relationship between church and state, Martin Luther King, Jr., once explained, "The church is not the master or servant of the state, but rather the conscience of the state." Most Americans would still agree.

Conclusion

The widening gap between falling national expectations and rising personal expectations is having disastrous consequences: individuals are pursuing bigger dreams while living in a society they perceive as increasingly unlikely to fulfill those dreams, either materially or spiritually.

The survey that forms the core of this chapter was undertaken with a number of assumptions: that the nation needs to change its course, that traditional prescriptions are inadequate for the task, and that the enduring elements of the American dream—such elements as freedom, opportunity, enterprise, family, neighborhood, patriotism, and color blindness—are well-suited to our new era and can guide our approach to today's issues. The findings suggest that the nation must indeed change its course, not only to renew the promise of American life, but also to ensure that the American dream itself endures, a fact that we may have previously taken for granted.

This is not America's first encounter with pessimism. There have been numerous periods when our citizenry thought that the next year would bring "worse times" (usually during economic hardship), not to mention occasional negative multiyear forecasts (during wartime). Today's pessimistic mood is unique, however, because it is compounded by a second phenomenon—a pervasive cynicism affecting the body politic. In a span of just thirty years, we have witnessed an erosion of confidence in our institutions that has finally taken its toll on the long-term national mindset.

Lack of confidence in our institutions has left us bereft of any hope of relief for what ails us as a nation. Although our individual moods may be buoyed by temporary good news (a sharp rise in consumer confidence, for example), our collective mood is trapped in a tailspin. In other words, while many of us may still hope that our personal dreams will be fulfilled, an allied vision for a greater America is slowly fading.

This allied vision of the American dream has taken several distinct forms (economic and spiritual), but the one thing that unites them all, unfortunately, is pessimism.

Those who define the American dream in *economic* terms blame government for its demise. To them, wasteful federal spending, excessive taxation, and a mounting federal deficit and debt have left a yoke around the necks of future generations, impeding their ability to achieve their dream. Given this confluence of developments, we are witnessing a phenomenon new to twentieth-century America—a profound intergenerational pessimism. A significant majority of Americans may assess their current personal situation in positive terms, yet their expectations for their children and the future are decidedly (and increasingly) negative.

Those who view the American dream in *spiritual* terms sense the moral decay of a nation besieged by crime and violence. To them, the American dream is dying along with the nation's spirit. Values such as community and responsibility, once so cherished and commonplace, seem abandoned. Institutions such as the family, church, and school that had once cultivated their hopes for a brighter future have been torn asunder.

While these two groups see the American dream through different lenses, they share a common belief that it is in serious jeopardy, and that something must be done now if it is to be saved. The challenge facing the nation today is to transform this cynicism and despair into trust and optimism. Meeting this challenge will depend in no small part upon the extent to which Washington can transform itself.

Since confidence in our nation's institutions is clearly at the core of the American dream, debate over more or less government misses the mark. The object of reform should be Washington itself. To renew the promise of American life, we must first and foremost restore public trust in Washington. Enacting federal government policy has become difficult not only because of legitimate ideological and political battles, but also because real reform inevitably runs into the brick wall of the entrenched bureaucratic and political establishment that arrived in Washington in the 1960s and 1970s and has refused to leave.

Since Americans believe that Washington exacerbates rather than alleviates the trends in modern life that concern them, it will be impossible to convince Americans to trust their institutions until they see Washington being streamlined and reformed. It is not just smaller government that Americans crave but better government, more honest government, and a government that is closer to home. None of these descriptions currently applies to Washington.

If Americans see scandal after scandal in the executive branch or in the halls of Congress, it will make no difference whether Vice President Gore is truly "reinventing government" or whether a conservative administration is slashing entire departments. Washington can regain the public trust only by doing little and doing it well, and returning all other responsibilities and power to the states, the towns, and the people themselves.

Washington must make a commitment to bring the decisionmaking framework as close to home as possible. Not only will the solutions then be more efficacious, but the American people will feel that they are again masters of their own fate. As government itself becomes more responsive, national issues (education, crime, welfare) will start to become what they truly are—local and individual issues. By affording people more control of the process, we can restore confidence in the entire system as a vehicle through which national problems can be solved. In short, there must again be government of the people and for the people, rather than in spite of the people.

There is another variable in the current ill health of the American dream. A nation built on a creed is most unified when that creed is challenged by an extraneous force. Common enemies become useful tools for downplaying our individual differences and uniting us in a common cause. Two New Yorkers may be mortal enemies, but for three hours at a Yankee–Red Sox game, they might as well be blood brothers.

The fall of communism has left America without a major external threat to combat, without an outside enemy to confront. In the 1950s and 1960s, international problems topped the list of the most important problems facing the country. In the 1970s and 1980s, foreign issues gave way to more domestic concerns. In this decade, international problems and concerns have all but disappeared from the public mindset. How incredible that a variant of the American dream is spreading through the former Soviet republics while it retreats here at home.

Throughout our history, we have dreamed of a better tomorrow, confident that we could face the challenges that lay before us. The twenty-fifth anniversaries of the landing on the moon and of Woodstock came at a time of national introspection. While each of us is optimistic that we will overcome our individual obstacles, the current challenges to our nationhood are more likely to divide us than unite us. Without unity of purpose we are forced to turn inward, confronting the fact that we are a nation divided in many ways: by race, ethnicity, and culture.

Americans, as individuals—and as a nation—have always had a preoccupation with being the best. Lately, however, belief in ourselves has waned considerably. When just one out of three Americans now regards the U.S. as the greatest country in the world, it is painfully obvious that the perception of American "exceptionalism" has been replaced with a more egalitarian position. Those who think that this humility is a positive development should recall Chesterton's dictum that a diverse population founded on a creed demands an exceptionalist mentality.

Perhaps recent world events will be seen by future historians to have come at a critical time in our history. Today's national introspection may give us the opportunity to address a national malaise—the spiritual decay of America—that would have become irreversible had we continued to ignore its symptoms. Saving our nation from itself may pose a greater challenge than the revolution from which America was born, may require more genius than putting a man on the moon, and may entail more fortitude than our inexorable struggle for liberty and democracy. But Americans were born for just such a challenge.

We are a nation of dreamers because we are a nation born from a dream. Thomas Jefferson once said, "Where there is no vision, the people perish." If the American dream dies, so too will the vision and dreams of all its citizens. For a nation entrusted with the mantle of human progress, that would be a tragic fate indeed.

Notes

1. Everett Carll Ladd, "Thinking About America," *Public Perspective* 4 (1993): 20.
2. This study was undertaken in August 1994 and commissioned by Hudson Institute. One thousand Americans nationwide, eighteen years and older, were contacted by random digit-dial telephone. Interviews lasted approximately thirty-two minutes and contained eighty-three questions. The study has a plus or minus 3.1 percent margin of error at the 95 percent confidence level.

    The results of the study were published in a Hudson Institute report entitled "The American Dream: Renewing the Promise," Indianapolis, Indiana, December 1994. The report also includes the results of two focus groups conducted in Baltimore and Denver. Unless otherwise noted, all data in this chapter are from this survey.
3. *Times Mirror,* 1990 and 1991.
4. *Times Mirror* for PSRA, 1990 and 1991.
5. Voter/consumer research for the Family Research Council, "National Family Values: A Survey of Adults," Washington, D.C., September 1993.
6. ABC News, September 16-19, 1993.
7. A poll of undergraduates at eight Ivy League institutions conducted between November 13 and November 22, 1992, with eighteen additional surveys completed on December 1, 1992. A total of 3,119 face-to-face interviews were conducted. The survey has a plus or minus 2.5 percent margin of error at the 95 percent confidence level.
8. Martin Luther King, Jr., "I Have a Dream," August 28, 1963.
9. James Bryce, *The American Commonwealth* (New York: Macmillan Company, 1924), 1.
10. ABC News, April 8–9, 1992.
11. Burns Roper poll in *Public Perspective* 5 (1994): 5.
12. ABC News, April 8–9, 1992.
13. Ibid.
14. CBS/New York Times, March 26–29, 1992.
15. ABC News, August 1993.

Part II

What Sort of Nation?

Chapter Four

The Future of American Pluralism

Diane Ravitch

"The average American is nothing if not patriotic. . . . The faith of Americans in their own country is religious, if not in its intensity, at any rate in its almost absolute and universal authority. It pervades the air we breathe. As children we hear it asserted or implied in the conversation of our elders. Every new stage of our educational training provides some additional testimony on its behalf. Newspapers and novelists, orators and playwrights, even if they are little else, are at least loyal preachers of the Truth. The skeptic is not controverted; he is overlooked." So wrote Herbert Croly in 1909, describing a people who shared a passionate belief in the future of their nation as "the Land of Democracy," "the Land of Promise," "the Land of Equality," and "the Land of Freedom." Americans also shared a general optimism that the future would be better than the past and that "an ever increasing majority" would enjoy the fruits of their hard work and be "relieved of the curse of poverty."

Croly doubted that "the promise of American life" could be achieved unless there was a general recognition of *national* interest and *national* purpose, as well as political institutions that would promote *national* development. His book helped to rationalize the need for an effective national government. In the ideological clash between Hamiltonian and Jeffersonian ideas, Croly sided with Hamilton. Croly associated "social amelioration" with "national development." He acknowledged that "We Americans are confronted by two divergent theories of democracy. According to one of these theories, the interest of American democracy can be advanced only by an increasing nationalization of the American people in ideas, in institutions, and in spirit. According to the other of these theories, the most effective way of injuring the interest of democracy is by an increase in national authority and a spread of the national leaven."

Progressive reformers embraced the nationalizing principle as the best means of improving society, and for most of the twentieth century, regardless of which party has won the presidency, the main trends in American life have moved in the direction of nationalization. It is clear that the national principle has had many important benefits—one thinks, for example, of landmark civil rights protections, the federal highway system, and medical insurance for the elderly—that few Americans would willingly jettison. Yet the Jeffersonian idea of keeping government close to the people continues to have enormous vitality. In 1800, the year Jefferson was elected president, he wrote:

> Our country is too large to have all its affairs directed by a single government. Public servants at such a distance and from under the eye of their constituents, must, from the circumstance of distance, be unable to administer and overlook all the details necessary for the good government of the citizens, and the same circumstance, by rendering detection impossible to their constituents, will invite the public agents to corruption, plunder and waste.

Most Americans react instinctively against rule by elites, whether the elites are royalty, plutocrats, or bureaucrats; even if they have never read Jefferson, they believe that they should have a large measure of control over their own lives. Skepticism toward governmental solutions is a hardy strain in the American character, and this tradition of skepticism is a Jeffersonian legacy. It was Jefferson who wrote:

> I am persuaded myself that the good sense of the people will always be found to be the best army. They may be led astray for a moment, but will soon correct themselves. . . . The basis of our governments being the opinion of the people, the very first object should be to keep that right; and were it left to me to decide whether we should have a government without newspapers, or newspapers without a government, I should not hesitate a moment to prefer the latter.

But I should mean that every man should receive those papers, and be capable of reading them.

Croly argued that small-scale democracy was no longer adequate, that times had changed, and that "the national advance of the American democracy does demand an increasing amount of centralized action and responsibility." Because of "the increasing concentration of American industrial, political, and social life," he maintained, it was necessary to create a national government capable of dealing effectively with national problems. Because of the aggregation of corporate wealth, the states were no longer capable of acting efficiently.

Croly's analysis had considerable merit in his time. In that era, it was necessary to empower the federal government to deal with national problems the states could not solve on their own. Nearly a century has passed since Croly published his speculations, and it is clear that there are some functions that only the federal government can perform. It is also clear, however, that there are important functions that are best performed by state and local governments or by families, communities, and voluntary associations. *The challenge of the early twenty-first century will be to sort out which functions are best performed at which level, and what kind of social organization will best promote a healthy polity, a just society, and a vigorous democracy.*

National Identity

One problem that did not trouble Herbert Croly was the question of America's national identity. He knew that there was an American people, that it was optimistic about the future, and that it was committed to realization of the democratic ideal. Were Croly alive in the 1990s, however, he would be less confident in defining the American people. He would stumble into contentious arguments about multiculturalism and diversity. He would search, perhaps in vain, to find the optimism he considered omnipresent in the first decade of this century. And yet he would still find—if he looked beyond the campuses and newsrooms—that most Americans believe in their country, love their country, and hope (though without a sense of inevitability) that the future will be better than the past and the present.

In Croly's era, the question of national identity was not at issue. The ideal was the sturdy Anglo-Saxon pioneer; all citizens were invited, encouraged, or directed to copy the Anglo-American model, to remake themselves in that image to the extent possible. In our own day, having experienced in the 1960s and 1970s the civil rights revolution, the black power movement, and the white ethnic revival, Americans are no longer sure that there is any civic ideal, common culture, or national identity. Nor can we be sure of the values that once seemed typically American: a generation of revisionist histories, adversarial journalism, and cinematic portrayals of political corruption (such as Oliver Stone's *JFK)* has gnawed away at the nation's self-confidence and eroded American society's sense of itself as a nation devoted to ideals such as justice, freedom, democracy, and equality.

As we appraise "the new promise of American life," we must consider a problem that never entered Croly's consciousness, specifically, the relationship between group identity (for example, race, ethnicity, gender, and religion) on one hand, and nationality on the other. This is not an unimportant issue: the tensions generated by differences among peoples fed the fires of two world wars in our century, as well as hundreds of regional conflicts. The new promise of American life will be made or unmade by our ability to address this issue in a way that honors democratic traditions. Are we a people or not? Do we have a common culture? Are there ties that bind us together as a nation and a people? What are the costs of not having a common national identity? How can we honor both our differences and our common purposes? How should our understanding of nationality and identity affect public policy?

I begin with a simple proposition: the United States is one nation, not a confederation of independent states or a collection of disparate nationality groups. It has a common civic culture that can be briefly summarized in a single sentence: "We the people of the United States, in Order to form a more perfect Union, establish Justice, insure domestic Tranquility, provide for the common defence, promote the general Welfare, and secure the Blessings of Liberty to ourselves and our Posterity, do ordain and establish this Constitution for the United States of America."

That sentence, surely the most important in American history, implicitly poses a question: who are "We the people of the United States"? At the time the sentence was written, only a minority of the population—white males— enjoyed the full rights of citizenship. And yet the sentence said "We the people," not "We the white male citizens." Much blood has been spilled over the years to expand the definition of "We the people" to include African Americans, women, American Indians, and other previously excluded persons. Today the multicultural advocates prefer to think of "We the peoples," but the Constitution reminds us that we are one nation and one people.

Today, the principle is well established that anyone born in the United States or naturalized as a citizen is an American. Citizenship is not conditioned on race, religion, ethnicity, language, or gender. For generations, the promise of American life was predicated on the pursuit of equal rights for all American citizens and on efforts to eliminate all forms of discrimination based on race, ethnicity, gender, or other group characteristics. But just as we seemed to be approaching that ideal, those who once sought it most fervently turned against it. At the very time that barriers based on race, ethnicity, gender, and cultural heritage were being swept away, remedies were devised that effectively distributed benefits and burdens based on race, ethnicity, gender, and cultural heritage.

The process of moving from unacceptable group-consciousness to acceptable group-consciousness was gradual but decisive. Executive orders, court decisions, regulations, and legislative mandates accumulated step by step, first suggesting, then permitting, then requiring the selection of persons on grounds of race and ethnicity. The remedies designed to help blacks were soon extended to include American Indians, Hispanics, Asians, and women. Over time, it became well established that individuals applying for a job, a scholarship, or admission to a university were expected to declare their race, ethnicity, and gender on their application, knowing that this information would improve or narrow their chances.

Does anyone recall that it was once the goal of the civil rights movement to remove photographs—and all other evidence of racial identity—from applications for jobs or college? Is it totally forgotten that the overriding aim of the civil rights movement was to make suspect any and all racial classifications? The idea of color blindness was and remains a democratic aspiration, and crusaders for civil rights liked to quote Justice John Marshall Harlan's dissent from the *Plessy v. Ferguson* decision of 1896, which said: "In respect of civil rights, common to all citizens, the Constitution of the United States does not, I think, permit any public authority to know the race of those entitled to be protected in the enjoyment of such rights. . . . Our Constitution is color-blind, and neither knows nor tolerates classes among citizens. In respect of civil rights, all citizens are equal before the law. The humblest is the peer of the most powerful. The law regards man as man, and takes no account of his surroundings or of his color when his civil rights as guaranteed by the supreme law of the land are involved."[1] For decades, these words were the rallying cry of civil rights litigators, who sought in case after case to remove from the states (as well as from all agencies that received public funds or served the public) the power to use racial classifications.

That was then, this is now. Now our institutions have embedded group preferences in their way of life. Now color blindness is perceived not as an ideal to be vigorously pursued, but as "laissez-faire racism," a covert way of removing from the state its power to improve the condition of disadvantaged minorities. Providing special assistance to disadvantaged black Americans would at least have historical logic on its side. But over time preferences have been extended to include Pakistanis, Chinese, Japanese, Sri Lankans, Mexicans, Salvadorans, Argentineans, Ecuadorians, Cubans, women, and many others whose only common characteristic is that they are not white males. Some of those who are eligible for special preferences in hiring or admissions are not even economically disadvantaged but are the children of successful professionals and entrepreneurs. Distributing rewards and burdens solely because of race, ethnicity, or gender refutes basic principles of American democracy; this was, we should recall, the evil against which the civil rights movement struggled.

A letter to the *New York Times* in 1994 commented on this state of affairs:

> My wife (a citizen of China) and myself (a citizen of Britain) have recently settled in your country. We like it here very much and hope to be accepted as citizens one day. But we are both utterly baffled by this business of "racial classification" on which your Government seems to expend so much time and effort. . . . For example, our daughter is precisely one-half English and one-half Chinese. When the time comes to fill out a Census form, which box do we check for her? Are we allowed to check both "white" and "Asian"? Or what? American friends tell us that most universities here operate quota systems against Asians, so our daughter's future may be adversely affected by an "Asian" classification. On the other hand, there are, we are told, certain jobs in which Asians are underrepresented (police, mail carriers), so an "Asian" classification will benefit her if she decides to pursue one of these careers. . . . There seems to be no legal obstacle to changing my name to Gonzalez and taking up Spanish as my language of choice. Do I thereby become Hispanic? Perhaps Americans sorted these things out long ago. To newcomers, the whole business seems unfathomable.
>
> Most of all, we wonder why the Government of a nation dedicated to equality is concerned with "race" at all. Our daughter is, by birth, a United States citizen. What else does her Government need to know? Perhaps you should consider following the example of South Africa and get out of the racial classification business altogether.[2]

In his book *Idols of the Tribe,* Harold Isaacs asked, "How can we live with our differences without, as always heretofore, being driven by them to tear each other limb from limb?"[3] Isaacs described the continuing fragmentation of human society as "an ironic, painful, and dangerous paradox: the more global our science and technology, the more tribal our politics; the more universal our system of communications, the less we know what to communicate; the closer we get to other planets, the less able we become to lead a tolerable existence on our own; the more it becomes apparent that human beings cannot decently survive with their separatenesses, the more separate they become."[4] Isaacs listed thirty-four bloody intergroup conflicts between 1945 and 1974 that had taken more than ten million lives. The list included two million people killed in clashes between Hindus and Moslems during the partition of India and the creation of Pakistan; two million killed in civil war in Biafra; half a million Sudanese blacks killed by Sudanese Arabs; more than half a million Pakistanis killed by other Pakistanis; 200,000 slaughtered during the separation of Burundi and Rwanda; and 150,000 Kurds killed by the Iraqis. An updated list would surely include many millions more slaughtered in racial, ethnic, and religious conflicts around the world. These are not, unfortunately, remote or unknown events; in 1994, the world watched in passive horror as hundreds of thousands of innocent people were massacred in Rwanda because they belonged to one tribe rather than another.

Racial, ethnic, and religious tensions have caused nations to disintegrate. Prime examples in recent history are the Soviet Union, Yugoslavia, and Czechoslovakia. Ethnic tensions have also caused murderous conflict in Ireland, Hungary, Romania, India, Somalia, Lebanon, Israel, Syria, Egypt, Liberia, Sri Lanka, Cambodia, Burma, Indonesia, Iraq, and elsewhere.

Let us not forget: it is hard, very hard, for people to live alongside others who are different from themselves. Sometimes conflict erupts because of racial, religious, or linguistic differences. Sometimes it explodes between peoples who are more alike than different, as in Northern Ireland. A recent *New York Times* article about the psychological roots of ethnic violence noted that when differences between neighboring groups are small, minor distinguishing features assume great importance. Daniel Goleman cited Cyprus, a hotbed of ethnic conflict, where both Greek and Turkish men wear identical black baggy pants and shirts; the Turks, however, always wear red sashes and smoke cigarettes from a red pack, while the Greeks wear blue sashes and smoke cigarettes from a blue pack.[5]

It should be clear: a successful multiethnic society is a rare and wondrous achievement. Scholars, public officials, educators, journalists, parents, and other citizens must ask, "What should we do to encourage a spirit of mutual respect and tolerance among people who may differ in many ways?" and "How can public policy nurture comity among the nation's citizens?"

The Civic Culture

As Emerson, Melville, and Whitman long ago prophesied, America has become the world's first universal nation. We count as citizens people from all the world's regions, races, religions, languages, and cultures. This remarkable demographic diversity may prove a source of enormous vitality, as many hope, or it may prove a source of perpetual tension and conflict, as many fear. Which is it to be? The answer is not obvious, nor is it foreordained. It will be determined by our own institutions, policies, and values. Diversity does not necessarily promise either harmony or conflict, although experience here and abroad suggests that it is more likely to be associated with conflict than with harmony.

If we seek to build a society that pursues brotherhood and social progress, rather than hatred and division, we must have a shared sense of the common good. It is not likely that we will be able to forge a sense of the common good unless we identify and build a common civic culture that overrides our particularities. Absent such a common civic culture, the people who live within our borders are neither a people nor a nation. The population then becomes only a random collection of unrelated groups and individuals, sharing nothing but geographical space in the middle of North America. Were this the case, there would be no reason for anyone to pay taxes to help anyone outside his own group; there would be no patriotic spirit on which to draw for the common defense or the general welfare; there would be no grounds on which to appeal to vindicate anyone's rights. Each group would be left to fend for itself, unable to call upon the pocketbook or conscience or fellow feeling of anyone belonging to another group. The practical effects of such fragmentation would be most disadvantageous to those who are socially and economically in need. Without a common civic culture, a shared sense of national identity and purpose, Americans would relate to each other with as much concern and interest as they do to people in Brazil, Romania, Zaire, or Taiwan.

Fortunately, the United States does have a common civic culture, which provides the foundation for American national identity. It is vital and real, and it holds the allegiance of the overwhelming majority of Americans. This civic culture is the sum of the institutions, values, and ideals Americans share. Our recognition of our failure to live up to our ideals reminds us that we accept the reality of common ideals. Even the most severe critics of this nation ultimately invoke the nation's ideals as a benchmark for their critique.

The institutions, values, and ideals that comprise the American civic culture are familiar to all Americans. Their sources are to be found in the Declaration of Independence, the Constitution, and the Bill of Rights. These documents espouse certain fundamental ideas: liberty, equality, justice, limited government, and government based on the consent of the governed. The democratic and rational ideas contained in these documents can be traced to ancient Greece and Rome and to Enlightenment thinkers; they are rooted in the historical experiences of Western Europe, England, and the English-speaking colonies in North America. They have inspired countless reform movements seeking justice and equal treatment for everyone who has been excluded from the full protection of the laws. From these documents has emerged a vibrant democratic civic culture that respects the principles of majority rule, protection of the rights of minorities, representative and limited government, the rule of law, and the equal rights of every citizen. Democratic institutions establish fair processes for resolving disputes at the ballot box and in courts of law. They promote certain values: tolerance, equality, freedom, fairness, individualism, optimism, civic participation, and self-reliance.

Because Americans treasure their own rights and freedoms, they tend to give a wide berth to people with whom they disagree, saying, "It's a free country," or "Live and let live." Most Americans are undisturbed by people who do or say what they please, so long as they do not trample on anyone else's basic rights. But most are also willing to lend a hand, to pitch in. The extent to which Americans volunteer to help out in their communities and through their associations has always amazed foreigners; volunteer activities in church, synagogue, school, workplace, and neighborhood continue to be a staple of American civic culture. Of course, some Americans don't share in these consensual values; some people are bad citizens; they are unfair, intolerant, and unwilling to do their share. But they are not typical.

The civic culture is the heart of the American common culture. It is not grounded in race, ethnicity, religion, gender, or anything else peculiar to a group or individual. It belongs to all Americans. It is widely shared among native-born citizens, naturalized citizens, and newcomers. It promises freedom, opportunity, equality, and the right to be a self-governing member of a self-governing polity.

Pluralisms

Real as it is, the civic culture is not the totality of American culture. People are defined in many ways, only some of which are included in the civic culture. The civic culture assures that no one can be excluded from participation in civic duties because of race, religion, ethnicity, or gender, but it does not make those characteristics unimportant in people's lives. On the contrary, those characteristics are frequently the basis on which people organize to participate in public as well as private life. For many Americans, for example, their religious affiliation directly influences how they live and what they value. Thus, a paradox: How should the civic culture relate to group life when part of the purpose of civic culture is to treat each individual without regard to group identification? Should it encourage group differences? Or should it attempt to minimize them?

The extensive literature that has addressed these issues recognizes that American nationality includes tendencies toward both assimilation and differentiation. Some advocates embrace only one definition of American identity, but experience demonstrates that Americans can assimilate and be different from each other at the same time. Typically, the definitions of American identity range across the following spectrum:

First, *assimilation.* The chief argument for assimilation is that the United States will be a stronger, more unified society if differences among its citizens are minimized. When immigration reached a peak in the early years of the twentieth century, public policy and private actions promoted the rapid assimilation of all citizens. Historically, there have been at least two varieties of assimilation: one was an idealistic appeal to Americans to merge and become a new race and a new nation, different from any other in the world. I call this idealistic because it presumed that everyone—whatever their race, religion, or culture—had something of value to contribute to the emerging new America. The metaphor for this kind of assimilation has been the melting pot, which suggests the melting and blending of disparate cultures into a new whole. The other version of assimilation, familiar to many today from their experience in public schools of the first half of the century, was Anglo-assimilation. This approach pressed newcomers to embrace the culture, history, and literature of our Anglo-Saxon Founding Fathers. This was a fairly mild sort of assimilation, however, since non-Anglo immigrants were free to speak their native language outside of public school, to worship as they chose, and otherwise to live in accordance with their own choices.

Second, *cultural pluralism.* Reacting against assimilationism in 1915, Horace Kallen called for "a democracy of nationalities."[6] His view, which he later called cultural pluralism, was posited on the belief that cultural groups were distinct, that individuals achieved their greatest sense of freedom and satisfaction as members of a cultural group, and that public policy should encourage distinct national groups to flourish. He wanted the United States to become a nation of nations. The metaphor for cultural pluralism, as Kallen envisioned it, was an orchestra composed of many different groups, each playing its own instrument in a grand national harmony. In our own time, Kallen's concept of cultural pluralism is represented by the metaphor of a mosaic, a collection of stones linked together in a common project; the stones, however, are each distinct and relatively unchanging.

Third, *dynamic pluralism.* Over the decades the concept of cultural pluralism evolved. Today it refers to the ways in which groups influence one another. Lawrence H. Fuchs uses the metaphor of the kaleidoscope to describe a situation in which cultural groups intersect, interconnect, and interact; in contrast to a melting pot, it might be called a stir-fry or a lightly cooked stew, each ingredient seeping into the other while retaining its own distinctive flavor. Dynamic pluralism describes the ways cultures blend and change one another, creating the restaurants in central Texas that serve both bratwurst and tacos, the Puerto Rican bagel factory in Manhattan, and the near-universal popularity of jazz, ragtime, salsa, reggae, the blues, and the polka, all of which began as ethnic musical expressions.

Fourth, *separatism.* A tiny minority of Americans choose to avoid intermingling with other groups. Most of the groups in this minority are held together by common religious beliefs. They include the Amish, Hutterites, certain Orthodox Jewish sects, and certain Muslim groups. These groups maintain their own schools to avoid the assimilating effects of American public schools. They do not wish to assimilate, and they limit their interactions with other ethnic and religious groups.

Which of these ways of life best describes the national identity? Are we a melting pot, an orchestra, a salad bowl, a mosaic, or something else? Whatever the metaphor, the fact is that all these ways of life coexist and that all are viable in modern American society. All these paths intersect with the civic culture, which nurtures and protects them. Even those who choose to live in separate groups are not entirely separate; they too make use of public roads, the common currency, the judicial system, and other protections supplied by the state, such as the fire department, police, and military. One person may even simultaneously adopt several of these ways of life. An American citizen today can at one and the same time be assimilated in some facets of his or her life (for example, at work or at college); a member of a vigorous ethnic culture; and a participant in dynamic pluralism who happily enjoys the products of other cultural groups. Americans do not have to choose among these ways of living; most move easily from one mode to another or live simultaneously in several. As American citizens, we are free to make our choices, unconstrained by government, so long as we do not break the law or injure others.

For all practical purposes, assimilation (voluntary and unconscious) goes forward every day in the United States. As people in other nations frequently remark, American popular culture is a powerfully assimilative instrument; the movies and television disseminate common ideas about dress, behavior, language, music, clothing, and values. Most people, regardless of their racial, religious, or ethnic origins, work in settings that have no racial, religious, or ethnic dimension; as workplaces become more diverse, workers adapt to one another, and assimilation continues apace. Without legislation or regulation, English is the language of the public sphere. The melting pot keeps on melting.

Among new immigrants, assimilation moves ahead, slowly but surely. Even what appear to the outsider to be intensely ethnic communities are almost always multicultural. Asians live side by side with other Asians from very different cultures, because the word *Asian* encompasses diverse cultures; so do Hispanics. Similarly, urban black communities contain people who trace their origins to many different cultures in the Caribbean, Latin America, Africa, and the American South. It is only public policy that sees a single culture, defined by race or language, when in fact most of these ethnic communities contain many cultural groups living side by side. For newcomers, exposure to American schools, workplaces, television, and politics also has an assimilative effect. Within a generation or two, newcomers are very different from those they left behind in their native lands, even though they are still bearers of the ethnic culture.

There is another sense in which it must be said that the melting pot did work. Many Americans are products of mixed marriages that long ago crossed racial and ethnic lines; some do not even know their ethnic origins. Can it be that we celebrate ethnicity because we fear that it is slipping away? Can it be that the homogenizing effects of American culture cause many Americans to magnify or recreate ethnic attachments that make their lives more interesting? When almost everyone wears green on St. Patrick's Day, when almost everyone eats pasta, and when almost everyone sings music of African American origin (for example, jazz, the blues, spirituals), we must acknowledge that ethnic experiences have been transformed and made available to those outside the group. The melting pot keeps bubbling.

At the same time, cultural pluralism also persists. There are many ethnic groups that have chosen to retain their group identities. These identities may not be the same as in each group's country of origin, but they are still quite different from the assimilated identity of most urbanites and suburbanites. There are many Americans who, for reasons of their own, choose to live in close proximity to members of their own group. Americans who prefer to live with easy accessibility to their own ethnic foods, ethnic churches, ethnic schools, and ethnic companionship maintain their culture on their terms, without diminishing their sense of identity as American citizens.

It is also true that dynamic pluralism has become a common experience in modern America, especially for people who live in metropolitan areas. They may be Protestant, Catholic, Jewish, Muslim, or Hindu, but their religious affiliation does not define their circle of friends or their place of residence. They may be of German, Irish, Korean, Italian, African, Polish, Lebanese, or Cuban descent, but they regularly interact with people who are not, whether at work, in school or college, or in their social life. Their interaction with other cultures is not simply accidental. They like to eat foods from a variety of ethnic cuisines; to go to movies, exhibits, or plays about people different from themselves; to live in neighborhoods where ethnic diversity is the rule. They enjoy their own ethnic origins, but they also enjoy experiencing those of others.

In the midst of all this vigorous pluralism, separation survives too. It appeals to a very small number of Americans, but most Americans respect the rights of those who choose to live apart. Live and let live. No matter how peculiar they may seem to others, those who separate are still Americans. In most instances, their ancestors came here to find freedom, and there is a general presumption that they should have it.

Unity

The civic culture is not threatened by the coexistence of these different ways of life. On the contrary, these different ways of life rely on the civic culture to provide the mechanism to resolve disputes as well as the consensus that allows individuals to shift easily from a cosmopolitan world to an ethnic world and back again, without undue psychic stress.

Yet it should be noted that the civic culture is not an impregnable fortress, impervious to assault, needing no defenders. It has been jeopardized in the past and will surely be jeopardized in the future by demagogues who set group against group; who seek out, exploit, and fan the grievances that can easily be found in a pluralistic society. Every generation has known its nativists, Ku Kluxers, anti-Catholics, anti-Semites, racists, and ethnocentrists. They define themselves by whom they are against. They reject the values of the common civic culture: tolerance, fairness, equality, respect for those who are different. Instead, they preach hatred and conspiracy. In our own time, the common civic culture has been assaulted by ethnocentrists and tribalists (some of whom are tenured academics) who demand not the right to be let alone but the power to impose their vision of ethnic separatism onto the public sphere.

Fortunately, ethnocentrists and tribalists usually have limited staying power; they gain a hearing and may even affect the curriculum in certain universities or school districts, but none has ever prevailed for long. Most Americans do not like to be told that they must think and act on the basis of their blood. Most prefer the freedom the civic culture provides. The alternatives are not appealing.

The all-encompassing civic culture is the best guarantee of our individual liberties; few are willing to exchange them for an ethnic cocoon. The civic culture assures us that our ethnic worlds are not ghettos or shtetls; the elders cannot force us to stay against our will. We are free to leave our ethnic enclaves, bound by nothing more than our internal sense of commitment to family and heritage. In recent years, the civic culture has reassured us, too, that it is praiseworthy to celebrate our ethnic diversity. We do not have to straighten our hair, change our names, shorten our noses, or discard our distinctive garb. Indeed, given the voracious appetite of the American consumer culture for variety, we may expect to see the ethnic garb that was cast away by our grandparents featured in national advertising as the latest fashion.

There are paradoxes aplenty in the emerging American identity. The American common culture is pluralistic. Even academic celebrations of diversity seem slated to feed the hunger of the common culture for new heroes, new models of American accomplishment. The cultural mainstream is a broad stream indeed, one that encompasses people of every race, religion, and ethnic group. The American of our generation who does not know the poetry of Langston Hughes, the fiction of Isaac Bashevis Singer, the paintings of Georgia O'Keefe, the music of Scott Joplin, the architecture of I. M. Pei, or the films of Spike Lee is out of touch with the common culture. We can be sure that the next generation of Americans will add to and subtract from the common culture we know. The great instrumentalities for shaping the common culture—films and television—celebrate diversity, individuality, and talent. The remarkable success of American movies in a world market testifies to the fact that they were produced for an audience that finds universality in particulars.

Years from now, when historians review this period in American life, they are likely to be struck by the blending of and borrowings among the nation's cultures, by the way Americans of different origins peacefully exchanged art, literature, humor, music, cuisine, dress, technology, and ideas. Living in the present, we worry about tribalism and ethnocentrism and the dangers they pose to genuine pluralism as well as to the possibility of building political coalitions for social improvement. But future historians are likely to see instead the absorption, domestication, and commodification of these movements. They will contribute in unimagined ways to the common culture, providing new fodder for books, films, T-shirts, and academic conferences.

I do not suggest that fundamentalism and particularism are to be taken lightly; much of the ethnic slaughter described earlier in this chapter was the result of unrestrained fundamentalism and all-encompassing tribalism. The American civic culture is not comfortable with extremism: the Constitution is a testament to the virtues of checks and balances; the national motto, *e pluribus unum,* requires a balancing of opposites; the American people are themselves a demographic refutation of the principle of racial, ethnic, or religious purity.

What I am proposing as public policy has two components. First, we must teach the civic culture that belongs to all of us and that protects our basic rights. Second, the government must adopt a stance of tolerance and noninterference regarding group life, recognizing that the civic culture is not the whole culture and does not dictate only one way to be an American. It is not the role of government to impose assimilation, cultural pluralism, dynamic pluralism, or separatism on its citizens. Essential to our freedom as Americans is our right as individuals to define our way of life for ourselves.

This proposal may be summarized as *e pluribus unum,* with equal weight given to *pluribus* and *unum.* It draws upon the shared civic culture for the values of tolerance and liberty, as well as for certain obligations and responsibilities of citizenship. Yet it is a *pluralistic* approach, for it accepts that there is no single pattern of group life that is right for everyone. Every citizen is entitled to exactly the same rights and liberties, and every citizen is entitled to make his or her own choices about how or whether to participate in group life.

Probably the area of American life in which we have been most successful in achieving a policy that balances government protection on the one hand and respect for liberty on the other is religion. Because of the widely acknowledged separation of church and state, it is well understood that the law protects religious freedom and prohibits religious discrimination, but that government has no power to interfere with religion; it must not support it, hinder it, or decide whether anyone should embrace it. Regarding religious freedom, government does not interfere, other than to protect expression and prevent discrimination. Government noninterference protects both those who are devout and those who are not.

Similarly, government noninterference is the best way to protect pluralism in other areas of American life. Government should not force people to abandon their ethnic ways, nor should government use its power to preserve those ways. Public policy should not interfere with the choices of those who differ from the majority, whether for reasons of religion, race, or ethnicity. The best policy is limited government, or "live and let live." And the best guarantee of real diversity—in which many different cultures persist and thrive by their own efforts—is pluralism. Modern American life is so relentlessly assimilative and so aggressive in promoting cultural blending, that those who are different should be left alone so long as they respect the law.

A forward-looking public policy must seek to expand the promise of American life to all citizens. As Croly pointed out, American optimism was founded on the faith that everyone who worked hard would escape the curse of poverty. That promise must not be abandoned. Public policy should aim to provide maximum opportunity for all American citizens: economic opportunity, educational opportunity, and social opportunity. Government must stand firmly against any kind of racial or ethnic exclusionary policy without resorting to group preferences or quotas. Public policy should forbid all forms of racial segregation, whether in college dormitories (built with public funds or inhabited by students receiving public scholarships) or in publicly assisted housing. Public policy should help people not because of their race, ethnicity, or gender but because of their economic disadvantage.

At the conclusion of World War I, John Dewey spoke about the ideas Americans might contribute to the reconstruction ahead. First, he recommended to the devastated nations the principle of *e pluribus unum,* "where the unity does not destroy the many, but maintains each constituent factor in full vigor." Then, he offered an idea gleaned from the American experience:

> One of the greatest problems which is troubling the Old World is that of the rights of nationalities which are included within larger political units—the Poles, the Irish, the Bohemians, the Jugo-Slavs, the Jews. Here, too, the American contribution is radical. We have solved the problem by a complete separation of nationality from citizenship. Not only have we separated language, cultural traditions, all that is called race, from the state—that is, from problems of polit-

ical organization and power. To us, language, literature, creed, group ways, national culture, are social rather than political, human rather than national, interests. Let this idea fly abroad; it bears healing in its wings.[7]

Dewey was wrong in that the United States had not done what he said; at that very time, it did restrict the rights of African Americans on the basis of their race, and it assertively classified people by race. But his statement should be read as a description of the American ideal, the American creed that Gunnar Myrdal later wrote about. Today the government regularly interferes in matters of language, group ways, and culture—matters that belong to the private sphere; I suggest, with Dewey, that it should not. The choice to assimilate must remain with the individual, not the state; the choice to preserve cultural traditions belongs to individuals and groups, not to the state.

If we are to fulfill the promise of American life, we must renew our egalitarian ideals, our commitment to individual rights, and our sense of civic responsibility. As our nation becomes a microcosm of the world, embracing as citizens people from every race and culture, we must teach the civic culture on which all of us rely. It should be a settled principle that the state must protect all American citizens against discrimination without interfering in private matters of creed, religion, ethnicity, race, gender, or culture. We must reinvigorate the processes of democracy in our neighborhoods, our communities, and our cities. We must revive our capacity at the local level for problem solving, for pitching in and helping our neighbors. And we must count on the resources of government to guarantee equal opportunity for individuals to improve themselves, regardless of who they are, where they live, or who their parents were.

Notes

1. *Plessy v. Ferguson,* 163 U.S. 537 (1896).
2. John Derbyshire, "Which Box to Check? White, Asian, or None of Them?" *New York Times,* July 17, 1994, 16.
3. Harold R. Isaacs, *Idols of the Tribe: Group Identity and Political Change* (New York: Harper and Row, 1975), 218.
4. Ibid., 2.
5. Daniel Goleman, "Amid Ethnic Wars, Psychiatrists Seek Roots of Conflicts," *New York Times,* August 2, 1994, C1.
6. Horace M. Kallen, "Democracy Versus the Melting Pot: A Study of American Nationality," *The Nation,* February 1915.
7. John Dewey, "America in the World," in *Essays on China, Japan, and the War,* Volume 11 of *The Middle Works of John Dewey, 1899-1924,* ed. Jo Ann Boydston (Carbondale: University of Illinois Press, 1982), 71.

Chapter Five

The Promise of Racial Equality

Abigail Thernstrom and Stephan Thernstrom

The public high schools in our nation's capital are virtually all-black. A few hundred white students, two-thirds of whom are concentrated in one school, intermingle with approximately fourteen thousand blacks. In the southeast corner of the city, African American kids wear T-shirts with the racially divisive message, "It's a black thing, you wouldn't understand." But no whites are even listening in that neighborhood, in which none lives.[1]

All-black schools need not be educationally disastrous; in Washington, however, despite per-pupil spending almost twice the national average, most of them are.[2] The problem in Washington goes well beyond education. The murder rate over the past fifteen years has roughly tripled. Public housing (home to twenty-four thousand families) is in disrepair, ravaged by drugs, crime, and abysmal maintenance—by residents and management alike.[3] And the middle class (both black and white) is leaving. The District of Columbia, a 1990 report concluded, has "the highest infant mortality rate of any similar geopolitical entity, state, or territory among the United States."[4]

The District is two-thirds black. Is the social disorder that plagues the city evidence that American life is promising primarily for whites? That the American dream, for blacks, is still deferred?

Yes and no. It often seems—and is often said—that the racial scene has
changed little, that blacks in American cities are a racially isolated, subordinate caste. "From the Emancipation Proclamation on, the Man been handing
us a bunch of bogus freedom checks he never intends to honor," Derrick Bell
writes in his best-selling *Faces at the Bottom of the Well*. "For over three centuries," he adds, "this country has promised democracy and delivered discrimination and delusions."[5] Andrew Hacker's *Two Nations* (also a best-seller) is subtitled *Black and White, Separate, Hostile, Unequal,* and racial
oppression is its central theme. Whites "scarcely acknowledge the common
features of humanity in this stranger whom slavery has brought among them,"
Alexis de Tocqueville wrote in 1830; that description, Hacker argues, "might
have been written today."[6] This is the view, as well, of the much-acclaimed
Lani Guinier, who sees African Americans as "a pariah group" kept in its
place by a "permanent" and "hostile" white majority.[7]

It is an odd perspective.

The Civil Rights Revolution

Perhaps Andrew Hacker cannot recognize "the common features of
humanity" whites and blacks share, but the twenty million viewers who made
the Bill Cosby show the most popular situation comedy in the history of television certainly could. Cosby—who earned NBC a billion dollars—was no
"stranger" to them.[8] It is not just that the antebellum America of which
Tocqueville wrote is long gone; the pre–World War I nation of which Herbert
Croly wrote in *The Promise of American Life* has also been transformed.
Croly's work was published in 1909, the year the NAACP was founded, yet
the question of racial equality failed to catch his attention. Such indifference
was not special to Croly. For northerners, blacks were largely out of sight and
out of mind. Even twenty years later, blacks were almost entirely ignored in
Middletown, Robert and Helen Lynd's classic study of American small-city
culture.[9]

In the South, where roughly 90 percent of the nation's blacks lived, the
prevailing white attitude toward blacks was not indifference but active hostility and implacable determination to keep African Americans confined to
"their place." Blacks were disfranchised, denied basic legal rights, forcibly
segregated, economically subjugated, and socially invisible. In fact, lynchings
averaged seventy-five per year in the decade in which Croly wrote.

Except for a rapid decline in the number of lynchings, the basic elements
of that picture remained unchanged for another thirty years. Traveling in the
South in the late 1930s, Gunnar Myrdal was appalled to learn that any white
could "strike or beat a Negro, steal or destroy his property, cheat him in a
transaction and even take his life, without much fear of legal reprisal."[10]

Black people, he discovered, were "excluded not only from the white man's society but also from the ordinary symbols of respect."[11] It would, for instance, have been a major violation of the caste order to address a black woman as "Mrs. Washington"—"Mrs." being a term reserved for whites. African Americans still could not vote, and blacks and whites were kept apart on streetcars, buses, and railroads, as well as in schools, waiting rooms, restaurants, hotels, boarding houses, theaters, cemeteries, parks, courtrooms, public toilets—and every other public space.

In the North, public accomodations were not segregated by law. Blacks could vote and run for office, use the local hospital and the public library, sit at the front of a bus, share a lunch counter—and even shake hands—with whites. Perhaps most important, they lived free of the terror that stalked the lives of southern blacks; they had rights which whites, too, had to respect. But a color line kept them out of the best paid and most desirable jobs, the better restaurants, and white neighborhoods and therefore white schools. In fact, some states allowed local communities to operate dual educational systems; *Brown v. Board of Education,* it may be recalled, involved segregated schools in Topeka, Kansas.

The curtain came down on the Jim Crow South in the 1950s and 1960s. In the North, too, the status of blacks began to improve dramatically—the consequence not of judicial decisions and congressional action but of a revolution in racial attitudes that began in the 1940s. In 1942, half of all northern whites believed that blacks were not as intelligent as whites, that they could not "learn things just as well if they [were] given the same education and training." Four years later, the skeptics were down to less than 40 percent, and by 1956 their numbers had dropped to 17 percent. Asked whether they would object to a black "with the same income and education" moving into their block, in 1942 almost two-thirds of the nation's whites said yes. By 1956 the figure was down to 49 percent, and to 42 percent among northern whites.[12]

Those were questions asked before sickening scenes of German shepherds and water from high-pressure hoses, used to quell peaceful demonstrators, had flashed across American television screens in the early 1960s. The civil rights revolution changed hearts and minds, as well as the law. By 1972 there was almost no dissent—even in the South—from the notion that whites and blacks should have an equal opportunity to get "any kind of job"; moreover, 84 percent of whites agreed that black and white students should attend the same schools.

Has racism disappeared? Of course not. But overt discrimination is now the great exception rather than the rule. The discovery in 1994 that a number of restaurants in the Denny's chain were treating black customers badly made national news. The story was rightly considered shocking. Restaurants were abruptly "closed" when blacks showed up; those not turned away were often harassed in a variety of ways. They were kept waiting, asked to pay before being served, seated in the back, treated with disrespect, or told there were minimum-purchase requirements. But Denny's paid dearly for the contemptible behavior of some of its personnel: its parent company coughed up $54.4 million to settle the litigation.[13]

In the South prior to passage of the 1964 Civil Rights Act, white-patronized restaurants didn't keep black customers waiting; they did not serve them at all. Today, there is much talk of federal overreaching—of too much federal legislation touching too many spheres of life. But the civil rights legislation of the mid-1960s was designed to remedy a real wrong. It changed the South, and thus changed the nation. That seems all but forgotten by skeptics who doubt that sweeping federal action is ever necessary and by those who—like Derrick Bell—think it did no good.

Progress Since the 1960s

Much was promised in the 1960s—and much delivered. In fact, as Frank Luntz shows in chapter 3, that fact has not escaped a majority of black Americans; 56 percent now describe themselves as either having achieved or being "close" to achieving the American dream. Only 28 percent of blacks say they are either "very far" from achieving that dream or never expect to get there—a figure almost indistinguishable from the 25 percent figure for whites. These very striking findings suggest a puzzle: why is the voice of the black leadership and the black cultural elite so pessimistic? And why do the white-run media take that pessimism so seriously?

The doors of opportunity are open, and blacks are walking through them. The gains are apparent in the nation's capital. Reports of inner-city distress fill the press; in fact, the city contains one of the greatest concentrations of affluent, college-educated African Americans in the country. The District is two-thirds black, and yet, until very recently, median family income was slightly above the national average. (Black and white middle-class flight to the suburbs has now resulted in some slippage.)

Much of the national picture is also heartening. Most African Americans are not poor; two-thirds have incomes above the poverty line—a marked contrast with the picture in 1940, when the poverty rate for black families was a staggering 87 percent.[14] More important, the median income of black *married* couples with children in 1992 was $36,357, a mere 1.2 percent below the average for all American families and *more than double* the figure for white single-parent families. The main determinant of family income is thus not race but family structure.[15] Persistent black poverty is the result in large measure of the extraordinarily high proportion of female-headed black households.

The gap in social status between the races has been closing. One-third of black families remain mired in poverty, but the upper third now resembles more closely the top third of whites. In 1940, 8 percent of black men earned more than the white male median income; in 1980 29 percent did.[16] Today, there are twenty-seven thousand black lawyers and judges, eleven times as many as there were just three decades ago. The number of black engineers has increased fourteen-fold over that same period. There are sixteen times as many black editors and reporters as there were thirty years ago.[17] This list could obviously be extended; indicators of black progress abound.

The doors of opportunity are not simply ajar; black advancement has become a national project. In 1909, the year *The Promise of American Life* was published, the governor of Mississippi told the state legislature that "money spent today for the maintenance of public schools for negroes is robbery of the white man, and a waste upon the negro."[18] And indeed not much money was "wasted" on the African American. Today, per-pupil spending in heavily black inner-city schools is generally above the state average, and racial sensitivity, black history, and other such workshops are a regular feature of the educational landscape.[19]

The commitment to black progress runs through the major institutions of American society. Elementary and secondary schools compete for black teachers, elite law schools for black students, newspapers for promising black journalists. The major corporations not only have "goals and timetables" that guide their hiring decisions; many give a special helping hand to small minority firms. Thus in recent years the Ford Motor Company has made a big effort to recruit minority suppliers. As part of that push, it guaranteed business to a black-owned trucking firm that needed Ford's support to secure a $100 million financial package that enabled it to expand. As the *Wall Street Journal* reported in November 1994, even companies that are downsizing and trimming costs are often buying more goods and services from minority-owned businesses.[20]

Residential Patterns

Black progress—impressive in many respects—flunks an acid test, it is often said. If blacks and whites work together, they live apart. Neighborhoods are still color coded. Substantial portions of our urban landscape remain white turf or black turf. No signs are posted to indicate which is which, but none are needed.

There is some truth in this, but it is far from the whole truth. Virtually all large American urban centers have overwhelmingly black neighborhoods in which a large fraction of their African American population lives; the sharp residential separation of the races is undeniably one of the most glaringly

obvious features of the typical American metropolis today. But not all blacks
live in large cities, and in smaller communities the level of segregation is
lower. More important, the suburbs that surround the city core are no longer
lily-white.

Whites are still to be found living in suburbs much more commonly than
blacks, but since 1970 the black suburbanization rate has outpaced that of
whites. Between 1970 and 1990, the number of whites living in suburbia rose
by 46 percent; but the black rate of increase was almost triple that—125 percent. In 1990, more than one out of four African Americans was a suburban-
ite, still well below the 50 percent figure for whites but a huge gain when
compared with less than a sixth just twenty years ago.

In 1970, for instance, 85 percent of the whites in the Atlanta metropolitan
area lived in suburbia, compared to barely a quarter of the blacks. By 1990, the
white figure had moved up a bit to 94 percent, while the black rate had soared
to 64 percent. Similarly, a quarter of the blacks in the Washington, D.C., metropolitan area had suburban addresses in 1970, as compared with 90 percent
of the whites. Over the next two decades the white concentration in the D.C.
suburbs rose by three points, while the black figure more than doubled, to 61
percent. Over the same years, the proportion of black suburbanites in the
Cleveland area climbed from 14 to 34 percent; in Dallas from 13 to 29 percent;
in San Diego from 15 to 35 percent; in Seattle from 8 to 36 percent.[21]

As a result both of the mass movement of middle-class blacks to suburbia in the past quarter century and of a blurring of the color line within cen-
tral-city neighborhoods, overall levels of residential segregation by race have
declined perceptibly. The most common measure employed by scholars
studying the matter is the "index of dissimilarity," which shows how differently two or more groups are distributed across urban space. If the black-
white index of dissimilarity for a particular community stood at zero, it would
mean that blacks and whites were randomly distributed and there was no segregation at all. An index of 90, on the other hand, means very severe segregation—nine out of ten blacks in the city would need to move to attain random
distribution.

If we look at the fifteen metropolitan areas with the largest black populations, we find that in 1970 the dissimilarity index was below 80 in only two
of them, and not much below 80 at that (78 for Houston, 73 for New Orleans).
In the other thirteen of our largest metropolises, at least 80 percent of the
black residents would have had to move to another neighborhood to eliminate
residential segregation altogether. This would seem to be a pretty strongly
segregated pattern.

Has anything much changed? By 1990, segregation had diminished in all
but two of these fifteen major black population centers. New York was the
only one in which racial separation had increased, and there the rise was by

just a single percentage point. Detroit, very highly segregated in 1970, was completely unchanged two decades later. Of the remaining thirteen cities, two—Chicago and Cleveland—had only very modest declines in their indexes of dissimilarity, drops of just six points. In the other eleven urban giants, though, the level of residential segregation of blacks from whites fell sharply—by 24 points in Dallas, 18 in Los Angeles, 15 in Washington, D.C., 14 in Atlanta, and 13 in both Miami and San Francisco.[22]

The index of dissimilarity measures how much various groups deviate from a purely random distribution. But is random distribution a meaningful standard? Virtually all ethnic groups in American society show some tendency to cluster together residentially; a random distribution of African Americans is thus an unreasonable expectation. In fact, another measure of segregation may be more illuminating. Our common-sense notion of life in "the ghetto" is that its black inhabitants live nowhere near whites. A recent survey asked how many blacks live in "the same neighborhood" as white people. The answer for 1987 was a remarkable 82 percent! This was a leap of 14 percentage points in just five years. Furthermore, almost six in ten blacks lived on the same block as whites in 1987, up from 46 percent a mere five years before.[23]

Our cities still contain strong concentrations of black populations that can reasonably be called ghettos. But the common impression that our society is becoming increasingly polarized, with blacks locked into the inner city and shut out of the all-white suburbs, is mistaken. The residential color line has not disappeared, but it has become much more blurred than it was only two or three decades ago.

Flight from Integration?

Blacks and whites may be both living closer and drifting apart. That is, even as residential integration becomes more common, the races' *sense* of separation may be increasing. That is certainly the picture most often drawn in the media and by black political and cultural celebrities.

For instance, in the summer of 1993 the widely respected *Economist* reported, "for every middle class black making his way though a white corporation, going to a white college, or mowing his lawn in a white suburb, many more are consciously seeking out black schooling and black culture." After the Rodney King verdict, it went on, "blacks *en masse* began to withdraw their money from the (white) commercial banks, putting it in black banks, and started a drive to support black businesses."[24]

How the usually authoritative *Economist* came to write such an erroneous story is a mystery. No growing hunger for "black schooling," for example, shows up in the data on college enrollment patterns. Only a quarter century ago, half of all black college students were enrolled in historically black institutions. By 1975 the proportion was down to 30 percent. It has continued to edge downward ever since, and was a mere 16 percent at last report.[25] Some African Americans have been celebrating Kwanzaa, a Christmastime holiday invented in 1966 by the leader of a black nationalist group, but how many? The number is probably very small—although no one has been able to count it.[26] And some blacks are undoubtedly making an effort to patronize black firms, but "it's not a major factor in their purchase decisions," according to Timothy Bates, an economist who studies black entrepreneurship. Undoubtedly more common is the view of one young black woman who told a reporter that she buys the shampoo that works.[27] A group of black Washingtonians have revived an early 1950s ritual, the annual "Capital Classic weekends," which featured a football game between two black colleges, marching bands, parties, and motorcade. But again, this is a minor show of black pride—hardly part of a clear separatist trend.

In fact, some survey data suggest confidence about the state of race relations and an impressive commitment to integration on the part of both blacks and whites. In a 1994 poll of Washington, D.C., residents, 82 percent of blacks and 62 percent of whites said they thought the two races got along "well."[28] In a national poll taken that same year, 70 percent of whites said that racial integration had been good for the society, a view echoed by 65 percent of blacks.[29] And again in 1994, a majority (54 percent) of blacks denied that there was "ever a circumstance in which it would be better for a black student to attend an all black school."[30]

In 1989 two out of every three whites reported having a "fairly close" friend who was black, a substantial jump from the 50 percent who said so eight years earlier. And the number of blacks who claimed to have a fairly close white friend rose from 69 percent in 1981 to 80 percent eight years later.[31] (We have no data from the 1950s and early 1960s, but clearly those numbers would be much lower.) Moreover, in 1993 a mere 3 percent of blacks surveyed said that Louis Farrakhan was the most important national leader in the black community; 39 percent named Jesse Jackson—the voice of the Rainbow Coalition.[32] By 1994, the percentage of blacks who opposed interracial dating had dropped from 18 percent in 1987 to 11 percent; in that same period white opposition dropped from 51 to 32 percent.[33]

That is the good news; there is, however, some conflicting evidence. Between 1983 and 1991, the percentage of blacks who approved of interracial marriage decreased from 76 to 71. (In the same period, the proportion of approving whites rose from 38 to 44.)[34] The same pattern—modest increases in support for integration by whites and modest declines in support by blacks—appears in studies of attitudes toward neighborhood integration in Detroit between 1978 and 1992. While Detroit's whites were becoming more accepting of having black neighbors, blacks were becoming less willing to live in predominantly white parts of the metropolitan area.[35] In 1993, 52 percent of blacks (but only 33 percent of whites) agreed that "our nation is moving toward two societies, one black and one white—separate and unequal."[36]

A 1992 poll conducted for the Anti-Defamation League showed more pessimism about the state of race relations than those cited above. Eighty-one percent of blacks and 76 percent of whites said race relations were "not so good" or "poor." Most blacks (68 percent) and whites (73 percent) agreed that "about half" of whites in America were "basically prejudiced."[37] Asked in 1993 whether they thought "relations between blacks and whites [would] always be a problem" or that "a solution [would] eventually be worked out," only 44 percent of blacks were optimistic that "a solution" would be worked out, a dismaying drop of 26 percentage points since 1963—a year before the 1964 Civil Rights Act was passed![38]

In addition, black pride can get ugly. In 1980, the Association of Black Psychologists passed a resolution declaring that "the Divine Images of Caucasian flesh constitute an oppressive instrument destructive to the self-esteem of Black people."[39] In the same spirit, the National Association of Black Social Workers has condemned the adoption of black babies by white families as "cultural genocide" against black infants. A number of best-selling black authors depict all whites as enemies. Thus Nathan McCall in his much celebrated book, *Makes Me Wanna Holler,* writes that "white men are the most lying creatures on the face of the earth," and that whites have "oppressed people of color whenever they encountered them."[40] Are such angry and alienated voices ominous signs of things to come? We do not know. This is very murky territory.

Public Policy and the Racial Divide

The polling data are hard to read, but this much can be said with confidence: if blacks and whites are indeed drifting apart, if the racial divide is in fact getting wider, our "enlightened" public policies are in part to blame. For the past quarter century, in places of employment, in institutions of higher education, and even in the political arena, blacks and whites have been treated not as individuals but as members of distinct racial groups. The state has been pasting racial and ethnic labels on all citizens, sorting them out accordingly, and conferring special benefits on blacks and members of other designated groups.

For example, law schools at the University of Texas and elsewhere have been admitting black students by standards entirely different from those that apply to whites.[41] Public elementary and secondary schools judge black applicants for teaching positions by separate criteria. Corporations that do business with the government are required to set racial and ethnic hiring goals. Such race-conscious policies are of course not confined to the public sector, but it is the classification of citizens along lines of race by the state— publicly sanctioned discrimination—that is most troubling.

Quotas divide the races. They do so literally, by creating separate, racially defined categories. And they do so indirectly, by increasing racial tension. White anger about preferential policies is widespread and has been documented with unusual rigor in Sniderman and Piazza's *The Scar of Race*. Analyzing five public-opinion surveys, the authors find that affirmative action "is so intensely disliked that it has led some whites to dislike blacks—an ironic example of a policy meant to put the divide of race behind us in fact further widening it."[42]

Backlash is the widely acknowledged problem, but there is another. Affirmative action policies protect black candidates from white competition. That is their point. They create a system of reserved seats in classrooms, places of employment, and legislative bodies for members of designated racial and ethnic groups. They thereby suggest, loudly and clearly, that blacks cannot make it without special arrangements—that, for instance, teaching certification tests "present a greater challenge" to black men and women, as an officer of the American Association of Colleges for Teacher Education suggested in 1990.[43] It is a poisonous, demeaning message, and it clearly labels blacks as a people apart.

In fact, African Americans do not need extraordinary protection; in a competitive world, they can make it. If preferential policies ended tomorrow, the total number of black law school students—and thus of future black attorneys—would not change. The distribution of those students among the schools would be different (fewer at Harvard, more at Boston College)—but for how long? The racial gap in educational achievement has been closing; we have no reason to believe that over time the applicant pools of whites and blacks will not converge.

A view of blacks as permanently crippled seems permanently embedded in the arguments made by affirmative action proponents. The fast-changing racial scene is stagnant, in their view. And thus they continue to believe, for instance, that, without extraordinary protection from white competition, black candidates for public office would almost never win, that they need the racially gerrymandered legislative districts—the safe black enclaves—that have now become such a pervasive part of the electoral landscape. But those districts not only smack of segregation; they are unnecessary. That is not wishful thinking; the evidence is all around us.

Whites not only vote for black candidates; they frequently support an African American running against a white opponent. That choice is most often available in mayoral contests. Conventional wisdom has it that the overwhelming majority of black mayors have been elected from majority-black cities, but most of those black "cities" are in fact tiny majority-black towns in the South. Eliminate those small urban dots on the southern map, and focus on cities of fifty thousand or more in population, and quite a different picture emerges. Eighty-three percent of the black mayors elected in such cities over the last thirty years have not had the benefit of a majority-black constituency. Sixty-one percent were elected in municipalities less than 40 percent black, and 43 percent took office in cities less than 30 percent black.

Thus in the 1989 mayoral race in New York City (29 percent black), Rudolph Giuliani lost between 25 and 30 percent of the white vote to David Dinkins. At least 38 percent of whites deserted Jon Derus in Minneapolis (13 percent black) in 1993 and cast their ballots for the victor, Sharon Sayles Belton, the black president of the city council. That same year, 31 percent of the white electorate in St. Louis (48 percent African American) had three white candidates to choose among and went instead for Freeman Bosley, Jr.; in fact, his overall vote total was precisely that of his white predecessor.

Belton and Bosley were making their first try; incumbents (with the obvious exception of David Dinkins in 1993) generally do even better. In the racially divided, minority-black Chicago of the late 1980s, even Harold Washington picked up more white support his second time around, especially in five lakefront liberal wards. The 1991 mayoral contest in Memphis was extremely racially polarized, and Willie Herenton won by only 142 votes, but a year later the mayor had a 60 percent approval rating among the city's whites.

It is not only in races for a mayor's seat that white voters choose black candidates over white. L. Douglas Wilder, in his successful gubernatorial run in 1989, got an estimated 40 to 43 percent of Virginia's white vote. Skeptics will say that figure still represents only a minority of the white electorate, but Charles Robb, the white Democratic governor who preceded Wilder, did only a shade better—45 percent.[44] Illinois (11.6 percent black) elected Carol Moseley-Braun to the U.S. Senate in 1992. In 1994, Ohio elected J. Kenneth Blackwell as state treasurer, and New York chose H. Carl McCall as state comptroller. Also in 1994, J. C. Watts won a congressional seat in a mostly (83 percent) white Oklahoma district. This is not a new phenomenon. Andrew Young was elected to Congress in 1972 from Georgia's fifth district, which was then majority-white.

Does this mean that, without the race-conscious districting that creates safe black legislative seats, the racial composition of, say, the U.S. House of Representatives would remain precisely the same? Probably not. Most members of the Congressional Black Caucus are too far to the left to win election in majority-white settings. But the doors to political advancement are open, and over time more centrist black candidates would walk through them. The districts, as currently drawn, divide whites from blacks; they imply two nations within our nation. If racial tension and racial isolation are together our greatest domestic threat, every public policy that widens the racial divide is dangerous.

Some Guidelines

It is relatively easy to describe the racial landscape and point to the problems within it. It is obviously much harder to suggest where we might go from here—what public policies would make sense. There are no easy answers. Or at least there are none that we—two authors who have been struggling with the issue of race for some time—feel entirely confident about.

We have, at this point, a few modest suggestions about directions this country should take, rough guidelines that may be helpful in thinking through the issue.

First, the government should stop classifying Americans along lines of race and allocating resources on the basis of race. It is time to endorse the view of the first Justice Harlan that our Constitution is color-blind, and rearrange our public life in accord with that view.[45]

Public policies deliver messages about what sort of society we want. In the 1960s we passed civil rights legislation not only to force white Americans to treat black citizens decently, but also to make a statement about what we, as a nation, stood for. Judge people by the content of their character, we said; skin color is irrelevant. Was Martin Luther King's phrase too simple? Of course. King knew being black was different from being white in American society. But he also knew it was the right message. And it remains the right message today.

This is the most elementary of points—forgotten, however, by both political parties. Republicans have talked a race-blind lingo but have often embraced color-conscious policies—in part believing it was politically impossible to do otherwise.

Second, civil rights laws should be vigorously enforced—but *as they were understood at the time of their passage.* There is nothing wrong with the 1964 Civil Rights Act that cannot be fixed if Congress will declare once again that the intentional, disparate treatment of individuals on the basis of race, religion, or national origin was the sole concern of the act. Likewise, the 1965 Voting Rights Act is still a good law, but neither it nor any of its amendments was intended to create a right to safe black (and Hispanic) legislative seats, and Congress needs to make that clear.

Racial equality was not part of the grand national scheme that Herbert Croly envisioned, but the great civil rights statutes of the 1960s suggest that he was partly right. Some national problems do require national solutions. The civil rights acts of that decade did, in fact, summon Americans away from selfish interests and parochial allegiances, toward a commitment to an overarching national ideal. Those statutes made us a better nation. The grand national project they constituted, however, got all bent out of shape in the process of enforcement. It's not too late to move forward by turning back.

Third, quality schools and safe streets are the real civil rights issues today—insufficiently recognized as such by the Congressional Black Caucus, which pays more attention to Haiti than it does to Harlem. We should experiment with a wide variety of the educational reforms that have recently been proposed, including vouchers, which would (at the very least) allow some inner-city students to leave schools that no middle-class family would tolerate. But no public money should be allowed for the racially exclusive schools that some proponents of Afrocentrism have called for. As to crime, we leave that question to John DiIulio in chapter 15.

Fourth, no one has a surefire or quick solution to inner-city problems. It is tempting to try to return to an earlier era, but we cannot reverse course on a road that is not clearly marked. In truth, we do not really know why, for instance, the black teen homicide rate has skyrocketed since 1987, or why so many very young, unmarried black women are choosing to have babies. And even if we could accurately identify the sources of the current mess, that would not necessarily point to a clear remedy. We may have mixed a combustible brew that feeds on itself once ignited. Understanding what is burning won't put the fire out.

The best we can do is keep our eyes out for the rescue operations that work, insist on rigorous evaluation of programs that seem to have promise, and insist as well that state action can do only so much to solve the problem of broken families and broken lives. The absence of rigorous evaluations of existing programs is a serious problem; Outward Bound's inner-city efforts, for instance, have a great reputation, but no one really knows whether they work.

Fifth, we must face the fact that our policy choices will often involve difficult trade-offs. Fourth Amendment rights may be compromised in exchange for safe public housing. Vouchers may result in some academically weak or ideologically offensive schools; parents do not necessarily choose well. The number of homeless may increase with a scaling down of Aid to Families with Dependent Children payments. The list goes on. These prices may be worth paying, but they should be acknowledged and discussed. We are such a trendy, nervous, credulous society that we tend to rush from one enthusiasm to another; it is better to greet every new idea with a healthy dose of skepticism.

A Final Word

In 1909 Herbert Croly saw a nation full of promise—but for whites only. Blacks were beyond his horizon of concern. Much has changed since then; no one today could write a manifesto for political and social change while ignoring the status of blacks.

Many would argue that America has hardly begun to fulfill its essential commitment to blacks. We see a different picture—unfinished but looking pretty good. Lots of success in meeting the nation's promise, some distance to go in fulfilling it, on the road to doing so. We worry most about public policies that divide the races. Change those policies, and much else will fall into place.

Notes

1. Katherine Boo, "Washington: Divided, Even Where the Races Meet," *Washington Post,* October 21, 1994, A1.
2. Per-pupil spending in the District for 1991–1992 was $9,549, while the national average was $5,421.
3. Serge F. Kovaleski, "Tight Rules Pushed for Public Housing," *Washington Post,* October 28, 1994, B1.
4. The Infant Mortality Review Progress Report, quoted in Sally Quinn, "Childhood's End," *Washington Post,* November 20, 1994, C1.
5. Derrick Bell, *Faces at the Bottom of the Well: The Permanence of Racism* (New York: Basic Books, 1992), 18, 97.
6. Andrew Hacker, *Two Nations* (New York: Charles Scribner's Sons, 1992), 215.
7. Lani Guinier, *The Tyranny of the Majority: Fundamental Fairness in Representative Government* (New York: The Free Press, 1994), 37, 55.
8. The size of the Cosby viewing audience is reported in "CBS Stays Right on Top of Ratings," *Chicago Tribune,* March 8, 1985, C8; and Laura B. Randolph, "Life After the Cosby Show," *Ebony,* May 1994, 100.
9. Robert S. Lynd and Helen Merrell Lynd, *Middletown: A Study in American Culture* (New York: Harcourt Brace, 1929). The introduction contained the only reference to black residents of Muncie, Indiana, noting they were 6 percent of the population.
10. Gunnar Myrdal, *An American Dilemma* (New York: Harper and Row, 1944), 559.
11. Ibid., 65.
12. These figures and those in the next paragraph come from surveys by the National Opinion Research Center, as reported in Herbert H. Hyman and Paul B. Sheatsley, "Attitudes toward Desegregation," *Scientific American* 195 (December 1956): 35–39; and Howard Schuman, Charlotte Steeh, and Lawrence Bobo, *Racial Attitudes in America: Trends and Interpretations* (Cambridge, Mass.: Harvard University Press, 1985), table 3.1, 74–75.
13. The Denny's story is told at length in Howard Kohn, "Service With a Sneer," *New York Times Magazine,* November 6, 1994, 43–47, 58, 78, 81.
14. U.S. Bureau of the Census, Current Population Reports, P-60-185, *Poverty in the United States: 1992* (Washington, D.C.: U.S. Government Printing Office, 1993), 3; James P. Smith, "Poverty and the Family," in *Divided Opportunities: Minorities, Poverty, and Social Policy,* ed. Gary Sandefur and Marta Tienda (New York: Plenum Press, 1988), 143–44.

15. U.S. Bureau of the Census, Current Population Reports, P-60-184, *Money Income of Households, Families, and Persons in the United States: 1992* (Washington, D.C.: U.S. Government Printing Office, 1993), 68, 71–73.
16. James P. Smith and Finis R. Welch, "Black Economic Progress After Myrdal," *Journal of Economic Literature* 27 (June 1989): 522–23.
17. U.S. Bureau of the Census, 1990 Census of the Population, Supplementary Reports, 1990 CP-S-1, *Detailed Occupation and Other Characteristics From the EEO File for the United States* (Washington, D.C.: U.S. Government Printing Office, 1992), table 1.
18. Quoted in Earl Black and Merle Black, *Politics and Society in the South* (Cambridge, Mass.: Harvard University Press, 1987), 88.
19. Michael B. Boozer, Alan Krueger, and Shari Wolkon, "Race and School Quality Since *Brown v. Board of Education,*" National Bureau of Economic Research Working Paper Number 4109, Cambridge, Mass., 15.
20. Udayan Gupta, "Minority Suppliers Get Aid at Big Firms," *Wall Street Journal,* November 10, 1994, B2.
21. 1970 figures from John F. Kain, "Black Suburbanization in the Eighties: A New Beginning or a False Hope?" in *American Domestic Priorities: An Economic Appraisal,* ed. John M. Quigley and Daniel L. Rubinfeld (Berkeley: University of California Press, 1985), 260; 1990 calculated from U.S. Bureau of the Census, 1990 Census of Population, *General Population Characteristics: United States,* 1990-CP-1-1 (Washington, D.C.: U.S. Government Printing Office, 1992), tables 266, 276.
22. Segregation indexes as given in Douglas S. Massey and Nancy Denton, *American Apartheid: Segregation and the Making of the Underclass* (Cambridge, Mass.: Harvard University Press, 1993), 222. The authors interpret the evidence quite differently than we do. As their lurid title suggests, they deny that residential segregation is "fading progressively over time" (1), though this seems to be the pattern evident in the tables that are the heart of their book.
23. William Feigelman and Bernard S. Gorman, "Blacks Who Live Near Whites: 1982 and 1987," *Sociology and Social Research* 74 (July 1990): 202–207.
24. Editorial in the *Economist,* July 10, 1993, 14.
25. Reynolds Farley, *Blacks and Whites: Narrowing the Gap?* (Cambridge, Mass.: Harvard University Press, 1984), 23; U.S. Department of Education, National Center for Education Statistics, *Digest of Educational Statistics: 1994* (Washington, D.C.: U.S. Government Printing Office, 1994), 208, 224.
26. The Hallmark card company estimates that five million blacks (one-sixth of the black population) celebrate the holiday ("Only in Afro-America," *Economist,* December 17, 1994, 32). This figure seems very inflated. In 1994 a Kwanzaa exposition in five heavily black cities drew a total (five-city) crowd of ninety thousand, which was probably about 5 percent of the combined black population of those cities. The ninety thousand figure comes from Ann Scales, "Kwanzaa's Message Hits Home," *Boston Globe,* December 30, 1994, 29.
27. Leon E. Wynter, "Business & Race" column, *Wall Street Journal,* August 17, 1994, B1.

28. Katherine Boo, op. cit.
29. Gerald F. Seib and Joe Davidson, "Whites, Blacks Agree on Problems," *Wall Street Journal,* September 29, 1994, A1. Neither whites nor blacks named integration as one of their top priorities, however.
30. Leslie McAneny and Lydia Saad, "America's Public Schools: Still Separate? Still Unequal?" *Gallup Poll Monthly,* May 1994, 24.
31. Richard Morin and Dan Balz, "Shifting Racial Climate," *Washington Post,* October 25, 1989, A1.
32. C. Gray Wheeler, "Thirty Years Beyond 'I Have A Dream,'" *Gallup Poll Monthly,* October 1993, 6.
33. Times Mirror Center for The People and The Press, *The New Political Landscape,* October 1994, 31.
34. Gallup News Service Poll, *Los Angeles Times,* August 16, 1991.
35. Reynolds Farley et. al., "Continued Residential Segregation in Detroit: 'Chocolate City, Vanilla Suburbs' Revisited," *Journal of Housing Research* 4 (1993): 23, 26.
36. George Gallup, Jr., ed., "Civil Rights and Race Relations," Survey #GO 422008, in *The Gallup Poll: Public Opinion 1993* (Wilmington, Del.: Scholarly Resources Inc., 1993), 178.
37. Anti-Defamation League, *Highlights from an Anti-Defamation League Survey on Racial Attitudes in America,* poll conducted by Marttila & Kiley, Inc., November 1992, released June 1993, 36–37, 40–41.
38. C. Gray Wheeler, op. cit.
39. Laurie Goodstein, "Religion's Changing Face," *Washington Post,* March 28, 1994, A1.
40. Nathan McCall, *Makes Me Wanna Holler: A Young Black Man in America* (New York: Random House, 1994).
41. The separate admissions criteria for blacks, Hispanics, and whites at the University of Texas Law School came to light in the case of *Hopwood et al. v. State of Texas,* decided by U.S. District Judge Sam Sparks (Western District, Texas) on August 19, 1994. See Center for Individual Rights, *Docket Report: Special Issue on Hopwood v. Texas,* Washington, D.C., 1994.
42. Paul M. Sniderman and Thomas Piazza, *The Scar of Race* (Cambridge, Mass.: Harvard University Press, 1993), 109.
43. Kenneth J. Cooper, "Seeking Better Teachers," *Washington Post Education Review,* November 18, 1990, 20.
44. R. H. Melton, "Wilder's Demographic Strategy Led to Win," *Washington Post,* November 12, 1989, A1.
45. For a history of our flirtation with the notion of a color-blind Constitution, see Andrew Kull, *The Color-Blind Constitution* (Cambridge, Mass.: Harvard University Press, 1992).

Chapter Six

Immigration

Francis Fukuyama

There are few issues as emotional and divisive in America today as immigration, and few have defied traditional left-right dichotomies to a similar extent. While opposition to immigration in Europe has been an almost exclusive province of the right, the United States, with its long and largely successful history of immigration, finds both liberals and conservatives divided against themselves on this issue. This schizophrenia was evident in the civil war among conservatives over Proposition 187, the California ballot measure limiting educational and health benefits that passed in November 1994 by a margin of 59 to 41 percent. Support for Proposition 187 and greater federal subsidies to states like California with large immigrant populations had become a keystone of Republican Governor Pete Wilson's successful reelection campaign. Proposition 187 also received support from Michael Huffington, who narrowly missed taking Democrat Diane Feinstein's Senate seat away in the other major statewide race.

In contrast to his views on bread-and-butter issues like taxes or welfare, however, Wilson's position on immigration was not universally shared by conservatives. Proposition 187 was opposed by former Reagan official Lyn Nofziger, as well as by William Bennett and Jack Kemp.[1] Wilson was also sharply criticized on his anti-immigrant stance by Ron Unz, the Silicon Valley entrepreneur who ran against him in the Republican primary on a generally more conservative platform and received 34 percent of the vote.[2] Despite efforts by some Republicans to make opposition to immigration a litmus test of conservative orthodoxy, it is unlikely to become one. While Pat Buchanan has faithfully anchored the position of the far right in opposition to almost all immigration, the *Wall Street Journal's* editorial page has equally steadfastly made the case for relatively open immigration.

Positions on immigration would appear to be heavily class based. That is, immigration is held to harm primarily low-skill workers who compete with recent immigrants for minimum-wage jobs. Hence immigration tends to be opposed by the same groups—blacks, unionized labor, environmentalists, and so forth—that are against trade liberalization measures like the North American Free Trade Agreement (NAFTA) and the General Agreement on Tariffs and Trade (GATT). This makes immigration a target of opportunity for populist conservatives like Ross Perot and Pat Buchanan, but also makes it a difficult issue for Democrats. A substantial proportion of the votes for Proposition 187 came from people who otherwise voted for Democratic candidates. But while free trade is a more divisive issue for Democrats than Republicans, the reverse is true for immigration. The reason for this, I suspect, is that immigration embeds a cultural issue not present in free trade, that is, the threat immigrants pose not just to American jobs, but to traditional American cultural values.

In my judgment, immigration overall confers great benefit on the United States. Economically, it brings talented, energetic, and entrepreneurial people to the country. Culturally, it reinforces the traditional social values now under attack, because those are the values that most immigrants bring with them. Some immigrants, particularly undocumented ones, also cause problems because many are poor, uneducated, and tend to be concentrated in certain cities and states where they put strains on public services like education. The immigration problem is not one that can be solved once and for all, least of all by a 1923-style closing of the doors to most foreigners. Rather, it is a problem (and an opportunity) whose various parts need to be managed pragmatically, so that the country can exercise a greater degree of control over who enters its borders. Republicans in particular may be tempted to exploit short-term electoral advantage by riding this issue, but that will undercut their long-term chances with middle-class Hispanic and Asian voters who will make up an increasingly large part of the swing vote in future elections.

Economics

The current immigration debate is taking place behind a tremendous veil of ignorance. Many of the supporters of California's Proposition 187, for example, thought they were voting to end the eligibility of illegal aliens for welfare benefits. Yet undocumented aliens have long been ineligible for welfare and other social benefits in California; the problem has always been one of enforcement.

The economic impact of immigration has been argued at length, and by now there is sufficient empirical data available to come to some conclusions. A recent report by the Urban Institute summarizes the results of a large number of empirical studies of immigration done over the past decade.[3] In addition, the Manhattan Institute has published a compilation of statistics on immigration that serves as a useful summary of our empirical knowledge of immigrants in the U.S.[4] The bottom line of these studies is not that immigrants are an unambiguous benefit to the American economy, but that their impact has to be disaggregated for differences in legal status, length of residence, and country of origin, and for whether one is considering public-sector impacts in specific states and localities or broader economic outcomes.

Immigrants as a group are poorer than the native born. But all earlier immigrant groups, including successful ones like the Jews, Chinese, and Japanese who arrived in the first half of this century, were much poorer than natives when they first arrived. The real issue is the rate at which their socioeconomic status rises as they assimilate. The most recent data indicate that the foreign born who arrived before 1980 have substantially higher incomes than those arriving thereafter, indicating upward mobility over time. If one excludes countries sending large numbers of illegal immigrants and "refugee" countries, average income for pre-1980 immigrants is actually higher than for native-born Americans.

The Urban Institute study indicates that there is also a major difference between legal and illegal immigrants in terms of educational status, hence of future economic prospects. Over 75 percent of immigrants from the major source countries for illegal immigrants have less than a high school diploma. The number of immigrants (whether documented or not) living in concentrated poverty areas has grown twice as fast as for natives during the 1980s. On the other hand, recent *legal* immigrants are significantly more likely to hold college degrees than the native born (33 versus 20 percent). Hence there is an hourglass-shaped distribution in the immigrant population, with legal immigrants clearly adding substantially to America's human capital base, and others (mostly illegal immigrants) lowering its average.

It is very hard to calculate the total impact of immigration on American GNP or the job market, since immigrant capital, labor, and entrepreneurship produce positive externalities not measured by most economic statistics. A third of all the engineers in Silicon Valley are foreign born; had they not been allowed into the U.S., the negative effects would have rippled far beyond the computer and semiconductor industries to the economy as a whole. Not only would there be no Borland International, founded by an illegal French-Jewish immigrant named Phillippe Kahn, but all the companies using Borland software products would presumably be less productive. The "brain drain" experienced by foreign countries, some in the Third World but others, like England, that are highly developed, is the counterpart to the enormous "free" additions to America's stock of human capital caused by the immigration of skilled individuals. It is clear that, at the upper end of the social scale, the American dream continues to operate full force: a mere cataloguing of high-tech executives born abroad, including Andrew Grove of Intel, Eric Benhamou of 3Com, Phillippe Kahn of Borland, as well as the approximately twelve thousand engineers of Chinese origin working today in Silicon Valley, indicates the significance of immigration to the American economy. Some 15 percent of Asian immigrants come to the U.S. with advanced degrees, double the proportion of the native born.

Those who argue that immigrants take jobs from natives assume that there is a fixed number of jobs to go around. In fact, many low-skill native-born workers would not work at the jobs or wages that similarly skilled immigrants accept. James Q. Wilson has noted that public buses in Los Angeles are ridden by Latinos way out of proportion to their numbers in the population, as they commute from inner city to suburb in search of employment. By contrast, African Americans, whose jobs the Latinos are supposedly stealing, are underrepresented among bus riders. Critics of immigration discount the positive effects of the wealth created by immigrant labor on native standards of living. The fact that immigrants are willing to work long hours for low wages shows up in lower prices for everything from fruit and vegetables to car washes, hospital visits, and meals at McDonald's.

Studies of the impact of immigration on specific labor markets indicate that it may have depressed wage rates for low-skill workers, particularly in economic downturns and in areas with concentrated immigrant populations, like California. Given that immigration has been of undoubted benefit to high-income workers who buy the services of countless nannies and busboys, low-skill foreign labor has contributed to the worsening of income distribution in the United States. (There are, of course, other, more powerful, forces such as the globalization of trade and investment and technological change moving the U.S. in this direction in any case.) For the nation as a whole, however, immigration has neither displaced a significant number of jobs nor depressed wage rates.

The greatest misperceptions concern immigrants and their impact on the public sector, particularly with regard to welfare. Overall, immigrants pay more in taxes than they consume in government benefits, so they help in reducing the federal deficit. (This occurs, if for no other reason, because immigrants tend to be younger than the population as a whole, and hence below-average consumers of Social Security and health benefits.) While many Americans believe that immigrants are heavy users of welfare, only 2 percent of immigrants (excluding refugees[5]) arriving after 1980 receive public assistance, compared with 3.7 percent of the native population. The reason for this is that most immigrants, particularly undocumented aliens, are not eligible for most public assistance benefits (although their American-born children are).[6] Legal immigrants are not eligible for benefits for a period of five years. The studies showing a huge fiscal impact of illegal immigration on Los Angeles and San Diego, cited by Governor Wilson in support of his pro-Proposition 187 platform, have methodological problems; they tend to overestimate benefits paid and seriously underestimate tax revenues generated by immigrants.

The real economic problem with immigration is that its costs and benefits are not evenly distributed around the country. Wilson is quite right that the federal government captures proportionally more in tax revenues from immigrants than it pays out in benefits. California and its municipalities, as well as other regions with large immigrant populations, therefore have some grounds for seeking federal subsidies.

Culture

For many people, conservatives in particular, the cultural threat posed by immigration is far greater than the economic one. Indeed, the cultural problem should logically come first. If one believed that immigrants would somehow destroy or dilute important values on which the American community depends, then it would take an extremely high level of economic benefit to allow them in; conversely, if immigrants actually reinforced key American values, then one should be willing to tolerate a certain economic cost in exchange. For most Europeans, the immigration issue is almost entirely cultural: in Western Europe's liberal democracies, the country usually corresponds to a more or less homogeneous ethnolinguistic nation, whose homogeneity is directly threatened by non-European immigrants.

The problem for the United States is somewhat different, because American national identity was not based from the outset on a single ethnolinguistic group whose ancestors inhabited the territory of North America from time immemorial. (Such groups existed, of course, but were killed or shouldered aside by European immigrants.) Our identity was embodied instead in a set of universalistic liberal political principles. The American "nation," in other words, did not exist prior to its being established as a liberal democracy, unlike the French, English, and Japanese nations.

Many would say that those universalistic principles, embodied in the Declaration of Independence, the Constitution, and the system of law founded upon them, are all there is to American national identity. This argument is made on two levels. First, obedience to this universalistic law is deemed sufficient in practical terms to create a viable political community and society under which citizens can peaceably interact. But second, in normative terms the country is said to be better off not trying to impose a common culture on the diverse populations and cultures that make it up, instead permitting each group the maximum of freedom to establish and pursue its particularistic cultural ends within the framework of the law.

There is no question that the universalism of our constitutional system is the foundation of political life in the United States, and a key to the success of the American experiment. But claims that constitutionalism alone is sufficient to create a livable society are flawed on both practical and normative grounds. Historically, it is not the case that Americans had no common culture beyond the constitutional-legal system; up to the middle of the twentieth century, the cultural tone for the country as a whole was set by its first and once-dominant immigrant group, white Anglo-Saxon Protestants. Thus, many WASP virtues are synonymous with what have commonly been regarded as American virtues, such as a vigorous work ethic, Puritan moralism with a strong sense of guilt, the ability to associate easily with one another in local communities, distrust of overarching authority, and openness to innovation and to modern science, as well as tolerance, optimism, universalism, belief in the perfectibility of man, and a complicated attitude towards family that takes family responsibilities seriously while not letting family loyalty stand in the way of broader community. These are not universal cultural constants; some cultures value leisure over work, emphasize family to the exclusion of citizenship, are hostile to innovation, discourage individualism in favor of conformity, or promote distrust of people outside of kinship groups. On the other hand, possession of these WASP virtues is not limited to WASPs. Descendants of the early New England Puritans could lose those virtues over time, while non-WASP groups could possess them in great abundance, either because their native cultures promoted analogous virtues, or because they became assimilated.

Many thoughtful theorists of modern democracy in general, and of the American polity in particular, have argued that a democratic community cannot exist on the basis of a pure social contract.[7] That is, a society conceived solely as a compact among self-interested individuals with aims no higher than enlarging their own private well-being could not field soldiers in self-defense, deliberate on matters of public policy, raise children, or, perhaps most importantly, defend itself from tyranny. What transforms a group of self-seeking, atomized individuals into a community is the presence of a common set of moral values transmitted through a national culture. While American culture is not tied to a specific ethnic group and hence is far more open and absorptive than other national cultures, its role in creating a viable society is no less important. If Americans had no basis for relating to one another except through the legal system, there would be no grounds for social trust and no vigorous associational life. In their place would be contracts, a thicket of formal rules, centralized bureaucratic solutions to problems of human interaction, litigation, and coercive enforcement. The decline of a common American culture can be seen, in fact, in the spread of all these phenomena.

In assessing the impact of immigration on American culture, then, we have to be clear that culture itself is important, and that while pluralism is deeply ingrained in the American political system, it needs to be moderated by some degree of common cultural language through which Americans can relate to one another. This is not to say that the country can or should turn back to seventeenth-century Puritanism; what aspects of that cultural heritage are salvageable today is an important and difficult question. But just as excessive conformity can be stifling, so too can excessive diversity make social structures and a national polity impossible.

The perceived cultural threat posed by immigration is that poor and ill-educated immigrants from the Third World, particularly illegal Latino immigrants, bring with them less-desirable values that add to the accumulation of social problems in America today.[8] In the eyes of many Americans, Third World immigrants have joined the black underclass in one large, threatening inner-city population plagued with pathologies from gang violence to drug use to single-parent families. There is indeed some basis for these fears: in New York, the rate of Puerto Rican illegitimacy comes close to that of African Americans at comparable income levels, while on the opposite coast Hispanic gangs have been highly visible.

The similarities between Latinos and the black underclass breaks down when the former is disaggregated by country of origin. When looked at as a whole, Latino family structure stands somewhere between that of whites and blacks. For example, the rates of female-headed families are 13.5 percent for whites, 46.4 percent for blacks, and 24.4 percent for Hispanics. If we adjust these figures for income level, however, Hispanics turn out to be much closer to the white norm. Family breakdown is correlated with poverty for all races and ethnic groups; part of the reason for the higher percentage of female-headed Latino households is simply that there are more poor Latino families. If we compare families in comparable income strata—for example, below the poverty level—the Hispanic rate of female-headed families is very close to that of whites (45.7 versus 43.6 percent), while the comparable rate for blacks is much higher than either (78.3 percent). Considering the substantially higher rate of family breakdown within the sizable Puerto Rican community, this suggests that the rate of single-parent families among Cuban- and Mexican-origin Latinos is actually lower than for whites at a comparable income level. Moreover, Latinos as a group are somewhat less likely to be single than either whites or blacks.[9]

In their broad cultural characteristics, Mexican immigrants in many ways resemble the Italian immigrant wave that arrived in the United States in the decades immediately before and after the end of the nineteenth century. These Italian immigrants were predominantly from the impoverished south of Italy, and arrived in the U.S. with very low levels of skills, education, and capital. Like today's Mexican-Americans, however, they had relatively strong family values. The culture of rural southern Italy has been described by Edward Banfield in his classic study *The Moral Basis of a Backward Society* as characterized by "amoral familism," in which the bonds of the nuclear family were the only grounds for sociability, and in which there was a high degree of distrust of those outside the immediate kinship group.[10] This overly strong familism hindered upward mobility by Italian immigrants because parents would discourage their children—particularly daughters—from seeking a higher education that would take them away from the family home. In the early decades of this century, Italians had lower incomes and higher rates of delinquency and crime than many other European ethnic groups. Yet despite the flatter trajectory, this group continued to advance, and by the 1970s, the per capita income of Italian-Americans was higher than the national average, and higher than that of native born Anglo-Saxon whites.

The two groups have other similarities as well. Mexican immigrants have a lower rate of citizenship than do other ethnic groups, reflecting the intention of many to return eventually to families and homes in Mexico. Similarly, many Italian immigrants at the turn of the century intended to return to Italy once they had made their fortunes in the U.S. Many initial immigrants were not families but single men, intending to be temporary guestworkers. And the Italians brought with them criminal gangs like the Mafia, which were more highly organized than the Chicano gangs in Los Angeles.

I see no convincing cultural reason why most of the recent Latino immigrant groups should be harder to assimilate than were the millions of southern Italians who poured into the United States a hundred years ago. In this respect, the U.S. is lucky that it has a Latin Catholic country to its south rather than a Muslim one, as in the case of Europe; Mexico's cultural distance from the United States is comparatively small, and the assimilability of its population comparatively great. The problems that arise in assimilating Latinos as opposed to Italians lie not with the groups themselves, but with changes in the American environment into which they have entered.

New Obstacles to Assimilation

The cultural differences between Mexicans and Italians are not great, and in terms of numbers, the U.S. should theoretically be in a better position to assimilate the newer arrivals. While the absolute numbers of immigrants are approximately the same as during the peak immigration years at the turn of the century, the country is also larger. Hence immigrants constitute only half the percentage of the total population that they did at the turn of the century.

But a number of changes that have taken place in American society in the decades between the arrival of these two Latin Catholic groups makes the problem of assimilation much greater today. The first and most important is the decline of an assimilationist ideology in the public school system and among key American elites. Italian children entering New York schools in the early decades of this century did not find a host of bilingual programs await-ing them, nor did they have a political leadership urging them to hold on to as much of their Italian cultural identity as they could. It was, of course, possi-ble for Italian schoolchildren to enter the parochial school system, and many of them did, but its control by the Irish Church hierarchy made it somewhat less than ideal as a locus of ethnic identity.

The origins of multiculturalism in the United States in the past genera-tion are complex and beyond the scope of this essay. One important political stimulus for greater cultural diversity came, however, from the experience of African Americans after the civil rights movement. Virtually alone among racial and ethnic groups up to that point, American blacks found assimilation into mainstream white culture extraordinarily difficult, and today many mid-dle-class blacks who have "made it" in terms of income or occupational sta-tus have nonetheless forsworn assimilation as a goal. This experience had a critical impact on minority groups that began their struggle for recognition later, by setting as a goal not assimilation but equal respect for a separate cul-tural identity.

The second respect in which the American environment is different today has to do with the changing nature of economic activity. It has been widely noted that, as the technological sophistication of modern economies increas-es, the returns to "human capital"—that is, investments in skills and knowl-edge—increase. At midcentury, it did not pay in strictly economic terms for a young person to go to college, since the income differential was not great between jobs for which higher education was necessary and a high-paying job in an auto or steel plant. Today, this situation is very different: wage dif-ferentials between low- and high-skill jobs have been widening steadily, plac-ing an ever increasing premium on skills and knowledge. The stagnating real incomes of low-skill workers in the United States over the past generation have been much remarked. While there has also been much debate as to how the blame for this phenomenon is to be allocated among government policies, immigration, globalization, and technological change, few question its reali-ty or deny that income stratification is likely to increase in the coming years.

The issue of declining wages of low-skill workers has been brought into the immigration debate because many low-skill workers blame their problems on competition from Third World immigrant labor. As the previous section on economics indicates, this may be true during economic downturns in areas of concentrated immigrant populations. Jack Miles has noted in the *Atlantic Monthly* that Latinos have pushed blacks out of low-skill jobs from chambermaids to busboys all across California.[11] But overall, competition from immigrant labor is a small contributory factor to the general phenomenon of declining low-skill wages.

The problem may actually be more severe in reverse: the declining returns to low skills make upward mobility harder for all groups, including immigrants. In the days when nearly everyone worked on a farm or in a low-tech manufacturing job, a person could overcome a deficit of skill or education through hard work, thrift, and other related virtues. Many immigrant European groups did precisely that in the first couple of generations; it was up to their children or grandchildren to assimilate fully by obtaining higher levels of education. Strong work habits and savings remain important, but their value relative to skills and education has been declining. Jewish and Asian immigrants have short-circuited this problem because their cultures value education as an end in itself, and have consequently shot ahead of not only Hispanics and African Americans but also most European ethnic groups. Absent these cultural advantages, however, life at the bottom promises to be harder to overcome than it was one hundred years ago.

A third change in the American environment is the broad decline in the quality of public education in the United States at the very time when increasing economic returns to skills and knowledge make education an ever more important priority. The causes of and possible solutions to this problem are discussed in chapter 16 of this book. Suffice it to note here that the politics of immigration have contributed to the problem. Bilingual education is a questionable means of promoting English fluency to begin with, and a number of recent studies have indicated that it slows down rather than advances assimilation.[12] In addition, such programs are expensive and take money away from the central programs of schools that are not doing a great job of basic education in the first place. Bilingual programs have become a political priority for many Hispanic political leaders, however, people who are sometimes less interested in promoting English skills than in preserving a separate Latino culture and their own segregated political base.

The fourth factor making the present environment different from earlier periods has been pointed to by Peter Skerry and other observers: the decline of local government and other mediating institutions that previously served to draw immigrants into the broader American community. Earlier ethnic immigrant groups, the Irish in particular, could achieve a high degree of political participation relatively quickly by taking over local governments. With the liberal reform movements of the postwar period, however, Tammany Hall, the

Daley machine, and similar political machines simply disappeared. While these machines were often corrupt and violated standards of "good government," they also were effective providers of political patronage, social mobility, and community-based social services. Other mediating institutions like churches and labor unions, which historically played an important role in socializing new immigrants to American values, have also been declining.

The Latino immigrant groups generally arrived after the undermining of the big urban political machines, when this form of self-organization at a local level was in bad odor. In keeping with other trends in American politics, local issues were escalated to the state and federal levels. This reinforced the tendency of Latino political leaders to opt for influence over what Skerry calls "post–civil rights" institutions, that is, highly centralized institutions like the courts or federal affirmative action programs as means of achieving social mobility. As Linda Chavez points out, certain Hispanic advocacy groups have used the court system effectively to obtain every conceivable expansion of entitlements possible for illegal aliens. The perception that they are doing so has legitimately fueled anti-immigrant sentiment among natives.

The final environmental factor that makes the last decade of the twentieth century different from the first is the growth of the welfare state itself. It is hard to account for the significantly poorer performance of Puerto Ricans when compared to other Hispanic groups (in terms of income, education, family breakdown, crime, and related measures) except to point out that they, as American citizens from the start, had access to New York City's generous welfare system for much longer. Welfare dependency was simply not an option during earlier periods of immigration. While it is doubtful that many Third World immigrants come to the United States simply to be on welfare, the welfare option is always there once they achieve citizenship.

An Agenda

Any sensible immigration policy has to start from the proposition that immigration has been and continues to be, on balance, very good for the United States. Our society is fundamentally different from other industrial democracies in Europe and Asia because the American nation does not correspond to ethnicity, and because we can assimilate energetic and talented people from a wide variety of cultures.

The changes that have taken place in the United States between the earlier and present large waves of immigration suggest that the chief problems we face are not due to immigrants per se, but rather result from counterproductive or mistaken social policies that would continue to harm American society even if the flow of new immigrants were cut off tomorrow. We would have no doubts about the assimilative powers of American society but for the existence of bilingual and multicultural educational programs whose intent is to foster a separate sense of cultural identity. There would be no worries about the low skills and incomes of newly arriving foreigners were there not a serious problem with public education in the United States that has been failing native-born Americans as well. We would not have to worry about socializing immigrants to American values and institutions were our mediating institutions not in serious disarray. And we would not have to worry about immigrants and welfare were there not serious problems with the welfare system in the United States.

Dealing with the immigration problem therefore means, in the first instance, dealing with these other issues as an urgent priority. Immigrants should not become scapegoats for a host of social problems brought about by the misguided policies of elites born in this country.

To say immigration is good "on balance" means that its effects are not uniform: while America has done well by being a nation of immigrants, some individuals, groups, cities, and states have been hurt by it. While some immigrants have added economic and social value to the U.S., others have contributed to social problems. A sensible immigration policy must make these distinctions carefully.

The Urban Institute's findings indicate that there are significant differences between legal and illegal immigrants in terms of education, skills, social habits, and the like. Legal immigration policy has worked relatively well in selecting people who can make useful contributions to American society, while many of the social problems associated with immigration are concentrated among undocumented aliens. There is nothing wrong in principle with a society insisting on exercising some control over the rate and quality of its new entrants. Indeed, many Americans are inclined to support initiatives like Proposition 187 because of the belief that we have simply lost control of our borders, reflecting a broader breakdown of law in the society. Note, however, that the desire to have greater control over illegal immigration is compatible with a policy generally supportive of immigration.

The problem with controlling illegal immigration is not one of principle, but rather of effective means of implementation. Here the problem becomes much more complicated, because it is not clear what combination of policies and practices will allow us to reduce the flow of undocumented aliens without endangering other values and civil liberties. The measures contained in Proposition 187—primarily denying access to public schools and medical aid—would seem to be blunt and ineffective instruments. The risk that poor, uneducated aliens pose for our society is that they will remain that way and not assimilate; refusing to educate them will simply perpetuate them as an underclass. It seems unlikely that undocumented aliens come to the United States primarily to get better educations for their children (as opposed to seeking employment), so denial of this benefit would have little deterrent effect. Proposition 187 does not explain how its provisions will be enforced in a manner consistent with constitutional safeguards of equal protection, and without creating yet another large and intrusive government bureaucracy to make it work.

As noted earlier, illegal immigrants are not entitled to welfare benefits in California to begin with, and to the extent they are receiving them, it is because fraudulent documents are easy to obtain. The problem of identification—today twenty-nine documents can be used to prove employment eligibility—has led to proposals for a national ID card that would be required for employment, public schooling, or benefits. The U.S. Immigration Commission has suggested tying documentation to Social Security numbers, which have in recent years increasingly taken on the role of a national ID. It is certainly desirable to streamline the documentation process and make fraud less easy to commit, and tying employment and benefits to a Social Security number may be workable. But a national ID card brings dangers of its own: Americans would be turning over to a federal bureaucracy a great deal of power over their lives, a power that would be sure to expand over time as more and more activities were tied to possession of what amounts to an internal passport.

Despite the failures of the past, more can be done to increase the effectiveness of border patrols. The "Operation Gatekeeper" effort near San Diego has shown signs of success. (It should be noted, however, that six out of ten illegal aliens initially enter the country on legal visas rather than by making clandestine border crossings.) A rethinking of the border patrol needs to happen in tandem with a major overhaul of the INS bureaucracy, which (as anyone who has dealt with it can testify) is one of the most inefficient, ungracious, and in some cases corrupt units of the federal government.

The 1965 Immigration Reform Act, which replaced the earlier quota system for legal immigration, based on country of origin, with an admissions policy based primarily on family reunification, needs to be rethought. Family reunification is a desirable goal, but it tends to bias the system in favor of countries of origin with large family networks, as opposed to other criteria like education, skills, capital, and the like. Immigrants can help bolster family values, to be sure, but it is also possible to have too much of a good thing.

The processing of people seeking refugee status is impossibly backlogged in the court system, with many cases taking years even to come to a hearing. This process could and, in fairness to all involved, should be speeded up substantially. Deportations of illegal aliens could also be made more rapid.

The final measure that is the only effective long-term solution to the problem of Mexican immigration has already been put into place: NAFTA. Ironically, those people most opposed to immigration tend to be the same people most opposed to NAFTA. This reflects shortsightedness and a lack of vision: Mexico under President Salinas moved decisively towards trade liberalization, and while President Zedillo's term has begun with a major currency crisis, the country's long-term prospects remain good. Mexican wages, employment, and living conditions are all likely to rise substantially in the next few years as economic integration proceeds, sharply reducing the incentive of Mexicans to come to the United States.

Finally, as noted earlier, it seems reasonable to subsidize those states bearing an undue share of the burden of caring for immigrants—California alone has 38 percent of the national total—but *only* if those states begin to face up squarely to their own welfare, education, and budget problems. California's public schools are in perilous condition not just because of broad economic factors beyond California's control, but also because the state itself has been unable to get its wide variety of spending programs and taxes under control. It would be all too easy for high-immigration states to waste federal subsidies.

All of these suggested remedies taken together may not be sufficient to end illegal immigration, and may take effect only after an extended period of time. But even if they are not effective, we need to keep the problem in perspective: the numbers of illegal immigrants are not huge, and the vast majority of them make positive contributions to the economy, usually by taking jobs that other Americans are not willing to do themselves. The need to control illegal immigration should not be allowed to jeopardize the substantial benefits brought by legal immigrants. Nor should it legitimate an ugly form of nativism. Governor Wilson is doubtless sincere when he rejects the charge that his support for Proposition 187 is motivated by nativism, but that may not be true of many of his allies. It is all too easy to make immigrants scapegoats for social problems that native-born Americans have brought upon themselves.

The country's gravest problems lie in education, welfare, the mindless promotion of "diversity," and a weakening of the values that are necessary for maintenance of a dynamic American civil society. If the immigration question can refocus the country on the need to solve these problems, it will be to the good. Immigration itself, however, is something to be promoted and managed, not a problem to be once and for all solved.

Notes

1. See William J. Bennett and Jack Kemp, "The Fortress Party?" *Wall Street Journal*, October 21, 1994, A14.
2. See Ron Unz, "Immigration or the Welfare State," *Policy Review*, Fall 1994, 33–38. Unz argues, among other things, that it will be suicidal for the Republican Party to become identified as a nativist, anti-immigrant party, given the sizable minority populations in key states like California that could potentially be persuaded to vote Republican.

3. Michael Fix and Jeffrey Passel, *Immigration and Immigrants: Setting the Record Straight* (Washington, D.C.: Urban Institute, 1994).
4. John J. Miller, ed., *Strangers at Our Gates* (Washington, D.C.: Manhattan Institute, 1994).
5. Refugees are admitted to the country on the understanding that they will be supported by the U.S. government until they get themselves established.
6. It is not surprising that the rate of pre-1980 immigrants on welfare rises to 3.2 percent, though this figure is still below that of native-born Americans.
7. The most important of these, for a variety of reasons, was Alexis de Tocqueville.
8. Lawrence Harrison, an observer with considerable experience in Latin America, makes this case in "America and Its Immigrants," *National Interest*, no. 28 (Summer 1992): 37–55.
9. Figures taken from U.S. Bureau of the Census, *Poverty in the United States: 1991*, Series P-60, Number 181 (Washington D.C.: U.S. Government Printing Office), 7–9. The percentages of people in families for whites, blacks, and Hispanics are 84.5, 84.8, and 89.0, respectively. See 2–3.
10. Edward Banfield, *The Moral Basis of a Backward Society* (Glencoe, Ill.: Free Press, 1958).
11. Jack Miles, "Blacks vs. Browns: The Struggle for the Bottom," *Atlantic Monthly*, October 1992.
12. For a discussion, see Linda Chavez, *Out of the Barrio: Towards a New Politics of Hispanic Assimilation* (New York: Basic Books, 1991).

Part III

Government and Civic Institutions

Chapter Seven

The Politics of Liberty, the Sociology of Virtue

William Kristol

The 1994 election marked the end of an era. In narrow political terms, it ended sixty-two years of Democratic Party dominance.[1] In a broader sense, it marked the end of the New Deal/Great Society era of big government liberalism. It would be too strong to say that the 1994 election represented a repudiation of that era, for much that was accomplished during those years will— and should—survive. But the election did mark the closing of a historic period—a period whose roots in turn lie in the Progressive movement. In a sense, then, November 8, 1994, could be said to cap and conclude the Progressive Era of American history. We have fulfilled the "promise" of Herbert Croly's vision—and in doing so have brought to light its limitations and even its pathologies. We now have a chance to shape a new era, informed by a new promise.

It won't be easy. It is entirely possible that the Progressive Era will simply be followed by an era of deconstruction, and deconstruction not just of progressivism but of much that is solid in American life. We can all too easily imagine an American future consisting of a politics of dealignment, a culture of decomposition, and a society of disenchantment. But perhaps not.

Perhaps we can move on and up from progressivism, informed by a new vision that returns, with suitable modifications, to the principles and understandings of the Founders. In Federalist No. Thirty-Nine, Madison refers to "that honorable determination which animates every votary of freedom to rest all our political experiments on the capacity of mankind for self-government."[2] Vindicating the capacity of mankind for self-government implies a political system that protects our liberty, and a society that fosters in its citizens a character capable of self-government, in both the political and moral senses. Self-government therefore implies both a politics of liberty and a sociology of virtue.

The construction (or reconstruction) of a politics of liberty and a sociology of virtue is at the core of the promise of post-progressive America. For as the sociologist Robert Nisbet points out, "a conservative party (or other group) has a double task confronting it. The first is to work tirelessly toward the diminution of the centralized, omnipotent, and unitary state with its ever-soaring debt and deficit." This task—the relimiting of government—is the politics of liberty. "The second and equally important task," says Nisbet, "is that of protecting, reinforcing, nurturing, where necessary, the varied groups and associations which form the true building blocks of the social order."[3] This task—strengthening the institutions of civil society that attend to the character of the citizenry—is the sociology of virtue.

The Politics of Liberty

The phrase "politics of liberty" suggests that the preservation of liberty is a political task. Conservatives and libertarians have on occasion neglected the implications of this fact. We have sometimes acted as if making the theoretical case for liberty, and decrying restrictions on liberty, would convince our fellow citizens to relimit government. But we have given less thought to the matter of structuring institutions and incentives to preserve and strengthen the system of liberty. We have criticized big government's usurpations and lamented its continued growth. Many—a majority of Americans—share this criticism. But how do we go about relimiting government?

In the wake of the election of 1994, this question has come to the fore. It is now clear that there is far more popular support than before for rolling back the huge expansion of government of the past half-century. The American people now believe the federal government is too big, too intrusive, and too meddlesome. They are open to more than criticism of particular government policies; they are now willing to address the issue of the size and scope of government itself. And we have learned that it is not enough simply to make the case against big government; we have to think politically and institutionally about how to rally support and create incentives for limited government.

Such thinking begins with an appreciation of the institutional obstacles to cutting government policies and programs. Electing conservative or Republican presidents in recent years, after all, has not changed things very much. Nor, so far, has the movement of popular opinion toward greater skepticism about government policies and programs. This is because the liberal welfare state has built up sets of relationships and patterns of behavior that are hard to break once they have formed and congealed. George Bernard Shaw said early in this century, "A government that borrows from Peter to pay Paul can always depend on the support of Paul." And if the government doesn't rob Peter *too* much, and if there are a lot of Peters dispersed throughout the society and only a few Pauls, there will be an endless process of little robberies of Peter to give benefits to Paul. And if the Pauls are organized as an interest group, and are strong in several congressional districts, and if, in the name of "progress," the notion of principled limits on governmental action disappears, then the welfare state just keeps on growing.

And yet it has become discredited. Poll data, and the recent election results, show that the American people now have a deep distrust of the federal government. In fact they believe, by substantial margins, that the government is more likely to do harm than good. We now have a public opinion that could support a broad attack on unlimited government. But because particular policies have beneficiaries who will fight to keep them, while the opposition to these particular policies is often diffuse, the best strategy for containing and rolling back the liberal welfare state may be to look for ways to cut the Gordian knot, rather than trying to unwind it one string at a time. Thus the attraction of proposals such as a balanced budget amendment, term limits, tax and spending limitations at several levels of government, the devolution of power to states and localities, and the privatization of government functions. Such policies are radical in the sense that they do not seek simply to contain some of the damage done by the welfare state, or to address its particular pathologies one by one. Rather, they seek to change the patterns of behavior of the political system as a whole to make it more supportive of relimiting government.

Such institutional reforms are, of course, in the spirit of the Founding Fathers' attempts to create structures, incentives, and relationships that would preserve liberty. In this sense, the new politics of liberty is an attempt to find new remedies for diseases that have grown up over our progressive century, as we abandoned the older constraints on government. Some of these new remedies are in fact traditional ones—for example, federalism, or devolution of power. But what conservative reformers now understand is that we do not need more "New Federalism" efforts in which state and local governments simply become ever more dependent extensions of the federal octopus. We need *real* federalism, understood as part of a general program of relimiting government. And that means that the devolution effort must occur at the state level as well. State governments are no more immune to capture by interest groups than the federal government, though they are more constrained by the need to balance the budget and by popular pressure. Teachers' unions in Albany or Sacramento are as strong as they are in Washington, D.C. Thus, it is not enough to kill the federal Department of Education and return power to states and localities; that is but a *step* on the road to real devolution of power to citizens—in this case, to greater parental control of and choice in their children's schools. The point, after all, is not to get power back to the state governments; it is to get power back to parents and citizens.

Similarly, the new politics of liberty does not simply seek to *restore* the old ways of governing. In 1995, the accumulated departures from those ways have acquired such weight that we need to think more imaginatively about cutting through the jungle of the modern welfare state with fresh populist remedies. Most striking in this respect is the emergence of the movement for term limits. This idea, rejected at the Constitutional Convention, had virtually disappeared from our politics for almost two centuries. Today, however, term limits may be the most popular movement in the country. Few in Washington like this idea very much—but voters in all twenty-two states where it has been on the ballot have passed such limits. If the Supreme Court now strikes down state-imposed term limits on federal officials, the issue will be driven to the national level, and could trigger a broader debate about what we want from our representatives and what their relationship to limited government is to be.

The reason for the interest in term limits, after all, is not simply a general belief that Congress will work better if there is greater turnover of its members. The case for term limits rests on a critique of what "representation" has become in the world of big-government/interest-group liberalism, in which "iron triangles" of politicians, bureaucrats, and interest groups establish and benefit from welfare-state and corporatist programs. This triangle seems at once virtually impervious to change from above—from a popular president—and to change from below—from public opinion. Term limits strike at the iron triangle. The incentives for individual congressmen will change under term limits, as the seniority system and committee baronies disintegrate and the balance of power changes within Congress, between Congress and the other branches of government, and between Congress and the electorate. Term limits thus offer the promise of addressing some of the pathological tendencies of interest-group liberalism.

The politics of liberty, therefore, goes beyond a politics informed by a generalized hostility to big government. It means thinking imaginatively about structural, legislative, and constitutional changes that would restore both the principle and the practice of limited government. Above all, the politics of liberty does not imply that we reinvent government; it requires that we relimit it.

We must relimit it not simply because big government is a threat to our economic well-being. It is a threat to free society, because it corrupts such a society by making its people less able to govern themselves. Self-government means that communities and citizens and families are able and willing to govern themselves. This requires the reassertion of the old-fashioned presumption that civil society should exist more or less free of government regulation, even regulation for desirable policy ends. The "pursuit of happiness" will be left primarily to citizens acting freely in civil society; government will secure some of the conditions of such a pursuit, but it will not try to make "happiness"—or even "security" in an extended sense—its direct object. And politicians in this new era will have to be able to articulate and live by this stern message of the limits to proper government action.

The Sociology of Virtue

The sternness of this message can be softened, however, by the hope embodied in the other pillar of the post-progressive agenda, the sociology of virtue. Critics of progressivism have long been concerned with the effect of modern political and social developments on our character, on our virtues. But we have tended to speak primarily of "preserving" our wasting moral capital from the depredations of modern life, of "defending" traditional ideas of law and morality against the assaults launched by a new doctrine of personal liberation, of "shoring up" old institutions that were under modernist assault. Our concern for virtue has been profoundly "conservative," even defensive.

Today's task—and possibility—is radical rather than conservative, proactive rather than defensive: it is to foster a sociology of virtue rather than merely stemming further erosion of virtue's moral capital. That erosion has today gone too far for a merely "conservative" approach. A new sociology of virtue thus implies a thinking through of the ways in which social institutions can be reinvented, restructured, or reformed to promote virtue and foster sound character. This won't happen merely because of a few political victories. Relimiting government would help us deal with our social and moral problems; a successful politics of liberty would make a sociology of virtue easier to pursue. But even a sound political order will not be sufficient for a good society. Such a society also requires a resurgence of efforts within the private and voluntary spheres to grapple directly with our social problems, problems that are ultimately problems of character, problems of virtue.

Such efforts are in fact already happening. They are not waiting for the success of the politics of liberty. Despite all the social destructiveness around us, there is ample evidence of a resurgent sociology of virtue at work. There are efforts by inner-city pastors to relegitimize and redignify fatherhood, for example, as a beginning to solving the terrible problems of our inner cities. There is an authentic religious revival going on in the land, despite the continuing efforts of progressives in the public sphere to delegitimize religion and reduce its role. The right-to-life movement provides counseling and homes for unwed mothers, trying to convince women to shun the exercise of a right they have won thanks to a "progressive" Supreme Court. Citizens are banding together to deal with even so fundamental an area of government responsibility as crime. It is clear that we will see ever more such efforts to deal with our social problems through social and civic actions, efforts that simply leave government aside or incorporate it as one part of a larger enterprise.

These efforts will ultimately have a political effect, of course. Take the area of education. Following on the successful models in Indianapolis and Milwaukee, there are increasing numbers of privately funded voucher programs that enable students from lower-income families to go to a school of their parents' choice. Those who wanted to help young people at risk to escape from dreadful government schools decided they could not wait for the political system to act. But ultimately, this kind of nonpolitical activity does put pressure on the political system to allow school choice, for the evidence of the success of the private efforts is itself a powerful political argument. In fact, such activity in the private sphere may be the most effective way to spur efforts to reform government policies.

This approach might be called the Federal Express model of reform. Critics of the post office tried for decades to reform it, decrying it as an inefficient monopoly dominated by unions. Americans agreed that the post office did not work well, but it seemed impossible to make any progress legislatively or administratively. Then, in the early 1970s, Fred Smith started Federal Express. The post office and its allies made an effort to strangle this upstart in its cradle. But Federal Express prevailed, since it is politically easier to defend a small business from the government than to break up a huge government monopoly. Now, thanks also to technological developments (such as the fax machine), we have a situation where, with no real legal change, the delivery of mail in America has been transformed. The post office is still big, unwieldy, and sluggish, but it is not a major obstacle to American competitiveness; and it is now weaker politically, because of the growth of private-sector competitors and to the demonstrated superiority of the private sector. The opportunities for fundamental political reform are far greater today thanks to autonomous actions in the private sector.

A similar approach can be taken in many other areas. Instead of waiting for success in changing government institutions, citizens simply begin to go around them. As that happens, these institutions either have to reform themselves, or they become relics that ultimately lose political support. Now, as the Federal Express example suggests, political action is often necessary to protect these private-sector efforts from government attempts to suppress them. That is, after all, how religious conservatives became politically active. During the Carter administration the federal government seemed to threaten the tax-exempt status of Christian schools; as a response to this perceived threat, the Moral Majority was founded to protect these private-sector institutions from the government. As this example suggests, defensive efforts on behalf of the institutions of civil society can ultimately become proactive ones that seek also to reform the political system and the political culture.

So while the sociology of virtue implies pursuing virtue primarily in the private sector through our social institutions, it ultimately has political implications. At the very least, it requires the defense of sound social institutions from attempts by a "progressive" polity to suppress or reshape them.

Liberty, Virtue, and the Family

The politics of liberty and the sociology of virtue might be said to be the twin tracks for a post-progressive American politics. They are, on the whole, consistent and complementary tracks—and they influence each other. A politics of liberty can allow for new kinds of common pursuits in the space cleared by the retrenchment of government. Thus these tracks run parallel to one another for a considerable distance, allowing libertarians to limit government and social conservatives to attend to the sociology of virtue.

But the two tracks cannot be kept forever parallel; the two efforts—though basically complementary—do come into some tension, especially around a core set of issues involving the family. Here the politics of liberty runs up against the impossibility of neutrality about the fundamental arrangements of society; and the sociology of virtue runs up against the limits of what can be achieved in the civil sphere without some legal or policy support.

This can perhaps be made clear by reflecting briefly on Charles Murray's famous October 1993 *Wall Street Journal* article, "The Coming White Underclass."[4] Murray argued that the problems of crime, illiteracy, welfare, homelessness, drugs, and poverty all stem from a core problem, which is illegitimacy. Illegitimacy is therefore "the single most important social problem of our time." Doing something about it is not just one more item on the American political and social agenda; it should be at the top of the agenda. The broad and deep response to Murray's article suggests that it struck a chord—and, in fact, it has implications for both the politics of liberty and sociology of virtue.

Murray argues that we need a politics of liberty. We do not need additional progressive social engineering to solve a problem such engineering has in part created; we need the state to stop interfering with the social forces that kept the overwhelming majority of births within marriage for millennia. While Murray is pessimistic about how much government can do (except for getting out of the way), he is optimistic about how little it needs to do. Perhaps government could make the tax code friendlier to families with children; otherwise, a politics of liberty, presumably supplemented by a private-sector sociology of virtue, would seem to be Murray's recommendation.

But near the end of his article Murray adds this: "A more abstract but ultimately crucial step is to make marriage once again the sole legal institution through which parental rights and responsibilities are defined and exercised." Indeed, "a marriage certificate should establish that a man and woman have entered into a unique legal relationship. The changes that have blurred the distinctiveness of marriage are subtly but importantly destructive."[5]

Murray's suggestion that we reverse these changes goes beyond a mere "politics of liberty." It implies legal "discrimination" against illegitimacy or nontraditional family arrangements. In other words, a pure politics of liberty seems insufficient to Murray to combat "the single most important social problem of our time." State welfare policies, for example, cannot today discriminate against illegitimate children. Part of this problem could be solved by undoing welfare as we know it. But if it is essential that the law explicitly support marriage and the family—if we can't depend on civil society in a climate of legal neutrality simply to produce healthy families and to see to it that children are mostly born into intact families—then we come to the point where the politics of liberty and the sociology of virtue intersect. At this intersection, the politics of liberty would have to accommodate the special status of the family, and the sociology of virtue would have to acknowledge its need for political support for the family as a social institution. In other words, the political sphere, whose primary goal is liberty, cannot be entirely inattentive to the claims of virtue; and the social sphere, whose focus is virtue, requires some political support. For the two spheres to accommodate one another, a common view of what is right and just must ultimately underlie and inform both our politics and our society.

To support the family, one must hold a certain view of human nature and possibilities, a view different from that animating the sexual revolution, whose effects Murray laments. Murray thinks that our public policy should lean against the sexual revolution. But Murray also alludes to the (differing) expectations we need to have for "little boys" and "little girls"; he would seem to want our public policy to lean as well against the other powerful revolution of our time, the feminist revolution. For Murray emphasizes that the burden of preserving the family inevitably must fall primarily on women, and he believes public policy has to recognize this fact.

The sexual and feminist revolutions sprang up in civil society, so to speak. Politicians did not invent them. But the polity helped them along by legitimizing them and delegitimizing those who tried to resist them. No politics can simply be neutral between the sexual revolution and those who would resist it, or between radical feminism and those who would resist it. So even though our new American politics should be overwhelmingly a politics of liberty, and the pursuit of virtue should be primarily a "sociological" matter, at the intersection of politics and society—especially at the family—some judgments will have to be made. These judgments will always be more problematic than the relatively clear and mostly separate agendas of the politics of liberty and the sociology of virtue; but they cannot be avoided. We can pursue the politics of liberty and the sociology of virtue for quite a distance before we reach their intersection, but they do come together at a point at which neither our politics nor our sociology can be neutral as to the content of "the laws of Nature and Nature's God." Ultimately, the return to nature, an ascent from the progressive view of history, underlies both the politics of liberty and the sociology of virtue.

Notes

1. This essay draws substantially on the Bradley Lecture delivered by the author at the American Enterprise Institute for Public Policy Research in December 1993.
2. James Madison, *The Federalist Papers,* ed. Clinton Rossiter (New York: New American Library, 1961), 240.
3. Robert Nisbet, "Still Questing," *Intercollegiate Review,* Fall 1993, 45.
4. Charles Murray, "The Coming White Underclass," *Wall Street Journal,* October 29, 1993, A14.
5. Ibid.

Chapter Eight

Changing the Culture of Washington

Philip M. Burgess

In November 1994, American voters swept out the old crowd and invited a new team to take the reins. They also gave the new team new instructions.

While Republicans have a spirited view of the election results, the tectonic shifts that occurred in November transcend the forces of party and partisanship. The majority that changed the face of Congress and the control of many state governments is not (yet) a new Republican majority. It's a new American majority—and Republicans are simply its temporary custodians.

Republicans were supported by most voters because Republican words and deeds were more closely aligned than those of the Democrats with the views of the new American majority in 1994, especially the view that government is too big, too costly, too intrusive, and too out of control.

Republicans will remain custodians of the hopes and dreams of the new American majority as long as that alignment persists and as long as they can deliver. If Republicans *can* deliver—if they can transform the revolution at the polls into a revolution in policy and government—they can turn the new American majority into a new Republican majority.

But that transformation hasn't happened yet. Whether it does depends on what happens in the next several years. The new American majority wants change. It especially wants leaders who will change the way Washington, D.C., conducts the public's business. The new team in Congress will have to produce that change in order to retain the trust and confidence of the people.

The needed changes—the agenda of the next several years—can usefully be thought of as the "Six Rs":

First, *refocus*. Can the new team successfully refocus the federal government on its primary responsibilities, which are national issues that *require* national solutions—for example, defense, commerce, international trade, immigration, and other functions that are enumerated in the Constitution and are vital to the wealth and well-being of the nation? Can the new leadership get the federal government to retreat from areas where it does not belong by withdrawing, for example, from the job-training, food-stamping, head-starting, and other "retail" operations best left to states, local governments, and the private sector? Can the federal government resist trying to micromanage every aspect of our lives and fix every problem, even disputes between professional baseball players and ball club owners?

Second, *restore*. Can the new team restore the spirit of the Tenth Amendment by returning power to states and to the people, recognizing that states are coequal members of the *national* government, not mere administrative units of the federal government? To do so, the federal government must forswear such pursuits as regulating outboard motors, lawn mowers, and weapons in the school yard. These and other "police power" issues are best left to the states, where the Constitution put them.

Third, *rebalance*. Can the new team rebalance the public-private mix by shrinking what Harold D. Lasswell called the "public order" (government in all its manifestations) and expanding the "civic order" (individuals, families, neighborhoods, churches, synagogues, and other voluntary institutions of the kind Tocqueville found so compelling)? Isn't it time to give society's "little platoons" of ordinary people a chance to win the battles lost by the big battalions of the welfare state?

Fourth, *restrain*. Can the new team restrain spending by saying "no" to pressures to raise federal taxes and boost federal outlays beyond levels required by cost-of-living and population increases? Will the new Congress stop issuing unfunded mandates that force state and local governments to increase their own spending on somebody else's priorities?

Fifth, *reform*. Can the new team make good on its commitment to reform the government itself—including a new initiative to pass a balanced budget amendment and term limits for members of the House and Senate to supplement the line-item veto passed in the 104th Congress? Can it enact session limits for Congress, replacing the full-time professional legislator with part-time citizen lawmakers who have real jobs in the real economy and who live in their districts at least half the year?

Sixth, *reengineer.* Can the new team reengineer both the processes and products of government in America? Can they buck the temptation to substitute Republican arrogance for the Democratic hubris that "Washington knows best"? Can Members of Congress resist intoning on issues like street crime, drunk driving, and the K-12 curriculum—sounding more like governors, mayors, or county commissioners than members of the world's most powerful legislature?

The Beltway Culture

The prospects for relimiting government are not good unless the new congressional leadership, following its instructions from the new American majority, also acts to change the big-government, expert-driven culture of Washington, D.C. For the culture of the nation's capital has itself become a major obstacle to achieving the aims of the new majority. That's why the problem is a "Washington" problem, not just a government or policy problem.

Elected officials—Republicans and Democrats alike—and senior public administrators who live and work in Washington do so in a cultural milieu quite different from that found in the rest of the country. Inside the Capital Beltway we find a self-absorbed professional class disconnected from the language and problems of everyday life and operating in a hothouse environment fueled by rumors, spin, and inflated self-importance. It is a place where *politics is everything.* To a far greater degree than Americans living anywhere else, people who live and work in Washington believe that government has a dominant role to play in most parts of life, including all the most important parts. Nearly every social or economic problem is seen as an agenda item for government policy. Only government solutions are considered legitimate.

Put another way, Washington is a place that both underestimates and, by its policies and actions, undermines the nation's civic order—including its civic culture and institutions. Meanwhile, Washington also overindulges the nation's dinosaur institutions (big business, big labor, big special-interest lobbies), which mobilize to bend government to their will, using it to invade the wallets of the taxpayer and to gain advantages through the regulatory process rather than the marketplace.

The culture of Washington also believes that *politics is process.* Journalists and commentators who live there focus more on tactics—who's up and who's down, who has what access to which staffer of which subcommittee—than on the substance of policy or its impact on people, communities, and institutions. (One illuminating exception is health care reform, where several hundred million dollars were spent to inform citizens of the substance of policy alternatives under consideration in Washington. The more people got to know about what was contemplated, the less they liked it. The result was a rare defeat for the expansion of government.)

Election coverage by Washington-based news media gives a lot more attention to the horse race—who's ahead and who's behind—than to substantive views of the candidates. Political analysis increasingly emphasizes the technology of elections, as journalists report on polling numbers (many of them generated by the news organizations they work for, and by the candidates whose interests the numbers serve) and on reactions of candidates and interest groups to each new set of poll data.

Media coverage of policy initiatives generally emphasizes who's for them and who's against them and whether officials' "positioning" on the issue provides tactical or partisan advantage or gives opponents an opening for attack. Far less attention is given to the merits of a policy proposal: will it work, is it cost-effective, is it a proper activity for the federal government?

The culture of Washington is *obsessed with self.* Elected officials and senior public administrators develop an exaggerated sense of their own importance to the future of the Republic and the well-being of their fellow citizens. The Washington political class has been likened to a log floating down the Potomac with two thousand ants on it, each one of which thinks it is steering. The ancient Greeks considered hubris the most dangerous of human failings. Political Washington confirms their wisdom.

The culture of Washington is *dominated by appearances*—and appearances have grown more important than reality. For example, the new American majority knows the Clinton crime bill will do little or nothing to increase the safety of people and their property. Nor will it much affect the gang violence, domestic violence, and drug-related crime that accounts for most of the crime that Americans experience and fear. Rather, the new majority knows the crime bill was an effort by the administration and the 103d Congress to make it appear that they were "tough" on crime, a fiction that most Washington-based journalists and their media organizations were willing to help perpetuate.

In truth, Congress has a dismal record in reducing the crime that affects most people—as shown by unconscionably high crime rates in Washington itself, the only city controlled by Congress. Yet making Congress the nation's top cop is good business for Washington's professional class, offering new programs, more staff, and new issues for Washington-based media to write and talk about—which brings us back to our first point: politics is everything.

This Washington culture itself needs changing. Indeed, changing it is prerequisite to the fundamental policy changes sought by the new American majority. That was true before the election and remains true today.

We learned from the election of 1980 that changing the faces of government is not enough. More is required: new ways of thinking must take root for real change to be possible—in the media and among the larger electorate, in state and local governments, and in our tens of thousands of civic institutions. These will help change the culture of Washington.

Many of the planks of the G.O.P.'s "Contract with America" promised to change the culture of Washington. However, the defeat of the balanced budget and term limits amendments shows the strength of the entrenched culture and its resistance to change.

That's why other reforms need to be considered as well. One would permit voters to select "none of the above" as an option on every general-election ballot for all major offices, requiring a new election whenever "none of the above" receives a plurality of the votes. Another would limit the influence of outside special interests by requiring that all campaign contributions originate in the state or district of the candidate. A third would permit two-thirds of the states to nullify a federal law or regulation.

One compelling reform idea is Lamar Alexander's proposal for congressional session limits (best known by the slogan "cut their pay and send them home"). Session limits, pension reform, and the resulting part-time "citizen Congress" would perhaps do the most to help change the culture—for two reasons.

First, session limits would change the perspective of lawmakers, who would be forced to spend more time living among their constituents back home and working at trades in which they must pay taxes and abide by the regulations that Congress imposes.

Second, session limits would change the culture of Washington because *they would yank away one leg of the "iron triangle"*—the well-known and all-too-cozy relationship that members of Congress and committee staffs enjoy with corresponding agencies and interest-group lobbyists that grease the process with money.

America's Backyard

The policy, procedural, and management innovations now on the table are good ideas, as far as they go. But we need to go farther still. We also need to pull another leg off the iron triangle to get at the real problem: the insatiable desire of Congress, the bureaucracy, most special-interest groups—and much of the Washington-based media who report on their activities—to enlarge the role of the federal government in the lives of Americans. The Washington problem, stated most simply, is this: we have a mainframe government in a PC world.

That's why *we need to reengineer and relocate government itself*—eliminating unneeded departments and agencies and realigning, consolidating, and relocating those that remain.

Relocation means actually moving most federal domestic agencies out of Washington. Executive-branch bureaucrats need to be separated from the culture of the Beltway and brought closer to the culture of the people they are supposed to serve. The telecommunications revolution, which has already dramatically changed the way things are done in the private sector, makes this possible. Preservation of representative government makes it desirable. Enforcing accountability makes it essential. Here is what that relocation might look like:

- The Department of Agriculture is supposed to serve farmers and rural communities. So put it in Des Moines or Omaha or Kansas City, close to farmers and farm businesses—or in California, America's largest agricultural state.
- A primary purpose of the Department of Interior is to manage federal lands. So, unless we are willing to auction off the public lands or turn them over to the states, let's headquarter the Secretary and the land managers in Denver or Salt Lake City or Reno—or perhaps Anchorage, where most public lands are located.
- The Treasury Department deals with financial markets headquartered in New York City. So move Treasury to the Big Apple.
- Department of Energy bureaucrats would do better in Dallas, Tulsa, Casper, or Las Cruces—closer to the oil and coal deposits and the nuclear waste sites they are supposed to develop and manage.
- Send the Department of Labor to Chicago or Detroit.
- Move Health and Human Services to Atlanta or Boston.
- Move Housing and Urban Development to Philadelphia or Baltimore.
- Relocate the Immigration and Naturalization Service to Laredo, Miami, or San Diego.
- Put the National Aeronautics and Space Administration in Houston or Huntsville, and the Environmental Protection Agency in New Orleans or Pittsburgh.

There are many benefits to getting the government out of town. First, moving government is a way to eliminate entire departments and agencies. The commission created to relocate agencies can also be given the task of identifying candidates for total abolition (for example, HUD, Commerce, Energy, Education, the Interstate Commerce Commission, Job Corps, and Rural Electrification Administration), agencies that are unnecessary or that carry out functions better performed by state and local governments or the private sector. The commission should also be empowered to consolidate, streamline, and realign remaining agencies and functions.

Second, it will downsize government. As agencies are eliminated and functions consolidated, overhead will be reduced. Many government employees will not want to move to Omaha, Detroit, or Casper. Based on experience in the private sector, where relocation is common, moving government will provide a significant opportunity to reduce the head count in the departments and agencies that move.

Third, it will improve working conditions. Federal employees who do move will frequently find themselves benefiting from a higher living standard and a better quality of life. They will enjoy lower costs and relief from many Washington-area pathologies—including lofty real estate prices, crime, high taxes, and bad schools.

Fourth, it will help to make public servants more responsive to elected leaders. Federal bureaucrats in the hinterland will be one step removed from the culture of Washington. Cozy relationships with congressional staffers will be more difficult. And the move will provide a booster shot of geographic immunization from Washington's enormous concentration of interest group power. These same forces will strengthen the ability of elected leaders—including the president—to manage and direct the work of public administrators, making the delivery of services more responsive to democratic control.

Fifth, it will improve press scrutiny of government. We will benefit from a division of labor among the press in its oversight of government operations. When an agency comes to town, local media will surely develop a special watchdog section to keep track of what it's doing, day after day. Today, the agencies are covered primarily by the trade press and special-interest publications—except when there is the scent of scandal, a major policy failure, or a "big" initiative. Otherwise, agencies escape day-to-day press scrutiny as the *Washington Post* and other jaded Beltway media concentrate their resources on Congress, the White House, and "who's up and who's down."

Sixth, it will spread the wealth. Government payrolls are substantial. Montgomery County, Maryland, and Fairfax County, Virginia, where many federal bureaucrats now live, are two of the wealthiest counties in the U.S. There is no reason why the substantial benefits of government payrolls should remain concentrated in a single region of this sprawling country.

Seventh, it will be more efficient. Office space is cheaper in America's hinterland, as are support services, employee parking, warehouse space, and nearly everything else.

Eighth, the move will make agencies more accessible to the ordinary citizens who may benefit from their services. It's a lot easier for a Minnesota farmer to do business in Des Moines than in Washington, D.C.—and a lot cheaper.

Ninth, the move will give agency staff an opportunity to eat lunch with working Americans, talk about crabgrass and Little League, and generally immerse themselves in the values and priorities of places where people live perfectly fine lives without worrying about "who's in, who's out; who's up, who's down"—to quote Bill Clinton's description of Washington in his inaugural address.

Tenth, the culture is generally healthier in the hinterland. With distributed government, public employees would be informed by the *Rocky Mountain News,* the *Des Moines Register,* or the *Atlanta Constitution*—rather than relying on daily doses of political correctness as promulgated by the *Washington Post.*

Finally, there's the effect the move will have on the iron triangle. By separating lobbyists from the bureaucrats and the Washington-based media from that now-cozy relationship, the triangle would be bent into a pretzel. When agencies move to America's backyard, Washington-based lobbyists will have to make a choice: concentrate on the career politicians and congressional staffers located in Washington or focus on agencies located all around America's hinterland. A Hawthorne effect, in which changes in the working environment tend to increase productivity, would generate fresh ideas, and those fresh ideas would replace the big-government smog that hangs over the nation's capital.

As for Washington, some agencies should remain there—for example, the Departments of Defense and State. But think of the possibilities as others vacate their imposing buildings near the Mall: these structures can be turned over to the Smithsonian to display more of the nation's treasures, including the *Enola Gay*, tainted by a controversy that exemplifies the hostility of Washington's culture to the values and sensibilities of mainstream America. There aren't many people outside the Beltway who believe Americans should feel guilt for the way we ended the bloodshed in the Pacific in World War II. The *Enola Gay* controversy was another dramatic example of how much the mandarins of Washington are out of touch with the culture they are supposed to serve.

Practicalities

The devil, as always, is in the details. Moving federal agencies out of Washington is an idea that Congress must approve in principle. But it should not be left to Congress to implement in detail, lest we see a huge pork festival not unlike the one that took place in the last few years as elements of the CIA and other federal agencies migrated to West Virginia under the guidance of the chairman of the Senate Appropriations Committee.

Fortunately, there is a model to follow: the Base Realignment and Closure Commission (BRAC), used by the Department of Defense to consolidate or shut down military bases in the post–cold war era. To ease tough choices and provide political cover, Congress authorized the president to impanel a special commission to make these decisions for it. Congress then accepts—or rejects—the entire package of BRAC recommendations by a simple up or down vote.

But getting the decisions made is just the beginning. The new arrangement must also work. For that to happen, government must embrace some of the practices of the private sector—and some of the most helpful developments of the information age.

People want smaller, more limited, less expensive, more user-friendly government; and they want the public order to shrink and the civic order to expand.

In short, the new majority wants government to stay out of matters better left to individuals, families, communities, and civic institutions. When government must act, the new American majority wants power exercised at the lowest possible level relevant to the problem—following what the Europeans call the principle of "subsidiarity." When the federal government must be involved—far less often than today—it needs to be efficient, responsive, and available.

Customers in the enterprise economy are making similar demands for responsiveness, speed, accessibility, convenience, choices, and control. That's why the private sector is using new telecomputing technologies to de-layer management operations, decentralize administrative operations, and devolve more decisionmaking authority to managers closest to the customer—linking networks of far-flung offices, managers, and workers in high-performance systems of distributed work. This can work for government, too. Even the federal government.

In today's environment, knowledge workers use computers, software, faxes, modems, express mail, and airplane tickets to stay in touch with customers, colleagues, and bosses. E-mail, the Internet, file-servers, and other networks and systems using advanced telecommunications technologies permit the integration of remote telework centers with a central office. It is no longer necessary to be in the same room as one's supervisor—or even in the same building or city. These new business practices indicate the richness of today's ways of working that are dramatically increasing productivity and decreasing costs in the private sector.

Experience in the private sector shows that distributed government can work. Everything from cultural trends to real estate economics, from citizen (that is, customer) expectations to growing experience with telecomputing networks, supports the idea of distributed government.

As we journey from the gridlock of the Beltway to the many paths to be found in America's backyard, we have plenty of successful examples to follow. Business has been hacking away at its excess for decades. Name one big company that doesn't have subsidiaries in other cities—a software division in Silicon Valley, for instance, and a service center in Atlanta. The telos of the global economy and the information age eliminates borders and shrinks distances as communications and information expand. Washington, no matter how hard it tries, cannot permanently resist adapting to America's technological revolutions.

We should take advantage of new telecomputing technologies, the information superhighway, and new management practices to change the culture of government by downsizing it, eliminating whole departments and agencies, moving much of what's left out of Washington, and substituting a more modern, decentralized, and networked approach for the old, centralized, industrial-age approach to governance. Surely a government of the people, by the people, and for the people would be a better government if it were spread among the people.

Chapter Nine

A New Citizenship, A New Civic Life

Michael S. Joyce and William A. Schambra

Government is too powerful; the citizen is powerless. Such was the unmistakable message of the electoral tidal wave of 1994. American voters signaled that they are fed up with large, aggressive national government and with the political party that has been, for much of this century, the embodiment of the "national idea." As President Clinton's own pollster, Stanley Greenberg, observed after examining his firm's surveys, "This was not a casual act on the part of voters. . . . Voters were very self-conscious that they were casting a vote of dissatisfaction . . . about the mess in Washington, about the nature of our politics, and they understood this to be a Democratically dominated politics."[1]

The underlying issues that drove the voters—skepticism about virtually any and all national undertakings, fear of crime, and general unease about the moral and spiritual decay so evident in the general incivility of American life—reflect a broad-based belief that, while the federal government has absorbed ever larger amounts of the nation's wealth and energy, things are nonetheless spinning out of control in America. As against a federal establishment that has far too much power, there stands the lonely, beleaguered citizen, who seems to have no power whatsoever to manage and order the daily affairs that concern him most. (Commenting on Greenberg's survey results, Al From of the Democratic Leadership Council noted that, in the face of these sentiments, his party must show the American people that it is "helping to repair the social fabric of our society," as well as "getting Washington and government under control.")[2]

More broadly, the elections of 1994 confirm the exhaustion of the grand political project for America that was outlined in 1909 by Herbert Croly's *The Promise of American Life,* elevated to electoral hegemony by Franklin Roosevelt and the New Deal, and pursued with single-minded resolve throughout most of this century by progressive liberal theorists and politicians alike. That project might be summarized as the effort to construct within America's borders a great national community, which would summon Americans away from selfish interests and parochial allegiances, toward a commitment to an overarching national idea or purpose. How this project came to be, how it came to collapse, and how civic life in America might be rebuilt on an older understanding of local community and citizenship are the topic of this chapter.

The Traditional Civic Order

The Progressive project of national community emerged at the turn of the century, in response to what appeared to be dramatic and permanent changes in the way Americans had traditionally conducted their everyday civic life.

Prior to the modern age, American life had been organized around what historian Robert Wiebe describes as "island communities."[3] As this apt phrase suggests, civic life was characterized by both its self-containment and its cohesiveness. Individuals were closely bound one to another by strong families, tightly knit neighborhoods, and active voluntary and fraternal groups. Through these small, local, human-scale associations, Americans not only achieved a sense of belonging and connectedness, they also tackled the full range of social and human problems that today have largely become the province of government. As sociologist Robert Nisbet notes, "the social problems of birth and death, courtship and marriage, employment and unemployment, infirmity and old age were met, however inadequately at times, through the associated means of these social groups" (or "intermediate associations," as he called them).[4] Citizens thus had a significant say—and *knew* they had a significant say—in the most important decisions affecting their own everyday lives. What we today call "public policy" was not a manufacture of government, but a lived, daily experience.

Thus, a citizen's churches and voluntary groups reflected and reinforced his moral and spiritual values and imparted them to his children, surrounding him with a familiar, self-contained, breathable moral atmosphere. Voluntary social welfare associations ministered to the community's vulnerable according to the tenets of compassion and charity implicit in those values. A citizen's schools, whether publicly or privately funded, enshrined and were run in accordance with those values, and with extensive citizen involvement and supervision. Critical public decisions were made in township meetings, ward conclaves, or other small, face-to-face gatherings in which the individual's voice was as important as his vote. In short, the most important decisions about citizens' lives were made not by faceless others in some distant state or national capital; they were made by and among citizens themselves, in gatherings of neighbors and acquaintances.

This, of course, is the America celebrated and immortalized in Alexis de Tocqueville's *Democracy in America.* "Americans of all ages, all stations in life, and all types of dispositions are forever forming associations," he noted, because this was how virtually every significant public problem was solved.[5] The weak central state, he pointed out, was not just an accident of history, but the design of the Founding Fathers, who understood that the civic and communal commitments and skills critical to a free society could be developed only by sustained interaction within small, intimate, decentralized settings. "The lawgivers of America did not suppose that a general representation of the whole nation would suffice," he noted. "They thought it also right to give each part of the land its own political life so that there should be an infinite number of occasions for the citizens to act together and so that every day they should feel that they depended on one another."

The Rise of the National Community Idea

This decentralized, self-governing, civically vital way of life, however, was doomed, in the view of the Progressives who emerged at the beginning of the twentieth century—theorists like Walter Lippmann, John Dewey, and, of course, Herbert Croly, and public figures like Theodore Roosevelt and (to some extent) Woodrow Wilson. In their view, the irresistible forces of modernity were beginning to sweep away the boundaries that historically had contained and preserved the island communities. Modern means of communication—telegraph, telephone, the high-speed press—had breached the small town's borders with a relentless barrage of information about the larger world, ending its isolation. Technology had given rise to vast corporate giants, whose operations reached far beyond the jurisdictions of any single state or city. Great cities had sprung up, populated by aggregates of isolated, disconnected individuals, rather than by tightly knit neighbors. Immigration added millions of people from threateningly alien cultures to these already forbidding metropolises. Political control all too often passed out of the hands of town meetings into the grasp of what were described as corrupt, boss-driven political machines. The duty of the citizen seemed to have been lost in the stampede for wealth, a stampede that was legitimated by new doctrines of emancipated individualism.

In short, the forces of modernity had precipitated a crisis of community in America: the small town and its civic virtues had been shattered. As Lippmann described it, modernity had forever and permanently "upset the old life of the prairies [and] destroyed village loyalties."[6] While it was pointless, in the Progressives' view, to try to preserve or restore the ethos of the small town (that had been the failed Populist response), it was now possible to move to a new and higher form of community: the national community.

The essential instrument of this new and higher form would be a powerful, active national government. In Croly's famous formulation, the Jeffersonian values of "community of feeling and . . . ease of communication" could now be established within the nation as a whole, using the Hamiltonian instrument of a vigorous central government. As Dewey described the Progressive project, the "Great Society created by steam and electricity" would have to be converted into the "Great Community."[7]

The central government, for instance, could tame through regulatory measures those great and disruptive concentrations of private wealth, the corporations, thereby turning them into "express economic agents of the whole community," as Croly put it. The government would also become "expressly responsible for an improved distribution of wealth," and would begin to alleviate, through the progressive income tax and social welfare programs, the inequalities of wealth that might imperil the sense of national oneness. A vigorous program of "Americanization" would serve to integrate diverse immigrant populations into a single, coherent people. "Scientific management" and other new developments in the social sciences held out the promise that enlightened, bureaucratic administration could order and direct the chaotic masses toward public purposes. (As sociologist Charles Horton Cooley put it, the era demanded "a comprehensive 'scientific management' of mankind, to the end of better personal opportunity and social function in every possible line.")[8]

Behind these specific developments and programs, however, lay a larger moral purpose: the creation of a genuine national community which could evoke from the American people a self-denying devotion to the "national idea," a far-flung community of millions in which citizens nonetheless would be linked tightly by bonds of compassion, fellow feeling, and neighborliness. In Croly's words, there would be a "subordination of the individual to the demand of a dominant and constructive national purpose." A citizen would begin to "think first of the State and next of himself," and "individuals of all kinds will find their most edifying individual opportunities in serving their country." Indeed, America would come to be bound together by a "religion of human brotherhood," which "can be realized only through the loving-kindness which individuals feel . . . particularly toward their fellow-countrymen."

The catalyst of the national community, the articulator of the "national purpose," in the Progressive view, was to be the president—the galvanizing, unifying voice of all the American people. The president's is the "only national voice in affairs," Woodrow Wilson argued. He alone could unite and inspire the people by combining their many views into one coherent whole: "The voices of the nation unite in his understanding in a single meaning and reveal to him a single vision, so that he can speak . . . the common meaning of the common voice." From the bully pulpit of the executive office, the president would summon from the American people the self-sacrifice, public-spiritedness, and compassion that the national community required.

This vision of national community reached its apotheosis in World War I. Suddenly, the Progressives discovered the awesome capacity of war to nurture public-spiritedness and national oneness. Dewey would speak appreciatively afterward of the "social possibilities of war." Lippmann noted approvingly that "the war has given Americans a new instinct for order, purpose, and discipline," and had served to "draw Americans out of their local, group, and ethnic loyalties into a greater American citizenship." Liberalism would never forget the lessons of 1917-18. Henceforth, in times of peace, it would search diligently for the "moral equivalent of war," a kind of war that would energize the national community without the actual spilling of blood.

The National Community and the Eclipse of Citizenship

At the level of the citizen, this new philosophy of national community began to introduce dramatic changes in the way everyday civic life was conducted and experienced. Whereas before public affairs were well within the grasp of the average citizen, easily comprehended and managed by everyday folk wisdom and common sense, now public affairs had allegedly been so complicated by modernity that, according to the Progressive elites, the average citizen could no longer hope to understand or manage them. Now it was necessary, in Frederick C. Howe's phrase, to "call in the expert."[9]

Thus, Dewey urged broad public education in the social sciences so that citizens would learn, in Timothy Kaufman-Osborn's formulation, "the radical insufficiency of the maxims of everyday conduct," as well as that "the roots of most problematic situations do not lie within the jurisdiction of the locality and hence that their commonsense analyses of those situations are unreliable."[10] The good citizen now accepted his "inescapable dependence upon those trained in the expert methods of the social sciences," and graciously backed out of public affairs in deference to the experts who alone knew how to manage the complexity of modern public life. As city management advocate Henry Bruere put it, "citizens of larger cities must frankly recognize the need for professional service in behalf of citizen interests. . . . Even efficient private citizens will evidence their efficiency by supporting constructive efforts for governmental betterment."

For the Progressive elites, "governmental betterment" meant reforms in governing systems that all but assured deference to the new professionals by structurally elevating public affairs out of the average citizen's reach. Historian Samuel Hayes points out that decentralized, localized ward and precinct systems of representation, which had "enabled local and particularistic interests to dominate" and had assured that elected officials "spoke for . . . those aspects of community life which mattered most" to the average citizen, now gave way to at-large, citywide systems of voting and representation, which handed over governance to corporate and professional elites possessed of an enlarged, scientific, rational view of governance.[11]

As Hayes suggests, structural revisions like the short ballot, initiative, referendum, recall, and the city manager system that familiarly present themselves as prodemocratic, antimachine reforms, might in fact be better understood as methods to subvert and undermine the private civic associations through which common citizens had previously expressed themselves, in the effort to ensure enlightened, elite rule. In Hayes' formulation, the earlier, decentralized system "involved wide latitude for the expression of grass-roots impulses and their involvement in the political process." The Progressive vision, by contrast, "grew out of the rationalization of life which came with science and technology, in which decisions arose from expert analysis and flowed from fewer and smaller centers outward to the rest of society."

The triumph of Progressive structural reform would mean, in essence, that citizen involvement in public affairs was reduced from active, intense, face-to-face problem solving on a daily basis, to passive casting of a lonely, solitary ballot once in a great while for a handful of offices. That ballot would be aggregated with vast numbers of other solitary votes into a mandate for an elite corps of professional experts, who would now conduct the real business of public life.

Similar "reforms" ensured that local schools were removed from the hands of ordinary citizens organized around religious or ethnic values. As Sol Cohen suggests, the decentralized, neighborhood-based management of the New York school system came under assault in the 1890s by reformers who were particularly anxious to drive religious expression and teachings out of the schools: "The reformers' battle cry, 'Take the school out of politics,' not only meant take the schools out of the hands of Tammany Hall, it also meant take the schools out of the hands of the Roman Catholic Church."[12] Joel Spring notes that "declining local control of the schools" was paralleled by "the increasing differentiation, specialization, and centralization of school administration," all of which "contributed to a decrease in lay influence on the schools."[13]

The anxiety about the presence of religious values in public schools arose, of course, from the conviction that traditional sectarian religion was but a benighted, retrograde system of myths that must be purged from common consciousness in order to establish the undisputed hegemony of the social sciences. Indeed, many of the Progressives understood the new sciences and their seeming capacity to reorder society into a coherent and orderly whole to be a secular evolution from or substitute for religion, a realization of the Kingdom on Earth—to recall Croly's formulation, a "religion of human brotherhood." J. David Hoeveler directs us to the view of the Progressive president of the University of Wisconsin, John Bascom, that "a theology which seeks the regeneration of society in ignorance of social laws is doomed to failure," and his consequent conviction that a government possessed of such laws was "a surrogate for the churches and voluntary societies."[14]

Bascom's evident hostility toward churches, voluntary societies, and other private civic institutions completes the picture of progressivism's understanding of public life in the new order. Experts needed to replace civic and voluntary social programs not only because those civil institutions represented backward, unsophisticated citizens hopelessly encumbered by retrograde values, but also because only the social sciences understood how to manipulate the powerful, subtle forces of modern society that in fact had produced social problems in the first place. The model for social policy was now a corps of professional social scientists organized into rational bureaucratic structures ministering to passive "clients," who were understood to be the blameless and helpless victims of those modern forces. This would replace what Bascom dismissed as a "rambling halting voluntaryism"—bumbling, amateurish, parochial, unenlightened voluntary charities, which mean-spiritedly insisted on holding those victims to a standard of personal moral responsibility, and expected them somehow to exert themselves on their own behalf.[15]

It should be apparent by now that progressive liberalism was not altogether forthcoming about its motives for moving toward a national community through bureaucratization, rationalization, centralization, and the centripetal moral impulse of the national idea. On the one hand, progressives insisted with sociologist Robert Park that "the old forms of social control represented by the family, the neighborhood, and the local community have been undermined and greatly diminished" simply as the inevitable and irresistible result of the forces of modernity.[16] On the other hand, as Robert Nisbet maintains, there is no mistaking the fact that the progressives were actively hostile to such intermediate associations, and worked hard to destroy them by shifting their functions and authority upward to the national state and its elite corps of experts.

The national community project thus was not somehow thrust upon reluctant progressive reformers by modern trends. It was in fact the culmination of human progress, in their view, the finest and most complete form of political and social organization imaginable, fully meriting every conscious effort to bring it to reality—even if that meant euthanizing civic institutions that might not be quite on their deathbeds.

The implications of the Progressive program were not lost on prescient observers at the time. Presidential candidate Woodrow Wilson sounded the alarm: "What I fear . . . is a government of experts," he noted in his 1912 Labor Day address in Buffalo. "God forbid that in a democratic country we should resign the task and give the government over to experts. What are we if we are to be [scientifically] taken care of by a small number of gentlemen who are the only men who understand the job? Because if we don't understand the job, then we are not a free people."

Before the decade was out, of course, Wilson would himself succumb to the charms of the Progressive project and the "social possibilities of war." After a hiatus in the 1920s, this project would be brought to political power by Franklin D. Roosevelt's New Deal, and then pursued relentlessly throughout the rest of the century by a succession of powerful, energetic, progressive liberal presidents.

The Reign of Progressive Community

Indeed, every great liberal president of the twentieth century following Wilson made the cultivation of the national community the central goal of his administration, expanding the power and reach of the national government, and calling upon Americans to put aside self-interest and local allegiances on behalf of the national idea (often invoking the moral equivalent of war.) The explosion of government power during the New Deal, for instance, proceeded behind FDR's call in his first inaugural address for Americans to "move as a trained and loyal army willing to sacrifice for the good of a common discipline." We must be "ready and willing to submit our lives and property to such discipline," he insisted, and pledge that "larger purposes will bind upon us all as a sacred obligation with a unity of duty hitherto evoked only in times of armed strife."

Samuel Beer notes that historians and economists have debated endlessly the intentions and effects of the vast outpouring of government programs during the New Deal. But "in creating among Americans the expectation that the federal government could and should deal with the great economic questions and that the nation could and should bear the consequent burdens, the achievement of the New Deal was close to revolutionary." (Beer brings an insider's perspective: as a young speechwriter for FDR, he notes, "I vividly recall our preoccupation with persuading people to look to Washington for the solution of problems.")[17]

Similarly, we remember John F. Kennedy above all for his stirring call to Americans to put aside self-interest on behalf of national purpose: "Ask not what your county can do for you—ask what you can do for your country." Concrete accomplishments aside, Kennedy promised to make us feel as a nation that we were together, united, "moving again." "These are times that appeal to every citizen's sense of sacrifice and self-discipline," he announced during the campaign of 1960. "They call out to every citizen to weigh his rights and comforts against the common good."

Liberalism's national community project reached its zenith in Lyndon Johnson's aptly named Great Society (though it would have been better named the Great Community). Again, there was the familiar explosion of federal government activity, justified by an equally familiar rhetoric: "I see a day ahead with a united nation, divided neither by class nor by section nor by color, knowing no South or North, no East or West, but just one great America, free of malice and free of hate, and loving thy neighbor as thyself." America, he insisted, must "turn unity of interest into unity of purpose, and unity of goals into unity in the Great Society."

The centerpiece of the Great Society was, of course, the "war on poverty"—selected with the careful progressive eye for "moral equivalents." "War," Johnson explained, "evokes cooperation . . . [and a] sense of brotherhood and unity." The "military image" of the war on poverty, he argued, would "rally the nation" and "sound a call to arms which will stir people . . . to lend their talents to a massive effort to eradicate the evil."

In this case, the people chiefly stirred to lend their talents turned out to be vast cadres of social scientists, armed with the very latest theories about the insidious social forces that "created" poverty and an endless array of federal programs designed to manipulate those forces on behalf of their putative clients, poverty's passive, helpless victims. Indeed, the Great Society probably came as close as any other period of this century to capturing progressivism's ideal: public policy securely in the hands of an elite cadre of professionals, dispensing programs through vast, gleaming, rational bureaucracies—a domestic version of Johnson's "best and brightest," who were busily designing another kind of war elsewhere.

The Assault on the National Community Idea

Beginning in the early 1960s, however, there were ominous rumblings beneath the apparently smoothly humming federal edifice. Powerful intellectual and political movements, spanning the ethnic and ideological spectrum, began to suggest that the national community was not quite so coherent or compelling as progressivism had hoped it would be. Indeed—in spite of six decades of progressive warfare against "parochial" civil institutions—there appeared once again a yearning for the intimate, face-to-face, participatory community to be found in small groups, family, neighborhood, church, and ethnic and voluntary associations.

The New Left, for instance, insisted that the Great Society was, in spite of its claims, radically anticommunitarian, characterized by (in the Port Huron Statement's formulation) "loneliness, estrangement, [and] isolation." This was inevitable in a society governed by what they now described as a massive, distant, alienating bureaucracy, linked closely with giant business concerns in that unholy alliance the New Left came to call "corporate liberalism." As an alternative, the New Left offered "participatory democracy." A society organized according to that principle would devolve major political and economic decisionmaking to small, tightly knit local groups, within which people would "share in the social decisions determining the quality and direction of their lives." (The communitarian strand of radical thought would ultimately be overwhelmed, however, by its companion doctrine of personal liberation and uninhibited self-expression, which would go on to play havoc with our civic institutions and values.)

The rejection of the national community and the impulse toward smaller, more intimate communities also characterized the Black Power movement of the 1960s and 1970s, and the subsequent flowering of similar movements centered around ethnic identity and community control that it inspired. According to Stokely Carmichael and Charles Hamilton in *Black Power,* blacks should begin to "recognize the need to assert their own definitions, to reclaim their history, their culture; to create their own sense of community and togetherness." Local social institutions like the schools and police should not be run by white liberals downtown, but by blacks in the neighborhood: "We must begin to think of the black community as a base of organization to control institutions in that community." By celebrating black culture and morality in neighborhood schools and other public places, a "growing sense of community" at the local level would be further encouraged.[18]

So powerful were these new doctrines that Senator Robert Kennedy seized upon them for his electoral challenge to Johnson's Great Society. In his campaign book, *To Seek A Newer World,* he argued that the nation's slums could be transformed only through "new community institutions that local residents control, and through which they can express their wishes." He called for a "decentralization of some municipal functions and some aspects of government into smaller units, no matter what the race or economic status of the governed."[19] This would, he noted, move us "toward [Jefferson's] vision of participating democracy," an objective that had otherwise become "increasingly difficult in the face of the giant organizations and massive bureaucracies of the age."

Perhaps the most politically potent expression of dissatisfaction with the national community in the 1960s and 1970s, however, came from the opposite end of the political spectrum, from lower-middle-class blue-collar neighborhoods, usually connected to the older industrial cities of the North and East, usually heavily ethnic (of southern and eastern European origin), Democratic, and Catholic. As they saw it, the national government seemed to have launched a massive assault—through cold, bureaucratic edict or equally cold judicial fiat—against the traditional prerogatives of locality and neighborhood to define and preserve their own ways of life. Suddenly, they could neither pray in their local schools, nor indeed count on sending their own children *to* the local school because of compulsory busing, nor ban from their community forms of expression or sexual conduct that they considered offensive, nor define the conditions under which abortion might be proper, nor even enforce the most rudimentary forms of civil order under the police power.

The most spectacular expression of this discontent came, of course, from George Wallace, who insisted that people were "fed up with strutting pseudo-intellectuals lording over them . . . telling them they have not got sense enough to run their own schools and hospitals and domestic institutions." Consequently, Wallace explained, there had been a "backlash against the theoreticians and bureaucrats in national government who are trying to solve problems that ought to be solved at the local level." His answer to this was "States' Rights and local government and territorial democracy."[20]

Describing the deeper impulses behind the white ethnic revolt, Michael Novak suggests in *The Rise of the Unmeltable Ethnics* that ethnics had historically been the primary victims of progressive liberalism's effort to eradicate particularist allegiances on behalf of one vast homogenized, rationalized, bureaucratized national community. Now they had made a dramatic and forceful "turn toward the organic networks of communal life . . . family, ethnic groups, and voluntary associations in primary groups."[21]

The Political Eclipse of National Community

Beneath the variety of intellectual currents of revolt during the 1960s lay this central truth: progressive liberalism's intention to eradicate "parochial" loyalties and allegiances on behalf of the great national community had failed miserably. That failure became ever more conspicuous during the 1970s and 1980s, when the nation's political landscape reshaped itself to accommodate this truth, along with the groups that had been roused to an angry political revolt over the assault on their "organic networks."

The often overlooked fact is that after 1964, *no one* would again win the presidency by boasting about building a Great Society, a great national community, in America. *No one* would again call proudly and forthrightly for a shift of power to Washington, and away from the local organic networks. Indeed, every president from 1968 to the present has placed at the center of his agenda the *denunciation* of centralized, bureaucratic government, along with promises to slash its size and power, and to reinvigorate states, small communities, and civil society's intermediate associations.

Thus President Nixon complained that "a third of a century of centralizing power and responsibility in Washington has produced a bureaucratic monstrosity, cumbersome, unresponsive, ineffective." He proposed a New Federalism in which "power, funds, and responsibility will flow from Washington to the State and to the people," through block grants and revenue sharing. During the presidential campaign of 1972—even after he had presided over four years of dramatically *expanding* government programs— Nixon would nonetheless insist that the "central question" of that election was: "Do we want to turn more power over to bureaucrats in Washington . . . or do we want to return more power to the people and to their State and local governments, so that people can decide what is best for themselves?" Similarly, President Ford characterized his programs as an effort to "return power from the banks of the Potomac to the people in their communities."

During this period, Republican presidential hegemony would be interrupted but once, by an "outsider" Democrat who insisted that the Republicans had, rhetoric notwithstanding, permitted the federal government to become too large and inefficient. What was needed, Jimmy Carter insisted, was an engineer's savvy to trim it back to size. Thus his schemes for reorganizing government, zero-based budgeting, and sunset provisions were meant to prove that government could "serve basic needs without proliferating wasteful, bloated bureaucracies." Cultivating his image as a man steeped in the moral and religious traditions of a small southern town, Carter promised a new emphasis on local community: "The only way we will ever put the government back in its place is to restore the families and neighborhoods to their proper places," because they can "succeed in solving problems where governments will always fail."

Carter, of course, eventually drifted away from his pledge to reduce government and restore the prerogatives of families and neighborhoods. Faced by shrinking popularity, he resorted to what almost amounts to a self-caricature of liberalism's "moral equivalent" ploy. In his now infamous "malaise" speech, Carter suggested that "We are the generation that will win the war on the energy problem and in that process rebuild the unity and confidence of America" (as if shivering in an underheated home, remembering to turn out the lights, or sitting in endless queues at gas stations would somehow restore our faith in the central government and sense of national oneness).

Americans were not particularly pleased to be told that they suffered from "malaise," nor were they up for a "war" that simply masked yet another expansion of federal power, in this case the nationalization of energy supplies. Thus was Carter replaced by this century's most consistent and eloquent critic of federal power and spokesman for reinvigoration of local community. Ronald Reagan promised an end to the state of affairs in which "thousands of towns and neighborhoods have seen their peace disturbed by bureaucrats and social planners through busing, questionable education programs, and attacks on family unity." He called instead for "an end to giantism, for a return to the human scale . . . the scale of the local fraternal lodge, the church organization, the block club, the farm bureau," and pursued this goal through budget reductions, block grants, a program of private-sector initiatives, and a (new) New Federalism. His successor, George Bush, followed Reagan in explicitly rejecting liberalism's project of national community, proclaiming instead a vision of "a nation of communities, of thousands of ethnic, religious, social, business, labor union, neighborhood, regional, and other organizations, all of them varied, voluntary, and unique," which would stand as a "thousand points of light" in America's struggle to solve social problems.

Republican ascendancy in the 1990s was terminated when President Bush not only failed to reduce government, but actually acquiesced in its expansion through significant tax hikes. His victorious opponent—like Carter, draping himself in the traditional values of a small southern town—swore that he had gotten the message about his party's traditional allegiance to big government.

Proclaiming himself a "New Democrat" by way of shorthand for this political epiphany, Bill Clinton pledged to end welfare as we know it, to get tough on crime, and to "reinvent" government (which insiders understood to mean "revive," but which the public could be counted on to mistake for "reduce"). Publicly, he would raise questions about reliance on big government, and suggest a return to the "organic networks": as he noted, "our problems go way beyond the reach of government. They're rooted in the loss of values, in the disappearance of work and the breakdown of families and communities." Problems will be solved, he continued, only when "all of us are willing to join churches and other good citizens . . . who are saving kids, adopting schools, making streets safer."

What explains an erosion of the idea of national community so severe that even the Democratic Party itself now hesitates to speak up for it? In part, the moral momentum of national community is extremely difficult to sustain. The project strains to create artificially, at the level of the entire vast nation, a sense of mutuality and oneness that appears readily and naturally only at the level of the family or local community. This transfer may be possible only in times of crisis, when the threat to the nation is sufficiently obvious that people do, indeed, feel obliged to pull together as one.

The United States has experienced its share of such crises since 1929— the Great Depression, World War II, the cold war—and liberalism has used them to maximum effect, to construct an ever more powerful central government. The extraordinary community-mindedness inspired by national crisis is extremely demanding, however, and therefore difficult to sustain, especially when real crises are not available, and liberal presidents must turn to moral equivalents. A war on poverty (to say nothing of a "war on the energy problem") is but a pallid substitute for the real thing. Today, with the end of a long and exhausting cold war, Americans seem distinctly unwilling to rally around the "national idea."

With the moral foundations of the liberal project thus eroding, its programmatic superstructure—a massive, centralized federal government—is left in a peculiarly exposed and precarious position. No longer understood to be the instrument of high national purpose, the federal government comes to be seen instead as a distant, alienating, bureaucratic monstrosity. In the wake of this development, it was inevitable that the American people would return to the idea of community that finds expression in small, participatory groups such as family, neighborhood, and ethnic and voluntary associations—an idea far more natural and easier to sustain.

That such a return is profoundly difficult and complicated after eight decades of liberalism's campaign of civil eradication is only to be expected. The consistent and ever intensifying message from our most "sophisticated" cultural and political institutions over that period was that such local civic institutions are at best sources of amusement, at worst hopeless, parochial backwaters of reaction, racism, and religious superstition and zealotry. In light of this unremitting barrage of cultural denigration, it is all the more remarkable that the American people nonetheless continued throughout the last quarter century to express themselves politically against the national community, and for local, organic networks.

Perhaps the only other political phenomenon evidencing itself as consistently as that expressed preference over the last twenty-five years has been the steadfast failure of our national leaders to respond substantively to it, solemn quadrennial promises to the contrary notwithstanding. Indeed, the dramatic and ever increasing gap between what the public *demands* and what federal officials actually *deliver* once in power has spawned whole analytic industries in political science, economics, and talk show punditry. Government programs have mysteriously acquired "lives of their own"; "runaway" entitlement spending has somehow passed beyond the realm of human control; a swarm of invisible but omnipotent special-interest groups are choking the life out of democracy; Congress's committee structure is hopelessly fragmented and can no longer discipline itself; government branches in different partisan hands collapse helplessly into "gridlock," "stalemate," "divided government"; we even hear today the patronizing psychopolitical hypothesis that the American people are fickle and self-contradictory, and do not *really*, in their heart of hearts, *want* to reduce government.

Again and again, for twenty-five years, our political elites have carefully and cleverly explained to the American people that, even if they no longer believed in big government or its higher purposes, big government was nonetheless here to stay. And again and again, for twenty-five years, the American people have trudged patiently, wearily, but—one clearly senses— ever more angrily to the polls to vote against it.

Viewed in this larger perspective, it is now perhaps easier to understand the tsunami of 1994. For the seventh time in a quarter century, the American people in 1992 had elected the presidential candidate who had persuaded them that *he* was the most sincere about reversing the growth of government (all three candidates had earnestly made that claim). And for the seventh time, early deeds such as proposing government absorption of the health care industry quickly gave the lie to words, and told the American people that, once again, they had been had.

What happened in 1994 was no infantile electoral tantrum, as has been suggested by some analysts. It was, rather, the culmination of twenty-five years of frustration, twenty-five years of promises made and broken. By 1994, the American people simply could not bring themselves, in the words of the ancient injunction, to "forgive, not seven times, but seventy times seven."

The Resuscitation of Civil Society

If we are to begin to restore faith in American institutions, understanding the full dimensions of the growing ill humor of the American electorate evident in 1994 is essential. Michael Sandel insightfully suggests that "the election was haunted by the fear that we are losing control of the forces that govern our lives, that the moral fabric of community is unraveling around us, and that our political institutions are unable to respond."[22]

As he implies, Americans have remained relatively untroubled about the abstruse macroproblems—workforce retraining for global competitiveness, the greenhouse effect, and long-term interest rates—our governing elites would like them to worry about (because these problems seem to call on scientific government expertise for solution). Rather, Americans are worried above all about the unraveling of the orderly, coherent, authoritative moral community they were once able to build around themselves within their own strong local civic institutions. They are deeply troubled by the sense that they are not safe from random violence in *this* house or *this* neighborhood; that they cannot send their children safely down *this* street to the local school; that they can no longer rely on *this* school to teach their children both rigorous basic academics and sound moral values in tune with *their* deepest spiritual and ethical commitments. And they have long since stopped trusting the experts who assure them that crime rates are really falling, or that children are really better off without pedagogy about right and wrong, or that disruptively immoral behavior is really just an alternative lifestyle.

As we have seen, our major governing institutions and elites have not only done little to prevent the erosion of local civic community—indeed, this has been their primary intention for much of this century. Our elites have spent eight decades explaining that modern circumstances are far too complex for the American people to hope to govern themselves—far better to shift public decisionmaking upward to sophisticated, rational elites who have scientifically mastered those circumstances. In this view, the local civic institutions to which the people cling are just backwaters of moral reaction—distractions from the grand national idea.

Further contributing to the erosion of those institutions has been the elite's ethic of unfettered self-expression, which they gladly inherited from the New Left. Beneath its dizzying variety of moral, political, and sexual manifestations, this ethic is at its heart nothing more than an in-your-face repudiation of the everyday, bourgeois moral code which the American people once counted on to preserve the immediate civic order. As Robert Nisbet observes, the embrace of the doctrine of hyperliberated individualism has added a potent weapon to progressivism's arsenal in its campaign to sap the power and authority of intermediate associations.

If the message of 1994 and of every presidential election since 1968 is that the American people have utterly lost faith in the project of national community and the elites who would construct it, then perhaps we would be wise at last to heed the other half of the last quarter century's message. For the American people have also been patiently and consistently telling us that they wish to get about the business of reconstructing the local moral and political institutions of civil society, and rebuilding the social order they ensure.

They understand that only strengthened local government and revitalized intermediate associations—families, neighborhoods, churches, schools, and ethnic and voluntary associations—will permit them to reestablish fundamental decency and basic civil order within their immediate surroundings. They wish to make the most important decisions about their own everyday lives for and among themselves, so that once again things are seen to be under control. In short, the American people will no longer settle for occasionally casting a ballot for one or another set of elites. They insist on becoming, once again, genuine, self-governing citizens.

The restoration of civil society will require nothing less than a determined, long-term effort to reverse the gravitation of power and authority upward to the national government, and to send that authority back to local government and civil institutions. Some of the proposed structural reforms currently before the public—term limits, line-item veto, the balanced budget amendment, and so forth—might be useful first steps in that direction. But they are only first steps, the damage-control measures that must be taken while a vastly more significant positive agenda is pursued in tandem.

That positive agenda is once again to empower civic institutions, local governments, families, and citizens genuinely to make the public decisions and carry out the public tasks that really count. These include especially the most significant decisions and tasks within the realm of social policy—the economic, social, educational, and moral sustenance of the youngest, oldest, poorest, and most vulnerable. As Peter Berger and Richard John Neuhaus suggest in their pathbreaking book, *To Empower People,* we must make intermediate associations (or "mediating structures," as they call them) the primary agents of social welfare once again.[23]

If such a shift of responsibility is to occur, however, resources must follow as well. Because the national wealth has been steadily siphoned upward for decades to support vast bureaucracies of service providers, some mechanism must be found to return resources as well as responsibility to individuals and local civic institutions. In the short term, the way to do that commensurate with the larger goal of revitalizing citizenship might be systems of vouchers, which would permit qualifying individuals to seek out the local educational and social service institutions that would best meet their needs as they themselves understand them, and that would reflect their own values. In many cases, such institutions will turn out to be church-based groups, which hitherto have been systematically excluded from social service networks by progressivism's antireligious prejudice, manifesting itself in a grotesquely rigid understanding of the Constitution's church-state doctrine.

Vouchers that go directly to individuals, not institutions, however, should meet any constitutional objection. The result would be individuals empowered to make decisions about which groups they wish to associate with, and local civic associations reinforced rather than undercut by federal resources. Meanwhile, the competition among such groups would ensure that public purposes are accomplished more effectively and less expensively. Over the longer run, of course, steady reductions in federal taxation would preempt the need for our resources to make this round-trip through Washington, D.C.

The faint of heart may flinch from the implications of this larger agenda, preferring to limit themselves to the negative agenda, the call simply to cut back government, or to shift power from one set of government bureaucrats to another through the latest version of "new federalism." This could well reflect a subtle suspicion, lurking in the psyche of even the staunchest government critic after decades of elite propaganda, that core social tasks *are* after all too important to be left to average citizens, and that government experts really *should* be left in charge, while less serious, symbolic decisions—school prayer, reciting the pledge of allegiance—may safely be turned back to local citizens.

American citizens, however, have had a bellyful of symbolism. As Nisbet reminds us, people "do not come together in significant and lasting associations merely to be together. They come together to *do something* that cannot be done in individual isolation" (italics added).[24] They will rally in revitalized civic institutions only if those institutions do something, and something significant—restore civic order, reflect and carry out deep moral convictions, and make and execute the most authoritative social and political decisions, especially in how we go about caring for the most vulnerable.

Serious discussions are already under way throughout society about ways to restore the authority of the most important civic association, the family. It is now becoming clear that the chief object of many of today's self-expressive, liberationist ideologies is precisely to discredit the traditional family, allegedly the most oppressive and backward of the parochial institutions of civil society. We are told that it stunts the potential of women by harnessing them to menial domestic chores, limits the intellectual development of children by subjecting them to the cramped moral perspective of the parents, and subjects both women and children to the tyrannical rule and predatory sexual impulses of men.

The counterattack, however, is in progress. Professional women have begun to realize that feminine fulfillment can be found either in careers, or in family life, or both. Family-friendly researchers have pointed out that children flourish, rather than wither, in strong moral atmospheres. And fathers are now beginning to be appreciated once more as providers of discipline and order within the family—especially as the consequences of rearing children without fathers become ever more apparent in the spread of gangs of rootless, violent young men throughout our inner cities.

Parents, in turn, have begun to fight back against a social service and educational establishment that has, for too long, treated them with contempt. Efforts by New York City's education elite to install a "rainbow curriculum," which would have introduced school children to doctrines of morally uninstructed sexual self-expression, met with a sharp rebuff, as Hispanic, black, and white parents of many faiths refused to permit the bureaucracy so to flout their deepest moral commitments. Similarly, parent uprisings around the nation have challenged the lax moral and academic standards of "outcome based" education curricula, and programs of sex education that implicitly sanction morally offensive sexual practices. In many state legislatures across the nation, "parents' rights amendments" have been introduced, which would confirm the prerogative of parents to direct the moral and educational upbringing of their children as they see fit. And the 1994 election makes it more likely than ever that the federal tax code will be revised to make it more family-friendly, and that larger portions of our resources will remain with parents, obviating the round-trip through Washington.

Closely connected to the rising cry of "parent power" is the movement toward parental choice in education, more commonly if less accurately known as "school choice." Perhaps no other aspect of public life so important to the everyday concerns of the citizen has been so thoroughly corrupted and distorted by the legacy of progressive liberalism. While nominally still under local control, the most important public school decisions about what is taught, how, by whom, and to whom, have long since gravitated upward into rigid, bloated education bureaucracies, and outward into powerful, well-financed public-sector unions of teachers and administrators, who act as the Swiss Guards of the bureaucracy.

Families have become increasingly aware of and disturbed by the education bureaucracy's low estimate of parental competence. (Progressive social worker Ellen Richards suggested as long ago as 1910 that the school is "fast taking the place of the home, not because it wishes to do so, but because the home does not fulfill its function.") Families are also alarmed by the eclipse of moral and spiritual discipline in public schools. Outraged by growing civil disorder and declining academic performance in the schools, parents in many locales around the nation have tried to take them back. Aside from occasional victories like the rainbow-curriculum insurrection, however, they have had little enduring success.

Consequently, we see growing enthusiasm for parental choice programs, under which vouchers would be issued to families, who could redeem them at the school of their choice. In a full choice system, that would include religious as well as secular schools. The contribution such a system would make to civic revitalization is substantial. The schools selected by parents would often reflect their moral and spiritual commitments. Parents would thus, for the first time in a long time, be making a vital, publicly supported decision that reflected their fundamental values. Children would again find themselves in morally rigorous, character-forming environments, free of the disorder that has stymied education in many public schools. And the local moral, spiritual, ethnic, or neighborhood community for which the school is often the institutional centerpiece would flourish, now with the help of, rather than in spite of, the state. Competition among schools for voucher-bearing students would ensure that parental demands for academic and moral excellence were met at costs dramatically lower than today, and even the public schools themselves might be driven to improve in order to capture their share of students.

Indeed, parental choice in education might be understood as a valuable prototype for the larger project of voucher-supported efforts to restore critical civic institutions. This is why it has found a place at the heart of the civic restoration agenda, as reflected in a large and growing array of choice initiatives at the city, state, and national levels. And this, of course, is precisely why the bureaucracies and public-sector unions have fought it so tenaciously.

They know full well that a fissure in the state edifice here could continue to widen, ultimately effecting its complete collapse.

Meanwhile, we would do well to explore applications of this prototype to other areas of social policy. The struggle to reform our welfare system, for instance, is complicated by the growing numbers of teenage girls—most of whom have not completed school and have minimal job and parental skills—who are nonetheless bearing children out of wedlock, with the assurance that the state will subsidize their households. For this skill-deficient population, "work not welfare" hardly seems to be a realistic alternative. And the growing sentiment simply to end all forms of assistance would not likely survive the first eagerly compiled media rumors of teen moms freezing in the streets alongside their babies.

A number of innovative private groups around the country—Sister Connie Driscoll's St. Martin de Porres in Chicago, for instance—already do superb work with this population, housing teen mothers and their children in disciplined moral and spiritual environments, teaching them parenting skills, and insisting that they pursue opportunities in education and work. By holding the teens to high standards of personal responsibility, such community-based groups teach the mothers to take control of their own lives, and to enrich the lives of their children. We should explore the possibility of converting cash assistance for teen mothers into vouchers, redeemable at such institutions. The young mothers would thus be drawn into association with the cohesive community institutions that cultivate the values necessary for self-directed living. And the institutions themselves—no doubt reflecting a vast array of moral, spiritual, and ethnic purposes—would now multiply and flourish with public support, becoming anchors of revitalized neighborhoods and civic life.

This sort of experimentation is already underway in the area of child care. Mothers who now must work to meet the Job Opportunities and Basic Skills (JOBS) requirements of the last welfare reform effort are given vouchers to secure child care from the full range of home-based, church-based, or large institutional providers. Thus far, no Constitution-threatening legal problems, serious abuses, or substantial performance failures have developed with this voucher-based, civically enriching approach.

We should now expand our experimentation throughout the current agenda of social policy, looking for opportunities to implement it in public and private housing, job training, and community development as well as education, welfare, and child care. The object would be to use public policy once more to encourage and cultivate, rather than to denigrate and undercut, the rich variety of vigorous civic, religious, ethnic, and voluntary associations once central to American social policy, as described in the pages of Marvin Olasky's superb *Tragedy of American Compassion.*[25]

Even without public assistance, neighborhoods across the nation are coming together to reestablish civic order within their borders. Fed up with cowering behind their bolted doors in fearful isolation, no longer satisfied with waiting for patrol cars to arrive at the scene long after a crime has been committed, citizens have formed neighborhood watch groups to retake their streets from drug dealers and petty criminals. In the process, they have begun to restore within their immediate vicinity the civic order that citizens require to feel that things are under control once more. These initiatives are often supported and encouraged by local "community-oriented policing" programs. As James Q. Wilson notes, these are simply efforts to get away from the centralized, bureaucratic policing model (yet another modern legacy of progressivism), and to return to the "neighborhood beat" approach, in which the street corner cop not only enforces the law, but works with the neighborhood to preserve civil peace, as well.[26]

Many localities have also begun to resurrect laws against loitering, vagrancy, panhandling, public intoxication, and other forms of disruptive public behavior. While such laws were early victims of our elites' judicial solicitude for uninhibited self-expression, they are now understood to be vital instruments for preserving order on the streets. Among the many legal reforms that would be helpful in the restoration of civil society, constitutional revalidation of such "order maintenance" laws will be important. Measures that would put the teeth back in the locality's police power and its traditional protection of communal health, safety, and morals would also be useful, as would other reforms that strengthen the hand of law enforcement officials, such as "good faith" exceptions to the exclusionary rule.

Neighborhoods are not only increasingly mobilized against crime, they are also taking larger roles in their own economic revitalization. As Mitchell Sviridoff pointed out recently, parts of our major cities that had long since been written off as hopeless because the usual top-down bureaucratic urban programs had failed (or made matters worse) have nonetheless come to life once again through coalitions of urban groups organized into community-development corporations (CDCs). At the heart of many of these efforts is a church that simply refuses to give up, even after the bureaucrats have thrown up their hands.[27]

Though the CDC process often focuses initially on development of housing, in the most successful cases it has gone on to embrace a full range of civic and community activities. The New Community Corporation in Newark, for instance, "has built, owns, and manages upwards of 2,500 apartments, and employs more than 1,200 people in a wide range of service areas including housing, public safety, health, child care, transitional housing for the homeless, employment and job placement," in Sviridoff's words. In short, the CDC itself becomes a vital, community-creating instrument of civil society.

Surveying the growing activity of neighborhoods across the country as they tackle housing, welfare, child care, crime prevention, and education, Robert Woodson points out that for virtually every social problem before us today, somewhere a community group has found an approach that works.[28] No matter which specific problem or activity they tackle first, the inevitable tendency of neighborhood groups is to incorporate ever more activities into their ambit, until they have grown into genuine communities, within which civic order has been restored, the humble bourgeois virtues reign once again, and the residents once again feel that they control their own lives and are fully self-governing citizens.

If this sort of civic restoration can proceed even under the most unfavorable of circumstances—in neighborhoods where the population is allegedly anomic, disorganized, and demoralized—then the possibilities for the rest of America should be apparent. If we are to reverse the cynicism and alienation of today's electorate, public policy should be directed toward seeking out and drawing attention to the most successful examples of civic revitalization, and encouraging local community leadership elsewhere to draw appropriate lessons from those models. Public subsidy may be necessary and useful, but only insofar as it reinforces, rather than erodes, the ability of citizens to govern themselves. That is, through vouchers and tax reform, public resources should be directed away from professional, bureaucratic service providers and toward ordinary citizens acting as community builders, who alone can recapture the civic vitality that once characterized America.

Through this approach, American citizens may once again come to feel safe in *this* home, to be certain that their children can walk without fear down *this* neighborhood street, to *this* school, in which real learning is going on and in which *their* deepest values are honored and passed on, not mocked. Americans may come to feel that they are in control once again of the forces that govern their lives, and that the moral fabric of community is being rewoven about them. Through the revitalization of civic institutions, Americans will once again be making the most important decisions in their lives for and among themselves. In the post-progressive era, Americans will shape for themselves a reinvigorated civil society, and a new citizenship.

The Coming Storm

The revitalization of civil society will not proceed smoothly or without opposition. Although the American people have grown cynical about great crusades or wars on behalf of the national idea, the martial image nonetheless retains considerable rhetorical power, having worked its way deep into our political imagination over the century. And powerful, deeply entrenched interest groups are poised to wield it. The towering bureaucracies and sprawling public-sector unions are full of clever, articulate, lavishly financed apologists for the state. Over the years, they in turn have persuaded significant segments of our population that the modern world is far too harsh and complex for its "victims" to survive beyond the walls of dependency on professional elites and government services. To ask such dependents to work toward becoming self-governing, personally responsible citizens is, in this view, to "blame the victim."

As soon as serious efforts are made to return power from the central state to localities and civic institutions, a full-throated cry of anguish will go up. The forces of darkness, the reactionaries, are striking at the heart of our sense of oneness, our great American family, our national community, we will be told. We will hear of a "new dark ages," in which caring and compassion are forgotten, and in which (as President Clinton put it) "greed, selfishness, irresponsibility, excess, and neglect" once again prevail.

In that moment of the national idea's counteroffensive, advocates of civic reconstruction must remind themselves that the critique of the liberal state is not some momentary, mean-spirited, irritable mental gesture on the part of reactionary Republicans. Indeed, the most insightful and effective critique of progressivism—to which this chapter is much indebted—ironically came from within the ranks of the liberal Democratic Party itself, over three decades ago. It was the New Left of the 1960s, not that era's hopelessly overmatched Goldwater conservatism, that was largely responsible for the initial disenchantment with the Great Society's intellectual rationale. For it persuasively and tellingly argued that the centralized, technocratic, bureaucratic state was inherently dehumanizing and alienating—inimical to rather than supportive of community, which could be realized only in small, participatory groups.

That critique from the left has been much diminished today by the state's ability to co-opt its critics and turn them into handsomely paid, if slightly cynical, employees and defenders (as the New Left itself warned.) Nonetheless, traces of it are still to be found in the radical skepticism of government cultivated by the Industrial Areas Foundation and other community organizing groups, in Harry Boyte's call for a revitalized local public life, and in Amitai Etzioni's communitarian movement.

Meanwhile, however, the central truths of the radical critique have been adopted, amplified, and refined by groups on both the left and right since the 1960s, as evidenced by the revolt of the unmeltable ethnics, both black and white; by the presidential campaigns of both Robert F. Kennedy and George Wallace; and by every one of the recent era's successful presidential candidates, both Democrat and Republican.

Consequently, when the counteroffensive on behalf of the national idea begins, we must recall that, after *three decades* of sustained and consistent critical analysis from *all points* on the ideological spectrum, the moral pretensions of the national community have long since been stripped away. Its elite defenders have long since been exposed for what they are—entrenched special interests desperately defending posts and perks that no longer have any connection to a larger public purpose. It is far too late for liberalism to expect us to heed their Oz-like plea to "ignore the man behind the curtain."

We must remind ourselves that to work for decentralization and the revival of civic institutions and values is not to turn our backs on community and compassion in the name of greed and self-interest. It is rather to reconstruct the most enduring forms of community that human beings and Americans have ever known—families, churches, neighborhoods, and civic and voluntary associations. Only within such rooted, human-scale communities, through concrete, everyday, face-to-face relationships, can genuine neighborliness, mutuality, and compassion be cultivated and expressed. Only within such communities may today's hapless "victims" shed the shackles of dependency, and come together as self-governing, personally responsible citizens, capable once again of running their own lives and affairs without the paternalistic oversight of the bureaucratic elites.

The American people have made quite clear where they believe the "new promise of American life" is to be found—basically, in standing on its head the dynamic described and promoted by Herbert Croly's *The Promise of American Life*. Indeed, Americans have already begun going about the business of reconstructing civil society in the very teeth of the disdain and contempt of Croly's now unmasked bureaucratic elite.

The message of 1994, however, is that they continue to look—as they have looked patiently but futilely for a quarter century—for national leadership that will reflect and support this quiet but powerful and growing grassroots movement. Over that time, they have grown weary of the substitutes for civil society proffered by their national leaders, and of the elaborate and sophisticated excuses for the state's continued growth. The next few years will tell us whether our leadership will stop making excuses, and fall into line with the task of building a new civic society, a new citizenship, in America.

Notes

1. Stanley Greenberg, remarks at Progressive Policy Institute, news conference with Democratic Leadership Council, Washington, D.C., November 17, 1994.
2. Al From, ibid.
3. Robert Wiebe, *The Search for Order, 1877 to 1920* (New York: Hill and Wang, 1967).
4. Robert A. Nisbet, *The Quest for Community* (Oxford: Oxford University Press, 1971), 54.

5. Alexis de Tocqueville, *Democracy in America* (Garden City, N.Y.: Doubleday, 1969), 513.
6. Walter Lippman, *Drift and Mastery* (Englewood Cliffs, N.J.: Prentice-Hall, Inc., 1961), 81.
7. John Dewey, *The Public and Its Problems: An Essay in Political Inquiry* (Chicago: Gateway Books, 1946), 98.
8. Charles Horton Cooley, *Social Process* (New York: Charles Scribner's Sons, 1918), 347.
9. Frederick C. Howe, *Wisconsin: An Experiment in Democracy* (New York: Charles Scribner's Sons, 1912), 38.
10. Timothy Kaufman-Osborn, "John Dewey and the Liberal Science of Community," *Journal of Politics* 46 (November 1984): 1157.
11. Samuel Hayes, "The Politics of Reform in Municipal Government in the Progressive Era," *Pacific Northwest Quarterly,* October 1964.
12. Sol Cohen, quoted in Joel H. Spring, *Education and the Rise of the Corporate State* (Boston: Beacon Press, 1972), 87.
13. Joel H. Spring, op. cit.
14. John Bascom, quoted in J. D. Hoeveler, "The University and the Social Gospel: The Intellectual Origins of the 'Wisconsin Idea,'" *Wisconsin Magazine of History* 59 (Summer 1976): 288.
15. Ibid., 292.
16. Robert Park, *The City* (Chicago: University of Chicago Press, 1967), 107.
17. Samuel Beer, "In Search of New Public Philosophy," in *The New American Political System,* ed. Anthony King (Washington, D.C.: American Enterprise Institute, 1978), 8 (footnote).
18. Stokely Carmichael and Charles V. Hamilton, *Black Power: The Politics of Liberation in America* (New York: Random House, 1967).
19. Robert F. Kennedy, *To Seek a Newer World* (Garden City, N.Y.: Doubleday, 1967).
20. George Wallace, quoted in Michael Novak, *The Rise of the Unmeltable Ethnics: Politics and Culture in the Seventies* (New York: Macmillan, 1972), 135–66.
21. Michael Novak, ibid., 273.
22. Michael Sandel, "This Election Was Haunted By the Fear That We Are Losing Control," *New York Times,* November 10, 1994, B5.
23. Peter Berger and Richard John Neuhaus, *To Empower People: The Role of Mediating Structures in Public Policy* (Washington, D.C.: American Enterprise Institute, 1977).
24. Robert A. Nisbet, op. cit.
25. Marvin Olasky, *The Tragedy of American Compassion* (Wheaton, Ill.: Crossway Books, 1992).
26. James Q. Wilson, *Thinking About Crime,* 2d ed. (New York: Basic Books, 1983).
27. Mitchell Sviridoff, "The Seeds of Urban Revival," *Public Interest* 114 (Winter 1994): 92.
28. Robert Woodson, ed., *On the Road to Economic Freedom: An Agenda for Black Progress* (Washington, D.C.: Regnery Gateway, 1987).

Part IV

Culture and Spirit

Chapter Ten

Retroculture

Paul Weyrich

The most important fact about the promise of American life is that it was fulfilled. Its fulfillment lies not in our future but in our past. By some time around the year 1950, give or take a decade, we had, on the whole, achieved the American dream. The task we face now is not building a new future, but recovering a lost past.

I grew up in that America. It was a wonderful place.

I say that as someone whose family was not well off. I can remember getting down on my knees in the living room with my mother to pray that God would send us warmer weather, because we couldn't afford any more coal for the furnace.

Being poor in 1950 did not mean what it means today, because in 1950 America was a vastly different country. Our neighborhood was as safe as a bank vault. A shocking crime was a kid—one of the really bad kids—throwing a snowball at an adult to knock his hat off.

My father earned his modest income firing the boilers at a Catholic hospital. He hardly ever missed a day of work. We never thought of accepting any form of public assistance. On the contrary, we gave to charity.

Our house was well cared for. My mother was always there waiting when I got home from school, and dinner did not come from the freezer via a microwave. My mother actually hated to cook, but she did it because it was her duty.

We were respectable members of the community. Beginning in the ninth grade, I always wore a suit to school. I liked doing so.

I also had a lot of fun as a kid. I loved riding the streetcars and the North Shore interurban line. At the age of thirteen, I walked into the North Shore offices in Milwaukee, pushed two hundred dollars of my own hard-saved money over the counter, and said I wanted to charter an interurban car for a private run. They said they'd never had a child charter a car before. I said, "There's my money; that's what you say a charter costs." I got my private car.

We lived in a decent neighborhood—not a rich neighborhood but a decent one. The houses were well kept, everybody on the street knew everybody else, and if one family got in trouble, everybody helped out. Part of our neighborhood was black and poor, and among my early memories is bringing things to those less fortunate than we were. People cared. We were all one community.

Our church, Holy Trinity, was another community. We went regularly for Mass, of course, but for a great deal more as well. A lot of our entertainment came through the church: church suppers, church picnics, church plays. This kind of entertainment had moral content—just as entertainment today has moral content, though of a very different kind. The kind offered by the church was wholesome and uplifting.

So was the Mass—the Latin, Tridentine Mass. My family never got over its abolition. My father always told me that when he arrived in America in 1923, not speaking a word of English, he immediately felt at home upon hearing the introductory words to the Latin Mass.

The point of this personal history is simple, yet in the America of 1995 remarkable, for some perhaps even incomprehensible. We were a relatively poor family, but we had a good life, because the society around us was rock solid. We were safe, we were free, we were respectable and respected. I went to excellent schools. I had many opportunities to develop my interests and abilities. I was surrounded by good influences, both in my family and in my church and community. I was helped in a thousand ways to become the person God intended me to be. I was sheltered from bad influences, not just by my family but by the whole community. Being poor did not prevent me from being richly endowed by the world around me, because that world was rich in righteousness.

And now that world is lost. Our task is to get it back.

To Americans, the idea that hope could lie in the past rather than in the future is revolutionary. When Herbert Croly wrote *The Promise of American Life*, he saw that promise being fulfilled in the future. So did virtually every other American writer, before or since. Ours has been almost entirely a future-oriented culture. If there has been one universal American belief, it is that the present is better than the past and the future will be better than the present.

In fact, that belief has been so pervasive that to consider its opposite—that the past may serve as a model for the present and the future—is difficult for Americans. Yet most cultures throughout history have been past-oriented. That is to say, they have looked to a past golden age as their model of how things should be, and they have seen both the present and the future as fallen from that high standard. Even within Western culture this has been largely true, and two of the West's most notable attempts to move forward, the Renaissance and the Reformation, were in fact attempts to recapture a lost past—the classical age in the Renaissance and the early church in the Reformation.

The experience of both the Renaissance and the Reformation illustrates a basic truth: no attempt to recapture the past succeeds fully. Renaissance Italy was not classical Greece or Rome, nor were the Protestant churches the early church. Yet in both cases, the attempt to recapture the past led to some notable gains. (In the case of the Reformation, the most notable gain was actually within the Catholic Church, in the Counter Reformation; most of the Protestants ended up with only half the liturgy of the early church.) The reason for these gains was that the past offered a model, an inspiration, and a goal to aim at, along with some very real resources such as rediscoveries of classical writings and a renewed emphasis on the study of Scripture.

Nor should we attempt to recreate every aspect of the American past. No one should want to return to racial segregation laws, for example. The civil rights movement was a good thing, as long as its goal was a color-blind society. But even here, a past focus is helpful, because at some point in the late 1960s or 1970s the civil rights movement lost its bearings. It changed its goal to a new system of racial discrimination, enforced by law in programs such as affirmative action. The vision of equal treatment of all races under the law is one we can and should recover from our more recent past.

For our time, for the United States of America at the end of the twentieth century, a past focus offers what we most need: a theme broad enough and powerful enough to serve as the basis of cultural revival. Retroculture[1]—an explicit attempt to recapture and recreate the best from our past—is the only theme, the only vision, that can compete with the cultural leitmotif that has laid us low: "If it feels good, do it."

It is not a coincidence that our national decline began in the mid-1960s. That "slum of a decade," as one writer called it, let loose civilization's oldest enemy, the desire for instant gratification. Coupled with moral relativism—the essence of "Do your own thing"—the legitimation of instant gratification has given us our "seven plagues": free sex, separated from marriage, family, and children; its consequence, widespread abortion; the drug culture; its consequence (in part), violent crime; the welfare culture and the underclass it creates; Yuppie materialism (a reminder that vice is not restricted by class); and the cultural dominance of the entertainment industry, itself based largely on sex, greed, and violence, which completes the circle by preaching an endless message of instant gratification and moral relativism.

It is a powerful and seductive message. It is also deadly. Regrettably, "If it feels good, do it" and "Do your own thing" cannot be countered by warning of their consequences. Conservatives have shouted warnings until they are hoarse, with little result. And warnings are no longer necessary, because the consequences are already visible all around us. They, too, have no effect. The culture continues its debauch.

The only tool that can save us from the false vision spawned by the 1960s is an alternative vision, one at least equally powerful, equally broad. That is what retroculture, the recovery of the past, offers.

For Retroculture to provide the basis for cultural recovery, Americans must respond to it. That in turn means they must already believe the past was better than what we have now, or at least be receptive to that argument. In fact, some very interesting polling suggests that they are way ahead of the intellectuals and the policymakers in that respect.

Early in 1992, in a poll commissioned by the Free Congress Foundation, Lawrence Research surveyed a thousand registered voters on their attitudes toward the past.[2] The results suggest that the shift from a future-focused to a past-focused culture was already under way by that time.

- 47 percent said that life in the past was better than life today. Only 17 percent said it was worse, and 30 percent said it was about the same.
- 47 percent said their grandparents were happier than they were; 29 percent said they were not as happy. Among black respondents, 62 percent said their grandparents were happier, a difference from the aggregate of 15 percent. This is striking, given that blacks are supposedly one of the groups that have benefited most from the social changes of the last forty years.
- 61 percent of all respondents said life in the 1950s was better than it is today; 20 percent said it was worse.
- When given a menu of five different places and times to live, 58 percent chose a typical suburb in 1950; the choice selected by the fewest respondents, 6 percent, was Los Angeles in 1991. When asked to make a second choice, the winner, with a plurality of 32 percent, was a small town in 1900. Los Angeles in 1991 again came in last.
- When asked if their impression of the Victorian period was favorable or unfavorable, 56 percent said favorable, 30 percent said unfavorable.

- 47 percent of those surveyed said they expect life in the future to get better; 48 percent said they expected it to get worse.
- Participants were asked, "Do you see signs today of people and things turning back toward the past?"; those answering "yes" were asked, "Do you feel this is a good thing or a bad thing?" 45 percent said yes, and it is a good thing; 7 percent said yes, and it is a bad thing; 45 percent answered no.
- Participants were asked, "Do you feel the country's leaders should or should not be trying to lead the nation back toward the way we used to be?"; those answering "yes" were asked, "Do you feel they are trying to do that?" Responses were:

Should/Trying To Do That	14 percent
Should/Not Trying To Do That	35 percent
Should/(No Opinion)	10 percent
Should Not	42 percent

The total for "should be trying to lead the nation back" is 59 percent.

More recently, Frank Luntz's survey "The American Dream: Renewing the Promise" offered similar evidence. Taken in August 1994, this survey found that 78 percent of Americans now think it will be harder, not easier, to achieve the American dream in the future than it is today. Forty-seven percent said future generations of Americans would be worse off than Americans today. Participants were asked, "If you could spend the next ten years in any decade this century, and you could take your family and friends with you, which decade this century would you choose?" Nineteen percent chose the 1950s, second only to 29 percent for the 1990s. In fact, 33 percent said they would want to live between 1900 and 1959.[3]

To a political establishment looking for potentially positive cultural changes, changes that might serve as a base for restoring the culture, these findings should be significant. They suggest that Retroculture may be a major wedge issue, one that anti-Establishment politicians could use to separate large numbers of voters from the Establishment. Clearly, within the Establishment the concept of a past-focused culture remains unimaginable, abhorrent, or both. But the polling demonstrates that the opposite is true with many voters.

The utility of Retroculture as politics is one question. Another is its viability as a tool for cultural recovery. Just what do we seek to recapture and restore through Retroculture?

A wonderful answer is offered by a novel that was a bestseller about ten years ago: *And Ladies of the Club* by Helen Hooven Santmyer.[4] Santmyer, who had published a couple of minor novels in the 1920s, wrote *And Ladies of the Club* over the course of most of her life. She wrote it specifically as an answer to Sinclair Lewis and his attack on traditional American middle-class culture. She loved and sought to defend that culture, as it had developed after the Civil War in her home town of Xenia, Ohio. The picture she paints of it might well serve as a blueprint for what Retroculture hopes to recover.

Two particular qualities of our traditional culture emerge most strongly from her book: initiative and virtue, both of which continually interact. Initiative forms the framework of the book; the club to which the title refers is a women's club, formed for the purpose of improving the minds of its members. It was most emphatically not merely a social organization, nor principally an organization to provide social services. It was about "uplift," through the creation of what was, in effect, a mini-Chautauqua. Its purpose was to help its members improve, educate, and develop themselves.

Nor was initiative confined to the club or its members. On the contrary, it was the means by which the community and those who comprised it continually tackled the problems inherent in human life. Usually it was individual initiative; virtually never was it initiative by government.

In effect, initiative is the book's alternative to the "nanny state," and to the modern notion that unless problems are solved by government they must fester and grow. In that sense, *And Ladies of the Club* is as effective an answer to Croly as it is to Lewis; not only does it refute Lewis's dark depiction of traditional American life, it also shows how traditional American communities addressed their problems without turning to government. People simply did what needed to be done, on their own initiative.

Their actions were guided by virtue. There was no notion in that past America of separating action from a moral code for fear of "imposing" a set of values. It was understood that effective action required a moral code and could only proceed from it. *And Ladies of the Club* does not present moral arguments in a didactic way; it simply depicts the fact that, in the past, Americans followed a shared moral code based generally on the Ten Commandments, and that it worked.

Sometimes a work of fiction can be more useful as a basis for social and cultural movements than many volumes of policy studies—*Uncle Tom's Cabin* comes to mind as one example. In presenting the past that Retroculture seeks to recover, *And Ladies of the Club* is worth many a scholarly monograph. The book, a runaway best-seller, clearly depicts the answer Retroculture offers to our culture's collapse: a revived culture based on the historical American strengths of initiative and virtue.

Of course, it must be expected that any attempt to recover virtue will be met with the question, "What is virtue?" Moral relativism is one of the most potent weapons in the hands of those who have brought our culture down, and they will not surrender it easily. In effect, Retroculture bypasses their question.

It replies that we should recover the past's definition of virtue. The question becomes historical rather than philosophical.

An interesting answer to the historical question is offered by Lawrence Harrison in his essay "Erosion of Values and Decline of the American Economy." He writes:

> America's historic success is, I believe, based on seven funda-
> mental values: freedom, justice, work, education, excellence, frugal-
> ity, and community. The seeds of those values were planted during
> the colonial period and flowered in the Revolution, independence,
> and the Constitution. Freedom and justice have flourished, and in
> several respects are more robust today than they were two hundred
> years ago. Work, education, excellence, frugality, and community
> have shown increasing signs of erosion since the 1960s.[5]

Harrison's list of key American virtues has the political advantage of being secular. A useful way to look at it is to ask what our future might be like if it were based on a determined effort to recover the virtues of work, educa-tion, excellence, frugality, and community—the values he believes we are losing.

It might look fairly bright. If we consider the problems America now faces, many of them are at least partially a result of the loss of these qualities. The condition of our inner cities is clearly in part a product of the absence of work, education, and community. The situation in our public schools reflects a loss of the values of excellence and work. The ever growing federal deficit is a massive reflection of the loss of the virtue of frugality. The crime problem is largely a product of a lack of justice (one of the virtues Harrison thinks is in good shape). In a just society, the law-abiding citizen need not live in fear of crime.

Others may argue that America's history points to a somewhat different list of central values. Certainly family might be added to the list, with its nec-essary companion, chastity; once sex is separated from marriage, family, and children, the latter face a major and perhaps overwhelming threat.

Moreover, although purely secular values have a political advantage in that they sidestep the charge that Retroculture wants to create a theocracy, they also have a central weakness. As Russell Kirk wrote, "Culture arises from the cult: that is, people are joined together in worship, and out of their religious association grows the organized human community."[6]

In no nation's history is that fact more clear than in our own. The Pilgrims did not come to these shores as an international business conglom-erate seeking new markets. They were a religious community, and from their shared religious beliefs—and their insistence on following them in their own way—grew the human community that became the United States of America.

Can the culture be revived without a major religious revival—in our concrete historical situation, a major Christian revival? Again, Retroculture looks to the past, not to abstract speculation, to answer the question. There should not be any question that Christianity played an enormous role in creating a successful American culture. Christianity was what motivated our forefathers to do many of the things that made this country great. It motivated them to remain faithful to their wives and raise their children to be solid, productive citizens. It motivated them to work, save, and build—the Protestant Ethic is not a reference to some social protest movement. It motivated them to tackle many of this country's real problems, such as alcoholism (the Women's *Christian* Temperance Movement), slavery ("Mine eyes have seen the glory of the coming of the Lord"), and ignorance (Catholic schools).

No doubt, there are individuals who can be good without religion; early Christian writers spoke well of the Stoics. But for society as a whole, our past argues eloquently for (as our present stands in mute testimony to) the truth of Russell Kirk's words: culture arises from the cult. Our historic virtues included religious faith, which for the large majority of Americans meant Christian faith. Any revival of American culture will almost certainly depend in part on a Christian revival—within the church as well as beyond it.

Just what does Retroculture—an explicit attempt to recreate the best of the past—have to do with these virtues? Can we not have the virtues without reference to the past?

Retroculture offers a vehicle that can bring the virtues—religious and secular, private and civic—back into the public square. Cultural and political commentators have been arguing for some years for the virtues. That argument has unquestionably picked up steam in the last decade, as more people—and more prominent people—have weighed in on its behalf.

But the efforts to date have not been decisive. They remain bogged down in all the old arguments: this is "imposing" values, all values are equally good, just let everyone "do their own thing." We are stuck in trench warfare.

Retroculture gets us out of the trenches and leads us around the cultural radicals' flank. The radicals use fashion as a powerful weapon; fine, we'll make "going retro" the latest fashion. They want to argue philosophy; we'll talk about history (which is solidly on our side). They can package their attack on the culture simply, as "Do your own thing" and "If it feels good, do it"; we will offer equally streamlined packaging, for example, "Enjoy the kind of life your grandparents led." They created a movement around "liberation"; we will create a new movement around "going back." They have sold the public on the idea that new is good; we will make old things new again—as truly our past is new to most Americans under fifty.

But Retroculture offers more than packaging—as important to success as that is. Retroculture enables us to offer a concrete rather than an abstract vision of the America we want. Any debate over values and virtues will be largely abstract, even if we can point to concrete consequences of the choices involved. The more concrete a vision, the more easily people can comprehend it, identify with it, and join the effort to bring it into being. Through Retroculture, we bypass the abstract by saying to the public that what we want is to recover how we used to live.

That means, first and foremost, recovery of the functional family—real families, with two married parents and children. It is easy enough to offer abstract arguments for the family, and the profamily movement has done that well. But it is far more powerful simply to say, "Wouldn't you rather have the kind of family your grandparents had? Wouldn't you like your children to grow up in the same kind of environment your mother and father grew up in? Well, that's what we want to make possible again." People's own memories, and their family's memories, are a more powerful answer to *Heather Has Two Mommies* than many monographs on functional child rearing.

Similarly, Retroculture offers a concrete vision of how we used to live in other areas. In education, the public will understand quite well what we mean when we say we want public schools like those we had in 1950. That vision doesn't argue against all the latest education theories; it throws them out (while keeping the computers, which schools would happily have used in 1950 had they existed). With reference to the crime problem, we want streets and neighborhoods like those we had while growing up. We want to be able to sleep with the windows and doors open on nice summer nights and not worry about anyone breaking in. To the reply of "That just isn't feasible," we in turn respond, "What we did once we can do again."

Three areas of widespread public concern are particularly ripe for a Retroculture approach: community, entertainment, and manners. In the past, we had strong communities, entertainment was decent, and a generally accepted code of manners and civility enabled people from widely different backgrounds to share the public space with minimal friction. Again, Retroculture can put it concretely: it's bad manners to play your radio so loud that other people must listen to your music. We want to watch *Father Knows Best* or *I Remember Mama* on television, not *Geraldo* or *NYPD Blue*. We want neighborhoods where kids can play safely in the street or in the neighbor's back yard without having to fear some paroled child molester living down the street.

Retroculture will not exactly duplicate the past. But the past offers a standard and a model people can understand and identify with. Despite the cultural radicals' efforts to obliterate history, people do remember. They remember best the real circumstances of their own lives and the lives of their families. If we make those memories the basis of our appeal, people will identify with us. They will understand what we want and what we are trying to achieve far better than if we only talk in abstractions, about this or that set of values. To be sure, Retroculture is only the vehicle; it was the virtues themselves that made our country work, and it is the virtues themselves that must be reestablished in both private and public life. But here, as elsewhere, the most direct route may not be the fastest or the surest.

A major question remains: How do we get there? How do we realize the potential of Retroculture as a theme broad enough and deep enough to replace the culture of instant gratification?

The first task is to frame the issue as this chapter has suggested: the choice is between an ever more degraded future or a return to a far better past. Our polling tells us this is no quixotic notion; a plurality of the public is already seeing things this way.

But making it happen requires building a Retroculture movement. There are parallels in other countries; we have seen similar movements in Ireland, in the Basque country, and in the modern state of Isreal, which was created by the Zionist movement. We are seeing a similar movement today in Russia. I have spent a lot of time in Russia since the fall of communism, and I have been struck by the way that much of what is happening there might be described as Retroculture. People know that what they had before 1917 was better than what they've had since, and they are striving in a thousand different ways to recover their past. Among the results is a massive flow of people back to the church. The type of religious revival we need so badly here may well be in progress there.

A Retroculture movement will not be primarily political. Although the cultural radicals have attempted to politicize the whole culture, they have not succeeded. Most of the cultural changes we need—the recovery of the virtues—will occur privately. Thus a Retroculture movement will be made up mostly of individuals and families reviving past ways in their own lives. In homes across the country, families will gather for dinner. Books will come down off the shelves—real literature, not the latest fluff about some celebrity. Parents will teach their children (the home schooling movement is thoroughly retro). Courtship will displace living together. Styles of architecture, even of clothing, will reflect past models.

Much of this is starting to happen. Such changes are visible in clothes, in theater revivals, even in food. Pick up an issue of *Victoria* magazine some time; it is now selling almost a million copies per month. Look at the homes going up in many new developments, with their front porches and gingerbread trim. Note that historic preservation and restoration are major concerns in a growing number of cities and towns. It should not be impossible to connect these superficial elements to what really matters, the values and virtues past generations lived by. Nor is it impossible: count the young people who are signing pledges of chastity.

A Retroculture movement will be broad, and that means it will have many variations. Individuals will choose their own models, the era they like best. They will "go retro" in a few or many aspects of their lives. That kind of variation is a strength, not a weakness. The most powerful cultural forces are not those that have a single leader and a disciplined following, but those that penetrate and permeate everything as individuals change their own lives.

Is there a role in Retroculture for government and politics? Yes. There is no such thing as value-free government; all government reflects certain values. At present, government is largely hostile to our traditional culture. That, too, must change.

The politics of Retroculture are what is known as cultural conservatism: a conservatism based on culture, not economics. The shift from economic to cultural politics is already well under way on both sides of the political spectrum. It began on the Left, in the 1960s. The conservative response was put together in the 1980s. I was personally involved in cultural conservatism by the mid-1980s, and by the early 1990s, several books describing it had appeared, most notably *Cultural Conservatism: Toward a New National Agenda* and *Cultural Conservatism: Theory and Practice.*[7] When the first of these was published, it came as something of a shock and was highly controversial. Now, cultural conservatism is widely seen as pointing the way to the future.

These books and subsequent writings lay out a wide political agenda aimed at moving government away from weakening our traditional culture and into a role supporting it. Examples include school voucher plans ending the monopoly of government-run schools, welfare reform, and revolving funds to help communities maintain their integrity while shifting their economic base.

But we cannot hope to restore our culture merely through government. Thankfully, government is not that powerful. Even when the most brutal governments have sought to make wholesale changes in culture, as in the Chinese Communists' so-called Cultural Revolution, they have failed.

By contrast, broad popular movements can alter cultures in significant ways. We have seen that, to our great detriment, in the cultural "liberation" movement that began in the 1960s. Now, we must construct our answer, the Retroculture movement: a movement to return to the culture we had before that catastrophic breakdown.

Perhaps Retroculture's greatest potential lies among our young people. We have a generation—perhaps more than one generation—that has followed the baby boom/"liberation" generation. So far, they have found no theme, no purpose, no vision of their own. For them, the past is largely an unknown territory. Television and the collapse of our education system have left them largely ignorant of who and what came before.

But this ignorance is exactly where the potential may lie. If we can open the book of our truly wonderful past to these young men and women, who see little of interest in the present and less to hope for in the future, they may grasp it with great enthusiasm. If they came to see as their generation's challenge the recovery and restoration of that past, then Retroculture would be on the road to triumph.

It is our challenge, the challenge of those who can still recall or recover our past, to offer it up to our youth. Ken Burns did a great job of it in his television documentary *The Civil War.* We need a massive effort to do more of the same, through every means available to us. If we can succeed in that, if we can present our past and the idea of recovering it to a majority of our countrymen, we will have a tool to save our culture. Neither politics nor philosophy alone can do that. Only Retroculture can.

Notes

1. This chapter draws a number of its themes from an unpublished book manuscript, *Retroculture: Taking America Back,* by William S. Lind.
2. These data are from a national telephone survey of registered voters prepared for the Free Congress Foundation, January 1992, Study Number 1141, by Lawrence Research.
3. These data are from a study conducted by Frank Luntz for Hudson Institute, published in a Hudson Institute report entitled "The American Dream: Renewing the Promise," Indianapolis, Indiana, December 1994.
4. Helen Hooven Santmyer, *And Ladies of the Club* (New York: G. P. Putnam's Sons, 1984).
5. Lawrence E. Harrison, "Erosion of Values and the Decline of the American Economy: Or the Fault, Dear Brutus, Is Not In Japan," in *Cultural Conservatism: Theory and Practice,* ed. William S. Lind and William A. Marshner (Washington, D.C.: Free Congress Foundation, 1991), 147–48.
6. Russell Kirk, "Variety and Unity in Culture," in *Cultural Conservatism: Theory and Practice,* 33.
7. William S. Lind and William A. Marshner, *Cultural Conservatism: Toward a New National Agenda* (Washington, D.C.: Free Congress Foundation, 1987); *Cultural Conservatism: Theory and Practice,* op. cit.

Chapter Eleven

Religion and Morality

James Nuechterlein

Herbert Croly is not normally thought of as a religious figure. Yet a certain kind of religious sensibility played a more central role in his thought than is often realized. More important, the dominant thread of American progressivism, of which Croly's *The Promise of American Life* was a significant source, has not been so relentlessly secularist as is generally imagined. Any attempt to understand Croly's vision, and to come to terms with where it has gone wrong, must take seriously into account its religious assumptions and trace their development—and the challenges to them—within the larger context of the development of progressivism. Beyond that, today's national concern over questions of public and private morality must, in a society in which morality is so firmly anchored in religion, take notice of Americans' religious beliefs and attitudes. If there is to be a renewed promise of American life—either in our political or our moral order—religion will necessarily be central to that renewal.

Croly's was an unorthodox religious faith. His parents, especially the father he revered, were devoted followers of Auguste Comte (1798–1857) and his positivist philosophy. Comte had sketched an evolutionary scheme of humanity's intellectual development, the "law of the three stages." The process of development moved from the theological to the metaphysical to the positive, the latter marking that culmination of thought in which phenomena were no longer understood supernaturally or philosophically but scientifically, that is, according to the method of observation, hypothesis, and experimentation. The sciences, in turn, were ranked on the basis of increasing complexity, in an ascending order of mathematics, astronomy, physics, chemistry, biology, and, at the unlikely pinnacle, sociology (a term Comte invented). Positivism was a program of social reform, and Comte believed that a sociology based on positivist principles would lead to harmony and fulfillment for individuals and nations alike.

At first glance, positivism would seem not merely nonreligious but even antireligious. Its scheme relegated theology and the supernatural to the lower stages of human intellectual development and associated progress with movement away from religion. Yet Comte was ambivalent on the subject. One of his late works, *System of Positive Polity*, actually placed religion above sociology as the highest science—but it was a religion removed from the transcendent, with humanity as the object of worship. It was in that ambivalence—religion without God—that his parents submitted the infant Herbert, in an obvious analogy to Christian baptism, to a "ceremony of presentation" that brought him within the fold of the "religion of humanity." From that ambivalence, Croly never disentangled himself. He was always half a believer, half a skeptic. Traditional religious belief was, for Croly, a delusion, but religious language, imagery, and conviction permeated his thought.

Croly's deepest belief was in democracy, understood not simply as a way of organizing and conducting government but as a way of life. Democracy was positivism made flesh, the process through which individual and collective desires would find their mutual fulfillment. The individual and the collective were never antagonists for Croly; individualism, rightly understood, realized itself in collective democratic purposes. And the future was illimitable. "Democracy must stand or fall," Croly insisted, "on a platform of human perfectibility."

That was no throwaway line for Croly, and it expressed more than an idiosyncratic view. The *New Republic*, which Croly helped found in 1914 and which he edited until his death in 1930, quickly established itself as the single most influential journal of opinion among American liberal intellectuals; and one can see in its pages, especially in the period up to 1920, the elaboration of what could be termed a religion of scientific democratic humanism. That religion was fueled by the dream of perfectibility, and it had as its end, its New Jerusalem, a rational, cooperative, and humane social democracy.

Throughout its early years, Croly's *New Republic* paid close attention to religion, and it was at all times the enemy of traditional orthodox Christianity, the Roman Catholic Church in particular. In the *New Republic's* view, Catholicism was the champion of obscurantism and the enemy of modern intellectual progress. It committed the great sin of "look[ing] for its truths in the past," and it stood stubbornly "against most efforts to advance scientific knowledge." In earlier times, democratic states had found such a situation tolerable, but that, the journal indicated (in an editorial almost certainly written by Croly), could no longer be the case, particularly when the question involved the education and formation of the young:

> Democracy has been evolving from a protest into a purpose. It is becoming a philosophy of life, no longer protestant but in its own way catholic. To be a democrat today is to be something more than a voter. It is to believe in a scale of human values, to have a morality and to think with certain assumptions. . . .
>
> The older view of eighteenth-century liberalism was that the democratic state must allow everyone freedom to practice almost any creed, even though the creed was opposed to freedom. . . . But twentieth-century democracy believes that the community has certain positive ends to achieve, and if they are to be achieved the community must control the education of the young. It believes that training in scientific habits of mind is fundamental to the progress of democracy. It believes that freedom and tolerance mean the development of independent powers of judgment in the young, not the freedom of older people to impose their dogmas on the young. . . .[1]

The *New Republic* (in another editorial bearing Croly's distinctive stamp) summed up its case against Rome in unequivocal terms:

> We deny the right of anyone, be he Catholic or Protestant or Jew, to remain consistently ignorant of the march of the human mind. . . . The Roman Church must realize that liberty is a relative concept and that we cannot each one of us do as we will. . . . We must demand the investigation of all things. We shall judge well of institutions like the Roman Church insofar as they contribute to the scientific conquest of our environment. . . . No church today can hope for survival if it provokes against it the forces of modern civilization. Only by alliance with their potentialities can it hope to exist.[2]

It would be difficult to overstate the audacity of the *New Republic's* presumptions. It saw modern scientific democracy as the true contemporary religion, and the *New Republic* liberals dreamed that they might be as gods. "The power to choose and control destiny," Croly magisterially proclaimed in 1916, "is the ambition of democrats educated in an age of science."

The religion of humanity, whether specifically positivist or not, was at its base a faith in science and, through science, in progress. Croly's generation of liberals was persuaded that history was moving inexorably in the direction of a more cooperative commonwealth. The logic of industrial development seemed to progressives obviously to point to a society more centralized, more regulated, more planned. The free market, laissez-faire, purely private enterprise—these things no longer made sense in a world of industrial consolidation, and those conservatives who continued to insist on them were not so much selfish or immoral as ignorant and irrelevant. For progressives, then, science and morality formed a seamless web. Conservatism would lose because it had to lose; it was simply inappropriate to modern reality. There was, in much liberal writing of the times, the unspoken assumption of an underlying progressive nature of things that science had but to uncover and demonstrate.

World War I and its aftermath dealt a severe, though not fatal, blow to the dream of scientific progress. The blow was the more severe because it was so unexpected and came so suddenly. For most American progressives, the war did not necessarily present itself as an impediment to reform. Indeed, modern warfare's requirements of centralized planning, allocation, and control coincided with the nationalist progressives' hopes for America. Those hopes were increased exponentially by the Russian Revolution in 1917 and, as the war approached its end in November 1918, by the apparent collapse of the old conservative order in Europe as symbolized by the fall of the Hapsburg and Hohenzollern monarchies. At the moment of peace and for a brief time thereafter, everything was in flux and anything seemed possible. The *New Republic* editors wrote in a spirit of apocalyptic expectation:

> Democracy will go forth with its faith in itself renewed. Institution after institution, now apparently as solid as human nature itself, will be judged anachronistic and condemned to destruction. For a century all history will pivot upon the great war, and the greater events of the past weeks. The French Revolution ushered in a new era. The European Revolution now under way is ushering in a new world.[3]

From that high point of anticipation and hope, things went rapidly downhill. There can have been no more disastrous year in the history of American progressivism than 1919. The Versailles Treaty that Woodrow Wilson brought back from Europe seemed a betrayal of liberals' hopes for a just peace; the nation dropped all the wartime planning and controls and drifted back to the old economic order; the labor movement, everywhere militant, was everywhere unsuccessful; by late in the year the great Red Scare had destroyed the meager forces of American radicalism and put liberals entirely on the defensive. The elections of 1920, with the victory of Warren G. Harding, completed the rout. In America as in Europe, the old order had turned out to be far more tenacious than expected.

Liberals like Croly found their faith in science shaken. The failure of the world to seize positively the great opportunities opened to it by war and revolution led Croly to perceive the limitations of the purely scientific approach to politics. Science by itself was "devoid of moral sanction" and thus devoid of effective force. The seamless web of science and morality had been rent. Scientific knowledge could show people the right, but it offered by itself no way to impel them to accomplish it. Knowledge had, after all, done little to liberate human life; indeed, knowledge applied without that moral purpose which only the religious spirit could provide would eventually destroy civilization. Total secularism robbed humanity of moral purpose. A fully satisfactory politics required a combination of modern knowledge with the Christian spirit. The scientific method, Croly concluded, had to be conjoined with the imitation of Christ.

This is not to say that Croly reversed his negative attitude toward orthodox Christianity. While he turned increasingly to the language of Christian exhortation, he specifically rejected "the old paths of baptism, dogma, [and] sacraments." America needed a religious revival, Croly decided, but the Christianity required was the Christianity of the Social Gospel. There was no element of transcendence in the faith that Croly preached. The uses of the gospel were the uses of its moral imperatives. As always, democratic reform required as its core doctrine a faith in human perfectibility, and in America Christianity was necessary to a revival of that faith.

Herbert Croly's positivism, even in its revised form, did not survive him. But his progressivism did, as did a significant element of his religious spirit. The secularized religious enthusiasm that informed *The Promise of American Life* stayed alive in the Social Gospel and in the liberal Protestant ethos embodied in the Federal and later National Council of Churches. (The former was established in 1908, the latter in 1950.) Even as Croly's *Promise* retains relevance as an outline of the enduring progressive mind-set and program, revised but not superseded, so one recognizes in his religious views the foundation of liberal moral understanding and striving as they were to persevere throughout the century.

Flash forward, briefly, to 1972 and the nomination of George McGovern for president. Like Croly, McGovern was devoted to his father; unlike Croly, McGovern did not share his father's theological perspectives. McGovern's father was a thoroughly orthodox Christian, a Wesleyan Methodist pastor. As a teenager, McGovern lost his faith. But a high school teacher, later reinforced by college and seminary professors, persuaded him that he could reconstitute the language and substance of Christian orthodoxy in social and collective terms, in terms, that is, of the Social Gospel. The symbols of sin and salvation, of judgment and redemption, could be translated from the traditional Christian understanding of fallen and redeemed individuals to that of fallen and redeemed societies. McGovern, though seminary trained, never entered the pastorate. He felt uncomfortable, he confessed, with the priestly—which is to say the religious—functions of that office. Instead, after a term in the professoriate, he became a politician. The progression followed naturally.

This is not to say that all those who embraced the Social Gospel did so as an escape from orthodox religious commitment. For a great many Christians, both before and after McGovern, the Social Gospel presented itself as the necessary adaptation of Christian orthodoxy to modern conditions. To be a Christian in modernity was to understand the gospel in collective terms. Even for many of those who still conceived of redemption in an essentially personal framework, the fruits of that redemption were collective. The duties that followed from the gospel had to do with healing humanity in the generality.

For those progressives who combined religious commitment with political conviction, the utopian vision came easily. Modern conditions had produced, for the first time in human history, the promise of universal abundance. Poverty was no longer the necessary condition of the run of humanity; and if poverty need not endure, how could it endure? Surely the answer to the problem lay in the equitable sharing of the social product, as determined by disinterested experts operating for the common good. The need was for cooperation, for overcoming irrational selfishness with reasonable benevolence. The obstacles to the realization of the kingdom of God lay with those who clung to the old order, who resisted the imperatives of the cooperative commonwealth. The structures of sin had to be overcome; capitalism, according to the Social Gospel preacher Walter Rauschenbusch, was "essential atheism." The solution—though most Social Gospelers were notably vague as to details—was some form of collectivism.

The evidence indicates that, for much of the period after World War I, the religious left had relatively little influence. It had, to begin with, many officers but few troops. Liberal Protestant leaders acted and voted one way, the people in the pews quite another. Despite the pleadings and pronouncements of church officials, most white Protestants remained Republican and conservative. (Roman Catholics, on the other hand, though culturally conservative, voted for Democrats and a certain form of liberalism for ethnocultural and economic reasons.) Beyond that, liberalism in the 1930s took on a predominantly secularist cast; relatively few on the Left defined themselves or their programs in religious terms. Those writing in the *New Republic* and other journals of the Left seldom had resort to religious language. To be tough-minded, as both the hard economic times and the reigning Marxist (or at least materialist) mind-set seemed to require, was to avoid the "soft" terminology of religious discourse.

Reinhold Niebuhr, a Protestant pastor in Detroit in the early 1920s and from 1928 onward a professor at Union Theological Seminary in New York, was among those uncomfortable with the perceived sentimentalities of the Social Gospel. Niebuhr, who was to become the most politically significant American theologian of the century, was always a man of the Left (he was a socialist during the 1930s, thereafter a social democrat), but he had little regard for the orthodoxies of either religious or secular liberalism. Liberal Protestantism, he concluded, had been weakened and corrupted by its failure to recognize the reality of original sin, of humanity's fundamental and enduring rebellion against God. Because of that failure, it continued to harbor illusions about the basic goodness or at least infinite malleability of human nature. From those illusions came dreams of inevitable progress—through education, moral exhortation, and institutional manipulation—toward the establishment of perfect social justice.

Against those illusions, Niebuhr posited his vision of Christian realism: facing up to the fact that the imperfections of the world stemmed from fallen human nature; that the realities of self-interest, aggression, and the human will to power had to be reckoned with; that to improve the world it would be necessary to work with those forces and not dream of obliterating them. The perversities of fallen humanity could not entirely be overcome, but they could, with considerable effort and ingenuity, be manipulated in the direction of the common good.

For Niebuhr, politics was the meeting place of power and morality; it was, therefore, inevitably a place of tension, ambiguity, and uncertainty. The central problem of politics was the problem of power: the inevitable temptation of people to use whatever advantages were theirs to further their own interests over those of others. That perennial temptation was compounded by the fact that under modern conditions power had more than ever to do with group rather than personal behavior, with the actions of collectives rather than individuals. Under such conditions, moral constraints on the use of power were the more uncertain, since group behavior was inherently less subject to moral control than that of individuals. It provided less restraint on egoism and self-interest. With individuals, there was always the possibility of the appeal to conscience, to compassion and concern for others. Individuals, however recalcitrant, maintain a capacity for self-transcendence and self-criticism. But how, Niebuhr asked, does one realistically appeal to the conscience of collectivities? Where is the conscience of General Motors or the AFL-CIO? There was, he concluded, an inevitable element of ruthlessness, even brutality, in collective behavior. Those who doubted that had only look to the history of nations. Again, those realities had to be faced. With great skill and effort one might manipulate collective behavior toward the common good; one could not wish it away or dispel it with moralizing rhetoric.

It is not surprising, then, that Niebuhr's argument for democracy differed so radically from Croly's. For Croly, democracy depended on the possibility of human perfectibility. Niebuhr, by contrast, insisted that while it was humanity's capacity for justice that made democracy possible, it was humanity's inclination to injustice that made democracy necessary. And by democracy Niebuhr meant not a grandiose way of life or an unbridled majoritarianism free to realize unbounded social purposes; he meant a constitutional order, with limited government, pluralism, checks and balances, separation of powers—arrangements that Croly had either scorned or minimized as restraints on all those good things an enlightened and energetic democracy might otherwise accomplish.

Niebuhr's liberalism, domestic or international, rested on the concept of the balance of power. A serious politics required at all times elements of deterrence, of checking power with counterpower. Realism, Niebuhr said, means that you achieve the common good not just by unselfishness but by the restraint of selfishness. Since power was never in stable equilibrium, so neither was politics: it was an ongoing process, not an achieved end. A realistic politics meant the acceptance of perpetual struggle and conflict, a constant balancing and rebalancing of social forces; and those involved in that struggle—one that Niebuhr thought honorable—would have to recognize its inevitable moral ambiguity. There could be no dream of perfect justice. Politics had to do with the relatively better, or even the lesser evil. At the heart of Niebuhr's politics was a resolute antiutopianism: there could be no perfectibility, no kingdom of God on earth, no New Jerusalem. The earthly city was always, in some sense, Babylon.

For those searching for a corrective to Croly, for a new promise of American life, Niebuhr is an obvious starting point. His theological (or at least anthropological) perspectives do invite the label of "realism" he attached to them. It is surely far more difficult at the end of this bloodiest of all centuries to take seriously the dreams of human perfectibility that Croly entertained at its beginning. But it is not simply at that high level of generality that Niebuhr commends himself to us. There is also the lesson of his evolving political judgment.

Since politics for Niebuhr always had to do with questions of power, his own politics changed in accordance with his changing estimates of the social configurations of power. Niebuhr's socialism in the 1920s and 1930s stemmed in no small part from his experience in the earlier decade as pastor in a working-class neighborhood in Detroit. Many of his parishioners worked for Henry Ford, and for the Niebuhr of those years and the Great Depression that followed, the problem of power was the problem of the power of capitalist oligarchs over the working class. He thought of power relations in terms of class relations, and he adopted a quasi-Marxist perspective. He was, in those years, an economic egalitarian. Existing socioeconomic inequalities could not be justified rationally and were explicable only in terms of the imbalance of power between social classes. (He never seemed to consider what, if any, degree of inequality might reasonably be justified.)

Economics was never Niebuhr's strong suit and, during his socialist years at least, he viewed economic wealth only in terms of distribution, not creation. He took economic plenitude as the natural state of things, and did not concern himself with the question of what conditions might be most conducive to generating the wealth he wanted available for distribution. His preoccupation was with the need, in the name of economic justice, to do away with private economic power and bring it under social control. So it was that during the years that conservatives assailed New Deal reform policies as destructive of capitalist enterprise, Niebuhr attacked those same efforts as halfhearted and unavailing in the effort to restrain capitalist power.

But Niebuhr was open to empirical evidence. Events in the postwar era persuaded him not only of the reality of Communist tyranny—which in any case he had had some understanding of earlier—but of the failure of Marxist analysis. The post-1945 prosperity of America and of the West in general demonstrated that capitalism could in fact deliver on its promises, and that the depression had been an episode, not a final judgment. Niebuhr came also to understand that if imbalances of economic power within capitalism constituted a problem, that problem was far worse in socialism, with its unification of economic and political power in the hands of the state. Pluralism, he decided, was required at least as much in economics as in politics. Niebuhr moved, one might say, from Marx to Madison—from a demand for power to the proletariat to a recognition of the need for a balance of power among the various sectors of society.

The Niebuhrian legacy is today in some respects uncertain. Progressives note that Niebuhr's journey away from radicalism never took him beyond the New Deal, that he never gave any evidence of repudiating the regulatory or welfare state. If he was in the end a sober, tough-minded progressive, he remained nonetheless a progressive. Neoconservatives, on the other hand, claim him for their own. Niebuhr's antiutopianism, they insist, would have estranged him from what became of liberalism during and after McGovernism. Had he lived, they argue (he died in 1971), he would have joined them in repudiating former left-liberal allegiances and followed their pilgrimage to a post–New Deal—or, more precisely, post–Great Society—suspicion of big government in any guise. The struggle for Niebuhr's political legacy is as earnestly contested as that for George Orwell's—and it is equally unresolvable.

Yet it is significant that the Niebuhrian legacy, however contested politically, remains philosophically indisputable. Niebuhr's theological perspectives can doubtless be made to consist with a number of political positions, but at whatever point on the political spectrum they are applied, their influence will inescapably tend in a conservative direction. Here the vulgar Marxian terminology applies: it is no accident that neoconservatives are more likely to cite Niebuhr than are progressives. Liberals recall him in program, but not in spirit. Niebuhr inspired a brilliant moment in progressive history—he was a leading intellectual and political force in the supersession of the 1930s Popular Front by the non-Communist left after 1945—but the post-1950s development of the Left suggests that Niebuhr's was a moment that never formed itself into an enduring mood. Certainly the voices of contemporary liberal Protestantism, and of progressivism in general, recall more of the Social Gospel than of Christian realism.

It might be objected that this whole argument—and by extension the analysis that preceded it—is fundamentally misguided. The proper antidote to the Social Gospel, it could be said, is not Niebuhrian neoconservatism but a principled withdrawal of religious faith from the political arena. Politics corrupts religion, and religion ought have nothing to do with the political order, other than to hold it under judgment.

There is much to be said for that argument, particularly in its warnings that religious sanctions should never be imposed on partisan positions. Religion, after all, is not a subcategory of politics. It has its own, indeed supreme, integrity. Religion is ultimately about worship and openness to the transcendent, not social or political utility. It is all too easy for those of either the Right or Left to invoke God on their side, to confuse the imperatives of, for example, the Christian gospel with the preferences of politics. We have all had enough of those who, whether in innocence or arrogance, serenely identify their conceptions of the common good with the beatific vision.

But that, finally, is only a partial, and potentially misleading, truth. If it is a fault to identify our political views too glibly with religious imperatives, it is an equally serious fault to suppose that our religious convictions have nothing to do with the public order. The relationship is complicated, however. Consider, once more, the example of Niebuhr. He was always a political activist, and he did not hesitate to make connections between Christian truth claims and the needs of the present moment. At the same time, he recognized that those connections were contingent and uncertain, and he always remained open to the possibility that on any particular issue he might well be wrong. Christian realism had deep theological roots in categories of grace and forgiveness, and it was always more a temper than a program. But it did not, for all that, withdraw entirely from political judgment.

America is a religious society, and for that reason there is an inescapable relation here between religion and public life. Those who imagine otherwise have been misled by a perverted version of another American commonplace: the separation of church and state. The confusion between these two sets of categories—religion and public life on the one hand, church and state on the other—has made a mess of our thinking in this area.

It takes only a moment's reflection to recognize that in America religion cannot reasonably be separated from the political order. The overwhelming majority of Americans say that they believe in God; they also say that they derive their moral principles from their religious beliefs. Since no one in his right mind wants a politics disconnected from morality, it follows perforce that for Americans religion and politics are intimately related. (Contrary to William James, religion is not simply what a person does with his solitude: it has public implications.) More particularly, politics in America is tied, historically and culturally, to the Judeo-Christian tradition. That is, for better or worse, the tradition that has formed us. To deny it is to succumb to multiculturally correct amnesia.

The confusion of many Americans on this subject has to do with the fog that our secular elites have spread over it: they wish that the nation's history were not as it is and they rewrite it accordingly. More particularly and more tellingly, the confusion stems from the bewildering and sometimes bizarre series of decisions on the subject that the U.S. Supreme Court has visited on the nation since World War II. This is not the occasion for a detailed description and analysis of those decisions, but their outline and impact can quickly be sketched.

In brief, the postwar Court has expanded out of all proportion the intended meaning of the First Amendment's prohibition of an establishment of religion and in the process has restricted its associated insistence on religion's free exercise. The result has been that Jefferson's mischievous metaphor of a wall of separation between church and state—which was not part of the original constitutional understanding and which in fact played little role in Religion Clause jurisprudence for 150 years after the Constitution was established—has become the cornerstone of the Court's understanding of church/state issues. The constitutional prohibition against establishment of any particular religion has, through an incremental interpretive process, come to mean that government must do nothing to encourage religion of any sort.

Take school prayer. It existed, in a variety of forms, from the earliest moments of the nation's existence. In 1962 the Court discovered that it violated the First Amendment because it transgressed the newly revealed rule that government must remain strictly neutral as between religion and irreligion. (The New York state prayer in question in *Engel v. Vitale* had no clear sectarian reference; it had in fact been approved by Christian and Jewish groups alike.) So zealous has the Court been in enforcing this rule that in 1985 (*Wallace v. Jaffree*) it struck down an Alabama law prescribing a "moment of silence" in the state's public schools on grounds that some legislators had harbored the unconstitutional desire that students might use the moment to pray.

Now school prayer is a legitimately contested issue, and not all who oppose it are antireligious. There are understandable concerns over possible coercion and intimidation as well as over the theological content of the prayers themselves (prayers arrived at by public consensus tend to be of the lowest-common-denominator sort). Indeed, many who support school prayer—and it does command substantial majorities in public-opinion polls—do so reluctantly; they resolve their conflicting views in its favor because they oppose the Court's obsessive insistence that religion can have no legitimate place in the public square. It has somehow become the case that freedom *from* religion is considered an American birthright.

The clear and present danger in America today is not the establishment of religion; it is rather the establishment, by default, of an all-pervasive secularism. Americans are instructed by the cultural elite to regard religion as a personal quirk, a practice properly indulged in, if at all, only in private and one that has absolutely no public significance or sanction. It is hardly surprising, in these circumstances, that those who aspire to any degree of worldly sophistication are led to understand (without the point having explicitly been made) that religion is a marginal enterprise engaged in—at least with any seriousness—mainly by those outside the respectable mainstream of society.

Fortunately, American society does not yet conduct its affairs in full compliance with the logic of the Court's jurisprudence. "In God We Trust" is still inscribed on our currency and the walls of our courts and legislatures; both houses of Congress employ chaplains and begin their sessions with prayer; schoolchildren still recite the Pledge of Allegiance, even though it invokes a nation "under God"; indeed, in a nice irony, the Court's own sessions begin with the words, "God bless the United States and this honorable court." None of these facts comports with what the Court's rulings would suggest ought to be the case. In light of this confusion, several members of the Court—in the company of a great many scholars and critics—have conceded that, with respect to church/state issues, both law and practice are in a state of inconsistency fast approaching incoherence. Some justices, though apparently not yet a majority, have gone on to suggest that greater efforts should be made to accommodate in law the religious sensibilities and preferences of the great majority of Americans.

The adamant refusal of the postwar secular elite to make those accommodations has been a central factor in the rise of the religious right. The secularist dogma that, as Richard John Neuhaus has argued, would exclude religion and religiously grounded values from the public square has become deeply entrenched; a great many Americans, however religious they might themselves be, have come to accept the notion that ours is and ought to be a secular society. But the secularist crusade has also generated among many Christians—by no means all of them fundamentalists or even evangelicals— something of a counterrevolution. They refuse to concede that in order to enter the public arena they must agree to check their deepest beliefs at the door.

The rise of the religious right has created no small amount of concern and protest. Some of the opposition is simply partisan. Those who cheered the liberal religious community's involvement in the civil rights and antiwar movements of the sixties express dread concern over the imminent revival of the wars of religion if today's religious conservatives are not somehow made to cease and desist. But such opportunistic hand-wringing is not the whole story. Not all those who express concern over the religious right's designs are doing so simply as a cover for the fear that, as the movement advances, their own political prospects will recede.

The concern, to state it bluntly, is that the religious right intends some form of theocracy. As it happens, there are theocrats on the margins of religious conservatism. They call themselves theonomists, and they do want to impose biblical law on the nation. But their influence is small to the vanishing point. They write prodigiously—one sometimes suspects that there are more theonomist books than there are theonomists—but beyond themselves they are taken seriously only by those who choose to conjure them as a threat to the nation's constitutional order.

There remains the more general concern that religious conservatives want to reconstitute a "Christian America." (Jewish Americans in particular shy from the phrase, and they are not comforted by the assurance that the term "Judeo-" will be attached to the Christian prefix.) There are indeed dangers of intermixing religion and politics, dangers that religious conservatives do on occasion exemplify. In addition to a general tendency among its adherents to identify their own views with God's will on issues—for example, the size of the defense budget or the design of tax laws—where the Almighty might better be left out of things, the religious right does not always successfully resist temptations to fanaticism and triumphalism. In a pluralist society like ours, people of minority religions—and of no religion at all—need to have ironclad assurances that their views and values will be respected by the religious majority. The religious right need not apologize for advancing its programs aggressively; but if it is to allay the fears of fair-minded critics, it should at the same time demonstrate that it poses no threat to democratic diversity.

In fact, most religious conservatives consciously avoid the term "Christian America," and even those who employ it do not in most cases intend it literally. They mean by it their hope that America will return to traditional morality, by which they mean, roughly speaking, the morality of the Ten Commandments—given to Moses, accepted by Christians, and subscribed to, at least in large part, by the overwhelming majority of Americans. Christian conservatives, by and large, seek to return Americans not to a particular theology but to a common morality. It is the dispute over that morality that is at the heart of our contemporary culture war.

The issue, indeed, is even more basic, and it involves far more than the fate of the religious right. It involves the very possibility of a stable morality, which is to say it involves the question of truth. The American proposition rests on the assumption of the existence of self-evident truths, and that assumption is today under attack as never before. At issue is not the proper definition of truth; it is whether truth itself can be said to exist. In a deconstructivist intellectual culture that assumes the death of God, radical relativism prevails, and in such circumstances neither truth nor morality has any firm basis. It takes an intellectual to believe that you can maintain a durable moral structure over time in a culture that denies the existence of God and the reality of objective standards of right and wrong.

Can people be good without God? That is an interesting philosophical question and one to which no simple answer can be given, at least if one takes "people" in the aggregate and over the long haul. But in America it is also an almost entirely theoretical question, since—a largely secular intellectual elite aside—most Americans rest their morality ultimately in their faith in God. The American reality is that religion and morality are inextricably tied together. Those who would encourage a revival of national morality both public and private—and who today would not?—have therefore little choice but to encourage a reaffirmation of religious faith and practice. Let the Supreme Court take note.

Again, the necessary cautions must be entered. It is essential that a reinvigorated sense of the transcendent not become an instrument of closure or coercion. Those of religious faith need to make clear their understanding that it is God's will that we not engage in bloody conflicts with one another over the nature of God's will. One can believe in moral absolutes and still insist on tolerance and compromise as the heart of pluralist democracy. Transcendent purpose can be only imperfectly discerned, and all apprehensions of ultimate reality should be marked by provisionality and modesty. Our goal should be the establishment not of a perfectionist religious order but of a religiously informed public philosophy, an ongoing discourse concerning the right ordering of society in which we search for unity and civilly engage the differences that divide us.

In that discourse religion has a legitimate but not privileged place. Expressions of religious conviction in the public arena must be accessible to nonreligious perspectives and accountable to public reason. It is not reasonable for those who are religious to expect to have their views accepted in the public sphere on grounds of special revelation or private understanding. Religious certainties must be translatable—as, for example, through the idea of natural law—into public arguments. The morality of the Ten Commandments, referred to earlier, is ultimately rooted in divine injunction, but its particular arguments concerning murder, theft, and the like can be made plausible to those who do not accept its theological foundations.

Religion, in any case, is not primarily about the ordering of public life. It performs its highest public function precisely by drawing people's attention to a different and higher order of things that judges, relativizes, and keeps in their proper subordinate place all our political projects. Thus is our politics best protected from utopianism and messianism. Religion, in reminding us of a Providence that both guides and judges, offers us grounds for hope even as it instructs us in humility. Meanwhile, people of faith pursue their Augustinian pilgrimage, in the world but not of it, contributing all they can to the civic order but with their vision ultimately fixed on that city where no politics intrudes. In that vision, however paradoxical it might seem, lies the surest hope for a new promise of American life.

Notes

1. "Father Blakely States the Issue," *New Republic,* July 29, 1916, 320.
2. "Catholicism Contra Mundum," *New Republic,* September 2, 1916, 104–106.
3. "The Pivot of History," *New Republic,* November 16, 1918, 59.

Part V

The Economy

Chapter Twelve

Economic Foundations of the American Dream

Alan Reynolds

It is often said, and apparently much believed, that living standards of typical Americans have stagnated or declined over the past decade or two, that the rich have gotten richer and the poor poorer, while the middle class has been up against a wall, going nowhere. These beliefs buttress another—namely, that today's young adults will be the first Americans not to do as well as their parents.

Edward Luttwak, author of *The Endangered American Dream*, wrote that "the great majority of individuals has experienced . . . an absolute twenty-year decline in personal incomes."[1] "A Vision of Change for America," a policy statement released by the Clinton administration in February 1993, made the following assertions:

- For about two decades . . . real wages have stagnated and family incomes have advanced at a snail's pace. . . .
- Throughout the 1980s, slow growth in living standards was accompanied by growing inequality. The rich got richer while the middle class paid more in taxes and fell further behind. . . .

• At today's anemic rate of growth, our standard of living will no longer double every generation—but once every hundred years.[2]

Surveys confirm that most people share these opinions. Yet truth is not a matter of opinion. A majority of Americans also believe that U.S. industry has been slipping behind that of other nations, for example. As the *Economist* points out, however, "America's industrial output expanded by 39 percent between 1980 and mid-1994, a bigger increase than in any other G-7 country [including Japan]."[3] In a similar way, the facts do not support many widely held beliefs and assertions about what has been happening to the growth and distribution of income since 1980. There may be a problem ahead for younger generations, but that risk lies in the soaring cost of government, not in any deep flaws in the private economy.

The "American dream" involves more than material things, of course. There are as many different dreams as there are Americans. But the concept does at least imply a widespread *opportunity* to raise one's living standard by some combination of hard work, study, frugality, and that subtle blend of innovation and daring that defines an entrepreneur. Nothing about the American dream ever implied that income gaps should not widen between those who work and those who do not, or between those who strive to become educated and those who do not. Yet income differences of this sort are, in fact, the subject of considerable academic anxiety about "inequality." The fact that college graduates have recently experienced better income growth than high school dropouts, for example, is often said to be unfair in some sense. Yet no country has ever provided broader opportunities for people to achieve whatever level of education their desires and abilities permit.

Americans are extremely self-critical—a venerable tradition that flows from impatience. Every social critic, whether on the Left or the Right, must first stir up some sort of "crisis" as the reason for adopting his or her favorite policies. Those inclined toward extensive government intervention are eager to persuade us that Americans are faring badly, in comparison with the past or with other nations, in order to argue for a more powerful, more expensive government. Those of the opposite conviction may nonetheless be as eager to argue that Americans are faring badly, or are unable to compete, in order to draw exactly the opposite conclusion: that government is too intrusive and burdensome. Such competition in crisis mongering would be a harmless and even potentially useful sport if people did not take it so seriously.

Measuring Living Standards

At the turn of each decade, we have almost always been inundated with gloomy forecasts of the future. The decade just past is always described as a disaster, and we are told in somber tones that the future will be even worse unless we mend our evil ways. By some quirk of fate, economic conditions happened to be unusually bad as each decade turned, with the economy in recession in 1920, 1930, 1949, 1960, 1970, 1980, and 1990. This cyclical bad luck has lent credence to the idea, enthusiastically expressed at the start of each decade, that the future is going to be terrible, in contrast to some earlier time that was supposedly marvelous.

Americans are regularly told how much better things were in the 1950s, or even in 1973 or 1979.[4] In the good old days, so goes the story, any high school graduate could easily afford to buy a brand new house and car and to put two children through college, all by doing mindless work in the local steel or textile mill. Only those who are too young to know better could possibly believe this. Anyone old enough to remember the actual fifties knows the U.S. economy was in recession almost as often as not (1949, 1953–54, 1957–58, and 1960). Anyone old enough to remember 1973 or 1979 should recall that both years were immediately followed by horrible inflationary recessions.

Rather than romanticize the past, it is time to take a closer look at claims that living standards have been falling for a decade or two, regardless of personal effort. The facts are so different that it is difficult to imagine how so many people came to believe these claims.

The best single measure of living standards is real consumption per capita. How much did people buy after adjusting for inflation? This is the measure of living standards adopted by both the U.S. Congressional Budget Office and the Organization for Economic Cooperation and Development (OECD) in Paris. Consumption is a better measure than income because: (1) people often under-report their actual income; (2) income can be quite variable from year to year; (3) some income, such as food stamps and public housing, is not in cash; (4) some income, such as capital gains, is not counted at all; and (5) consumption also takes into account changes in taxes and wealth. (Household net worth rose 35 percent in real terms from 1981 to 1989, a gain that can finance consumption or investment, just as income can.)[5]

What has happened to real consumption per capita? No progress occurred from 1929 to 1940 (see fig. 12.1). The postwar trend was certainly up, by about 2 percent a year. Moreover, *U.S. living standards from 1984 to 1989 were well above the long-term trend* (as fig. 12.1 illustrates with dots for 1985 and 1990 that are well above the long-term trend line), though gains were relatively disappointing from 1990 to 1993.

Using consumption rather than money income to measure "inequality" is particularly enlightening. As Christopher Jencks and others have pointed out, annual consumption by the poorest fifth of the population has risen much faster than their apparent money income. Each household in the poorest fifth

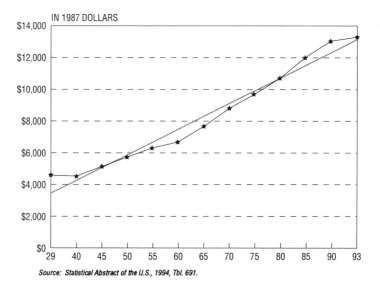

Source: Statistical Abstract of the U.S., 1994, Tbl. 691.

Figure 12.1. Real consumption per capita: 1929–93 trend

consumed goods and services totaling an average of $13,558 in 1988–89, though their average money income was supposedly only $5,588.[6]

One reason consumption by the poor is so much larger than their income is that measures of "money income" completely ignore nearly $200 billion a year of in-kind transfer payments (Medicaid, food stamps, public housing, school lunches, and the like). But even the consumption measure omits some of these same subsidies, including an average of over $4,000 per household in housing and Medicaid subsidies.[7] Another reason is that substantial income from the underground economy goes unreported, either because it is from illegal sources or because revealing the income would result in smaller government transfers, larger taxes, or both.

A third reason why consumption greatly exceeds income among the poor is that some of them are only temporarily poor, and therefore have assets or credit to draw upon in hard times. A self-employed businessman or salesman, for example, may have a loss in any given year, which (assuming the enterprise is a proprietorship, partnership, or Subchapter S corporation) is recorded as a personal income of *less than zero*. Although we do not usually think of shopkeepers, bond traders, and real estate salesmen as "the poor," thousands of such people are nonetheless included in a statistical count of the poor in any given year, even though their average incomes over several years may be relatively high. Many college students, if they set up separate households, are likewise apt to be counted among the poor if we look only at their money incomes and not at their consumption (which is often subsidized by parents or student loans).

Although spending by consumers is in many ways a more accurate measure of living standards than annual income, consumption nonetheless greatly understates the actual improvement in living standards because of dramatic gains over time in the quality and variety of goods and services. Thirty years ago, air-conditioning was very rare in homes, rarer still in cars. Houses were typically much smaller, and did not have Jacuzzi tubs and walk-in closets. Ordinary family cars did not have radial tires, disc brakes, air bags, or multivalve fuel-injected engines. In the sixties, those studying statistics or engineering did not have computers, or even calculators; they used slide rules. There was far less variety in food products and clothing, fewer choices among affordable restaurants. There were no video cassette recorders, or fifty-inch televisions with five speakers and access to two dozen cable channels. No compact discs, or CD-ROMS, or cassette tapes.

From 1970 to 1990, the average size of homes increased from 1,500 to 2,080 square feet, the percentage of homes with air conditioning rose from 34 percent to 76 percent, the percentage of families with two or more cars rose from 29 percent to 54 percent, and life expectancy at birth rose from 70.8 to 75.4 years.[8]

Even aside from such qualitative gains, living standards *never* doubled "every generation," as the Clinton administration claimed in "A Vision of Change for America." That is simply a myth. In the past, it has always taken almost two generations to double living standards (see fig. 12.1). But there is nothing in the experience of the eighties (when living standards were *above* the 1929–93 trend) that suggests it must take any longer in the future. The U.S. economy can still deliver the goods. The real question is whether the most productive and innovative economy the world has ever seen will eventually succumb to gradual suffocation by taxes, mandates, and regulations.

If there is a threat to living standards in the future, it does not lie in poor *economic* performance in the past decade, but rather in poor *political* performance over the next two decades. *The biggest risk to the living standards of future generations is, by far, federal taxes.* Unless we are very careful, taxes may grab an inordinate share of added output and income early in the next century, undermining incentives to work and save, encouraging even greater dependency on government handouts, and leaving tomorrow's workers with a meager share of the fruits of their efforts.

Falling U.S. Incomes?

Despite the fact that real consumption per person has continued to rise at a normal pace (*above* normal from 1983 to 1989), many people remain convinced that real incomes have stagnated or declined for most Americans. The statistic most often cited to make this point is median family income. By definition, half of all families earn more than the median income, while half earn less. But this average is likely to be a poor measure of changes over long periods, such as the two decades from 1973 to 1993, because the definition of "family" has changed so much. (Measures of "household" income are even less comparable across decades: in 1993, 44.8 percent of all households were headed by people who were not married, compared with 29.5 percent in 1970.)

If two people who each earn $20,000 get divorced, the result is to convert one family with a $40,000 income into two households (assuming that neither partner lives with parents) with $20,000 apiece. If there are children involved, and the woman has custody, then that new female-headed household falls into the category of a low-income "family." The same statistical result occurs if, as has increasingly been the case, the mother does not marry in the first place.

By 1993, *17.5 percent of all families were headed by a woman "with no husband present"*—up from 10.8 percent in 1970. Since a separate female-headed household that includes young children cannot possibly have more than one adult working (and most have *no* full-time workers), a rising proportion of such families must depress the measured average income. This can make it misleading to compare levels of family income, especially between ethnic or racial groups. Because 50.7 percent of black families were female headed by 1993, compared with 16.7 percent of white families, any average of "family" incomes is necessarily higher among white families. Ethnic and racial differences in median income *among married couples* are relatively small—$43,675 for whites in 1993, and $35,218 for blacks (who are younger, on average, and still catching up in educational attainment).

Although comparisons of income levels between black and white families are misleading (because the family structures are so different), the trends over time are nonetheless of interest. Larry Lindsey, governor of the Federal Reserve, notes that "during the 1973–81 period . . . the median income of black families fell by nearly 11 percent, far more than the 8.8 percent decline for white families. . . . By contrast, the 1981–90 period saw a rise in median black family income of 12.3 percent, compared with a 9.2 percent rise in white median family income."[9]

Ethnicity aside, when a rising percentage of "families" consists of women with children, this trend naturally holds down median family income for *all* families. The resulting dilution of median income does not mean that some "average" or typical family has had little or no increase in income.

Instead, it means that "family" income two decades ago cannot properly be compared with "family" income today, when some families are so differently constituted.

A 1992 Census Bureau study confirms that "the declining proportions of married couple households and rising proportions of single parent families and nonfamily households had a large negative impact on the nation's median income level [by] 1989."[10] This fact makes it all the more significant that median family income nonetheless increased by nearly 13 percent from 1983 to 1989.

The sizable increase in living standards in the eighties is often concealed by changing the subject and talking about what happened over a much longer period. The 1994 *Economic Report of the President*, for example, said "the median family today has virtually the same real income as the median family 20 years ago . . . . At the pace of income growth from 1973 to 1992, it would take centuries for real median family income to double." We have already noted one problem with comparing family incomes over such an extended period: the average family size has fallen, and its composition has changed, largely as a result of more female-headed families with children. That means incomes of "average" families in 1992 cannot be accurately compared with incomes of a quite different mix of families in 1973.

However, there are several other problems with comparing median income in 1992 with that of 1973. First, the use of 1973 as a basis for comparison is deceptive. In 1973, price controls repressed and disguised inflation—as was increasingly evident from widespread shortages and an explosion of inflation by 1974. Because inflation in 1973 looked artificially low, inflation-adjusted real income or real wages likewise look artificially high. In reality, 1973 was a frightening prelude to runaway inflation, though economists and politicians with short memories still portray that year as some pinnacle of prosperity.

Second, any statement about what happened to incomes over the past fifteen to twenty years fails to differentiate periods when income was rising from periods when income was falling. It is not true that median income was simply unchanged for such a long period. What really happened is that median income fell 8 percent from 1979 to 1982, then *rose 13 percent* from 1982 to 1989, and then fell once again, by 7 percent, from 1989 to 1993. The two periods of falling income do indeed offset the prolonged prosperity of the eighties, but that says more about the policies of the seventies and nineties than it does about the years in between.

The first three bars of figure 12.2 compress the 1970s into five-year intervals. From 1970 to 1980, there was only modest progress in median income. The annual figures show a cyclical drop in real income in 1980–82, as a result of serious inflation (which eroded real wages) and the subsequent Federal

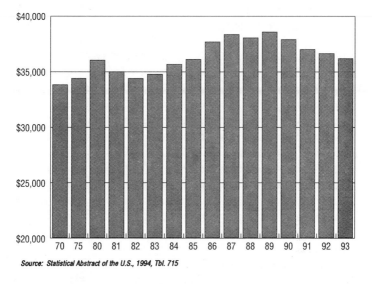

Source: Statistical Abstract of the U.S., 1994, Tbl. 715

Figure 12.2. Median family income in constant 1991 dollars

Reserve credit crunch. Median family income fell by 3.5 percent in 1980 alone (which explains why critics of "the eighties" always start counting from 1979, if not 1977 or 1973).

From 1983 to 1989, however, median family income rose by 13 percent—despite rapid immigration of relatively low-income workers, and despite the fact that more and more families were headed by females with no husbands to help pay the bills.

A mild recession at about the time of the Iraq War (July 1990 to March 1991) depressed income, which is to be expected. Yet *median income continued to fall (and poverty rates continued to rise) in 1992 and 1993—long after the recession had ended.*

It is obviously inaccurate to attribute the falling incomes in 1990–93, or 1973–80, to "the eighties," though this is done all the time. By any measure, income and living standards rose at an impressive pace from 1983 to 1989 and only declined after that. The drop in median family income after 1989 is even larger if income is measured after taxes. There were sharp increases in federal income and Social Security taxes from 1990 to 1993, and often in state income taxes as well.

Why does it matter in which years average incomes were rising and in which they were falling? Because getting the dates right provides a strong clue about which sorts of government policies are conducive to prosperity, and which are not. Federal policies were quite different in the eighties than they are in the nineties or were in the seventies. In 1982–89, major tax reforms were aimed at reducing tax penalties on extra work and savings; these policies were largely reversed in 1990–93. In the most recent years, transfer payments became more widely available and more generous (such as the earned income tax credit, and the Aid to Families with Dependent Children–Unemployed Parent [AFDC-UP] welfare program). Tax policy became progressively more punitive toward efforts to raise income by working or saving: three new tax brackets were added to the pre-1990 ceiling of 28 percent; a temporary 1990 law shrinking deductions and exemptions as incomes rise was made permanent in 1993, and 85 percent of Social Security benefits became taxable only for older Americans prudent enough to have put aside a modest pension. In short, incentives to work or save improved greatly in the eighties and worsened greatly in the nineties. We should not be surprised that the labor force grew twice as fast from 1981 to 1989 as it has since, or that personal savings fell sharply after tax rates on "the rich" were increased in 1993.

To describe the entire period from 1973 to 1993, or from 1979 to 1993, as one continuous period of stagnation or decline is to evade critical distinctions about which sorts of policies have been effective, in the U.S. and elsewhere, and which have not. From 1983 to 1989, the U.S. was moving toward policies similar to those pursued by such vibrant economies as Hong Kong or Singapore, with their top tax rates of 20 to 30 percent and minimal regulation of commerce. Since then, the U.S. has been slipping back to the pattern of the bureaucratic welfare state, emulating the sorts of policies that have made the economies of Sweden and Canada what they are today.

A Shrinking Middle Class?

Widespread confusion about when incomes rose or fell is exceeded by bewilderment about "inequality" in the "distribution of income" (a concept almost suggesting that income can and should be "redistributed" from those who earn it to those who do not). The mystification surrounding "inequality" is well illustrated by the often repeated anxieties about the "shrinking middle class."

Figure 12.3 illustrates the facts. From 1970 to 1989, the percentage of families earning between $15,000 and $50,000 a year—in constant 1992 dollars—shrank from 61 percent to 49 percent of all families. But *all* of that loss in the middle is fully accounted for by an increasing share of families earning *more* than $50,000. Some social scientists seem to regard this as a problem. Most Americans would regard it as progress—the American dream in action. From 1989 to 1992, however, the share of the population earning more than

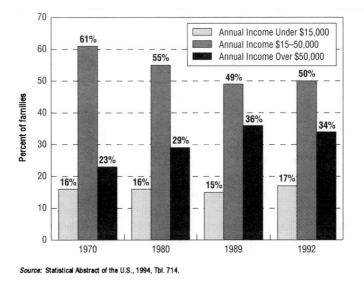

Source: Statistical Abstract of the U.S., 1994, Tbl. 714.

Figure 12.3. Changing fortunes of the middle class

$50,000 declined, while the share earning less than $15,000 increased. The decline in the number of relatively affluent families after 1989 may not prove to be a longer-term problem, but it is the opposite of what happened in the 1980s.

The fact that a rising *percentage* of U.S. families earned over $50,000 in the eighties is often confused with the idea that "the rich got richer." Actually, the middle got richer. (Even if 99 percent of Americans were in families earning more than $50,000, someone would undoubtedly complain that the gains were not equally distributed.)

One reason that a rising share of family heads enjoyed relatively high incomes in the eighties is that they had invested valuable time and money in acquiring an education, and those investments in human capital began to pay off. As Maury Gittleman notes, "The gains by more educated groups are in sharp contrast to trends in the 1970s, when . . . these groups lost ground."[11] Curiously, this has been the subject of much concern within the Clinton administration. "A Vision of Change for America" worried that "wages of college graduates have advanced far faster than those of high school graduates since 1978; similarly, the wages of high school graduates have risen faster than the wages of nongraduates. . . . Throughout the 1980s . . . people at the bottom of the income scale actually lost ground: measured in inflation-adjusted dollars, their incomes fell between 1977 and 1991."[12] (Note the creative dating of "the 1980s"as 1977–91.)

The 1994 *Economic Report of the President* likewise notes that "Starting some time in the late 1970s, income inequalities widened alarmingly in America. . . . One major factor is increasing returns to education and experience. The college-high school wage premium increased by . . . 20 percent for all workers eighteen years old and over."[13] A sensational *Business Week* cover story, moreover, complained that "the real wages of high school dropouts have fallen by up to 20 percent since 1979, while real incomes of employees with more than four years of college have grown by 8 percent, according to the Economic Policy Institute, a liberal think tank in Washington."[14] (Note the ambiguity of "up to" 20 percent.)

To understand why increasing returns to education in the eighties should not be regarded as an "alarming" or inequitable development, it helps to understand what happened in the seventies. Ramon Vilches points out that "In the 1970s . . . the earnings of young, college-educated males declined precipitously relative to the earnings of their less skilled counterparts."[15] It is surely much better for America to have *rising* financial rewards for getting an education (as in the eighties), than *falling* (as in the seventies). Better income opportunities are not the only reason for investing time and money in additional schooling, but they are certainly a very important motive. If society attempts to redistribute income from those who invest in their own human capital to those who do not, perverse incentives will follow. This is one reason to be concerned about the longer-term impact of higher marginal tax rates, which, Philip Trostel finds, greatly reduce young people's willingness to pursue additional schooling.[16]

There is some evidence that the relatively poor earnings growth among recent high school graduates is partly attributable to declining quality of public schooling, and better evidence that the rapid income gains among college graduates are largely due to relatively slow growth in their numbers, compared with the seventies.[17] Another factor pushing up the relative wages of college-educated employees has been the rapid growth of government—a sector that generates unusually heavy demands for educational credentials.

Improved primary and secondary schools would help lift earnings for those who do not go on to college, while pushing more young people through college might have the unintended effect of holding down future salary increases among college graduates. But how do we get better schools? In the case of any other product or service, economics teaches that the way to improve quality per dollar spent is to *maximize consumer choice and competition*. "Choice in education" is much more than a slogan. It is through choice and competition that almost everything *except public schools* is produced and distributed in a free economy.

More Workers, More Income

One simple but oft-neglected reason that some families earn more than others is that more family members work. A middle-aged working couple with two teenagers who work during the summer will report a much larger family income than a nonworking single mother with young children. This is an embarrassingly obvious observation, as is the fact that inexperienced young people almost always earn far less than they will when they are middle-aged. Yet such simple points are often neglected in discussions of "income distribution."

Families having four or more workers in 1992 had more than four times the median money income of families with no workers (see fig. 12.4). Few people would regard this as unfair, unless they were not informed why families on the right side of the graph in figure 12.4 earn more than those on the left. Yet such simple factors as the number and age of workers in a family have a huge impact on statistics that describe what average incomes are and how incomes are distributed.

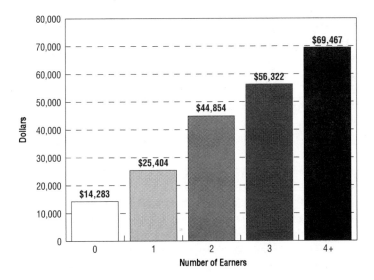

Figure 12.4. Median income by number of earners per family: 1992

One economist who did not overlook the importance of work to "inequality" is Alan Blinder, a former member of President Clinton's Council of Economic Advisers and now Vice Chairman of the Federal Reserve. In 1980, Blinder wrote a notable paper on income distribution that made the following observation:

> The richest fifth of families supplied over 30 percent of the total weeks worked in the economy in 1977, while the poorest fifth supplied only 7.5 percent. Thus, on a per-week-of-work basis, the income ratio between rich and poor was only 2 to 1. This certainly does not seem like an unreasonable degree of inequality.[18]

Blinder's comment is even more relevant today, because there is now a much larger percentage of two-earner families among the richest fifth of families than there was in 1977, as well as a much smaller percentage of families in the lowest fifth who work at all, much less work full-time all year. Christopher Jencks of Northwestern University notes that "the character of poverty has changed. It has become . . . more concentrated among families in which the head does not work regularly."[19]

Although median family income was only $36,812 in 1992, this figure blends the incomes of quite different types of families. Among married couples, median income was $42,064, or $59,286 if both husband and wife worked full-time. Among female-headed families with children under age eighteen, median money income was $13,445 (though many such families also receive in-kind income, such as food stamps and Medicaid).[20] Married men and women tend to earn more because they are (1) often older and more experienced than single people, and (2) much more likely to work full-time all year.

Married couples in which both husband and wife work full-time year-round have nearly three times the median income of couples in which neither works (see table 12.1). To the extent that tax and transfer policies encourage two-earner families to become one-earner families, encourage fathers to leave the support of their children to taxpayers, or encourage people to retire prematurely, median income is likely to fall.

The weakening of work incentives may help explain the otherwise anomalous drop in median income during the 1992–93 cyclical recovery. Participation in the labor force stopped growing from 1989 to 1994 among married women, and declined among single women and all men. Because of the reduced willingness to work, annual growth of the labor force slowed to 0.9 percent, compared with almost 1.7 percent from 1981 to 1989. Had labor force growth from 1990 to 1993 been only about 1.4 percent a year (rather than 0.9 percent), the number of job seekers would have been 2.5 percent larger, leaving unemployment at the end of 1993 at 7.9 percent (rather than the actual figure of 5.4 percent). In that case, the economy would have had considerably more room to grow without creating anxiety in the Federal Reserve or anywhere else about a shortage of qualified workers.

Table 12.1
Median Income of Married Couples by Work Experience (March 1993)

	Wife worked year-round full-time	Wife did not work
Husband worked year-round full-time	$ 59,286	$ 41,435
Husband did not work	$ 35,070	$ 21,105

The income distribution among people who work is a great deal more equal than it is between those who work and those who do not. According to the Census Bureau, of those families in the lowest fifth of the income distribution in 1992 (many of whom are poor only in a relative and often temporary sense), *45.3 percent had no family member who worked at all in 1992*, 42.6 percent worked part-time for less than half a year, and only 4.1 percent worked full-time all year. If real wages and salaries of workers increase over time, the gap between those who work and those who do not work must, of course, increase. This is what most of the controversy about "income distribution" is really about. The number of those counted as poor, at least in a relative sense, seems stubbornly constant. But the nature of poverty has changed. There are fewer and fewer "working poor," and more and more nonworking poor. However, as mentioned before, the distribution of *consumption* (living standards) is far more equal than the distribution of money income, thanks largely to in-kind transfers from those who work to those who do not.

To repeat, nothing about the American dream implies that income gaps should never widen between those who work and those who do not, or between those who strive to improve their education and those who do not. Yet the existence of such income "inequality" has become a major complaint among some who have borrowed the rhetoric of "restoring the American dream." In America, those who study hard and work hard still have an excellent opportunity to provide a comfortable living for themselves and their families, as well as a fair chance at becoming rich (which is also part of the dream). Unfortunately, a system that rewards industriousness and prudence does not satisfy the many social critics who wish to punish success with steeply rising tax rates, while subsidizing the absence of work effort or parental responsibility—all in the name of eradicating "inequality."

Anemic Productivity and Falling Wages?

When those skeptical of the American dream are not abusing statistics on median income, they often refer to labor productivity of nonfarm workers or average (mean) "real wages among nonsupervisory workers"—both of which have also supposedly fallen since 1973 or 1979. The 1994 *Economic Report of the President,* for example, asserts that "growth in productivity has been anemic for about two decades," and "U.S. real wages have hardly grown since the early 1970s."[21]

It is difficult to imagine a more roundabout measure of living standards than nonfarm productivity. Given the problems entailed in measuring output per hour of work in this regard, one would have to be terribly short of other statistics to choose that as the measure of how folks are doing. Why exclude farm productivity, for example? Doesn't higher farm productivity give us more and better food at a lower price?

As it happens, most of the apparent drop in nonfarm productivity after 1973 occurred *before* 1980, not since. Productivity also appears artificially weak because of an arbitrary assumption that productivity cannot possibly improve at all in financial services, among other important service sectors. As many valuable new services in finance, insurance, and real estate hired more people—the mutual fund industry, for example—this made overall productivity appear weak.[22] Productivity among *nonfinancial* corporations was *above* a thirty-year trend in the late eighties and early nineties, rising by 2.1 percent a year from 1981 to 1992 (see fig. 12.5).

What about wages? It is often said that real wages have been falling for two decades, that more full-time workers are earning below the poverty level, and so on. How can this possibly be true? We have shown that median family income rose at a brisk pace from 1982 to 1989, despite the inclusion within the average of hundreds of thousands of additional female-headed families and low-income immigrants. Real consumption per person—living standards—also grew substantially in the eighties, which would have been virtually impossible if wages had really been falling. Real income per capita also rose by 20 percent from 1980 to 1989.

Much of the mystification arises from lumping the seventies and eighties together by starting from the price-control year of 1973, or by defining the eighties as starting in 1977 or 1979. A graph in the 1994 congressional *Joint Economic Report*, for example, is titled "Middle Class Incomes Declined in the 1980s While the Rich Got Richer." Only a careful reader would notice that the period being described as the "1980s" is, in reality, 1977–1992. There is no question that the U.S. went through very difficult years from 1974 to 1982, with two bouts of double-digit inflation followed by deep recessions. As a recent Labor Department report points out, "During 1978–80 there was

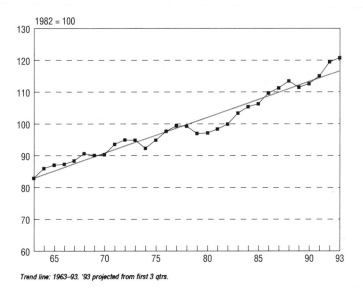

1982 = 100

Trend line: 1963–93. '93 projected from first 3 qtrs.

Figure 12.5. Productivity of U.S. nonfinancial corporations

a dramatic fall in wages and salaries adjusted for inflation. . . . Beginning in 1982, this pattern was reversed, with wages rising more rapidly than prices."[23]

There is also no question that median income fell from 1989 to 1993. However, real incomes, wealth, and living standards certainly increased from 1980 to 1989. It is not the eighties but the seventies and early nineties that offer some reason to be concerned. The distinction is important, because the economic policies of the early nineties—rising tax rates and a falling dollar—have more in common with the seventies than with the eighties.

A commonly cited indicator—"average real wages for nonsupervisory workers"—is extremely misleading. First of all, the percentage of jobs that are "nonsupervisory" shrank from 77 percent in 1985 to 68 percent in 1991. As more Americans were promoted, or moved into managerial and professional careers, they dropped out of the "nonsupervisory wage" statistics altogether. As the best employees move up and out of the "nonsupervisory" category, they may well depress the measured average wage among those still left. Their promotions cannot be recorded as a wage increase, because salaried workers are not in that job category any more.

Second, the mean average of wages is not at all the same as the wage of an average or typical worker. There have been millions of young people (including baby boomers) and immigrants starting entry-level jobs in the past two decades, which diluted the average (mean) wage. If entry-level workers had not been able to find jobs, then their wages would not have been included in the average, so average wages would appear higher. But that certainly does not mean that a wage of zero (unemployment) is preferable to starting at a low wage and working one's way up.

Third, the average wage figures *exclude all benefits*. Medical and pension benefits became much more generous in recent years, and are often preferred by workers because such perks are tax free. The employer's share of rising Social Security taxes must also depress wages, however. Given the choice, employers would rather pay higher wages than higher payroll taxes. It is not likely that many people would choose to pay a larger share of their income to Social Security if they had a choice. When benefits are included, and total compensation is properly adjusted by the newer, post-1983 consumer price index (CPI-UX1), average real wages and benefits rose by 22 percent from 1970 to 1992, though at a slow pace since the late eighties.

Fourth, there is some evidence that average work hours have fallen more than reported, so that incomes per hour are higher than the figures show.[24] Many people habitually report working forty hours a week, for example, when their schedule is actually 35 hours (9 to 5 with an hour's lunch break).

Fifth, many economists argue that the consumer price index overstates inflation by a percentage point or more, because it fails to account for rapid improvements in quality (for example, in computers, cars, and drugs). That is, better products are reported as simply costing more. If inflation has been overstated by about 1 percent in recent years, it follows that growth of real wages, real incomes, and real consumption has been *understated* by about 1 percent a year as well.

Sixth, it is another myth that workers are typically being pushed out of high-wage manufacturing jobs into low-wage service jobs ("McJobs"). Many have chosen to leave manufacturing jobs because of superior opportunities for wage increases in service industries. From 1980 to 1992, average hourly wages in manufacturing rose from $7.27 to $11.46, or 58 percent. In the same period, wage rates rose 80 percent in services, 64 percent in wholesale trade, and 87 percent in finance, insurance, and real estate.[25] Average wages in transportation and utilities, wholesale trade, health services, finance insurance, and real estate are now about the same as average wages in manufacturing.[26]

Too Many Low-Wage Jobs?

The 1994 *Joint Economic Report* says, "A recent Census report showed that the percentage of Americans working full-time but earning less than a poverty wage has risen about 50 percent in the past thirteen years." This report has been widely cited by those who argue that high-wage manufacturing jobs are being replaced by low-wage service jobs, or claim that the number of working poor is rising. Actually, the Census study does not support either interpretation. Indeed, the report explicitly notes that "most year-round full-time workers with low annual earnings are not in poverty," and that "husbands in married couple families have the smallest likelihood of receiving low annual earnings."[27] What the Census report really shows is that the percentage of jobs that do not pay enough to keep *a family of four* out of poverty ($14,343 a year) has been increasing. But $14,500 is *not* a poverty wage for a very young man living by himself in an apartment in a small southern town. Even young college graduates may not earn enough on their first job to support a family of four, but very few of them have that many dependents.

Most "low-wage workers" are either young singles—who do not *need* to earn enough to support a family of four—or teenage children of someone with a higher income. In 1990, over 61 percent of low-wage workers were age sixteen to twenty-four, compared with 34.5 percent in 1979. It should not be surprising to learn that nearly all of us earn less on our first job than we will later. Similarly, Ronald Mincy of the Urban Institute has shown that 21 percent of those workers receiving the minimum wage are in families with annual incomes above $50,000, while another 40 percent are members of families earning between $24,000 and $50,000.[28] Low wages are usually associated with *youth*, less often with poverty.

The federal minimum wage prohibits unskilled employees from offering their services, or employers from offering jobs, below some arbitrary hourly rate. The resulting artificial shortage of jobs at the legal minimum increases the supply of workers in sectors exempt from the minimum wage (such as farm labor) or easily able to evade the law (such as casual day labor, mowing lawns, and babysitting), and thus *depresses* the lowest wages of all. In 1993, nearly 1.7 million people worked at wages *below* the legal minimum of $4.25.[29] To the extent that the minimum wage is not circumvented, it prevents many young people with little formal schooling from establishing a record of reliable work habits and getting on-the-job training that would enhance their future ability to compete for better jobs.

Taxing Industriousness and Subsidizing Indolence

If the American dream means that hard work and study are well reward-
ed, that dream was alive and well in the 1980s, though less so since. Those
who dropped out of school and/or the labor force have not fared as well, but
there is nothing inherent in the American dream that suggests they should.

Economic growth is still the best antipoverty program ever devised. "A
rising tide lifts all boats," as long as people are willing to get in a boat and
row. More and better jobs cannot help those who choose not to work. More
and better investment opportunities, and a stronger market for U.S. stocks and
bonds, cannot help those who do not save.

Work experience, education, and savings are critical for financial success. That means the most important thing that public policy can do is to
avoid penalizing and discouraging work, education, and savings. In this
respect, the federal system of taxes and transfers was never helpful and has
become even more damaging in recent years.

Since 1990, three new tax brackets have been piled on top of the maximum 28 percent rate enacted in 1986 (in exchange for elimination of many
deductions). As family income rises (because of additional work, education,
and savings) the marginal tax rate at the federal level alone now rises to 31
percent, 36 percent, and 42.5 percent. Actual marginal rates can be even higher, because allowable deductions and exemptions are now reduced as family
income rises above $108,000.

The evidence is clear that such high and rising marginal tax rates discourage spouses from working (typically, wives whose children are out of
school), discourage saving among those who continue working, and encourage early retirement among primary breadwinners. There is also good evidence that the prospect of high tax rates on incomes after years of costly, difficult, and time-consuming study has a strongly negative effect on the
decisions of young people to extend their schooling (for example, to go to
college or to continue with graduate school). Here is some of that evidence:

- Robert Triest finds that "the [labor force] participation decision is
  more sensitive to economic incentives than hours worked." Despite
  problems with existing studies that tend to underestimate the response
  of work effort to after-tax income, Triest nonetheless finds that
  "increasing the higher tax rates results in sharply higher efficiency
  cost, and raises less revenue."[30]
- An econometric simulation by the International Monetary Fund estimates that "an increase of 1 percentage point in either consumption or
  labor income taxes may induce a reduction in the hours of work
  between 0.5 and 1.5 percentage points."[31]

- James Ziliak of the University of Oregon estimates that a 30 percent increase in marginal tax rates on the top 1 percent of U.S. taxpayers (smaller than the actual increase from 28 percent to 42.5 percent) would reduce hours worked by as much as 11 percent and reduce tax revenues by a comparable amount.[32]
- Martin Feldstein, president of the National Bureau of Economic Research, notes that increases in marginal tax rates "induce [affected employees] to alter their taxable income in a wide variety of ways including changes in labor supply, changes in the form in which employee compensation is taken, changes in portfolio investments, changes in itemized deductions and in other expenditures that reduce taxable incomes, and changes in taxpayers compliance."[33] Feldstein uses data from the 1986 tax reform to estimate that the 1993 increases in the higher marginal tax rates are quite unlikely to increase revenue in the longer run, as Ziliak and Triest also found, although he attributes the fall-off to greater tax avoidance as well as reduced work effort.
- Alan Auerbach argues that Feldstein's research on the surprisingly favorable effect on tax revenues of reducing the highest tax rates in 1986 is likely to *understate* the revenue losses from the 1993 increases in tax rates. "Because the 1993 Act is very progressive," Auerbach writes, "its income effects on labor supply and saving . . . would lead to a greater behavioral response . . . than occurred after the 1985 Act."[34] The Congressional Budget Office has observed that the tax schedule is now as steeply graduated as it was in 1977, though tax rates appear lower when we forget how many loopholes there were back then.

Disincentives to work are not confined to those in the higher brackets. There are severe work penalties in federal entitlement programs as well:

- Older Americans who earn more than about $11,000 a year have their Social Security benefits reduced by fifty cents for every dollar they earn. If their income exceeds $35,000 (from work or savings), 85 percent of their remaining benefits are then taxable (though the 1994 Republican Contract with America aims to phase out that tax).
- The AFDC-UP program, which Congress mandated the states to adopt in 1989, pays benefits only if the primary earner works fewer than a hundred hours per month.[35]
- The Earned Income Tax Credit (EITC), which was greatly expanded in 1986 and 1993, is phased out in a way that imposes a marginal tax rate of about 50 percent on at least two-thirds of the fifteen million families who are now eligible (working more reduces benefits and adds to

taxes). For eligible households with incomes between $11,000 and $27,000, the EITC check is reduced by twenty-one cents for every dollar of extra earnings, and added Social Security and income taxes collect another 30 percent. If the family also receives food stamps, the marginal tax on working additional hours can rise to 75 percent.[36]

- For single mothers on welfare, working means losing cash benefits, food stamps, Medicaid, and housing allowances. Each additional dollar of earned income can easily result in the loss of more than a dollar in government benefits, or a marginal tax rate above 100 percent. This creates a "poverty trap": efforts to work one's way out of poverty result in lower living standards. Efforts to save are even more sternly punished. For those receiving AFDC or food stamps, it is literally a federal crime to save more than $3,000. Other federal entitlements require people either not to save or to dispose of the assets they once had. As Hubbard, Skinner, and Zeldes note, "The asset-based means testing of AFDC, Supplemental Security Income, and Medicaid may ultimately affect . . . saving choices of low-income households by more than even extreme variations in explicit marginal tax rates."[37] Since many taxpayer-financed benefits are available only to those who do not save (as well as those who do not work), that effectively closes the only other escape route from chronic dependency—accumulating enough capital to start a small business, buy a computer, or finance an education.

The welfare state, in its broadest sense, is not kind but cruel. It has undermined the American dream for those who receive government transfer payments and for those who pay the bills. Punitive payroll and income taxes used to finance soaring benefits discourage work and saving by taxpayers, even as the conditions attached to government benefits have equally demoralizing effects on those dependent on taxpayers. Steep marginal tax rates, imposed on those with both the highest and lowest incomes, make it increasingly difficult to get ahead. Each step upward is punished by a higher tax bracket—greasing the rungs on the ladder of opportunity.

How might these disincentives be minimized? A simple low, flat rate of taxation, as proposed by Rep. Richard Armey, would minimize the many distortions and complexities involved with the current graduated income tax. Short of that, any move toward a flatter tax schedule, such as existed prior to the 1990 and 1993 tax bills, would be a substantial improvement.

Welfare reform could also be of considerable help in alleviating marginal penalties on work and saving among lower-income people, but only if it looks at the combined impact of *all* transfer payments (for example, the total marginal cost of losing welfare, food stamps, and Medicaid). That is, welfare reform should focus on restoring incentives to work and save. Allowing the states more latitude in the area of welfare reform is likely to bring about the experimentation that will lead to effective alternatives to the existing failed system of federal entitlements.

Taxes: The Real Threat to the Next Generation

The generation now coming of age has many advantages. For one thing, it includes relatively few young adults, unlike the baby boom generation, which overcrowded the job and housing markets in the recent past. The Bureau of Labor Statistics estimates that the number of men aged twenty-five to thirty-four will fall by nearly 2.9 million from 1992 to 2005, or 14.7 percent. It estimates that the number of women in this age group will decline by more than nine hundred thousand, or 5.8 percent. There will be more teenagers, but that only adds to the potential supply of full-time, year-round workers if many of them are not attending high school or college.

The young will inherit many debts, but also many assets. (For example, with a larger stock of military equipment, it becomes feasible, up to a point, to economize on future outlays of this sort.) There is nothing wrong with inheriting a mortgage if you also inherit the house. Although some argue that tax rates should be increased because paying interest on the national debt will otherwise burden future generations, higher tax rates would burden future generations in even clearer and probably more lasting ways. To keep raising tax rates to accommodate the federal government's appetite for revenues amounts to temporary capitulation to what is ultimately an impossible trend. In the not-so-long run, the government simply cannot keep growing faster than the incomes of taxpayers, or all of us will end up collecting more in government checks than we are paying back in taxes. Higher tax rates damage economic efficiency and incentives in ways that could easily make funding the government and servicing the debt even *more* difficult, because the tax burden would then fall on a smaller economy with fewer workers and savers.

The next generation will need more technical skills, but that does not necessarily mean that only those with college degrees will be able to realize the American dream. Indeed, if the supply of college degrees soared, their value would fall. Computers offer new sources and varieties of knowledge, skills, and information. Many middle-aged people now grappling with computers did not learn the relevant skills in college, and are amazed at how easily even very young children can master such modern technology. Multimedia software really is getting user-friendly, which makes certain forms of valuable education cheaper and more accessible to the next generation than ever before. Compare, for example, the cost of an encyclopedia on CD-ROM (with stereo sound) to the cost of a bound set of books a few years ago.

The biggest danger facing young people today is runaway growth of the welfare state, and the obligations it threatens to impose on current and future generations. Transfer payments have recently been growing much faster than private wages and salaries (see fig. 12.6). At the same time, annual growth of the labor force has slowed dramatically since 1989—to about 0.9 percent a year from 1990 to 1994, compared with almost 1.7 percent from 1981 to 1989. These are unsustainable trends which could end with very few people willing to work, because the rewards for work are unsatisfactory in comparison with government subsidies for not working.

At the very least, transfer payments will have to be financed efficiently—with low *marginal* tax rates—to avoid discouraging work effort, schooling, and saving. However, it is time for more fundamental reforms to reduce the cost of government, particularly the federal government. This will involve decentralization, deregulation, privatization, and outright elimination of programs, subsidies, agencies, and entire departments that cannot justify their costs. Federal politicians have spent many decades creating new programs. Taking a year or two to eliminate some old programs and agencies does not seem too much to ask.

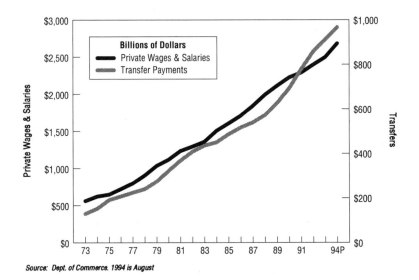

Source: Dept. of Commerce. 1994 is August

Figure 12.6. Growth of transfer payments versus private wages and salaries

In her 1991 book, *Reviving the American Dream*, Alice Rivlin (now Budget Director) proposed that "the states should take charge of the productivity agenda, especially education, training, infrastructure, and economic development, while the federal government should devolve its programs in these areas to the states."[38] The same could be said of many other activities, notably crime prevention, which are far more effectively handled by local government or by the private sector.

If we reduce the burden of federal programs and mandates, states and cities need not find their tax bases preempted by the seemingly insatiable appetite of the federal system. It is vitally important that the federal government *devolve the tax base*, however, and not simply the responsibilities for public spending. In recent years, the trend has been just the opposite. The federal government has taken larger and larger slices out of revenue sources previously used mainly by states and cities, such as taxes on gasoline and cigarettes. When the federal government raised the tax rate on capital gains, that reduced realization of capital gains (people held onto assets rather than selling them), which greatly reduced *state* revenues from this source. Since federal income tax rates have gone back up, states that have attempted to add their own income tax hikes (New Jersey and California) soon found that their revenues fell, thanks to a loss of employers and high-income taxpayers to more tax-friendly states.

As the federal government decentralizes and devolves responsibilities to levels of government closer to the people, it must also eliminate some federal taxes entirely and scale others back sharply. Herbert Croly's quaint 1909 vision of the merits of increased centralization was founded on the notion that "American state governments have been corrupt and inefficient largely because they have been organized for the benefit of corrupt and inefficient men." The federal government, by contrast, was apparently organized for the benefit of saints and angels. Still, Croly's idea of "big government" in Washington looks like a bargain by today's standards. He reasoned that a much stronger federal government could be financed out of a graduated inheritance tax: "The tax at its highest level," Croly wrote, "could be placed without danger of evasion at as much as 20 percent." Some recent estimates suggest that Croly may have been correct about how high the estate tax could be pushed without losing money.[39] In any case, if a 20 percent inheritance tax were the only federal tax we had to worry about, as Croly proposed, the states would have little difficulty in raising money for the services that are still almost entirely a state or local responsibility, such as police protection, public schools, and roads. (The federal government, by contrast, is almost entirely involved in taking money from some people and giving it to others).

States need more scope to develop their own alternatives to a wide variety of welfare benefits and pension/insurance systems. There is no shortage of bold proposals, but boldness is not a quality likely to emerge from any federal bureaucracy.

Choice and competition in welfare services, as in education, could encourage development of effective programs and could weed out failures. Taxpayers could be granted a credit for contributions to organizations that meet certain criteria, such as helping to feed, shelter, and find jobs for the poor, all with minimal overhead expenses. Government programs would have to meet the same standards, and taxpayers could earmark their credit for such programs, federal or local, or to private agencies, whether nonprofit or for profit.[40] Retirement and long-term care for the aged will have to rely much more on innovative private alternatives to tax-financed subsidies. Younger people might be permitted to allocate the employee's share of the Social Security tax to a private retirement account, for example, in exchange for reduced benefits from the government-run system.

The observation that punitive tax rates can do so much damage that even the government loses money is neither a new nor a uniquely conservative insight. Back in 1976, James Tobin of Yale, a former adviser to President Kennedy and candidate McGovern, observed that "there is a point beyond which higher surtax rates collect less—not more—revenue. . . . We have a great stake in maintaining the view that performance pays off, that indolence and inefficiency do not."[41]

The American dream is grounded in hard work and thrift, innovation and opportunity. By reviving the incentives to reward productive behavior, and by using American ingenuity to enhance opportunity and reduce dependency, this amazing country's greatest achievements could lie just ahead of us.

Notes

1. Edward N. Luttwak, "Will Success Spoil America?" *The Washington Post*, November 27, 1994, C1.
2. Executive Office of the President, "A Vision of Change for America," U.S. Government Printing Office, 93-0247-P, February 17, 1993, 6, 7, 13.
3. "Economic Indicators," *Economist*, August 13, 1994, 92.
4. In December 1994, when Congressman Richard Gephardt first proposed his version of a "middle-class tax cut," he claimed that "For the past 15 years [that is, since 1979], incomes in this country have eroded. Our standard of living has slipped."
5. *Economic Report of the President* (Washington, D.C.: U.S. Government Printing Office, February 1994), table B-113, 397.
6. David Whitman, "The Poor Aren't Poorer," *U.S. News & World Report*, July 25, 1994, 33–38; Robert Haveman, "Who Are the Nation's Truly Poor?" *Brookings Review* 11 (Winter 1993): 24–27.

7. Robert Rector, "The Facts About America's Poor," *Heritage Foundation F.Y.I.*, Washington, D.C., December 23, 1993.
8. Richard McKenzie, "Decline Dissertation Flunks Numbers Test," *Washington Times,* July 8, 1994.
9. Larry B. Lindsey, "Inflation and Economic Opportunity," *Federal Reserve Bulletin* 78 (July 1992): 513; Lawrence B. Lindsey, "Why the 1980s Were Not the 1920s," *Forbes*, October 19, 1992, 78.
10. Paul Ryscavage, Gordon Green, and Edward Welniak, "The Impact of Demographic, Social, and Economic Change on the Distribution of Income," *Studies in the Distribution of Income*, Current Population Reports, Series P60-183 (Washington, D.C.: U.S. Government Printing Office, 1992).
11. Maury Gittleman, "Earnings in the 1980s: An Occupational Perspective," *Monthly Labor Review* 117 (July 1994): 17.
12. "A Vision of Change for America," op. cit.
13. *Economic Report of the President,* op. cit., 25, 117.
14. Christopher Power and Howard Gleckman, "The Global Economy: Who Gets Hurt?" *Business Week*, August 10, 1992, 50.
15. Ramon Vilches, "Changes in the Structure of Wages: A Regional Comparison," *New England Economic Review*, Federal Reserve Bank of Boston, July/August 1991, 45.
16. Philip A. Trostel, "The Effects of Taxation on Human Capital," *Journal of Political Economy* 101 (April 1993): 327.
17. Gary Burtless, "The Payoff to Education in the Labor Market," in *Workers and Their Wages*, ed. Marvin H. Kosters (Washington, D.C.: American Enterprise Institute, 1991), 34–35.
18. Alan S. Blinder, "The Level and Distribution of Economic Well-Being," in *The American Economy in Transition,* ed. Martin Feldstein (Chicago: University of Chicago Press in association with National Bureau of Economic Research, 1980), 415–79.
19. Christopher Jencks, quoted in Don Lambro, "Liberal Study Refutes Underclass Statistics," *Washington Times,* April 10, 1991. See also Don Lambro, "Overrated Statistics on Underclass," *Washington Times,* April 15, 1991, D1.
20. *Statistical Abstract of the United States, 1994,* table 720, 472.
21. *Economic Report of the President,* op. cit., 23, 97.
22. "More Than Meets the Eye," *Economist,* December 26, 1992, 91.
23. U.S. Department of Labor, *Employment Cost Indexes and Levels, 1975–92* (Washington, D.C.: U.S. Government Printing Office, November 1992), 8.
24. F. Thomas Juster and Frank P. Stafford, "The Allocation of Time: Empirical Findings, Behavioral Models and Problems of Measurement," *Journal of Economic Literature* 29 (June 1991): 493–94.
25. Alan Reynolds, "Workforce 2005," in *Societies in Transition: The Future of Work and Leisure* (Paris: Organization for Economic Cooperation and Development, 1994), 47–80.
26. Gene Koretz, "Service Jobs Have Been Getting a Bum Rap," *Business Week*, February 15, 1993, 28.

27. Bureau of the Census, "Workers With Low Earnings: 1964 to 1990," Current Population Reports, Series P-60, No. 178, March 1992, 5–6.
28. Ronald Mincy, "Help for the Middle Class," *Fortune*, April 4, 1993, 24.
29. *Statistical Abstract,* op. cit., table 670, 432.
30. Robert K. Triest, "The Efficiency Cost of Increased Progressivity," National Bureau of Economic Research Working Paper Number 4535, Cambridge, Mass., November 1993.
31. E. Mendoza, A. Raaxin, and L. Tesar, "An International Comparison of Tax Systems in Industrial Countries," in *Staff Studies for the World Economic Outlook* (Washington, D.C., International Monetary Fund, December 1993), 101.
32. James P. Ziliak, "Three Essays on the Effect of Taxes and Tax Reform on Life-Cycle Labor Supply," *Proceedings of the Eighty-Sixth Annual Convention of the National Tax Association,* St. Paul, 1994, 126.
33. Martin Feldstein, "The Effect of Marginal Tax Rates on Taxable Income: A Panel Study of the 1986 Tax Reform Act," National Bureau of Economic Research Working Paper Number 4496, Cambridge, Mass., October 1993, 3.
34. Alan Auerbach, "The U.S. Fiscal Problem," National Bureau of Economic Research Working Paper Number 4700, Cambridge, Mass., April 1994.
35. Hillary Hoynes, "Welfare Transfer in Two-Parent Families: Labor Supply and Welfare Participation Under AFDC-UP," National Bureau of Economic Research Working Paper Number 4407, Cambridge, Mass., July 1993.
36. John Karl Scholz, "The Earned Income Tax Credit: Participation, Compliance and Antipoverty Effectiveness," *The National Tax Journal* 47 (March 1994): 63.
37. R. Glenn Hubbard, Jonathan Skinner, and Stephen P. Zeldes, "Expanding the Life-Cycle Model: Precautionary Saving and Public Policy," *The American Economic Review* 84 (May 1994): 179.
38. Alice M. Rivlin, *Reviving the American Dream* (Washington, D.C.: Brookings Institution, 1992), 180.
39. B. Douglas Bernheim, "Does The Estate Tax Raise Revenue?" in *Tax Policy and the Economy,* vol. 1, ed. Lawrence H. Summers (Boston: M.I.T Press in association with National Bureau of Economic Research, 1987).
40. Alan Reynolds, "Competition in Welfare," *National Review*, December 10, 1976, 1347.
41. James Tobin, "Considerations Regarding Taxation and Inequality," in *Income Redistribution*, ed. Colin D. Campbell (Washington, D.C.: American Enterprise Institute, 1977), 131–32.

Chapter Thirteen

The American Dream and the Spirit of Enterprise

William A. Schreyer

The Spirit of Enterprise

The United States today is the unrivaled leader of the global economy. No other nation can match the strength and dynamism of the $6.7 trillion American economic powerhouse. Our exports dominate markets from Bangkok to Budapest. Our productivity and living standards are the envy of the world.

What is the key to this remarkable economic success? For the most part, the essays in this volume focus on government and its decisions: policies that can be altered, programs that can be restructured. But as wise as any public policies might be, the *true* source of America's economic energy is not found at the Federal Reserve, the Treasury Department, or the Senate Finance Committee.

To understand the triumph of our economy, it is well to forget for a moment about the planners in the nation's capital and the fifty state capitals. Think instead about the "spirit of enterprise." The genius of the U.S. economy is rooted in *private* decisions: in the innovations, hard work, and entrepreneurship of millions of individuals—and thousands of companies—throughout the land.

That spirit of enterprise was alive and well in the first decade of the twentieth century, when Herbert Croly and other intellectuals were laying the groundwork for the Progressive Era. But while they struggled with theories about the relationship between government and the people, the people themselves were thinking about different matters.

For example, two Dayton brothers—one a few years older than Croly, the other a little younger—had a new hobby which they found time to tinker with on the margins of each day, when the "real" work in their small bicycle shop was completed. They were not necessarily out to get rich, but they did have a dream. Their project took all the skills and drive they could muster. The road they traveled was not easy. Failure awaited them at many turns. But they persevered. And eventually they succeeded.

Orville and Wilbur Wright built the first airplane. They were practical folks, trying to solve a problem. And through their industriousness and sheer determination these bicycle builders—on their own, without help from government—produced one of mankind's greatest inventions.

What could be more American, or a better illustration of the spirit of enterprise?

The achievement of the Wright brothers was indeed amazing. But it is hardly unique in our history. The spirit of enterprise they epitomized has been one of the nation's hallmarks from the start, and it remains so today. This is still a country where a young dreamer, working in his family's garage, can produce an invention that changes the world. In the 1970s, Steven Jobs did just this as he transformed a passion for computers into the Apple Corporation and launched the personal computer revolution. Twenty years later, we are not sitting and waiting for the federal government to "pave" the nation's information superhighway. Thanks to the spirit of enterprise—that uniquely American drive to solve problems and seek profits—creative individuals and aggressive companies are *already* building it themselves.

A small bicycle shop. A garage on a middle-class street. Two unassuming locations, at opposite ends of the twentieth century, linked by the spirit of enterprise. It is in millions of places like these, most of them far from Washington, where we should look for the source of America's economic strength.

Why do ordinary Americans do extraordinary things—like take risks, build companies, and create marvelous inventions? After spending a career in the private sector, and observing firsthand the workings of other economies around the world, I am convinced that our exceptional spirit of enterprise is driven by one thing above all: *the American dream.*

America has rightly been called the "land of unlimited possibilities."[1] For all the differences we may have with Herbert Croly's prescriptions for recrafting the political economy of the United States, Croly did recognize the power of the American dream—that quintessentially American conviction that each generation can do better than the one before it.

In business, it is essential to know something about risk and reward, about the tradeoffs that people demand before committing themselves to new ideas. The bottom line: if you want people to take risks, they have got to see the chance for clear rewards. The American dream is the ultimate reward, inspiring countless risk takers. With their eyes fixed on the dream, individuals begin new projects and build new companies. The dream means opportunity exists, profits can follow investments, and advancement can follow hard work.

This vision of a better tomorrow inspires innovation, extra effort, and entrepreneurship. It fosters our economy's dynamism and our people's optimism. In short, the American dream nourishes the spirit of enterprise. No one ever started a business or invented a new gadget because someone in Washington told him to. People are driven by the chance to get ahead. Our extraordinary spirit of enterprise is a direct result of the knowledge that we will reap the rewards of our labor.

Does the American dream still exist? Absolutely. Even now, while press and pundits make much of a new cynicism and pessimism spreading across the land, nearly 75 percent of Americans agree with the statement, "In America, if you work hard, you can be anything you want to be."[2]

Although national and global conditions change, the basic principles that govern the behavior of people do not. What is important is that we keep reinterpreting and reapplying these principles in ways that fit the changing environment. Croly tried to do this at the beginning of the twentieth century. It is time to reopen the debate about proper economic policy, in light of very different conditions, as the century draws to a close. Our nation's real economic challenge is to preserve the American dream, along with the spirit of enterprise it engenders, and to deliver it to generations yet unborn.

The Challenges

Early in *The Promise of American Life,* Herbert Croly wrote, "This vision of a better future is not, perhaps, as unclouded for the present generation of Americans as it was for certain former generations. . . ." That is not a bad way to put it. No one is more optimistic than I when it comes to America's destiny. But we cannot ignore the fact that the American dream, and therefore our nation's spirit of enterprise, face stiff challenges. The sooner we recognize which problems are truly important and start working on solutions to them, the sooner we will be able to reassure our grandchildren about their futures.

Our leaders in Washington engage in debate over a vast range of economic issues, from trade policy to worker training to new strategies for public investment. As I look ahead, however, two interrelated challenges stand out as fundamental to America's economic future. The first is the growth in the government's share of our economy. The second is the personal saving crisis in the U.S. Each of these has enormous implications for the prospects that await future generations.

Government Spending

In economics, few trends continue decade after decade. Markets are inherently cyclical and self-correcting; they tend to wring out excesses naturally. Looking back over the twentieth century, however, we can discern at least one pattern that has not diminished over the course of nine decades: the relentless increase in government's "take" from the U.S. economy.

Since Croly's day, the share of our economy devoted to government has more than quintupled. Combined federal, state, and local government spending has increased from less than *8 percent* of a $22 billion economy in 1902 to more than *42 percent* of a $6.3 *trillion* economy in 1993 (see fig. 13.1). That is an astounding increase.

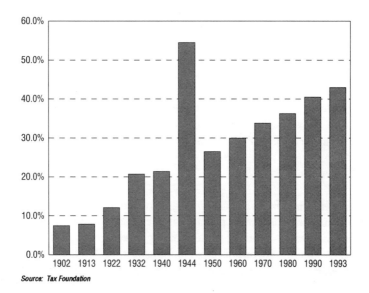

Source: Tax Foundation

Figure 13.1. Total government spending as a share of GDP

It is important to realize another, perhaps obvious, point about the growth of government during the twentieth century. It has not been driven primarily by a massive increase in spending near the people, at the state and local level. The overall expansion of American government is the direct result of an explosion of *federal* spending. Between 1930 and 1950, the U.S. witnessed a dramatic shift (see fig. 13.2). For the first time in our history, federal spending emerged as the dominant share of total government spending.

As we look down the road, it is the federal government that continues to pose the greatest threat of further expansion. Indeed, there are reasons to believe the trend toward a larger public sector might actually accelerate in the next century. At the federal level we have already made promises for future income-transfer programs that will grow increasingly expensive to keep as the huge baby boom generation reaches retirement age over the next few decades.

A recent study by the U.S. General Accounting Office (GAO) explored what would happen if the federal programs in place today were left untouched into the next century. The results were shocking: GAO projected that federal spending alone would reach *42 percent* of gross domestic product (GDP) by the year 2020.[3] Assuming that state and local spending stay close to where they are today (16 percent of GDP), government would take nearly *60 percent* of total U.S. economic output—a share greater than during the height of World War II.

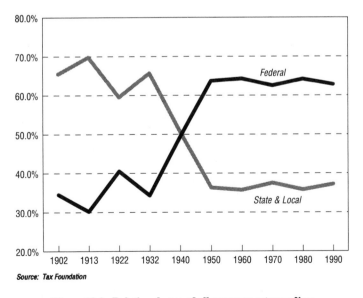

Source: Tax Foundation

**Figure 13.2. Relative shares of all government spending
(federal + state + local = 100%)**

There are two major reasons—the first strictly economic and the second more psychological or cultural—why this growth in government poses a grave threat to the American dream.

First, the economics. No one knows for sure whether we are on track to see government spending reach 50 percent, 55 percent, or 60 percent of GDP. It is impossible to predict what will in fact occur. All we can be certain of is that the public policies in place today, if left unchanged, will significantly expand government's share of our economy.

The reality is that every additional billion of GDP we devote to government is taken away from uses in the private economy. No one who believes, as I do, that the most productive investments are consistently made by the private sector rather than by government bureaucracies, and that people know how to use their own money better than planners ever will, can escape the conclusion that expanding government will limit Americans' future living standards. The more the government takes, the less the private sector has left. All those dollars of extra output devoted to government may generate an investment return just a little lower than what they would have produced in the private economy. But even those small differences will loom large over the long run.

All who doubt this have only to compare the economic track records of the United States and the United Kingdom.[4] At the end of the nineteenth century, per capita income in the U.S. was about 15 percent lower than in the U.K. Over the last 120 years, however, the average annual growth of real per capita income in the U.K. was 1.38 percent, while in the U.S. it was 1.86 percent. A small difference, many would say. But small differences compound and cumulate. The result: per capita income in the U.S. today is now *50 percent greater* than it is in the U.K. Less than half a point difference in the growth of income since the late 1800s was sufficient for the U.S. not merely to overtake the U.K. as the world's wealthiest, most powerful nation, but to outstrip it by half.

Anyone who says that devoting a little more of GDP to government will not affect our economic future is simply wrong. Over the long run, using more of America's output in the private sector than in the public sector will make a huge difference in terms of economic growth. And maintaining each generation's chance to do better than the one before it is easier in an economy that is rapidly expanding and generating broad increases in living standards.

My concern over the growth of government goes beyond economics and right to the heart of one of today's great tensions in American society: our devotion to unlimited individual opportunity on the one hand, and our concerns about "fairness" and "equity" on the other. Naturally, our interest in the former draws us toward *less* government interference in the marketplace, while our concern for the latter prescribes *more* government to make sure we distribute the nation's output "fairly."

The size of government is a pretty good proxy for how far we are tilting toward an arbitrary, politically defined notion of "equity" and away from opportunity. Looking into the next century, America seems to be headed toward bigger and bigger government. This is certain to be detrimental to individual opportunity, and therefore to the spirit of enterprise that drives our nation's private sector. Simply put, as a society we risk becoming so obsessed with how the pie is sliced that we neglect to bake a bigger one.

It is impossible to quantify with precision to what extent this cultural shift will influence our economic future. But I cannot help concluding that an expanding government and a shrinking spirit of enterprise will have an enormous effect. Letting this cultural shift continue unchecked is a risk too dangerous to take.

The Savings Crisis

It is no coincidence that, as government's role in our economy has grown, another problem has developed: a serious decline in U.S. savings rates. This personal savings crisis constitutes the second threat to America's continued economic success.

Personal saving has been locked in a downward spiral over the last twenty-five years (see fig. 13.3). While household savings rates exceeded 8 percent of disposable income in the late 1960s and early 1970s, today that rate

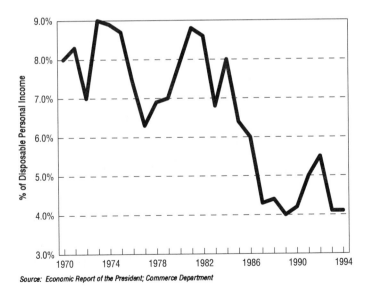

Source: *Economic Report of the President; Commerce Department*

Figure 13.3. U.S. personal savings rate

has fallen to only 4 percent. American families saved less of their income in 1994 than in almost any year since the 1940s.

Americans' current failure to save not only looks bad against our own historical record; it also stacks up poorly against the performance of our global competitors. Americans today save at less than *half* the rate of the British, Canadians, and Germans, and less than *one-third* the rate of the Japanese and French (see fig. 13.4).

One reason the personal savings crisis has developed at the same time that government's role in our economy has grown is this: government actions—on both sides of the ledger, taxing and spending—tend to confuse household saving decisions. When one steps back and looks broadly at the impact government has on our society, one can almost make out a coordinated strategy (especially at the federal level) to help Americans "kick the saving habit."

On the revenue side of the government's books, we have in place a tax system that is biased *against* saving and *in favor of* consumption. Most significantly, it double taxes all funds that are saved: first when they are received as income and again when they are saved and earn interest or dividends. Yet funds that are consumed are for the most part taxed only once, when earned. This double taxation imposes a steep penalty on saving and investment. Down the road, should policymakers decide to increase income tax rates to fund the growing role of government, the bias toward consumption over saving will only become more pronounced.

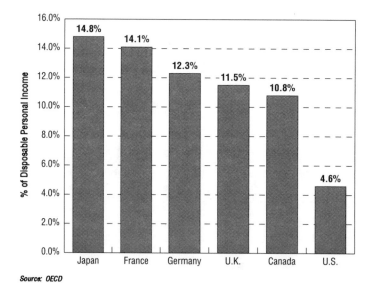

Source: OECD

Figure 13.4. Household savings rates in 1993

The government's spending policies also stack the deck against saving. A long list of current programs and policies tends to dampen the need to save. For example, Social Security has relieved some of the reason to save for retirement. Unemployment insurance has lessened the need to save for a rainy day in the labor market. Medicare has made saving up for old-age health costs much less of a concern. Many welfare programs (such as Aid to Families with Dependent Children) are means-tested, and one's means include savings. That is, if you save too much, you are out of the program—a reality which discourages many welfare recipients from building their own nest eggs and establishing some real financial security.

No one would seriously propose to eliminate all of these programs tomorrow. But it is time to recognize that the entire structure of government in the U.S. has conspired to depress personal saving. Together, the programs listed above plus countless others have helped to foster an ethos very new in American history: *"I'm not responsible for my own future."*

If government expands as rapidly in the next century as some have predicted, the personal savings crisis will grow even more acute. What does this portend for the future of the American dream? The savings crisis affects the dream on two levels.

The first level is macroeconomic. Personal saving provides a key source of U.S. investment capital. In today's economy, the fall in personal savings rates from 8 percent to 4 percent means that America has to make do annually without roughly $200 billion of domestic investment capital that would have been available had the 1970 savings rate been maintained.

Users of capital in our economy can make up for this in part by borrowing money from abroad, or canceling a planned investment or two. But there is no getting around the fact that low personal savings rates rob the U.S. economy of billions that could have been used to fund investments in new factories, equipment, and technology—all of which are needed to produce stronger economic growth and rising living standards. The American dream is much easier to keep alive in an expanding economy than in a society experiencing flat wages and stagnant living standards.

The second impact of the savings crisis is more personal. At the individual and family level, low saving limits financial security and makes the prospect of surpassing previous generations far more doubtful.

Figure 13.5 puts a human face on the macroeconomic figures generally used to illustrate the savings crisis. The graph shows the median net financial assets of American families in 1993—that is, the money they had in the bank in one form or another.[5]

Half of all American families headed by individuals age forty-five to fifty-four have less than $2,600 in net financial assets. It doesn't take an economist to point out that this is not nearly enough saving for genuine security.

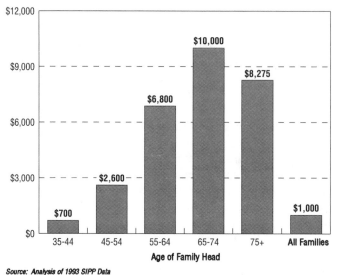

Source: *Analysis of 1993 SIPP Data*

Figure 13.5. Median net financial assets of U.S. families (1993)

Even among households closer to retirement, headed by individuals age fifty-five to sixty-four, median net financial assets are only $6,880.

This lack of personal saving has obvious implications for the future awaiting individual American families. It spells economic insecurity in the near term; a tough time making needed investments (in children's education, for instance) in the medium term; and the prospect of difficult changes in living standards in the long term, as retirement approaches. Indeed, with such limited personal resources, Americans are more reliant on government for assistance—today and into retirement—than ever before.

All of this suggests a vicious cycle affecting our society. As government's reach has spread, its policies have discouraged saving. The personal saving crisis, in turn, has left families with such meager balance sheets that they increasingly look to government for help. This bolsters support for ever more generous government programs—which, in the end, reinforces and perpetuates the cycle. The lesson is clear: expanding government not only promotes low personal saving; low personal saving also promotes expanding government.

Croly's ideas lured America in this dangerous direction. His vision, with its role for a larger public sector, clearly had surface appeal at the start of this century. It promised government would be there most of the time, protecting, providing for, and lifting responsibility from the individual.

It was not until America actually went down this road—toward an economy characterized by big government and low personal saving—that its pitfalls became clear. As reliance on government grew, individual responsibility and opportunity took a back seat. With saving discouraged, the fuel for long-term economic growth was sapped. And families, far from being more secure, found themselves more vulnerable—without the resources to provide for their own future should government promises not be kept.

After decades of travel, it is clear that the road Croly offered was a dead end.

Our challenge now? To find a more promising path to the economic future. Some specific policy ideas are outlined below. But the central elements of a new vision should already be clear: that is, a society with much more limited government and a far greater emphasis on individual responsibility and personal saving. The challenge is to transform the vicious cycle of big government and low saving into a virtuous cycle of small government and high saving. This is the direction that will lead to stronger economic growth and more abundant opportunity—helping to renew the American dream and strengthen the spirit of enterprise that fires our magnificent economy.

Looking to the Future

America has always been characterized by a national resolve to tackle problems. It was not until the 1990s that Nike popularized the phrase "Just do it," but observers of the United States have recognized our "get it done" spirit since the beginning. Tocqueville used these words to describe a typical nineteenth-century American: "In his eyes, what is not yet done is only what he has not yet attempted to do."[6] At the end of the twentieth century, our nation's will to solve the tough problems is just as strong as ever.

Any comprehensive strategy for a sound economic future must take on the growth of government and the decline of personal saving *together;* the two cannot be separated. Therefore, our approach to saving the American dream should be threefold. First, most obviously and immediately, we must cut government spending and free resources in the economy for productive private investment. Second, if we want to get a firm grip on the growth of government over the *long term,* we must rationalize our Social Security system. Third, we must press for fundamental tax reform, aimed at ending once and for all the bias against saving and investment. The following sections will sketch out these suggestions in a little more detail.

Cut Government Spending

William Kristol proposes in his essay a radical relimiting of government. Make no mistake—his ideas are not merely good social policy and an important lesson in public administration. They are also the foundation of growth-oriented economic policy. When we have a choice between investing dollars in more government or investing them in the most productive private economy in world history, it is really no choice at all.

In Washington, almost everybody focuses on the federal budget deficit. Unfortunately, deficit figures are an incomplete—and often misleading—way to think about fiscal issues. They are usually presented as single-year dramas. They do not tell us enough about the relationship between outlays and receipts over time. Thus, deficit numbers alone can lead us astray.

Figure 13.6, which shows federal budget trends since 1960, illustrates that there is indeed a gaping deficit. But as this chart also makes clear, our deficit problem has been created not by a revenue drought but by a flood of new spending. Federal receipts have been remarkably stable as a share of GDP over the last thirty-four years. The same cannot be said for spending. It has grown steadily, from an average of 19.1 percent of GDP in the 1960s, to 20.6 percent in the 1970s, to 23.1 percent in the 1980s. A steeper rise in government spending is scheduled to begin early in the next century.

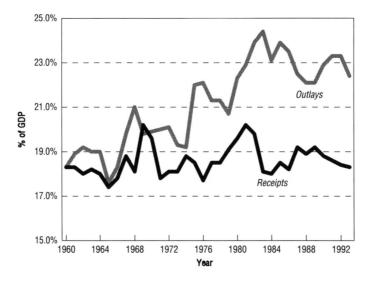

Figure 13.6. Federal receipts and outlays in relation to GDP

Let's not fall for the talk in Washington about "raising taxes a little here, cutting spending a little there" in the name of addressing the deficit as Public Enemy Number One. America's real fiscal debate should be over just one thing: federal spending. As we begin to cut that spending, the budget deficit can certainly provide a useful benchmark. Our first step should be to bring federal spending—debt service included—back down to approximately the 19 percent of GDP that revenues have averaged over the last few decades, thereby closing the deficit.

Then America should try to tighten its belt another notch or two, trimming government spending further at every level. The payoff will be hundreds of billions of dollars released for use in the private economy. Investing these immense resources in the private sector will mean expanding jobs, increasing productivity, growing wages, and rising living standards. Spending them on government accomplishes none of these things.

A dramatic rollback in government spending, especially federal spending, has to be our guiding strategic vision. While it is beyond the scope of this chapter to spell out the details of this vision, one reality does stare us in the face as we look down the fiscal road ahead. It will be tough to make much long-term progress in controlling the size of government unless we are willing to touch the "third rail" of American politics, Social Security. This is a hard fact that all policymakers—Democrat and Republican alike—must soon bring themselves to face.

A New Approach to Social Security

It may not be "politically correct" to talk about reforming the Social Security system. But the need for a new approach to Social Security is becoming more and more obvious.

Among experts on the Social Security system, there is a growing consensus that something must be done, and soon. Last year, perhaps the most respected new book on Social Security got to the point in the very first paragraph:

> The United States Social Security system is the largest and one of the most successful federal social policies. . . . Despite [its] tremendous achievements, the system is ripe for reform—so ripe in fact that we can state unequivocally that it *will* be reformed. Indeed the issue facing the nation is not whether, but how and when.[7]

Why the imperative for reform? First, demographic pressures are mounting. Americans are living longer and retiring earlier. After the turn of the century, the aging of the baby boom generation will dramatically boost the ratio of Social Security beneficiaries to workers, up from twenty-seven beneficiaries per one hundred workers in 1990 to forty-three per one hundred by 2030.

These population shifts are driving the program's enormous fiscal imbalance. In 1983, Social Security experts predicted the system would remain solvent until the year 2063; now that bankruptcy date has been moved up to 2030 under some assumptions, and to as early as 2017 under others. Because of earlier benefit cuts and tax increases passed to extend the program's solvency, it is increasingly forcing young people to pay in more money than they will ever take out. And some thoughtful observers have noted that—with Social Security's unfunded benefits to current and future retirees totaling $6.7 trillion—the system's liabilities are actually *larger* than the federal debt.[8] Is it any wonder polls have shown that young Americans today are far more likely to believe in UFOs than in the prospect that Social Security will be there when they retire?[9]

Social Security's balance sheet is not the only problem. In the year 2030, fully *one-fifth* of the American population is scheduled to receive Social Security retirement benefits. Under the current system—in which everyone's taxes go to Washington and benefits are paid from Washington—this means a further expansion of government's role in the U.S. economy, and a redistribution of our nation's wealth on an unprecedented scale. Annual Social Security spending is projected to total $2.8 trillion by the year 2030—more than $7.5 billion paid by government every day. We are on track to see a broader involvement than ever before by government in the financial affairs of American families. With this involvement will surely come enormous distortions to incentives to work, save, and invest in the U.S. economy.

It is hard to disagree with the experts. Social Security reform *is* inevitable. The challenge is to make sure it is done well. This means trying to accomplish three goals: restoring the system's financial balance, ensuring that all participants receive a fair return on their money, and limiting the role of government.

With these principles in mind, we can begin thinking seriously about changes by recognizing the two central goals of the Social Security program: 1) reallocating income from individuals' working years to their retirement, and 2) transferring resources from better-off to less well-off retirees.[10]

These are simple goals. Yet many problems with our existing Social Security system are rooted in the fact that we have tried to accomplish both of these goals within one program and with a single source of revenue: the payroll tax. This scheme has naturally led to confusion. Many Americans think they are participating in some type of mandated saving plan, where they will get their "contributions" back during retirement. Many others see the program primarily as a means to redistribute income to elderly Americans in need. As we enter the new century, it is time to end the widespread confusion.

There is a straightforward way to do this: restructure the Social Security program to achieve its two central goals separately. This would mean, first, establishing a true *compulsory saving program,* funded by a payroll tax. Such a program would allow people actually to set aside their own Social Security contributions for their own retirement, as many people think they are doing right now.

There is no reason why this new compulsory saving program should force individuals to keep their contributions in an account at the Treasury Department, invested exclusively in government debt, as required by the current Social Security system. The new program would provide for Americans' payroll taxes to be sent—either by the federal government or by their employers—directly to individualized *private* accounts, similar to existing IRAs. Funds in these accounts would be invested in a range of approved private investment vehicles and could not be withdrawn before retirement. Upon reaching retirement age, Americans would use the money in their personal accounts to buy an annuity, transforming their accumulated Social Security contributions into a steady source of retirement income.

One reason it is vital to establish *private* Social Security accounts: under the current arrangement, policymakers have shown that it is impossible for them to keep their hands off the cash. Today, the money Americans have paid into the Social Security "trust fund" is simply loaned to the Treasury, allowing the federal government to spend more every year without having the full impact of its spending register on the deficit. There is no real "saving" going on. No money is actually being set aside in Washington for the baby boomers' retirements. Indeed, this shell game has made the term "trust fund" especially apt, because that is all there is in the fund right now: no money, just trust. The current system is built on blind faith that the Treasury will return the money early in the next century, notwithstanding that the Social Security "trust fund" must pay out each year more than it takes in.

For Americans who had low earnings during their working years, and were unable to put enough money into their individualized accounts to meet a minimum acceptable level of retirement income, the second part of the new Social Security system would come into play: a separate *income maintenance program for the elderly.* For low-income retirees, this welfare-like program would make up the difference between the income provided by their individualized account and the minimum acceptable standard.

Since this part of Social Security would be explicitly designed to redistribute income, it would probably best be funded out of the government's general revenues, which are collected by a progressive income tax system, rather than a regressive payroll tax. Incidentally, a model for this "new" welfare program already exists: the Supplemental Security Income program, which currently makes transfers to lower-income elderly Americans.

A wide range of benefits would flow from this fresh approach to Social Security:

- First, this approach would facilitate the investment of Social Security funds in the private sector, where they would help provide capital for stronger economic growth.
- Second, individual Americans would be personally able to direct the investment of their own retirement resources. This would help ensure all participants a fair return on their retirement savings rather than the varied and arbitrary returns offered by the current system.
- Third, private investment of retirement savings also promises higher returns compared to the current system. Social Security is now projected to deliver only about a 2 percent return on the "investment" of average workers retiring early in the next century.[11] In contrast, even a relatively conservative private investment portfolio (50 percent stocks, 50 percent bonds) has experienced returns of roughly 9 percent over the last four decades. Better investment of Social Security's resources would lessen the system's financial strains and help it deliver the retirement income America will need in the next century.
- Fourth, the proposed Social Security system, with its private accounts, would take the bulk of Americans' retirement savings out of Washington, so that our policymakers would not be tempted to spend the money prematurely on other government programs.
- Fifth, the system is certain to raise confidence in the future of Social Security, given that Americans would be able to monitor the funds in their own personal accounts.
- Finally, with its freestanding cash assistance program, the new system would make the income redistribution role of Social Security explicit, allowing it to be evaluated by policymakers on the same footing as the other government transfer programs competing in Washington for scarce resources.

One more change to Social Security is badly overdue and would help alleviate financial pressure as we move toward a new system: *raising the Social Security retirement age.* The system's "normal retirement age" has been fixed at sixty-five since its inception. Yet the average life expectancy of a newborn has increased by fifteen years since the 1930s, and, over the same time period, the average remaining life expectancy of a sixty-five-year-old has risen by 25 percent.

Currently, the Social Security retirement age is scheduled to increase very slowly, only reaching age sixty-seven by the year 2025. In light of the longer and healthier lives Americans are leading, it would be reasonable to set the retirement age higher than this and to increase it more rapidly. Many have suggested a move toward age seventy over the next two or three decades. This would help both to balance Social Security's finances and to align the program better with today's demographic realities.

No doubt such reforms would have to be phased in. It would not be fair to change the rules overnight for millions of Americans on the verge of retirement. But there is no reason we cannot start shifting younger Americans into a program that makes better economic and political sense. These changes would take us a step closer to making the dream of a secure retirement a reality for today's young Americans.

Now that we have outlined a set of sound ideas, we should briefly mention one bad idea. A lot of people today talk about means-testing Social Security benefits (that is, reducing benefits as income rises). Without question, the idea has enormous intuitive appeal: *why should a retired couple with $150,000 in income be receiving Social Security payments?* Means-testing seems to make all the sense in the world—until you try to put theory into practice.

Unfortunately, means-testing regimes inevitably create a substantial new tax on private saving. As soon as we begin means-testing, the more saving that Americans do (and therefore the more private retirement income they will have), the more Social Security payments the government will take away. In effect, means-testing would slap a penalty on savers by lowering their Social Security benefits.

Some dismiss as insignificant the potential antisaving effect of means-testing. They are dead wrong. This new, implicit "tax" on saving could be prohibitive. Lawrence B. Lindsey, a Federal Reserve governor, has calculated that one widely discussed means-testing proposal—which would phase out up to 85 percent of benefits for people with between $40,000 and $120,000 in retirement income—would create an additional *39 percent* "tax" on each extra dollar of retirement income people saved on their own.[12] If we impose means-testing, many Americans will find that it doesn't make sense to fund that 401(k), Keogh, or IRA, since doing so will only lead to less in the way of Social Security when they do retire.

With the personal savings crisis in the U.S. continuing to worsen, the *last* thing we need is to give American families one more compelling reason not to save.

Fundamental Tax Reform

This brings us to the third, and final, area of reform: tax policies designed to increase America's low saving rate. It has been more than three hundred years since the English philosopher Thomas Hobbes observed that it is fairer to tax people on what they extract from the economy, as measured by their consumption, than to tax them on what they produce for the economy, as measured by their income. That wisdom is timeless. As we think about recrafting American tax policy, it is important to consider not only *how much* government is taking from our economy, but also *how* it is being taken. Some types of taxes are more equitable than others. Even more important, tax policies have a direct impact on the decisions people make, and some taxes encourage them to make bad decisions. As I have said repeatedly, one of the worst problems with the American tax code today is its systematic bias against saving and investment.

It is time to adopt a fundamentally different system, which focuses on taxing consumption rather than income. Hobbes explained why this would be more fair. A consumption-based tax system would also level the playing field for Americans trying to decide whether to save or spend that extra dollar.

The most exciting proposal to rebuild America's tax code is the unlimited saving allowance (USA) tax, which Senators Sam Nunn and Pete Domenici have advanced. The USA tax was introduced into the policy debate most recently in late 1992. It was the centerpiece of a bold and influential report issued by the Strengthening of America Commission, established by the Center for Strategic and International Studies (CSIS).[13]

This type of sweeping reform might take a couple of years to accomplish in Washington. For the near term, however, there are at least two quick fixes that will move America in the right direction, toward ending the bias against saving and investment.

The first is to reduce the capital gains tax rate, while indexing all capital gains for inflation. The capital gains reduction would lighten the heavy burden on savers imposed by our current income tax code and unlock capital in the U.S. economy to flow to the most productive uses. Indexing would end the taxation of inflation-created "profits," ensuring that the capital gains tax bite applies only to asset price increases above and beyond inflation. This would stop the current, unfair practice of taxing Americans for asset price increases that simply reflect economy-wide price increases rather than any real appreciation in the value of their property.

The second change is to expand individual retirement accounts (IRAs). The tax-deductibility of IRAs offsets the double taxation of saving created by the current tax code. Policymakers should reopen IRAs to all taxpayers, raise the contribution limits, and allow these saving vehicles to be used for more than retirement (for example, home purchase or education funding). Another simple, but worthwhile, change: give Americans an easy way to direct money to these accounts, by having the IRS offer to send their tax refunds directly to an IRA.

Desirable as they are, the improvements just described work at the margin of the tax code. Our ultimate vision should be a move to the USA tax. That would eliminate the tax bias in favor of consumption once and for all, by changing the basis of our tax system: instead of levying taxes based on income, the USA tax would levy taxes based on consumption. How? By allowing individuals a tax deduction for the share of income they save and allowing businesses a deduction for all of their new capital investment.

For individuals, the basics of the USA tax would be familiar. They would still receive an annual tax return, which allowed for various exemptions and included a table of tax brackets and rates that increased with income. Despite the surface familiarity of the new tax system, however, its impact would be radically different. Rather than taxing income, the USA tax would be based on consumption. When tax season rolled around, American families would total up their annual cash inflow from all sources—wages, dividends, capital gains, interest, proceeds from asset sales, and so forth—and then subtract the amount they saved that year. After this simple subtraction, the family would be left with a figure equal to their consumption (that is, income minus saving equals consumption). This measure of consumption is what the USA tax would be levied on.

In effect, the USA tax would create something like a universal and unlimited IRA for every family. All Americans would be able to deduct *all* their annual savings from the amount of money subject to federal income tax.

For businesses, the USA tax would replace the current corporate income tax with a cash-flow tax. To calculate the money subject to tax, businesses would simply add up all their sales during the year and subtract the cost of all purchases. Importantly, the cash-flow tax would allow investments in plant, equipment, and inventory to be fully expensed in the year they are made, rather than depreciated over many years. This change would create a powerful new incentive for productive investment in capital equipment.

Although the USA tax is consumption based, it should *not* be confused with the often discussed value-added tax (VAT). The VAT is a consumption tax generally levied at the point of transaction—added to individual purchases made by families and businesses. While VATs are common in the European Community and many other places, establishing a VAT in the U.S. would demand an enormous, costly new administrative machinery. Another problem: the VAT is regressive. Although the USA tax also taxes consumption, it can easily be made as progressive as desired, by imposing different tax rates on high earners (that is, high consumers) and offering generous personal deductions and exemptions to lighten the load on families struggling to get by.

One other attractive tax reform idea deserves mention: the flat tax that has been proposed by Richard Armey, the House majority leader. While they differ in mechanics, the flat tax and the USA tax share broad common ground. Most importantly, both are designed to eliminate the double taxation of saving and investment. The Armey flat tax would do this by excluding all interest, dividends, and capital gains from an individual's taxable income.

The USA tax—with the explicit deduction for savings taxpayers would make each year—offers a slightly more powerful way to get all Americans thinking about saving more. Yet the Armey flat tax certainly deserves support because, like the USA tax, it focuses attention on exactly the right policy question: how can we boost saving and investment in the American economy?

The USA tax would restore strong incentives for American businesses to invest and for American households to save. In the process, it would combat our saving crisis on both fronts, spurring the buildup of capital to increase growth of the U.S. economy, and encouraging American families to stash away more of their income for future use. The USA tax would get all this done by going back to the central concept advanced by Hobbes: a tax code focused on what people take from society—in the form of consumption—rather than what they contribute to the economy by saving and investing.

Conclusion

Throughout my business career, I have been proud to be known as an optimist. And it has served me well, especially because I worked for a firm known for its bullishness. But my unwavering confidence in the future has never come from donning rose-colored glasses. It has been rooted in one belief: as long as we can recognize the obstacles that confront us, we can figure out how to surmount them.

America faces serious economic challenges today. The answers are not all easy. But I have no doubt this nation and its leaders will ultimately do the right thing and address the threats to our economic future.

At the same time, we cannot let ourselves get so wrapped up in diagnosing America's ills that we lose sight of the exceptional strengths that have enabled our people to turn a wilderness into an economic and military superpower. The greatest of these strengths? That facet of American culture touched on by Frederick Jackson Turner in his timeless essay on the significance of the frontier: "Since the days when the fleet of Columbus sailed into the waters of the New World, America has been another name for opportunity."[14]

This nation has always been about opportunity and individual initiative. Our economic success has not been built on our vast markets, plentiful natural resources, or even our extraordinary capital base. America's real strategic asset is more obvious: its people. The triumph of the United States is a tribute to what individuals can achieve when they have the freedom to dream and the opportunity to succeed.

A market economy like ours is built on big ideas and sheer determination. No one can plan its future or predict where it is going; it lives on adrenaline. If I were a policymaker in Washington, I would be much less worried about "perfecting" the American economy than about smothering it with ill-advised policies adopted in the name of good intentions.

Since the early days of our history, we have had enough respect for the genius of our people and the potency of the spirit of enterprise to recognize that all that is needed to build a great nation is to inspire millions of individuals to pursue their own American dream. Whether we are talking about the Wright Brothers, Steven Jobs, or a million unknown American heroes, the formula for economic success endures: if we can preserve the spirit of enterprise and hold on to the vision of the American dream, the twenty-first century is bound to be another American Century.

Notes

1. Ludwig Max Goldberger, *Land of Unlimited Possibilities: Observations on Economic Life in the United States of America* (New York: Brentano's, 1903).
2. These data are from a study conducted by Frank I. Luntz for Hudson Institute, published in a Hudson Institute report entitled "The American Dream: Renewing the Promise," Indianapolis, Indiana, December 1994.
3. United States General Accounting Office, *Prompt Action Necessary to Avert Long-Term Damage to the Economy* (Washington, D.C.: U.S. Government Printing Office, June 1992), 59.
4. Council of Economic Advisers, *Economic Report of the President* (Washington, D.C., U.S. Government Printing Office, January 1993), 225.
5. Joseph M. Anderson, "The Wealth of U.S. Families in 1991 and 1993," Capital Research Associates, Bethesda, Maryland, December 1994. Dr. Anderson's definition of "net financial assets" includes checking, saving, and retirement accounts, including 401(k) accounts, plus stocks, bonds, and mutual funds, less unsecured debt (such as credit card debt) and stock margin debt. Employer pension fund accruals are not included in "net financial assets."
6. Alexis de Tocqueville, *Democracy in America* (Garden City, N.Y.: Doubleday, 1969), part I, chapter 18.
7. Eugene C. Steuerle and Jon M. Bakija, *Retooling Social Security for the Twenty-First Century* (Washington, D.C.: Urban Institute Press, 1994), 1.
8. Lawrence B. Lindsey, "The Big Black Hole," *Forbes*, November 21, 1994, 42.
9. These data are from the Luntz Research Companies and Mark Siegel, survey of five hundred Americans age eighteen to thirty-five, conducted for The Third Millennium, September 1994.
10. This section relies on insights provided by Dr. Harvey Rosen, professor of economics, Princeton University, and by Dr. Carolyn Weaver, director of Social Security and Pension Studies at the American Enterprise Institute. For some of their views on Social Security reform, see Harvey S. Rosen, *Public Finance*

(Chicago: Irwin, 1995), 211–13; Carolyn L. Weaver, "Social Security Investment Policy: What Is It and How Can It Be Improved?" American Enterprise Institute, Washington, D.C., August 1994; and Carolyn L. Weaver, "Social Security Reform After the 1983 Amendments: What Remains To Be Done?" American Enterprise Institute, Washington, D.C., May 1994.

11. Eugene C. Steuerle and Jon M. Bakija, op. cit., 290.
12. Lawrence B. Lindsey, op cit.
13. While the general idea of a consumed-income tax is based on decades of academic economic research, the version discussed here, called the "savings-exempt income tax," emerged from work by the Center for Strategic and International Studies' Strengthening of America Commission (see the commission's *First Report,* issued in 1992). For additional information, see Murray Weidenbaum, *The Savings-Exempt Income Tax* (St. Louis: Center for the Study of American Business, Washington University, July 1994); Laurence S. Seidman, "A Better Way to Tax," *Public Interest* 114 (Winter 1994); and Peter M. Taylor, "Savers' Tax Relief: Revisiting a Good Idea," *National Tax Journal* 46, no. 3 (September 1993).
14. Frederick Jackson Turner, "The Significance of the Frontier in American History," *The Frontier in American History* (New York: Henry Holt and Company, 1920).

Part VI

Domestic Concerns

Chapter Fourteen

The Social Safety Net

Robert A. Sirico

Every society includes a large and ever-changing group of people who are not in a position to be completely independent, whether physically, economically, mentally, or spiritually. They require the help of others. Children, the elderly, the sick and infirm, those who suffer mental and spiritual debilitations, those who are victims of unfortunate circumstances in family and professional life—they all require our aid. Many of these people are also poor, even if that is more often a symptom of their problem than a cause. Our society does not take the attitude once predominant in the ancient world, that the weak may not be worthy of our attention. Whatever the cause of people's weakness, we recognize our moral obligation to intervene, to have compassion, to act charitably, and to give of ourselves.

The philosopher John Rawls asks us to put ourselves behind a "veil of ignorance" and imagine that we could be any person in society, whether a well-paid and secure corporate executive or an unskilled person without a home who is unsure where his next meal will come from.[1] It is an interesting mental exercise. Rawls suggests that we seek the kind of society in which, no matter where we end up on the socioeconomic and generational ladder, we can be assured of basic rights to life, to liberty, and to the pursuit of happiness.

A decent society does indeed need structures to assure everyone of these rights, and surely a social safety net of some kind is essential. But what kind? For several generations, when Americans have thought about charity and welfare, we have thought of the federal welfare state—a vast apparatus consisting of more than a hundred programs, involving millions of workers in tax-funded bureaucracies, costing as much as $350 billion per year, and designed mainly to enhance the *economic* standing of the recipients. Although Americans are a very charitable people, the size and scope of the federal effort have led many to believe that the social safety net is sufficiently secure; thanks to government intervention, those in need require little of our private attention.

At the same time, there is wide public recognition of the omnipresent and multifarious failures of the welfare state, failures which have caused political movements from the Right and Left to seek fundamental reform. The social safety net, despite the best intentions of its architects and defenders, has in fact become a monstrous bureaucratic machine that eats both lives and property. Many people with entrenched interests in preserving the present system will resist this conclusion, but the average voter is not among them. Observe the fate of the Clinton administration's health care proposal. As it came to be viewed as a big-government solution to economic dislocation in health care, its fate was sealed, no matter how good the intentions of the plan's designers. Big government no longer sells, and for this reason, among others, change is inevitable in many of our accustomed arrangements. The giant welfare apparatus we have come to know all too well has probably played itself out; it is no longer compatible with American ideals. Judging from present trends in public philosophy, the general direction of reform will be away from dependence toward independence, away from Washington toward local communities, away from government solutions toward private ones.

As we begin to reform the welfare system—a process that is likely to last for years—let us reflect on the ends we seek to achieve and the means we must invoke to bring about those ends. The gospel tells us that the needy cannot be overlooked, and indeed must be served, in every society, here or abroad. As people of faith, we would not be fulfilling our dominion covenant (our mandate to use the earth on God's terms) if we were to ignore them. I would go so far as to say that a social order must be judged by the way those most in need, who are so by no fault of their own, are treated by others.[2] Likewise the system of economics—meaning the manner in which social resources are used and allocated—must be judged on the same basis.

Our society has been so infused with this ethic, which is essentially western, that almost everyone agrees with it, including social philosophers and theologians. People must not be left out, forgotten by society, denied opportunity, or ignored by the economic system, especially by those who have been blessed with wealth.

But beyond this point, I am afraid, the consensus falls apart. On ultimate ends, people agree. The dispute is on the means. Is it appropriate to deal with poverty and suffering solely through the coercive apparatus of the welfare state, the philosophy of statism and socialist democracy, or some other arrangement of government intrusion? Or is the natural order of liberty, created by free people within the overall structure of an entrepreneurial economy, exercising compassion within their communities and localities, to be preferred as the primary—and normative—means of help?

In thirty years of experience, we have learned that simply wanting to help the unfortunate is not enough to ensure that they will in fact be helped. Remember that, in the name of the poor and oppressed, governments all over the world have inflicted a tremendous amount of suffering on their people during this century. The Soviets ruled for seventy-four years in the name of the proletariat, while impoverishing an economy and culture to an extent unknown in world history. So it is in many Latin American, African, and western nations. Good intentions for the poor and oppressed, if in fact that is what the intentions were, have gone sorely awry.

If we are to help the poor and establish an authentic social safety net that really works, we must do more than will it with our hearts. We must also use our heads. I am not convinced the federal government has done much good for those most in need, in our time or any time. But the harm it has caused is incalculable. In fact, most important improvements in the lives of the least well off in society have been a result of two major forces: first, general improvement in the standard of living resulting from free exchange in markets combined with entrepreneurial initiative; and, second, the work of private charity exercised on a local level by people who understand the needs of those who genuinely require help. This manner of helping the poor and promoting the common good gets far less attention than the governmental kind. Because this method of social improvement is not designed by anyone in particular, or embodied in a particular program or agency, we tend to overlook it. Yet it is these largely unheralded remedies for human suffering that are most effective. Private solutions may not have the glamour of a new "jobs program" or be featured in press conferences, but they ultimately do more good.

I have had wide experience in working with charities, including homeless shelters, AIDS hospices, medical clinics, soup kitchens, meals-on-wheels, homes for unwed mothers, hospitals that serve the poor and elderly, and more. I have witnessed much suffering and pain on the part of those in need. And I have witnessed heroic acts of charity and generosity, as well as even more heroic acts of courage to overcome terrible odds.

But in my years of the ministry, the acts of charity I have witnessed that have really worked, that have actually met human needs, have been primarily those that rely on the voluntary efforts of people who care, not on programs administered from Washington, D.C. Nor does it take years of experience to come to this conclusion. We all know this intuitively, from what we read in the papers, and from reflecting on our own patterns of behavior. When any of us is in trouble of any sort, who are we more likely to call? A federal or state agency? Or a family member, local religious body or institution, or caring community group?

Among the least noticed effects of government programs is an increase in the price of charity itself, such that it is currently far more expensive to help people in need than it otherwise would be. The welfare state increases the cost of charity in two ways. First, government programs are inherently less efficient than private-sector provision, owing to the lack of institutional incentives to save on costs. It is no accident that cost overruns are endemic to government programs; it is a consequence of the nature of government itself, especially government that is distant from the intended beneficiaries. Second, government welfare perpetuates and even generates poverty by subsidizing it. Thus there are more "poor" people to be served by government programs because the programs themselves create incentives to become or remain jobless and to stay on the dole.

Health Care

This effect is not limited to government provision for the poor. It is apparent in any enterprise in which the government heavily involves itself, with health care constituting a classic case. When the Clinton administration was pushing its first version of health care reform, it often decried the rising costs of health care. Indeed, those costs make it difficult for anyone without insurance to "self-insure" against sudden and serious illness, especially anyone with limited financial means. But the Clinton administration failed to give a coherent explanation of why health costs have been rising. (It often blamed technological advances.)

The administration should have mentioned the excesses of Medicaid and Medicare, among the costliest and fastest-growing programs the federal government has ever undertaken. These programs not only put upward pressure on health care prices; they also encourage people to "overconsume" professional health care at the expense of preventive care. Another culprit is the linkage of health care provision to employment, which buffers consumers, even those in higher income brackets, from even knowing the cost of their consumption.

If these programs could be restructured so that they did not drive up the overall costs of health care, it would be all to the good. Many health care reform proposals have been on the table for several years, and—to the extent that they rely on individual choice as opposed to employer mandates and limitless, zero-price service—they are an improvement over the present system. The best way to rein in health care costs is to focus on the aspects of the system (notably zero-price service and employment-linked benefits) that are exerting upward pressure on prices.

We need not assert, as the Clinton administration did, that the way to health care utopia is through some sort of socialist planning. We need to seek ways to make the current system more market oriented, not less. Health care is not, after all, immune from the laws of supply and demand. It is as essential as housing and food, and the allocation of health care should be no more socialized than our present manner of allocating housing and food resources. Market-oriented reforms will make health care less expensive for all Americans and make it possible for the private sector to deliver better care at less expense to the most needy.

For this to be practicable, we must imagine private alternatives to government-controlled health care that will still meet the needs of those who cannot afford coverage. Under a market arrangement, not everyone would be guaranteed health care, but coverage would be in the reach of poor people if we eliminated the waste and abuse of the current system. Through tax policy, the government can also make it easier for private charitable organizations to provide health care for needy Americans. As we take steps toward greater privatization, new institutions will arise to answer the demand for coverage. Under the present arrangement, that demand is masked and the prospects for new institutional providers are squelched because the current system offers coverage blindly, without reference to need or cost.

Two potential mechanisms hint at a workable beginning to reform. First, with suitable tax incentives, private charities could develop medical IRAs for low-income individuals, with funding from nonprofit agencies. This would inject some responsible planning and foresight into a system that offers disincentives for seeking preventive care and incentives for milking heath care benefits for all they are worth. Second, as health care costs became more manageable, businesses could be offered tax incentives to take indigent people on their payrolls. How many they took would depend on the size of the business. As government disappears from the map of socialized planning, private institutions—including businesses—will have to step in and take the lead in addressing the new needs and realities. Market forces will ensure that we adapt quickly. Although these mechanisms for adding market elements to our health care system are no cure-alls, they are examples of the kind of fresh thinking about health care we need to engage in.

The Most Effective Welfare Program

The most effective welfare program of all is a growing economy. People who are able should become part of the economy's complex division of labor, thereby offering their unique talents to their neighbors and promoting the social process of economic production.

Economic liberty and the social forces associated with it make a rise in the general standard of living more likely and personal desperation and social deprivation less likely. The achievements of free enterprise since the Industrial Revolution have been enormous. In free enterprise, private property constitutes an institutional environment where each person can own and control the personal space around him. The private quality of private property is not primarily exclusionary; rather, it demarcates predictability and stability for the common destination of goods. The institutional setting constituted by private property is to be contrasted with one in which the property owner is defined as a collective entity such as the state. The purpose of property is not to acquire for oneself, but to serve others. In a free market economy, serving others is the principal use of property and the wealth it generates.

Some people say that wealth comes through using up natural resources, exploiting others, or making purely technological innovations. But these routes are the exception, not the rule, under free enterprise. The right of exchange itself is the major contributor to prosperity. Any time a market transaction takes place, goods or services of a lesser value are traded for goods or services of a higher value. If people agree to this exchange voluntarily, everyone involved in the exchange is better off. It is the great unappreciated fact of voluntary economic exchange that it allows people to trade a less desirable state of affairs for a more desirable one.

People must be secure in their property and the results of their exchanges in order for these institutions to contribute to the social good. When contracts are not enforced, the value of wealth in general begins to go down. A banker cannot lend money if there are no dependable ways of enforcing the obligations of all involved in the transaction. A laborer will not work for a business unless he or she knows in advance what the terms of remuneration are. Even charity must rely on contract.

The economic system appropriate to a free and compassionate society must also reward creative liberty, or what Pope John Paul II has called the right to private initiative.[3] Every person, by being created in the image and likeness of God, has within his heart and mind a capacity for thinking in new ways, for renewing the space around him, and for improving society. This desire which exists within us, and which virtue requires that we cultivate, is a reflection of a primary attribute of God as creator. In economics, this creative capacity is called entrepreneurship.

We are accustomed to calling charity work voluntarism, as in, "I am volunteering my time at the soup kitchen." And certainly this term applies, but not *only* in this context. "Voluntary" describes something undertaken without compulsion or coercion. In free enterprise, all labor and entrepreneurship are undertaken without compulsion or coercion. All trade is voluntary and all work is voluntary. Free enterprise and contract enforcement allow for the flourishing of a fully voluntary society, one where none of our labors are employed without our consent. The free enterprise system—different from all other, coercive systems—is the economic basis of a free society.

The institutions of free enterprise have permitted vast increases in wealth over the last centuries. We have benefited so greatly that even our standards of what we call "poor" have changed. Consider an illustration. A family has no indoor toilet and no running water. They have to use an outhouse, and have to boil water from far away just to get a drink or take a shower. Would this family qualify as poor? Probably. Is there a moral obligation to care for them, to provide for their well-being? What if this charity fails? Should the government come in to care for them and guarantee the bare minimum standards of sanitary conditions? The description I just gave applied to more than one-third of all American households in 1940. That is not in the eighteenth or nineteenth century, but 1940. Only 1 percent of Americans are in a similar situation today. It was not a massive government program administered from Washington that changed matters. It was an entrepreneurial economy.[4]

As we reform welfare, we need to reinforce these essential institutions—private property, free exchange, contract enforcement, and enterprise. Market restrictions such as the minimum wage, excessive licensure restrictions, high taxes, and job-killing regulations have effectively shut many out of markets in which they should be key participants.[5] Markets and property are the foundation on which true charity ultimately rests. When Aristotle considered the merits and demerits of collective ownership, he pointed out that the first casualty of common ownership is charity. "The abolition of private property," he wrote in *The Politics*, "will mean that no man will be seen to be liberal and no man will ever do any act of liberality; for it is in the use of articles of property that liberality is practised."[6] In order to provide the help that the less fortunate require, we must have sufficient property to make it possible. One of the many tragic effects of the welfare state has been to drain private capital that could have gone toward helping others invest in future prosperity.

Families

The most frustrating and deep-rooted problem of our society today is illegitimacy, and its pernicious consequences can be seen most clearly among teenagers who give birth out of wedlock. Illegitimacy—which has increased more than 400 percent since 1960—is the greatest contributor to the breakdown of the two-parent family. This trend is tearing the fabric of our society, and it is critical that we take radical measures, absent excessive government involvement, to restore the family unit as the organic extension of the natural order of private life. The family must be reclaimed as the fundamental unit of society. While there are certainly thousands of stories of heroic single mothers, most of these women would admit that their condition is not ideal. Choosing their lot in life from behind the Rawlsian veil, they would see the dependency and social devastation that follow single motherhood as undesirable. There is no reason to celebrate illegitimacy and family breakdown; these are probably the most tragic consequences of centralized, state-run, materialistic approaches to poverty and helplessness.

The links are quite clear between a missing parent in a child's life and poverty, illegal drug use, failure in school, violent crime, gang activity, and suicide. The single-parent family can no longer be considered simply one among many social norms, as the counterculture has tended to regard it. Instead, it must be considered a regrettable outcome of unfortunate circumstances. This experiment in family engineering, in short, has continued long enough.

Illegitimacy is not merely a technical problem, but also a moral one. To the extent that the federal government encourages out-of-wedlock births with its ill-conceived policies, it is morally culpable. When the government subsidizes out-of-wedlock births, it removes the structure of social and economic incentives and disincentives that serve to discourage promiscuity and irresponsibility.

While I hold the federal government partially responsible for the soaring illegitimacy rates since the beginning of the Great Society, we need not ask federal officials to solve the problem themselves. The federal government should not now try to tinker with its welfare programs to punish women who give birth to children outside of marriage. The problems are moral, but the federal government is not, and cannot be, an effective moral teacher.

The Welfare State and Private Charity

The very nature of the welfare state—with its bureaucratic, one-size-fits-all policies—prevents it from helping individuals become responsible parents and citizens. Indeed, it takes a much deeper understanding of human needs to encourage such responsibility. The very size and scope of the welfare state, moreover, deter private citizens from becoming personally involved in problems like illegitimacy. The presence of the welfare state diminishes their contact with and sensitivity to those in need. Under the current system, bad charity has driven out good. If and when bad charity comes to an end, we can expect an explosion of interest in helping those in need. We must begin to have faith in the good efforts of the American people.

Some people say that what is called the "private sector" cannot take care of the problem. It is necessary but not sufficient, some say. But we have forgotten just how powerful the forces of genuine charity are in American society. For too long, the federal government has crowded out private solutions. Once the government's budgetary woes begin to remind people of their own responsibilities to others, we will be astonished at the outpouring of energy. Government has no monopoly on compassion. Indeed, government is compassion's least able practitioner.

Let's allow and encourage real charities, not bureaucracies, to take on the illegitimacy problem, along with the myriad of social difficulties engendered by it. Along with material assistance for mothers who are pregnant out of wedlock, charities can administer individual care that is catered to a woman's specific circumstances, needs, abilities, and character.

Others say that lowering the dollar amount of parental aid will lead to an increase in abortion. That's not likely. Abortion is not a cost-free decision. It is the most difficult and painful decision a woman can make. Far from encouraging abortion, ending the present system of subsidies will discourage promiscuity and promote a more responsible approach to parenthood itself. For a person of free will, it will clarify the issue of whether to risk pregnancy in the first place. It will reinforce sexual restraint. We cannot, of course, guarantee perfect results in the near term. But we can stop the federal government from continuing to expand programs that are encouraging the current social crisis.[7]

The alternative to the current system of welfare is to organize the care of at-risk young people in a way that allows the influence of religious values. The government need only allow this to happen; it need not promote it. Federal benefits carry no concrete responsibilities on the part of the recipient; if this were changed, poor women who are pregnant out of wedlock would turn to more local organizations, which include church-run charities.

Think of the change in incentives that would result. If another child means no hardship and a bigger check, it is easy to see why this is not wholly undesirable from one point of view. Yet, if the individual's circumstance is being closely monitored by a secular charity or church ministry, the individual becomes acutely aware that sexual irresponsibility carries a price.

The church very likely views sex outside of marriage as a sin, and will not provide services without admonishing the sinner or requiring some type of work in return. Being an organic part of a church ministry makes the individual accountable to those who are providing the aid. Close contact with the providers discourages irresponsible behavior.

This model relies on the classical view of moral tutoring, which has two dimensions: we abstain from immoral behavior because we fear its effects, and because we love the good. Church-run charities hope to instill a love of good in the people they help. But they also rely on clients' fear of being reprimanded or losing services. Fear and love are both motivators. While the latter is a preferable motive, the former also works.

Newt Gingrich has praised Marvin Olasky's book, *The Tragedy of American Compassion*. It is indeed a great book. It details many of the thousands of charitable organizations that thrived in the nineteenth century to deal with social problems not unlike those we confront today. Let's look at just one case. The New York Association for Improving the Condition of the Poor (AICP) was established in the 1840s, and related societies appeared in Baltimore, Boston, Chicago, St. Louis, and other cities.[8] It was founded in response to the "indiscriminate charity" of government programs, a result of government being "bound to relieve all not otherwise legally provided for."[9] Because government programs were small, the private system could be large and effective. The Baltimore AICP, for example, had 2,000 volunteers who made 8,227 visits in 1891 to 4,025 families.[10] Half of these families were headed by widows who tended to receive material aid, while most of the others were headed by able-bodied men who were counseled on how to break addictions to alcohol or opium, and on how to get a job.

AICP promised to "aid all those whom it can physically and morally elevate, and no others." Its contributors gave of their own resources to aid people authentically, and not simply to reinforce poverty through material subsidy. Its founders said that if the AICP failed in this "discrimination" and had "no higher aim than the Almshouse, why should it exist at all? and why should those already heavily taxed for the public poor entrust funds to this charity?"[11]

AICP's rule was that relief should be a temporary state of affairs. "Many once learning to lean on public or associated relief, not only neglect to exert the powers God has given them, but continue to call for aid long after it is right," the group wrote. This leads on the broad road to pauperism. Individuals or societies can hardly guard too watchfully against it."[12] The group emphasized training and improvement of the poor over material relief. Its volunteers visited homes to "guide in matters of religious observance" and to encourage and train the families to be thrifty, hardworking, and temperate.

In general, it promoted four key principles: first, poverty must be distinguished from pauperism, which is an "unnecessary dependence"; second, entitlement relief tends to pauperize because it offers disincentives for independence and discipline; third, there exists a moral obligation for those financially independent to become "personally involved with the poor"; and fourth, those who are poor due to their own character flaws must show that they are willing to change the behavior or thinking patterns that have kept them impoverished. If they did not show that they were willing to change, then the volunteer had to leave them for a while, return to renew the offer, and be willing to leave again if the individuals' "hearts had not changed."[13]

Robert M. Hartley, secretary of AICP for over thirty years, saw alcoholism as a large part of the problem, and saw in it a much deeper collection of moral and spiritual problems. In order to raise a person out of poverty, he sought to "remove the causes; and these being chiefly moral—whatever subsidiary appliances may be used—they admit only moral remedies." Hartley quoted St. Paul's Letter to the Thessalonians: "We hear that some of you are idle. They are not busy; they are busy-bodies. Such people we command and urge in the Lord Jesus Christ to settle down and earn the bread they eat." AICP leaders knew that helping to elevate the poor was stressful and often overwhelming work, and that many would be discouraged from participating in it. They realized that to most volunteers the effort would seem worthwhile only if the goals went beyond providing for material needs to include spiritual uplift as well.[14]

Comparable institutions are today not as large, nor do they thrive as they once did, precisely because they have been supplanted by government programs. But it is not just such private institutions that need to be recovered. It is also the philosophy that AICP and others used to assist people in time of need. Since the advent of the welfare state, and during its growth over the decades, we have forgotten basic facts from the past that were once commonplace among social workers and professional charity workers.

Past Wisdom

Mary Conyngton's 1909 book *How to Help* was a standard reference manual for many years. In addition to being a wonderful manual of practice, it pointed to a number of principles that should guide any "who contemplate undertaking any charitable work, even though his projected activity is small." The first is "seriousness of purposes." Charity work "means influence upon the lives of others, for good or for ill, and no one has the right to touch another's life carelessly or lightly."[15]

Another qualification is "a sympathetic imagination, which will permit the worker to share the point of view of those he is endeavoring to help. Whoever goes among the poor with a preconceived idea of what is the cause of their trouble and what should be its cure," she tells us, "is liable to meet many disappointments."[16] In a point that could be made against Washington's bureaucracies, she says: "the poor obstinately refuse to form one class, all amenable to the same treatment." Because the poor come from every nationality, and because their styles of life and standards of behavior differ widely, the solutions must be specifically tailored to the individuals in need.

Conyngton also mentions the need for "a sense of proportion." We should seek not perfect solutions, but "the highest practicable good attainable in each case." This requires looking at the long run, not just reaching for the first available, or easiest, answer.

It seems an obvious question: does the federal welfare system display seriousness of purpose, the capacity for imaginative solutions, and a sense of proportion? The answer is obvious, too: it does not. The present system comes up with all the wrong answers. Yet the problem of government aid was also present when Conyngton was writing. In a section that could have been labeled "How Not to Help" she has some strong comments about public aid.[17] "So long as an applicant can do anything for himself, or his friends can give help, it is better to refuse him public assistance, leaving private charity to piece out his insufficiencies." The reasons are several. "Public relief authorities must deal with large numbers of applicants, with whom their relation is purely official and formal." Thus "it is not possible" for them to "become so well acquainted with the circumstances of the individual case as can the agents of private societies," who "bring more of the personal element into their dealings." There is also the danger that the recipient of public funds will be used as "political capital," she says.[18]

Then there is the largest danger of all, one that has become most conspicuous in our day. "Many people," Conyngton says, "are inclined to look upon public help as a right and to apply for it without hesitation, while they would regard themselves as a losing caste if they appealed to private aid." That is the good thing about private charity, and the essential moral hazard associated with public charity. (She also notes cases in Brooklyn and Philadelphia when the number of poor *declined* after the abolition of public relief.)

The Art of Helping People Out of Trouble, a 1924 book by Karl Deschweinitz, confirms how important it is that charity always take account of a person's self-worth and attempt to preserve his self-respect. Otherwise, charity may cause "the humiliation of the man who is obliged to confess his failure to meet" his obligations "by taking as a gift the livelihood that other men are earning for themselves. It matters not whether the amount of money involved be great or small. His self respect has been invaded."[19] When a person has financial difficulties, says Deschweinitz, whoever helps him should do as much as possible to help without actually giving money as a gift. "Perhaps he can be aided to find more remunerative employment. Perhaps a wiser household management will fit his present resources to his needs." Only after every other path has been tried should someone in need be given cash, and then only to "stimulate his sense of responsibility."[20]

Again, the present government welfare system seems to reverse these priorities, giving money first, then fostering dependency, forgetting entirely about self-respect, and discouraging a path to independence. The point here is not simply to condemn federal welfare but to highlight the long tradition of private provision, and to suggest how much more effective it can be than the current system. Just getting government out of the way as a competitor to the genuine exercise of compassion would be a good start.

Subsidiarity

There is a principle that should guide any efforts to reform welfare. It is called "subsidiarity." The concept is this: those social functions that can be accomplished by a lower order of society should not be usurped by a higher order. When it comes to caring for women who are pregnant out of wedlock, or for anybody with needs, the resources of first resort should be individuals, churches, neighborhoods, towns, and cities. The federal government has failed to solve American family problems. Now it must allow these lower, mediating institutions to take over.

The idea of devolving social responsibility to the states is in keeping with the principle of subsidiarity. It is a step in the right direction. By itself, however, it is not enough. We do not want bureaucracies in Washington to be replaced by equally intrusive government bureaucracies in state capitols. "If you take power and independence from a municipality," Alexis de Tocqueville wrote, "you may have docile subjects but you will not have citizens."[21]

Indeed, the primary font of social power and authority must be in communities. Tocqueville spoke of the brilliance of New England townships, but his observations are applicable to communities in all parts of the land. Communities work because we have a close interest in them and share in their management; we love them because we are part of them and put our labors into them; we invest ourselves in the community, knowing that our futures are intertwined; through the community we understand basic concepts like freedom, justice, order, charity, enterprise, and social harmony; it helps us to generate practical ideas about how to serve others, and the presence of others serves to remind us of our moral obligations.[22]

Can some of the functions of government welfare provision actually be returned to the communities? Can we afford to take the risk that doing so will not work? Tocqueville noted that "a very civilized society finds it hard to tolerate attempts at freedom in a local community; it is disgusted by its numerous blunders and is apt to despair of success before the experiment is finished."[23] We must guard against this tendency. Before we condemn local solutions as unworkable, let's be careful not to compare the likelihood of local success with an idealized—but unrealizable—model of central government programs. The socialists used to condemn the failures of existing capitalism as compared with an idealized socialism. So it is with decentralization. The relevant comparison is between a federal system that has failed, and a humane local system that, though less than perfect, will have the ability to be flexible and learn from its mistakes.

We should remind ourselves: we cannot centrally plan authentic charity any more than we can centrally plan the direction of the economy. We must trust private individuals and rely on the goodness of the American people to reach out to help others, as they will be inspired to do if the government allows more room for the spontaneous actions of the nongovernmental sector. There is no need to expect a dollar-for-dollar replacement of government funds by private funds. That would not be necessary, since private efforts are so effective.

With private charity assuming a greater role, will some people fall through the cracks of the social safety net? The short answer is yes. They also fall through cracks in the existing statist, centralized, expensive welfare system. We cannot create utopia, and one is tempted to quote Jesus about the perpetual presence of the poor in every society. Older people, children, the poor, and the disabled will continue to experience personal suffering and may need assistance that will not always be there.

The issue is not how we can create a perfect world without poverty, but how we can create a system that is most adept at finding those who need help, meeting their needs, and, when possible, helping them to a life of independence. When we evaluate private versus public charity, and fairly consider the merit and demerits of each, we must conclude that the government system has proven a failure.

Must we continue to try to resuscitate a failed system, tinkering with this or that aspect of it for decade after decade, as the Soviets did in trying to make communism work? Or is it time to transfer the obligation and opportunity for caring for people to those who have their best interest at heart and can do the job at far less expense? The answer is clear. The social safety net will never be perfect. But with a greater burden being borne by the private sector, we can make people more aware of their obligation and bring to an end some of the innumerable problems of today's failing system.

The people who are most generous with their time and money in the service of others also tend to be most frustrated with the present system of welfare provision. Those who give are mostly married, employed, college educated parents with small children, according to data from Independent Sector and the U.S. Labor Department. According to analyst Karl Zinsmeister, people politically classified as conservative "are more than twice as likely to volunteer time for the carrying out of good works. They also give more than twice as big a proportion of their annual incomes to charity" than others.[24]

Americans are among the most generous people in the world. Each year, individuals donate $125 billion to philanthropic efforts. Foundations give another $100 billion, and corporations give $8 billion.[25] The first beneficiary of these funds are churches, which are in an excellent position to pick up where the central state leaves off in its charitable provision. Already, ninety million Americans volunteer at least three hours a week at nonprofit groups. Nearly one million nonprofit organizations now exist.[26]

Yet further steps must be taken to increase contributions and allow private charities to flourish. Even when tax deductible, individual and family charitable contributions are made from discretionary income, that is, from funds left over from the family budget. When taxes go up, the choice of where to put the marginal dollar cuts against charitable contributions. Over the last several decades, it has become more difficult to give to private charities and religious bodies of all sorts. Indeed, charitable contributions fell in 1994, according to an Independent Sector report.[27]

In addition to passing tax reforms that will promote economic growth, we need to make charitable giving more financially rewarding. For example, we could allow individuals to deduct 110 percent of their charitable contributions, thereby increasing the incentive to give.[28] Or tax deductions could be replaced with a tax credit, which would allow people to choose to use their money to support either public or private systems of welfare provision.[29]

We also need to make it possible for private and religious charities to minister to those in need without the government regulations that have impeded some innovative efforts in the past. Food, housing, safety, and marketing order regulations (which govern the size and quality of agricultural goods that can be distributed by the private sector) have forced small charities to choose between providing for people and complying with bureaucratic mandates. At the very least, these regulations must be relaxed for smaller charities that serve meals, give shelter to the homeless, and provide counseling services.

Data from 1950 to the present show that when government spending on welfare increases (or the public perceives that it is increasing), the percentage of personal income given to charity decreases. The postwar peak of charitable giving, 2.6 percent of personal income, dates from the beginning of the Great Society. The opposite is also true; charitable donations increase as governments cut back and the public is reminded of its moral obligations to serve others.[30]

The issue is not how to expand the federal welfare state, or even how to make it work better, but how to make private charity an effective alternative that can better achieve our shared goals. Even in health care, individual empowerment through the private sector would appear to be the most desirable path.[31] Whatever policy routes are taken, we should focus on returning responsibility to individuals, churches, neighborhoods, towns, and cities. Every case of family tragedy, dependency, or deprivation is different, and the individuals involved have different resources, abilities, and weaknesses. A faceless bureaucracy cannot take all of these into account. Nor can it encourage moral renewal. What people need is not layers of public agencies, but other human beings who have knowledge of their real needs and a commitment to help them become responsible and independent citizens. The future is with the private sector and its proven ability to help those in need.

Notes

1. John Rawls, *A Theory of Justice* (Cambridge: Harvard University Press, 1971), 136–37.
2. National Conference of Catholic Bishops, "Economic Justice for All: Catholic Social Teaching and the U.S. Economy" (Washington, D.C.: United States Catholic Conference, Inc., 1986), v.
3. Pope John Paul II, "Centesimus Annus," *Origins,* CNS Documentary Service, Washington, D.C., 1991, chapter 4, section 43.
4. Shelby Siems, "New Report Tracks Fifty Years of American Dream," *Christian Science Monitor,* September 13, 1994, 9.
5. Walter Williams, *The State Against Blacks* (New York: New Press, 1982).
6. Aristotle, *The Politics,* trans. Hugh Tredennick (Cambridge, Mass.: Harvard University Press, 1976), 1263b7.
7. Charles A. Donovan, "Capping Welfare Payments: Subsidizing Illegitimacy Isn't Pro-Life," *Family Policy* (Washington, D.C.: Family Research Council, October 1994).
8. Marvin Olasky, *The Tragedy of American Compassion* (Washington, D.C.: Regnery, 1992), 27–34.
9. Ibid., 27.
10. Ibid., 80.
11. Ibid., 27.
12. Ibid., 49.
13. Ibid., 27–28.
14. Ibid., 27–32.
15. Mary Conyngton, *How to Help: A Manual of Practical Charity* (New York: The MacMillan Company, 1909), 26.
16. Ibid.
17. Ibid., 36.
18. Ibid.
19. Karl Deschweinitz, *The Art of Helping People Out of Trouble* (Boston: Houghton Mifflin Company, 1924), 175.
20. Ibid., 176.
21. Alexis de Tocqueville, *Democracy in America* (Garden City, N.Y.: Doubleday, 1966), 68–69.
22. Ibid., 70.
23. Ibid., 62.
24. Karl Zinsmeister, "Resources to Build a World Without Welfare," *The Washington Times,* January 10, 1995, A17.

25. *Statistical Abstract of the United States* (Washington, D.C.: Government Printing Office, 1994), chart 604.
26. E. Thomas McClanahan, "Nonprofits: 'The First Line of Attack,'" *Orange County Register,* November 23, 1994, M9.
27. Independent Sector, *1994 Report on Non-Profit Organizations* (New York: Independent Sector, 1994).
28. Peter Drucker, quoted in McClanahan, op. cit.
29. John C. Goodman, Gerald W. Reed, and Peter S. Ferrara, *Why Not Abolish the Welfare State?* (Dallas: National Center for Policy Analysis, 1994).
30. Alan Wolfe, *Whose Keeper: Social Science and Moral Obligation* (Berkeley: University of California Press, 1989), 88.
31. John C. Goodman and Gerald L. Musgrave, *Patient Power* (Washington, D.C.: Cato, 1992).

Chapter Fifteen

New Crime Policies for America

John J. DiIulio, Jr.

Crime and the Failure of Representative Democracy

The Promise of American Life is widely regarded as one of the best commentaries on American political thought published in the twentieth century. But as is true of many great or near-great books, Croly's *Promise* has been more quoted than read and more interpreted than understood. Contrary to what many have asserted, Croly did not argue that America needed a strong, centralized national government to promote democracy and equal rights. Metaphorically speaking, Croly's *Promise* is not a waltz composed so that Hamiltonians and Jeffersonians could dance hand in hand.

Rather, as Harvard University's Samuel H. Beer has keenly observed, "Croly's emphasis was on the Hamiltonian purpose of nation-building as a goal different from, but complementary to, Jeffersonian democracy." Croly argued that the Constitution was "made not only by but also for the democratic nation." For Croly, the Constitution derived its authority not from the states but from "the sovereign people. Its purpose was to promote their excellence both as individuals and as a nation."[1]

Yet even Beer's superb analysis of Croly's *Promise* misses the book's most important legacy, namely its tacit restatement of the theory of representative democracy contained in James Madison's contributions to The Federalist Papers, most especially Federalist No. Ten. At a time when other Progressives were calling for fundamental changes in America's constitutional system, Croly neither departed from nor denounced the constitutional vision of Madison.

Madison's constitutional vision has three main parts. First is the belief that, while average citizens lack the time, energy, information, and interest to decide well on public policy, they can make reasonable choices among competing leaders or groups of leaders. Second is the idea that representative institutions should be structured in ways that make them politically and legally resistant to temporary popular majorities but responsive to persistent popular majorities. Third is the prayer that the American republic's size, variety of economic interests, diversity of religious opinions, and constitutional contrivances such as staggered elections will render persistent popular majorities rare and unlikely to threaten either individual liberty or public order. In the language of Federalist No. Ten, the hope is that, whatever the issue around which they form, persistent popular majorities will transcend partial, immoderate, or fleeting ("factional") interests and embody a true concern for "the permanent and aggregate interests of the community," both national and local, public and private.[2]

Beer and many other Crolyites of the World War II generation have long cherished the New Deal as an example of Madisonian representative government at work. As they see it, during the Great Depression, a popular national majority wanted government action on a wide range of social and economic issues. This majority persisted, and government action consistent with popular policy preferences followed. Through acts of the national government, the promise of American life was extended, if only symbolically, to the poor, the working poor, blacks, immigrants, and others who had not previously participated in "the common life of the nation."[3] But the New Dealers did not trample needlessly upon the "first object of Government," which Madison defined as protecting the "diversity in the faculties of men from which the rights of property originate."[4]

Whatever one thinks of this unbenighted Crolyite view of the New Deal in relation to representative democracy, it simply does not work for the Great Society or for the several decades of big-government policies, programs, and personalities that consolidated and extended it. Some of the original leaders of the Great Society, most notably President Lyndon B. Johnson, may have believed that they were merely putting the final stitches in the New Deal's social safety net. From a constitutional perspective, however, they were guilty of advancing the power of government into many areas where there existed no persistent popular majority in support of major national action. Over time, their crisis mongering led to social welfare and tax policies predicated explicitly on the anti-Madisonian notion that "an equal division of property" was a proper end of America's constitutional government rather than an "improper or wicked project" to be avoided at all costs.[5]

Today, however, the greatest domestic threat to the promise of American life and public trust in representative democracy resides not in what government does in realms such as social welfare and tax policy, but in what government has failed to do in response to a persistent public plea for action to protect law-abiding citizens of all races, creeds, colors, incomes, and ages from being victimized by predatory street criminals. Here a persistent popular majority exists. Here the government has sorely failed to heed it.

The American people have never asked government to "solve" the nation's crime problem. Most anticrime efforts in this country have been, and continue to be, private, not public or governmental. They consist of the countless financial, locational, and organizational decisions made each day by families, businesses, and neighborhood groups in an effort to render the environments in which law-abiding people live, work, shop, attend school, and recreate relatively impervious to crime. We lock our doors and install burglar alarms. We tell our teenagers to be careful and to avoid driving through "bad neighborhoods." We relocate our families and our businesses. We watch a neighbor's home when he's on vacation. We hire private security guards. We form neighborhood watch groups. All of these behaviors and numerous others are part of the everyday anticrime regimen of the American people. Were it not for these private anticrime efforts, America's crime problem would be far worse than it is.

With respect to crime control, all that the American people have ever demanded from government, and all that they have been demanding since the mid-1960s, are commonsense policies that result in the detection, arrest, conviction, and punishment of violent and repeat criminals. All they have asked for are policies that do not return persons who assault, rape, rob, burglarize, deal drugs, and murder to the streets without regard for public safety. All they have wanted from their representative democratic institutions are policies that do not positively encourage crime or invite tragedies that could be averted simply by keeping convicted criminals behind bars or under intensive community-based supervision.

In short, for three decades now, a persistent national public majority, one encompassing majorities of citizens in every region of the country and of every demographic description, has merely asked their "proper guardians of the public weal"[6] to do no harm on crime. In a comprehensive review of post-1965 survey research and polling data on crime and how government should respond to it, William G. Mayer concluded:

The conventional wisdom on this issue is that . . . public opinion became increasingly outraged by horror stories about brutal criminals set free on legal technicalities or through the ministrations of misguided social workers. And, in this case, the conventional wisdom turns out to be quite accurate. From the mid-1960s to the late 1980s, there is clear, strong evidence that American public opinion became substantially more conservative in its assessment of how to deal with crime.[7]

Today majorities of both blacks and whites favor the death penalty for persons convicted of first-degree murder; doubt that most violent criminals can be rehabilitated; demand that juveniles who commit violent crimes be treated the same as adults; oppose the legalization of marijuana, cocaine, and other illicit drugs; believe that there is too much graphic violence on television and that it contributes to crime; strongly favor making parole more difficult; and support paying more taxes if necessary to build more prisons and put more cops on the beat.[8]

The problem, however, is that this persistent and broad-based public outcry for sane crime policies has not been heeded by most elected officials and civic leaders. There are, to be sure, many areas of American government where one can find a gap between persistent majority preferences and existing public policies.[9] But the size and duration of the gap with respect to crime is American government's opinion-policy Grand Canyon.

Since the early days of the Great Society, as the American people have become ever more aware of and frustrated by the failure of government to do its share by keeping violent and repeat criminals at bay, politicians have done little more than attempt to pacify the electorate by putting new names on existing revolving-door policies. Meanwhile, radical and liberal judges, journalists, academics, activists, lawyers, and lobbyists have served as apologists for policies that permit convicted criminals in state custody to violate the life, liberty, and property of average citizens. Adding antidemocratic insult to palpable injury, these elites have derided the people's fear of crime as reactionary, lambasted elected officials and other civic leaders who dared to argue in favor of reasonable anticrime policies, and waged an organized, devious, and, until recently, largely successful campaign of anti-incarceration propaganda. At every step along the way, their anti-incarceration agenda has been aided, abetted, and enforced in its particulars by activist judges, who have unfailingly undone the few sound anticrime policies the people and their faithful representatives have managed to etch into federal, state, or local law over the last three decades.

America's crime problem, therefore, must be understood first and foremost as a failure of representative democracy. In the remainder of this essay, I will attempt to document this failure, explain why it has occurred, and summarize its disastrous consequences. By way of conclusion, I will suggest how this failure might be reversed so that crime does not extinguish the new promise of American life and, with it, the light of representative democracy itself.

Crime Fears: Rational, Not Reactionary

There are at least four things to know about crime in America today. First, national victimization rates for many types of property crimes have been declining over the last few years. Still, American citizens of every regional and demographic description are more likely to be victimized by most types of crime today than they were in the 1950s, and far more likely to be victimized by violent crime today than at any time on record (see table 15.1).

Table 15.1
Crime Rates, 1962–92: Offenses Per 100,000 Residents

Year	All Crime	Property	Violent	Murder	Rape	Robbery	Assault
1962	2,019.8	1,857.5	162.3	4.6	9.4	59.7	88.6
1972	3,961.4	3,560.4	401.0	9.0	22.5	180.7	188.8
1982	5,603.6	5,032.5	571.1	9.1	34.0	238.9	289.2
1992	5,660.2	4,902.7	757.5	9.3	42.8	263.6	441.8

Source: *Crime in the United States, 1992 Uniform Crime Reports* (Washington, D.C.: Federal Bureau of Investigation, October 3, 1993), 58; data for 1962 and 1972 supplied upon request by FBI Program Support Section, July 7, 1994. Note: "All crime" includes the categories listed plus burglary, larceny, and motor vehicle theft.

Second, many crimes (some believe more than half of all crimes) are never reported to the police, so that existing data understate the nation's crime problem. The FBI's Uniform Crime Reports (UCR), begun in 1929, are based strictly on a count of crimes reported to state and local law enforcement agencies. Since 1973 the U.S. Bureau of Justice Statistics (BJS) has conducted a National Crime Victimization Survey (NCVS). The NCVS contains data from a nationally representative sample of households and accounts for victimizations whether or not they were reported to the police. But for technical reasons having to do with the design of the NCVS, the NCVS has discounted the actual incidence of and increase in several types of violent crime.[10]

Third, it is clear from both the UCR and the NCVS that black Americans have been, and continue to be, much more likely to be victimized by crime than white Americans, and that most crime in America is intraracial.

According to the NCVS, by 1992 blacks and whites had virtually identical risks of being victimized by personal theft. But the household crimes rate for blacks remained about 33 percent higher than the rate for whites. And in 1992 the violent crime victimization rate for blacks was the highest ever recorded.[11]

Between 1973 and 1992 the rate of violent victimization of young black males (ages twelve to twenty-four) increased about 25 percent, and the average annual rate of handgun victimization was three to four times higher for young black males than it was for young white males.[12] The gap between white and black victimization rates persists across age categories but is especially wide for the young (see fig. 15.1).

Racial disparities in violent crime rates have run highest for murder. In the nation's seventy-five most populous counties in 1988, blacks were 52 percent of all murder victims and 62 percent of all murder defendants, but they were only 20 percent of the general population in these metropolitan jurisdictions.[13] By comparison, whites were 44 percent of all murder victims and 36 percent of all defendants, but they were 77 percent of the general population in these urban areas. About 84 percent of all single-offender violent crimes committed by blacks are committed against blacks, while about 73 percent of all such crimes committed against whites are committed by whites.[14] This intraracial pattern holds most strongly for homicides: about 94 percent of all black murder victims and 76 percent of white victims are killed by someone of the same race.[15]

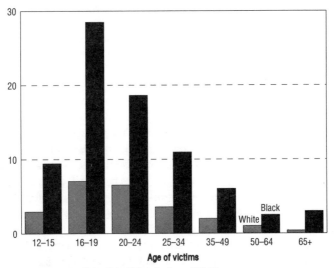

Source: Data drawn from *National Crime Victimization Survey, 1987–92*

Figure 15.1. Number of victimizations per 1,000 population, 1987–92

What do such numbers mean in a particular place? Consider Philadelphia, where 433 people were murdered in 1994, 340 of them black. Blacks were 39 percent of the city's population but 78.5 percent of its murder victims. Only 5 of the 89 murder victims under age twenty were white. Citywide, the number of murders per 100,000 residents was 27.6. But in the predominantly white, working-class Greater Northeast region of the city, the murder rate per 100,000 residents was about 2; in predominantly poor, black North Philadelphia, the rate was 66; and in the heart of North Philadelphia, in an area known to residents and police as "the Badlands," the rate was over 100.[16]

Fourth and finally, certain demographic changes make contemporary America itself, and not just the nation's inner cities, a ticking crime bomb. Alfred Blumstein has calculated that between 1985 and 1992 the rate at which young males murder increased by about 50 percent for whites and tripled for blacks (see fig. 15.2).[17] At the same time, it is virtually certain that by the year 2000 there will be five hundred thousand more American males ages fourteen to seventeen than there are today. Based on numerous crime cohort studies, there is every reason to expect that at least 6 percent of these young males (thirty thousand) will become high-rate offenders and will account for roughly half of all the serious crimes committed by this increment to the cohort, while tens of thousands more of them will become medium- or low-rate offenders and account for the other half.

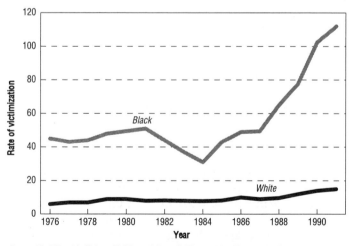

Source: *Alfred Blumstein, "Prisons," in Crime, ed. James Q. Wilson and Joan Petersilia (San Francisco: Institute for Contemporary Studies, 1994), 413, reporting data compiled by Glen Pierce and James Fox of Northwestern University*

Figure 15.2. Male homicide victimization rate per 100,000 for ages 14 through 17

Thus, there is really little good news about crime patterns in America today. James Q. Wilson has observed that as "the costs of crime decline or the benefits increase, as drugs and guns become more available, as the glorification of violence becomes more commonplace, as families and schools lose" whatever little restraining power they have left, at-risk boys become even more crime-prone than their uncles or grandfathers once were.[18]

One certain result of these ongoing demographic and social changes will be a continued increase in random and remorseless youth violence. Another result, almost as certain, will be an increase in the chance that America's crime problem, which remains concentrated in the nation's black inner cities and white lower-class urban neighborhoods, will spill over into America's suburbs and rural areas. To date, that has not happened to a statistically significant degree—but worse is surely yet to come.

Public Awareness

The American people do not know the exact crime statistics, but they do know the reality behind the numbers. For example, while all Americans now feel more threatened by crime than they did in the past, urban Americans feel more threatened than suburban or rural Americans, and urban black Americans feel more threatened than urban white Americans (see fig. 15.3). Moreover, in a recent survey conducted by the Black Community Crusade for Children, black children, who are now far more likely than black adults to be murdered or victimized by many types of violent crime, were asked to state their concerns about children they know. Their top concerns were as follows:[19]

- kids carrying guns (70 percent)
- drugs (68 percent)
- violence in school (68 percent)
- living in a dangerous neighborhood (64 percent)
- involvement with gangs (63 percent)
- involvement with people who are a bad influence (63 percent)

For these kids, for their parents, and for most Americans, street crime is making the promise of American life an impossible dream.

Even those Americans least likely to be victimized by street violence—highly affluent whites and the high- and middle-income elderly—can hear America's crime bomb ticking. They are justly worried about what it means for them, their families, their businesses, and their country.

What these Americans sense is that, for all of the private, corporate, and community-based anticrime initiatives of the last several decades, for all the disposable income spent on security devices, for all the behavioral changes,

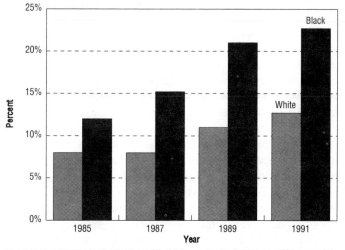

Source: Crime and Neighborhoods *(Washington, D.C.: U.S. Bureau of Justice Statistics, June 1994)*, 1, *reporting data compiled from the American Housing Survey*

Figure 15.3. Crime fears in black and white: Central city residents citing crime as a major neighborhood problem

and for all the neighborhood rallies, crime remains a real and growing problem in America. Having pushed the envelope on nongovernmental efforts to combat crime, Americans are awakening to the grim fact that they have gained only marginal and temporary relief from murder and mayhem.

It is no surprise, therefore, that Americans are now demanding that the government meet them at least halfway in doing whatever can be done via police, prosecutors, judges, and corrections officials to take back the streets. The much publicized rise of crime as the number one political issue in 1993 and 1994 reflects the public's growing awareness that existing government policies simply do not protect law-abiding citizens from violent and repeat criminals.

Even now, however, the American people are not fully aware of how utterly perverse government's crime policies are.

Revolving-Door Policies

One reason for this lack of public awareness is that the federal and state governments generally do not collect, and the elite print and broadcast media almost never report, the full range of facts about government's revolving-door policies.

For example, if you want to know how many federal and state sex offenders receive what type of "treatment" behind bars, you can easily find the answer in the relevant federal government sourcebook.[20] But if you want to know the ages or other objective characteristics of rape victims, you will discover that thirty-six states do not even keep such statistics.

If you want to know how much time convicted murderers spend in prison on average, you can consult the latest federal government report on felony sentences in the United States (the answer is about nine years).[21] But if you want to know what fraction of persons convicted of murder in any given year were on probation, parole, or pretrial release at the time that they committed the murder(s) for which they were convicted, you can forget it. The federal government keeps data that enable one skilled in statistical analysis to make tentative estimates. But there is no national data set on murderers who have been freed by the system, and many states do not keep any sort of relevant tallies either.[22] At present, therefore, we do not know precisely how many of the over 350,000 murders that took place in this country from 1980 to 1994 were committed by people on probation, parole, or pretrial release at the time that they did the murder(s) for which they were convicted.

Based on existing data, I would estimate that about one-third of those convicted for murder between 1980 and 1994 were on probation, parole, or pretrial release when they committed the crime. If this estimate is in the ballpark, then freed offenders were responsible for thousands of post-1980 murders, most of which could have been averted had the criminals served just 85 percent of their sentenced time in confinement (in the case of probationers and parolees) or been detained (in the case of pretrial releasees) rather than being released back onto the streets.

But the problem is not simply, or even mainly, a lack of relevant facts and figures. The problem is also that only a few of the relevant numbers ever get reported, and then only in the most misleading ways. In October 1994, for example, the headlines and airwaves crackled for a few days with the news that America's prison population had passed the one million mark. Almost all of the "expert" commentary on this fact was negative. Virtually every comment by "experts" quoted in the stories suggested that the increase was a very bad thing for America: it means rising costs but provides no social benefits; results in more "petty" and "nonviolent" offenders behind bars; is a reflection of racist sentencing policies; makes America the most "punitive" society in the world (or most punitive after South Africa); promises no positive impact on public safety or any reduction in crime rates; supplies further evidence that the public is hysterical and that politicians are simply playing politics on the crime issue; runs counter to the need for more alternatives to incarceration; represents a continuation of the failed "get-tough" sentencing policies of the 1980s; and so on.

Not one of these reports, however, mentioned any of the following ten sets of highly relevant contrary facts, virtually all of them compiled in published reports produced regularly by the BJS or available in easily accessible and widely respected sources:[23]

1) Of the over five million persons under correctional supervision in America today, 72 percent are *not* incarcerated. Instead, they are on the streets, most of them under loose probation (average officer caseloads of between 150 and 300) or parole supervision.

2) Over 90 percent of all prisoners are held by the states. While "only" 49 percent are now serving a sentence for a violent crime, 62 percent have been convicted in the past of one or more violent crimes, and 94 percent have been convicted of violent crimes or sentenced in the past to probation or incarceration. Thus, only 6 percent of state prisoners can be meaningfully classified as nonviolent nonrecidivists.

3) Over 90 percent of all criminal cases now result in a plea bargain. There are no studies that systematically analyze what the plea bargaining "discount rate" is, but some estimates would place it at or above three. In other words, for every three felony crimes for which an offender could be tried and sentenced, he "pleads out" and is convicted and sentenced for just one.

4) Likewise, the official criminal histories do not account for the amount of undetected, unprosecuted crime committed by prisoners in the year prior to incarceration. But the two largest, most up-to-date scientific prisoner surveys found that half of all prisoners committed twelve serious crimes, *excluding all drug crimes*, in the year prior to their incarceration.

5) Prisoners who are classified by many "experts" as "mere" property offenders are generally career criminals. In one of the surveys noted in point 4 above, a prisoner-property offender at the 25th percentile (that is, 75 percent of the sample committed more, and more serious, crimes than he did) had the following "petty" criminal profile: he committed auto thefts at the rate of three a year, burglaries at the rate of six a year, and petty thefts at the rate of twenty-four a year.

6) The mandatory-minimum sentencing policies of the 1980s have done little to keep violent or repeat criminals behind bars. The mean sentence for state prisoners is seventy-five months, of which they serve on average 38 percent, or twenty-nine months. The average time actually served in prison for various crimes is seventy-four months for rape, thirty-five months for aggravated assault, and twenty-three months for all property crimes.

7) Measuring the incarceration rate relative to the total U.S. population is less germane in policy terms than measuring it relative to the crime rate. By the former measure, the rate per 100,000 residents has more than doubled from 139 in 1980 to 344 in 1992. But over the same period the number of persons sent to prison per thousand arrests for murder, robbery, assault, and other

serious crimes increased only from 128 to 148. The probability of going to prison for a felony crime today remains far lower than it was in the 1950s and 1960s. Indeed, between 1950 and 1988 the cumulative probability of being arrested for a serious crime, being prosecuted if arrested, being convicted if prosecuted, and going to prison if convicted fell by nearly 33 percent while the crime rate quintupled.

8) Cross-national comparisons of imprisonment rates are grossly misleading unless one accounts for demographic, legal, and administrative differences. For example, while American prisoners receive longer sentences for comparable offenses than inmates in England and Wales, the gap shrinks when the comparison is made in terms of time actually served rather than time imposed at sentencing. Nor has there been a single major empirical study to support the assertion that the justice system is full of racial disparities in sentencing. In a recent report, a National Academy of Sciences panel rejected the argument that the current gap between black and white levels of imprisonment is mainly due to discrimination in sentencing or any other decisionmaking processes in the criminal justice system. A recent study based on a sample representing over forty-two thousand defendants in large urban counties found no evidence that the system treats blacks more harshly than whites. And a comprehensive 1994 review of the empirical literature on racial disparities in death sentences found that, once one controls for all relevant legal variables (for example, eyewitness present, aggravating circumstances), there is absolutely no evidence of discrimination in contemporary capital sentencing.

9) There is a wealth of evidence to indicate that imprisonment cuts crime. For example, given what is known about prisoners' criminal records, tripling the prison population from 1975 to 1989 prevented a conservatively estimated 390,000 murders, rapes, robberies, and aggravated assaults in 1989 alone. Even more crimes would have been averted if even more violent and repeat criminals in state custody had spent half or more of their time incarcerated. And if data are not enough, try this thought experiment: what would any sane person suppose would happen to crime rates tomorrow night if we released at random half of all prisoners tomorrow morning?

10) The cry for "alternatives to incarceration" has been answered by placing over four million persons under correctional supervision on the streets rather than behind bars. Between 1980 and 1993, the nation's prison population increased by 184 percent but its parole population increased by 205 percent. Likewise, the cry for "intermediate sanctions"—substance abuse counseling, house arrest, community service, victim restitution programs, and the like—has been answered: about 90 percent of the nation's three million probationers are already a part of this graduated system of punishment. The fact, however, is that about half of them never comply with the terms of their

community-based sentence, and only one-fifth of the violators ever go to jail for their failure to comply.

Who Keeps the Revolving Door Open?

If the facts about government's revolving-door policies are so over-whelming and so well established, then why are they not more widely known and cited, and why have policies not come into line with the realities? Part of the answer is that the elite media systematically underreport or distort the facts about revolving-door justice in deference to "studies" which argue that America incarcerates "too much" and that prisons are terribly "crowded."

To cite just one example, in 1991 *New York Times* columnist Tom Wicker penned a column entitled "The Punitive Society." In it, he summarized the results of a "study" conducted by the National Council on Crime and Delinquency (NCCD). NCCD is one of several anti-incarceration advocacy groups that are routinely cited as a sources of "nonpartisan" data and "expert" commentary on crime and punishment in America. Wicker asserted that "80 percent of those going to prison are not serious or violent criminals but are guilty of low-level offenses: minor parole violations, property, drug, and public disorder crimes."[24] One still hears this figure cited today.

This NCCD "study" was based on exactly 154 loosely structured interviews with incoming prisoners in three states. By contrast, the 94 percent figure cited earlier—49 percent of prisoners are in jail now for a violent offense, 62 percent were convicted of one or more violent crimes in the past, and 94 percent are violent or repeat criminals—is based on a scientific survey representing 711,000 state prisoners![25] The data from the latter study are in public and university archives; anyone who has the inclination can go and analyze or reanalyze them to his heart's content. Moreover, Professor Charles Logan of the University of Connecticut found that while NCCD claims in its summary that the "vast majority of inmates are sentenced for petty crimes," in the body of the report "vast majority" refers to 52.6 percent, and "petty crimes" means criminal acts that majorities of Americans of every demographic description believe it is appropriate to punish by incarceration.[26]

Still, NCCD and its many anti-incarceration comrades in arms—the Sentencing Project, the Prisoners' Rights Project of the American Civil Liberties Union (ACLU), and others—are given the lion's share of credibility and attention by the national media covering crime and corrections issues, adult and juvenile.

Indeed, only two national sources of news consistently report on the extent and consequences of government's revolving-door policies, namely, the *Wall Street Journal,* on its op-ed pages, and *Reader's Digest,* in articles by Robert BiDinotto and others. These publications matter, the former because it addresses the debate among elites, the latter because it takes the facts to a mass audience. But they are no match for the rest of the media, and it remains too easy for policy elites who are so inclined to dismiss as "sensationalistic" local television news programs (which often lead with dramatic crime stories) and nationally syndicated programs like "Cops" and "America's Most Wanted" (which have probably done more than we know to stimulate public awareness about revolving-door policies).

Even in cases where the facts about the human and financial toll of revolving-door policies almost seem to speak for themselves, the facts rarely get heard. For example, I have yet to see a single major national media reference to the stunning data presented in the August 1994 report of the Virginia Governor's Commission on Parole Abolition and Sentencing Policy. Among its numerous findings, the report indicates that in Virginia "68 percent of all murders, 76 percent of all aggravated assaults, and 81 percent of all robberies" are "the work of repeat offenders," and that between 1986 and 1993 over one thousand violent crimes, including seventy-three murders, would have been averted if nondrug felons out on parole had served their time in prison.[27]

Likewise, I have not been able to find a single major national media reference (other than my own) to a Florida Department of Corrections study which found that 127,486 (87 percent) of the 146,956 persons released from the state's prisons between January 1, 1987, and October 10, 1991, were released early. After early release, they committed over 15,000 violent and property crimes and over 9,000 drug crimes. The violent crimes included 346 murders and 185 sex offenses.[28] Most of these crimes, including the murders, would have been averted if the convicted criminals had served out even 85 percent of their jail time instead of being released after serving less than half of their sentenced time behind bars.

Taking such data seriously does not end the debate over whether, for example, to abolish parole for all categories of repeat offenders (for example, low-level drug dealers whose only crimes are minor drug crimes).[29] Nor does it end the debate over the long-term social costs and benefits of life imprisonment for thrice-convicted violent felons (the "three strikes and you're out" laws).[30] There is plenty of room for reasonable disagreements, competing interpretations, and different inferences about policy. But there is absolutely no room for the cavalier and callous disregard for the human and financial toll of lax parole policies that has characterized most "expert" commentary on and most elite media analyses of crime and punishment in America.

Irresponsible Judges

The elite media and their "experts" are hardly the only forces that keep the revolving door open. The main doormen of this system are activist judges.

In 1970, not a single state prison system was operating under sweeping court orders to change and improve. Today, most states and scores of municipalities are operating their prisons and jails under some type of court order. The legal, political, and administrative history and consequences of judicial intervention into prisons and jails have been debated time and again.[31] In some cases, judges have intervened in a responsible way, protecting prisoners' rights without sparking prison violence, micromanaging operations, or greatly increasing costs. Not every act of judicial activism is irresponsible; not every intervention is a debacle.

But in far too many cases, judges have made themselves sovereigns of the cell blocks, forcing changes in operations that have resulted in inmate-on-inmate and inmate-on-staff murders, a dramatic increase in spending on amenities and services for inmates, and the early release of literally hundreds of thousands of violent or repeat criminals.

In Federalist No. Seventy-Eight, citizens are instructed not to worry about the power of federal judges who have neither "the purse" nor "the sword" but only "will." But as the Anti-Federalists warned, these judges, and their activist peers at the state and local level, can wield great power contrary to the public interest. In this case, they may lack both purse and sword, but they have managed over the last generation to steal the keys to the prison gates.

The main excuse for judicial intervention has been empirical, not jurisprudential. Prisoners have asserted that "crowding" has resulted in "cruel and unusual punishment" behind bars. But there is no empirical evidence to demonstrate that "crowding" causes violence, inmate health problems, or other tangible or psychological harms. In a recent review of the relevant empirical literature, Dr. Gerald Gaes, chief researcher for the Federal Bureau of Prisons, found that despite "the prevailing sentiments about the harmful effects of crowding, there is little consistent evidence supporting the contention that short- or long-term impairment of inmates is attributable to prison density"—and that is stating the case against the conventional judicial wisdom on "crowding" mildly.[32]

But activist judges have the luxury of ignoring the facts when it suits them. Indeed, they can ignore basic constitutional and legal doctrines as well. To cite just one example, for the last decade the city of Philadelphia has labored under a prison cap enforced by U.S. District Court Judge Norma L. Shapiro. As is the typical judicial modus operandi in such cases, Judge Shapiro bullied and cajoled the city into signing two consent decrees, one in 1986 and one in 1991, which gave her virtually unfettered control over the system and its finances. This relieved her of the necessity of ever having to issue a finding that any particular inmate in the system was suffering from any specific violation of his constitutional rights. Edward Rendell, Philadelphia's Democratic mayor and a former district attorney, has been battling for years to get Judge Shapiro to relinquish her control. She has successfully resisted.

The main consequence of Judge Shapiro's intervention has been to decriminalize drug and property crime in Philadelphia. Data compiled by the Philadelphia District Attorney's Office and by two independent researchers show that some 67 percent of all defendants released because of the prison cap simply fail to appear in court. In just one recent eighteen-month period, 9,732 arrestees out on the streets because of the prison cap were rearrested on new charges, including 79 murders, 90 rapes, 701 burglaries, 959 robberies, 1,113 assaults, 2,215 drug offenses, and 2,748 thefts.[33]

Among those murdered by offenders who had been released because of the court's prison cap was Danny Boyle, a thirty-year-old rookie Philadelphia police officer. And the prison cap has played havoc with the city's downtown redevelopment efforts and forced local businesses to spend even more on security. It has also turned Philadelphia into a major drug smuggling port.

Yet in a statement issued on October 31, 1994, Judge Shapiro did what activist judges all around the country have been doing in such cases for the last three decades: she rejected the people's public safety concerns, ruled out of bounds any counterevidence on the effects of "crowding," and, most significantly of all, ignored the language of a democratically enacted law (in this case an act of Congress, the Violent Crime Control and Law Enforcement Act of 1994) which mandated that consent decrees in such cases must be reopened.[34]

This brazen judicial action, and the hundreds like it that have been taken in prison and jail cases by activist judges since 1970, explains why laws passed in the 1970s that were supposed to cut funds for ineffective "rehabilitation" programs never took effect, and why mandatory-minimum sentencing laws passed all across America in the 1980s left us in 1994 with over four million persons on probation and parole and with state prisoners who served an average of only 38 percent of their sentenced time in prison. Supported by an elite research, media, and prisoners' rights establishment that takes the "sophisticated" view that America cannot solve its crime problem by tough measures, the judges have short-circuited all such measures by imposing prison caps, micromanaging prison operations, and guaranteeing that most violent or repeat criminals will be released early or not go to prison at all.

The central lesson here is that it is not enough to raise public awareness or pass new laws. For representative democracy to work on crime policy, for the new promise of American life to be protected against the ravages of street crime, more fundamental changes are needed.

Taking Back Our Streets, Taking Back Our Government

The first and most crucial step is to prohibit judges from becoming de facto legislators and corrections czars. The provision of the 1994 federal crime bill mentioned earlier was a step in the right direction, but only a baby step. Title III of the Violent Criminal Incarceration Act of 1995—the "Stop Turning Out Prisoners" (STOP) provision—is a bigger step. That bill passed the House in February 1995. Whatever the ultimate fate of the STOP provision, certain facts about the constitutional propriety of such laws should not go unaddressed.

Article III, Section 2 of the Constitution states that "the supreme Court shall have appellate Jurisdiction, both as to Law and Fact, with such Exceptions, and under such Regulations as the Congress shall make." But Article III also makes not only the jurisdiction, but even the very existence, of federal "inferior courts" purely the province of Congress. Any reasonable doubts about the meaning of Article III vis-a-vis the power of Congress over lower federal courts is answered plainly by Edward S. Corwin's classic, *The Constitution and What It Means Today:* "[T]he lower Federal courts derive *all* their jurisdiction immediately from acts of Congress. . . . Also, all writs by which jurisdiction is asserted or exercised are authorized by Congress. . . . The chief external restraint upon judicial review arises from Congress's unlimited control over the Court's appellate jurisdiction, as well as of the total jurisdiction of the lower Federal courts."[35]

Indeed, the Supreme Court has declared over and over that federal courts must restrain themselves with respect to "conditions of confinement" cases. To cite just a few key decisions, in *Bell v. Wolfish* (1979), the Court declared that double celling did not violate due process. In *Rhodes v. Chapman* (1981), the Court held that double celling was not cruel and unusual punishment. In *Wilson v. Seiter* (1991), the Court ruled that constitutional violations had to be based on specific conditions rather than "totality." And in *Rufo v. Inmates of Suffolk County Jail* (1992), the Court endorsed flexible standards for modifying consent decrees in light of changed circumstances.

Yet within weeks of the passage of the 1994 crime bill, the National Prison Project of the ACLU issued a memo on how to "confront" the provision. With great smugness, the memo chided Congress for "taking a stand in favor of God, motherhood, and locking up criminals."

In response, in December 1994, the National District Attorneys Association, a nonpartisan body representing concerned prosecutors throughout America, approved a resolution calling on federal lawmakers to adopt more detailed legislation to deal with the reality that "federal court orders in prison litigation often have severe adverse effects on public safety, law enforcement, and local criminal justice systems." This resolution became the basis of the STOP law.

Judge Shapiro and her like-minded brethren on the bench are right that "Congress can't do whatever it wants."[36] But they and the prisoners' rights and anti-incarceration lobby need to be reminded of the clear language of the nation's seminal political document with regard to the power of Congress to set the jurisdiction of the lower federal courts. No one wants a return to the "slave of the state" doctrine. Most Americans do want prisoners to have basic amenities (decent food, adequate medical care) and services (educational opportunities, drug treatment). But they do not want prisons to be virtual resorts and they certainly do not want another generation of violent and repeat criminals returned to the streets because of some judge's political ideology, statistical illiteracy, jurisprudential ignorance, or stubborn delusions about the consequences of "crowding."

Thus, Congress should pass legislation that unambiguously defines and further limits appropriate remedies in prison and jail cases. Unless and until the courts are curbed, no mere changes in the law—truth-in-sentencing reforms, "three strikes" mandates, new death penalty provisions—will survive the judicial gauntlet that has effectively stymied every major democratically enacted anticrime measure of the last quarter century.

The Thin Blue Line

Whatever happens with the courts, and whatever reforms are made with respect to the excessive legal fetters on the capacity of police and other law enforcement officials to book and incarcerate offenders (for example, the exclusionary rule), the simple truth is that "there's never a cop around when you need one." That is doubly true for Americans who live in high-crime, inner-city neighborhoods. Much-touted strategies such as community-oriented policing are all well and good, but they are "do more with more," not "do more with less," strategies.

Today America's thin blue line is stretched incredibly thin. Consider the New York City Police Department (NYPD). Despite its problems, the NYPD remains one of the nation's finest police departments. And now that it is led by Police Commissioner William J. Bratton, it is also one of the country's most innovative. But at full strength, the NYPD has about thirty-one thousand officers, only ninety-seven hundred of whom are deployed on one of three eight-hour shifts on any given day. (The rest of the officers have the day off, do supervisory or desk work, work at the training academy, do detective bureau or investigative work, are on vacation, call in sick, or have other assignments.) This means that there are, on average, only about thirty-three hundred patrol officers on duty in the city at any given moment. And "on duty" does not mean "on the streets." (Officers must spend a certain amount of time doing paperwork, attending court, and so on.) These officers are spread thinly across the city, and there is no evidence to indicate that deployment patterns are strongly connected to crime patterns. This is equally true for other big cities, including many where the actual street enforcement strength per capita runs much lower than it does in New York City.[37]

The federal crime bill of 1994 contained billions of dollars for policing, though nothing even approaching what it would actually take to recruit, train, and retain one hundred thousand police officers, as the bill's proponents claimed. Moreover, the history of federal programs designed to advance state and local law enforcement goals is abysmal. This is as true for programs launched on the watches of Republican presidents as for initiatives by Democratic ones.[38]

The voters clearly are willing to have their state and local governments spend more to thicken the thin blue line. The real obstacle here is a common one in contemporary American federalism: subnational governments cannot spend in accordance with persistent popular majority preferences because Washington has loaded them down with so many heavy unfunded federal mandates. The hard truth is that the only way America will get more cops on the streets, and the only way that new policing dollars will be spent wisely and efficiently, is if Washington gets out of the way, lightens the unfunded mandate burden on subnational governments, and lets state and local officials raise and allocate new law enforcement dollars accordingly.

Much the same thing is true with respect to state and local corrections. Right now, for example, it is fiscally impossible for most states to incarcerate most violent and repeat offenders for 85 percent or more of their terms. Prison costs can be cut once irresponsible judicial mandates are lifted, possibly by as much as half. (As a result of judicial intervention, in many states today about half of every prison dollar goes to prisoner amenities and services, not security or custody basics, food services, and physical plant maintenance.) But to meet the public's legitimate wishes for incarcerating dangerous criminals, unfunded federal mandates will have to be reversed so that state and local spending priorities can be effectively reordered.

Tracking America's Most Wanted

In the meantime, Washington can help combat crime by investing in genuine interjurisdictional criminal-background information systems. To cite just one example of the need for this investment, many big cities today often make decisions about whether to release a crime suspect or arrestee without reference to criminal history data from counties or states other than the one in which the suspect or arrestee is being held.

Whatever one's view of the antigun provisions of the 1993 Brady
Handgun Violence Prevention Act (or of gun-control laws more generally),
the Brady law (or some new law modeled on the relevant provisions thereof)
could be used to establish a real national criminal-background information
system for use by county police, prosecutors, courts, and corrections departments. This is properly a national responsibility and would require sustained
cooperation between the federal government and the states.[39]

Today, however, while the computer technology for a first-rate system of
this kind is at hand, the public policies, the administrative mechanisms, and
the funding necessary to track America's most wanted are not. The price of
inaction: countless criminals will continue to slip through the justice net and
victimize innocent citizens because of simple, avoidable information failures.

Rescuing Children

Such basic changes in the justice system's capacity to detect, prosecute,
and punish violent and repeat criminals can make a positive difference. But
perhaps the biggest thing that Washington can do to ameliorate the nation's
crime problem is to reverse the perverse social policies that fuel it.

Every study shows that a majority of the most violent juvenile offenders—tomorrow's high-rate adult criminal predators—begin life in homes
where they are severely abused and neglected. But in the name of "family
preservation," the federal government now mandates and subsidizes policies
that keep severely abused and neglected children with the deviant, delinquent,
and criminal adults who brutalize them. Recent reports on the "child welfare"
systems of New York City, Philadelphia, and other jurisdictions make plain
that severely abused and neglected youth are being sentenced to lives of welfare, joblessness, illiteracy, and crime by the present system. Existing laws
governing the conditions under which battered and brutalized children are to
be removed from their parents simply are not being followed in most places.

While a disproportionate fraction of severely abused and neglected children are inner-city blacks, such kids can be found within every race, creed,
and ZIP code. Federal social policy needs to foster rather than forbid the formation of group homes (call them orphanages, boarding schools, or whatever you prefer) where severely abused and neglected children can be loved,
educated, and given a decent chance in life by adults who are ready, willing,
and able to care for them.

As the leading criminology textbook concludes, we must "rivet our attention on the earliest stages of the life cycle," for "after all is said and done, the
most serious offenders are boys who begin their careers at a very early age."[40]
Very bad boys *do* come disproportionately from very bad homes in very bad
neighborhoods. If it were to happen soon, ending federal "family preserva-

tion" policies that trap severely abused and neglected children in horrible homes, uncaring foster-care complexes, corrupt youth and family services bureaucracies, and dysfunctional juvenile corrections systems could help to defuse America's ticking crime bomb.

Restoring Representative Democracy

There are, to be sure, other measures that government at all levels could take to help the American people in their fight to curb the nation's crime problem and rescue its most vulnerable children. I have outlined but a few.

One thing is clear: the stakes could not be higher. We are talking not only about reducing the horrific human and financial toll of street crime in America. We are talking as well about ways of restoring representative democracy in America.

The decline of public trust and confidence in representative institutions has been led by the decline of public trust and confidence in the government's response to the crime problem. In 1993 and 1994, there was only one public institution that elicited less public confidence than did the Congress, namely, the criminal justice system.[41]

The rise of crime to the top of the public issues agenda at a time of increasing voter anger at liberal Democratic incumbents is no mere coincidence. But crime need not be a partisan issue. In the historic midterm congressional elections of 1994, voters who ranked crime as one of the issues that mattered most to them in deciding how to vote split their votes about evenly between Democrats (49 percent) and Republicans (51 percent).[42] This reflects the healthy fact that the crime planks of the candidates were largely indistinguishable from one another. On the electoral stump, candidates of both parties sounded as if they had finally gotten the people's message on crime: more cops, incarceration of violent and repeat criminals, and no more policy subterfuges or nonsense.

But will the nonsense stop, and what if it does not? In America, the failure of representative democracy will not produce a mob. But it can strengthen impulses toward direct democracy that threaten to derange the constitutional system established for America by the Founding Fathers. On crime as on other issues, our system is not designed to give the people whatever they demand. Nor is it designed, in the language of Federalist No. Ten, to ensure that "enlightened statesmen" will always be "at the helm" of government. But it is designed to carry forward into law and action the will of a persistent popular majority that embodies a legitimate conception of the public interest.

Those unenlightened leaders who continue, in the words of Federalist No. Ten, to "betray the interest of the people" on crime will be responsible not only for the wounds of crime victims, but also for the erosion of our constitutional heritage. Taking back the streets is a necessary but insufficient condition for restoring public trust and confidence in the limited republican government envisioned by Madison and accepted by Croly.

Returning to our representative democratic roots on crime, here and now, may be the one certain way to reclaim the promise of American life, and to make new promises that we, the people, and our constitutional government can keep.

Notes

1. Samuel H. Beer, *To Make a Nation: The Rediscovery of American Federalism* (Cambridge, Mass.: The Belknap Press of Harvard University, 1993), x, xi.
2. James Madison, Federalist No. Ten (November 22, 1787), reprinted in *The Federalist Papers,* ed. Clinton Rossiter (New York: NAL Penguin, 1961), 78.
3. Beer, *To Make a Nation,* 17.
4. Madison, Federalist No. Ten, 78.
5. Ibid.
6. Ibid.
7. William G. Mayer, *The Changing American Mind* (Ann Arbor, Mich.: University of Michigan Press, 1992), 19–20.
8. U.S. Bureau of Justice Statistics, *Sourcebook of Criminal Justice Statistics, 1993* (Washington, D.C.: U.S. Bureau of Justice Statistics, 1993), section 2.
9. "Forum: Public Opinion, Institutions, and Policy Making," *PS: Political Science and Politics* 27 (March 1994): 538.
10. Ronet Bachman and Bruce Taylor, "The Measurement of Family Violence and Rape by the Redesigned National Crime Victimization Survey," *Justice Quarterly* 11 (September 1994): 701–714.
11. U.S. Bureau of Justice Statistics, *Highlights from Twenty Years of Surveying Crime Victims* (Washington, D.C.: U.S. Bureau of Justice Statistics, October 1993), 22.
12. U.S. Bureau of Justice Statistics, *Young Black Male Victims* (Washington, D.C.: U.S. Bureau of Justice Statistics, December 1994), 1.
13. U.S. Bureau of Justice Statistics, *Murder in Large Urban Counties, 1988* (Washington, D.C.: U.S. Bureau of Justice Statistics, May 1993), 2.
14. U.S. Bureau of Justice Statistics, *Criminal Victimization in the United States, 1992* (Washington, D.C.: U.S. Bureau of Justice Statistics, 1994), table 47, 61.
15. *Murder in Large Urban Counties,* 3.
16. Adapted from Don Russell and Bob Warner, "Fairhill: City's Deadliest Turf in '94," *Philadelphia Daily News,* January 9, 1995, 4–5.
17. Alfred Blumstein, "Prisons," in *Crime,* ed. James Q. Wilson and Joan Petersilia (San Francisco: Institute for Contemporary Studies, 1994), 412.
18. James Q. Wilson, "Crime and Public Policy," in *Crime,* ed. Wilson and Petersilia, 493.

19. Black Community Crusade for Children, "Overwhelming Majority of Black Adults Fear For Children's Safety and Future," Black Community Crusade for Children, Children's Defense Fund, Washington, D.C., May 26, 1994, 2.

20. *Sourcebook of Criminal Justice Statistics, 1993*, 638–40.

21. U.S. Bureau of Justice Statistics, *Felony Sentences in the United States, 1990* (Washington, D.C.: U.S. Bureau of Justice Statistics, September 1994), 8.

22. I am now in the early stages of a research project designed to answer this very question about convicted murderers and other questions related to it.

23. See Patrick Langan, "Between Prison and Probation: Intermediate Sanctions," *Science,* May 6, 1994, 791–93. See also John J. DiIulio, Jr., and Anne Morrison Piehl, "Does Prison Pay? Revisited: A Benefit-Cost Analysis of Incarceration," *The Brookings Review* 13 (Winter 1995): 21–25.

24. Tom Wicker, "The Punitive Society," *New York Times,* January 12, 1991, section 1, 25; James Austin and John Irwin, *Who Goes to Prison?* (San Francisco: National Council on Crime and Delinquency, 1990).

25. U.S. Bureau of Justice Statistics, *Survey of State Prison Inmates, 1991* (Washington, D.C.: U.S. Bureau of Justice Statistics, 1993), 11.

26. Charles H. Logan, "Who Really Goes to Prison?" *Federal Prisons Journal* (a publication of the Federal Bureau of Prisons), Summer 1991, 57–59.

27. Calculated from *Governor's Commission on Parole Abolition and Sentencing Reform: Final Report,* State of Virginia, August 1994, 72.

28. Florida Statistical Analysis Center, *SAC Notes: Study Examines Inmate Recidivism* (Tallahassee, Fla.: Florida Statistical Analysis Center, July 1993), 3.

29. See DiIulio and Piehl, "Does Prison Pay? Revisited."

30. See Peter Greenwood et al., *Three Strikes and You're Out: Estimated Benefits and Costs of California's New Mandatory-Sentencing Law* (Santa Monica, Calif.: RAND Corporation, 1994).

31. See John J. DiIulio, Jr., ed., *Courts, Corrections, and the Constitution* (New York: Oxford University Press, 1990).

32. Gerald G. Gaes, "Prison Crowding Research Reexamined," *The Prison Journal* 74 (September 1994): 329–63.

33. *Defendants' Motion to Vacate the 1986 and 1991 Consent Decrees,* Office of the District Attorney, Philadelphia, Pennsylvania, October 1994.

34. Henry Goldman, "Judge Open to Prison Hearing, But Says Crime Bill is Crowding Her," *Philadelphia Inquirer,* November 1, 1994, B3; John J. DiIulio, Jr., "A Philadelphia Crime Story," *Wall Street Journal,* October 26, 1994, A21.

35. Edward S. Corwin, *The Constitution and What It Means Today* (Princeton, N.J.: Princeton University Press, 1978), 213, 225.

36. Judge Shapiro, as quoted in Goldman, "Judge Open to Prison Hearing."

37. Commissioner Bratton confirmed these data in a conversation with the author in Williamsburg, Virginia, October 8, 1994. The data were reported in the *New York Times,* August 7, 1994, 36. For data and estimates on other cities, see John J. DiIulio, Jr., *Community-Based Policing in Wisconsin: Can It Cut Crime?* (Milwaukee: Wisconsin Policy Research Institute, October 1993).

38. John J. DiIulio, Jr., Steven Smith, and Aaron Saiger, "The Federal Role in Crime Control," in *Crime*, ed. Wilson and Petersilia, chapter 19.

39. Carol DeFrances and Steven Smith, "Federal-State Relations in Gun Control: The 1993 Brady Handgun Violence Prevention Act," *Publius: The Journal of Federalism* 24 (Summer 1994): 1–14.

40. James Q. Wilson and Richard J. Herrnstein, *Crime and Human Nature* (New York: Simon and Schuster, 1985), 508–509.

41. The Gallup News Poll Service, Princeton, New Jersey, April 25, 1994. The number of respondents saying they had a "great deal" or "quite a lot" of confidence in Congress was 18 percent in 1993 and 18 percent in 1994; for the justice system, the numbers were 17 percent and 15 percent, respectively.

42. "How They Voted—And Why," *National Journal*, November 12, 1994, 2632, reporting data from Voter News Service Exit Polls.

Chapter Sixteen

The Promise of Quality Education

Carolynn Reid-Wallace

In the opening pages of *The Promise of American Life,* Herbert Croly presents a paradox. How do we maintain the essential elements of our "national tradition" while changing our ways enough to make the promise come true? And he offers a resolution: cling to the goal but boldly discard the accustomed means of attaining it.

"The better future which Americans propose to build," Croly wrote, "is nothing if not an idea which must in certain essential respects emancipate them from their past. . . . [T]he American of today and tomorrow . . . must be prepared to sacrifice to that traditional vision even the traditional American ways of realizing it. Such a sacrifice is, I believe, coming to be demanded; and unless it is made, American life will gradually cease to have any specific Promise." What justified that sacrifice, of course, was the importance of the promise itself.

For most Americans, education has long been a way to achieve the promise of American life. And despite the complex problems facing our schools today, education still offers the greatest opportunity for the largest number of people to realize their goals. But there is growing evidence of decline in our nation's schools.

As early as 1983, an alarm was sounded when the National Commission on Excellence in Education reported to the country that our educational system had fallen into critical disrepair. The pedagogical structure upon which our national security and prosperity relied, the commission stated in *A Nation at Risk,* was no longer fulfilling its basic purposes.

According to the commission, America's elementary and secondary schools had become so fettered by bureaucratic constraints and regulatory inertia, so weakened by eroding standards, and so inundated by extraneous preoccupations that they were no longer able to carry out their primary responsibilities with acceptable efficiency. Our school boards, administrators, and teachers had ceased to insist upon levels of performance that were once routine. Many classrooms had degenerated into dead-end confinements for ill-trained, overextended, and dispirited instructors. In these cheerless surroundings, far too many of our adolescents were allowed to atrophy into idlers, underachievers, or functional illiterates. How had this happened?

Of course, schools competed with rock music, athletics, commercial television, and even gangs for the attention of children. But there was more to it. There were problems with motivation and discipline. Our community leaders and parents were having to push harder to persuade marginal students that there was any object to their enduring a tedious treadmill long enough to collect diplomas they could scarcely read; our teenagers were spurning the values of elders they had come to regard as petty jailers; and our graduation certificates were losing their capacity to guarantee even minimal competence in such indispensable subjects as reading, writing, mathematics, science, history, and geography.

In light of these troubling developments at the precollegiate level, it was scarcely surprising that many of our postsecondary facilities were being overrun by students who had felt compelled to seek further schooling, yet who arrived on campus with inadequate motivation and intellectual foundation for baccalaureate studies of any depth or complexity. The competitive job market demanded a college degree for positions that once warranted only a high school diploma. Institutions of higher learning were easing their admission criteria, augmenting their remedial services, diluting their accustomed course offerings, softening their grading practices, and downscaling their exit requirements. Meanwhile, the nation's unemployment and public assistance rosters grew more bloated, the streets were infested with drug dealers and derelicts, and our crime rates and penal expenditures were accelerating. Our workplaces were experiencing "a rising tide of mediocrity" at the very moment when employers from Connecticut to California clamored for young adults with substantially more "skilled intelligence" and adaptability than their predecessors.

Though it occasionally used the metaphors of national security, *A Nation At Risk* defined America's vulnerability not in military terms but in terms of eroding economic and social conditions. The report said, in effect, that the promise Croly had urged us to cherish and uphold was now imperiled. Its authors warned that millions of Americans were in danger of becoming "effectively disenfranchised," not only from the opportunity to enjoy "the material rewards that U.S. citizens had long regarded as their birthright," but also from "the chance to participate fully" in the pursuits and prerogatives of a "free, democratic society." America's "once unchallenged pre-eminence in commerce, industry, science, and technological innovation" was rapidly yielding to rivals from other parts of the world. They maintained that the United States was neglecting to equip its upcoming generations for success within the uncompromising global marketplace, and they forecast that the years ahead would call for a populace with appreciably more analytical capability, communications prowess, intellectual breadth, and creativity than most of our schools, colleges, and universities believed it conceivable to instill in their charges.

Twelve Years Later

The commission's words rang out with unimpeachable authority, reverberating through every corner of American society. *A Nation at Risk* stimulated philosophical rumination and the creation of new goals and standards. It prompted statistical surveys, enrollment projections, and policy appraisals by all sorts of agencies. It galvanized professional associations, corporations, and private foundations to examine their procedures and priorities. It instigated curricular adjustments and program changes and catalyzed new cooperative ventures. In short, it fostered a varied and wide-ranging reform movement, one that has begun to alter the way Americans think about the importance of education.

During the twelve years since the commission reported, much has been done. Though it is still too early to expect the most acute problems to have been solved, we can see signs of modest progress among hundreds of schoolhouses, lecture halls, and laboratories that are now humming with unaccustomed vigor. But there have also been disappointments and setbacks. And even the most optimistic of today's educators would maintain that far more needs to be done. Most agree on the need for renewed commitment to radical educational reform if we hope to arrest the decay that will otherwise undermine the new promise of American life.

It is by no means too late to aspire to a more productive, equitable, and sustainable social order. If we are truly to act upon such aspirations, however, we must do so boldly and with minimal regard for political consequences. We must prepare ourselves to do what Lincoln urged upon America in 1862: "The dogmas of the quiet past are inadequate to the stormy present. The occasion is piled high with difficulty, and we must rise to the occasion. As our case is new so we must think anew. We must disenthrall ourselves." If today we respond to the nation's educational peril with less wisdom and resolve than Lincoln, we may discover that our polity has succumbed to an insurgency of apathy and mediocrity which threatens the national ideals we cherish.

A Better Future For All

What can we do to turn things around? In formulating a new approach to America's education problems, we had best start with essential attitudinal changes. Only then will we be able to make the sizable institutional and organizational reforms that are necessary to fulfill the promise of a better future.

Schools should not ignore the rich diversity of their students or the larger world civilization. American public education clearly should provide all students with a curriculum that explores the diversity of cultures and peoples that has shaped our national character and the world we inhabit. But it would be a grave mistake to capitulate to factions that seek to use the public schools as a means of inculcating their own separatist philosophies based on race, ethnicity, or gender.

If our children are to realize the promise of American life, we must accept the premise that standards are the surest route to excellence. Parents and educators should inculcate that ethic of excellence in schools by raising standards of performance for both students and education professionals.

This may be difficult, but it's plainly possible. Standards and expectations work. Anyone who has ever watched the Olympics knows exactly what we expect of our top athletes. It is not enough that they made the trials. We are sorely disappointed when they miss the gold and have to "settle" for a silver or bronze medal.

We hold our athletes to lofty standards. We recognize the time and effort they put into being the best they can be, and we support them in these efforts. We expect excellence from them, and by and large we get it. Why, then, can't we have similar expectations for the academic success of students in our schools? Is education less important than athletics? It takes every bit as much individual effort, desire, and parental support to excel in academic subjects as in sports. Yet today our standards for academics are far lower. We settle for much less, and the result is troubling—weak literacy levels, poor job performance, and low productivity.

Perhaps the reason for this double standard lies in the nature of the standards themselves. In athletics, our standards are clear, objective, and measurable. In academics, they tend to be more subjective and equivocal. But understand why: They are subjective because they are designed to ensure that almost everyone will meet them without a great deal of effort. They are equivocal because they are not consistently enforced. Rather, they are subject to different interpretations, often depending on a student's race, ethnicity, or socioeconomic status.

Excellence in education demands objective and unequivocal standards, too. Standards must be measured and quantified to be effective, which means some form of consistent testing or assessment. We must require that our students read from classic texts, become familiar with the natural sciences and the fundamentals of mathematics, and develop logic and reasoning skills. They should also engage in rigorous study of the ideals of democracy and the source of those ideals, namely western civilization.

But it is essential to examine more than the standards that students are expected to attain. We must also look at performance standards for teachers, and, indeed, for each school as a whole. Are standards for teachers fairly applied and rigorously enforced? Are administrators held to account for the results achieved by their students and their schools? Does the school help its teachers keep abreast of changes in their disciplines? How easy is it for a student and his parents to talk to a teacher after class hours? Is the library stocked with high-quality materials? Does the school have access to up-to-date technology? Are the classrooms and other physical facilities clean, well lit, and adequately furnished? Are the school and its environs free from drugs, violence, and other disruptions? Parents should insist that the school environment encourage the kinds of discourse, debate, and reflection mandated by its curriculum.

Diversity and Uniformity

E pluribus unum is not just a maxim by which to construct the curriculum. It is a sound principle for reforming the education system itself. Despite the curriculum experts who seek to magnify the *pluribus* at the expense of the *unum,* Americans must stand firm on behalf of both parts of this brilliantly balanced phrase, which precisely evokes an essential aspect of the promise of American life. We should not expect all schools to be alike, precisely because people and communities differ. In our society, one size cannot fit all. By acknowledging that diversity and insisting that our education system accommodate and reflect it, we are far more likely to produce national unity.

There is no single way to achieve the educational goals outlined above. Standards may be national, but local communities must be empowered to develop the educational strategies that best suit the needs of their citizens. That was the essential logic of America 2000, the school reform strategy advanced by President George Bush and his education secretary, Lamar

Alexander. They knew the difference between a national project and a federal program. They understood that real, lasting change will come to American schools only when every community in the land realizes that the responsibility for renewal rests with it, not with a distant government at the state or national capital.

Communities and parents need to be empowered. Parents are generally in the best position to select the optimal educational arrangements for their children, since they are the ones who care most about their children.

But parents differ, too. All efforts to force families and communities into the same educational mold will produce greater conflict than learning. While it is critically important that standards not be sacrificed, it is just as necessary to recognize that the places and methods of teaching and learning do not have to look alike.

But we should be wary of romanticizing the capacity of parents. Most do an acceptable job of organizing their children's education. Some youngsters, however, are victimized by home environments. Controversial as this precept is, some circumstances justify the state's intervention on behalf of children. Regrettably, too many young children do not stand a chance of extricating themselves from the lure of the streets and the pitfalls of their parents' dysfunctional condition.

Until we can solve our other social problems—in particular, until we succeed in persuading people who are not ready to be good parents that they ought not have babies—we will continue to wrestle with broken families, foster homes, and boarding schools. Some youngsters come from homes where parents are unable or unwilling to provide for their basic needs—adequate food, health care, safety, love, and guidance. Why shouldn't they be guaranteed a safe harbor, at least until such time as their parents or adult guardians are able to provide them a stable, nurturing environment?

While the concept of orphanages has recently come under attack, the idea of boarding schools should not be dismissed. It worked for thousands of black families who sent their children to boarding schools during the 1930s, 1940s, and 1950s, when public schools were plagued with racial segregation and discrimination. It works today at residential institutions such as Boys Town, the Milton S. Hershey School, and the Laurinburg Institute.

The cost of establishing such institutions is substantial, but the financial costs are secondary to the human costs that accrue when the needs of young children are not met. Here we should be clear: more money alone won't cure what ails American education, but some of the cures we need to consider will cost more than we're spending today. No one should doubt the willingness of the American people to dig into their pocketbooks for education, as long as they feel they are not being asked to pay more for more of the same.

Addressing a Systemic Problem

In devising reform strategies, we must bridge the educational divide between precollegiate and postsecondary, remaining mindful of what Ernest Boyer has termed the "seamless web" of education. The deficiencies in our universities are the direct result of the dilapidation of their feeder institutions. The flaws in any one level of our educational structure tend to cause—and be caused by—failures at other levels. Only if we think systemically can we meet the challenge in its entirety. Harold L. Hodgkinson gave voice to this caveat in 1985 when he predicted that reformers would be frustrated in their attempts to mend any of the nation's instructional units until they acknowledged that it was necessary to treat all of them simultaneously, as elements of "one system" that extended from "kindergarten through graduate school."[1]

Unfortunately, the "system" Hodgkinson referred to is anything but systematic in the way it conducts a student along its twisted paths. With a topography whose fault lines make it resemble a fissured maze more than a clearly delineated road map, American education can intimidate even the intrepid with its perplexing and overlapping detours and cul-de-sacs.

Those who linger in the shadowy corners of America's bleak ghettos may be the most conspicuous detritus of our country's dysfunctional hodgepodge of instructional domains. But they are not the only casualties of our wasteful educational "system." For every bored, impoverished, crime-prone, alcohol-abusing, or drug-dependent adolescent who leaves a poor rural or inner-city school before the age of sixteen, there are dozens who end up with little to show for the effort that keeps them trudging to class long enough to garner a diploma they cannot be proud of but often take to college. It can be a debasing charade.

Even as the taxpayer is asked to make a short-term sacrifice in the name of a long-term gain, that same taxpayer has the right to insist that high academic standards be upheld at every level of the education system.

The ideal of the university as a place where one cultivates the intellect has been replaced by the reality of the university as a fee-for-service institution. Here, admission standards are elastic, depending on the number of students who desire to enroll and the institution's capacity to accept them. In other words, the laws of supply and demand prevail. That explains why admission standards run the gamut, with some schools accepting anyone who has finished high school and can fork over the tuition, and others accepting only those students whose test scores, essays, transcripts, and extracurricular activities demonstrate a track record of success.

The risk facing the fee-for-service university today is one of excess capacity. American higher education has the capacity to educate 14 million students. There are only 2.7 million graduating high school seniors per year.

What this means in economic terms is that some universities may close down—and a few already have. Other institutions will have to collaborate and even merge with nearby institutions in order to avoid going out of business. And some institutions will have to eliminate programs and units. These actions, although generally healthy in economic terms, are painful in institutional terms. Therefore, many institutions of higher education do whatever it takes to avoid or defer them, including lowering admission standards to attract more students.

Access and Excellence

There are, of course, other reasons why admission standards have been lowered. Some people believe that high standards are barriers to the kinds of students needed to diversify campuses. An official of one of the largest higher education associations put it this way: "If we try to impose standards now, we run the risk of leaving huge sections of the population behind."

Some fear that setting and enforcing high academic standards will mean that minorities or poor children will be excluded or caused to fail. Such thinking not only contributes to a self-fulfilling prophecy but is the cruelest form of racism and classism. Low-income and minority parents want the best for their children, too. They, like the majority of Americans, still believe in the promise of American life. And they, perhaps even more than the middle classes, know that today's education system imperils that promise for their children.

The sort of defeatism that makes some people reluctant to enforce high academic standards is premised on a false dichotomy between access and excellence. Specifically, many assume that achieving excellence requires limiting access for low-income and minority children, and that providing access requires compromising excellence. These people are wrong. Access and excellence are in no way antithetical—they represent two noble goals that are both worthy of our best efforts.

Our policies should reflect the Jeffersonian ideal that education be available to all our citizens. We have made tremendous strides in recent decades to increase the access of racial and ethnic minorities. But our policies should not let access get in the way of excellence. Our prospects for realizing the new promise of American life will rely heavily on our capacity to maintain broad access to education, while generating excellent results.

The alternative is simply unacceptable. Increasing participation by lowering standards—or scrapping them altogether—demeans an institution of higher education by devaluing its core purpose: to provide a first-rate education. Perhaps more regrettably, institutions that lower standards in order to meet racial or other quotas demean the students who believe their acceptance indicates their ability to do college-level work. No one benefits—neither the student nor the institution, let alone the prospective employer—when colleges and universities compromise standards of excellence.

If a college degree is to mean what it should, standards must be raised rather than lowered. This does not mean simply making subjects like foreign languages, science, mathematics, or English more rigorous. It also means expanding what is taught in these subjects. It is not enough to learn the grammar and syntax of a foreign language; one must learn to speak the language fluently, and one must read great literature written in that language. Moreover, it is not enough for American students to explore the history and culture of foreign nations without a solid grounding in the history and culture of western civilization.

The Challenge of Setting Standards

Several years ago the National Alliance of Business asked twenty-five hundred small business firms how difficult it was for them to find job applicants with basic skills. The results were striking: 70 percent of the companies said their applicants lacked writing skills; 61.8 percent said they could not do basic arithmetic; 64 percent said they could not listen or follow oral instructions; 59.2 percent said that applicants did not understand manuals, graphs, schedules, and other business forms; and 58.4 percent said they could not speak well enough to be understood.[2]

In addition to undermining our colleges, mediocre standards in our schools are weakening American competitiveness and the prospects of new entrants in the global job market.

Several years ago, one might have concluded that we were getting serious about standards. A 1991 Gallup poll showed that 81 percent of the American public supported the idea of strengthening standards.[3]

In 1992 the national movement to strengthen standards really picked up momentum:

- With support from the U.S. Department of Education and the National Endowment for the Humanities, the National Center for History in the Schools began crafting standards for elementary and secondary school history curricula.
- A coalition of science groups, including the National Academy of Sciences, the American Association for the Advancement of Science, and the National Science Teachers' Association set forth to develop standards for their discipline.
- The National Council for Geographic Education announced its intention to create national standards for geography.

- The National Council of Teachers of Mathematics, which pioneered the movement for standards and which issued standards in 1989, began moving to help teachers implement these standards in the classroom.
- Standards for English also seemed to be just around the corner, with the National Council of Teachers of English and the International Reading Association leading the charge.
- Along with the federal arts and humanities endowments, the U.S. Department of Education, under the leadership of Secretary Lamar Alexander, was supporting the development of voluntary national standards in the arts by a consortium of music, dance, theater, and visual arts education groups.

Support for strengthened standards was also being translated into action at the local level. The New York City public schools announced in 1992 their intention to require all students to study algebra. In the same year, the District of Columbia announced that it would increase graduation requirements to include the study of algebra as well as two years of a foreign language.

But somewhere along the line things went awry. The effort to set outcome standards became the object of intense criticism and political controversy. Problems arose when policymakers moved from the broad principle of setting high academic outcome standards for all students to the practical details of specifying those results.

There is one primary reason for this standards backlash—the controversy over outcome-based education. Regrettably, the outcomes defining what all students should learn often turned out to be heavy on behaviors and beliefs that are vaguely worded and largely affective. They showed little concern for core academic content and described mental processes such as attitudes, dispositions, and sentiments—behavioral and social outcomes rather than knowledge and skills.

Much of the problem can be traced to the process and mechanisms for setting the standards. Elected officials typically give responsibility for defining outcomes to panels dominated by people whose views on education differ from those held by most average citizens. The consequence is standards that are antithetical to those the public officials thought they were mandating.

While all is not yet lost, we find ourselves, once again, trying to convince people that standards represent a vision of what is possible, not an impossible obstacle or noisome intrusion. As a goal toward which students are expected to strive, standards can foster self-discipline, self-denial, and hard work, all habits essential for success in today's competitive world.

Institutions of higher education have a crucial role to play in the process. If they do not set and enforce high standards for students and faculty, there will be little incentive for high schools and elementary schools to raise theirs.

By insisting upon meaningful standards that define passage from one point to another along the academic continuum, we are taking seriously our responsibility toward American schoolchildren.

We make a big mistake if we abandon the effort to set goals and standards that will hold students, educators, and schools accountable for their performance. A results-oriented reform effort that has any possibility of overcoming the outcomes backlash will have four essential elements:

- *Standards.* States and communities should develop a core list of academic standards that define knowledge and skills all students are expected to master by the end of high school. Efforts by national professional associations may or may not be of help in this process. But as the debate about outcome-based education shows us, this process should not be controlled by education experts. While experts should have ultimate authority for the means of education, ordinary citizens should determine its ends.
- *Assessments.* For standards to make a difference, good tests and other measures of student, teacher, and school performance are needed. All these measures must carry consequences for those involved. For example, students should not be promoted or graduated, nor should they gain admission to college or into the work force, unless they have met prescribed standards of achievement.
- *Family choice.* All families, particularly poor ones, must be able to select the school that best meets the needs of their child. They must have the right to leave a bad school for a good one. And they should be given the consumer power—the dollars—to do this. Those whose beliefs clash with the core academic standards established by the community must also have the option of private or home schooling.
- *Creating new "public" schools.* While all schools should embrace a common core of academic outcome standards, they should be encouraged to differ in other dimensions. We are too big and diverse a country to expect a single model to fit everyone. We must welcome educational pluralism and competition. And we should encourage teachers and other educators as well as other community leaders to create and manage schools. This would make a "public" school one that serves the public, teaches to core standards, and agrees to be held accountable for results.

Those four guidelines create a framework for real education reform, but our efforts cannot stop there. There are also some promising practices that will accelerate our movement toward a radically improved system. They include:

- *Starting early.* We need to focus on the care of children before they begin school. We need to protect children even before they are born, so that on their arrival in this world they will be free of drugs and safe from other forms of prenatal abuse or neglect.
- *Making schools safe.* All parents want good and safe schools for their children. But the streets around many schools are dangerous. Every school should have a zero-tolerance policy for violence, weapons, and drugs. Alternative schools should be available for troublemakers who disrupt the school life of teachers and students.
- *Keeping schools open longer.* Our schools are in a time warp. Their hours of operation don't fit today's family schedules. There is no excuse for closing schools at three o'clock every day and for three months every summer, leaving children unattended and parents scurrying to find adequate supervision (beyond the television set) for their children.
- *Connecting with the world of work.* Students don't learn about real careers and real work in today's schools. A school created for an agrarian age and still functioning in that paradigm cannot produce a workforce equipped for the information age. Schools must work with the business community to ease the transition from school to work. And schools must integrate the use of new technologies into what both students and educators do.
- *Supporting and rewarding professionalism.* Educators should be given much more freedom to decide what happens in their schools and classrooms, including how fiscal and human resources are allocated. As long as students are attaining the desired standards, a school staff should be free to organize itself as it thinks best.
- *Starting from scratch to charter new schools.* Eleven states have now allowed for the creation of new kinds of independent public schools. Through a charter agreement, educators, parents, and a variety of public and private entities can start from scratch to design a school that fits the needs of today's families and today's children. These "educational entrepreneurs" are free from many of the rules and regulations that have stifled the system. A true revolution in education means creating schools never before imagined.

At every level, achieving the new promise of American life means bringing a strong sense of purpose to our efforts to revitalize the education system. We can no longer afford to accept "circumstances beyond our control" as an excuse. We dare not rest on custom, daunted by institutional inertia or terrorized by self-interested factions that for too long have held sway over the policies and practices of our schools and colleges. We must use all our personal and institutional resources to redirect our collective energy and rewrite the ground rules by which the education system operates. Irving Kristol reminds us that:

> One of the most critical challenges to leadership is to read the signs that announce the status quo has outlived its time. Established habits of thought always tend to prevail over the candid recognition of emerging realities. What is involved is not a failure of intelligence—or even a weakness of will—but a deficiency of imagination, that rarest of faculties in any leadership. It is rare because it is not usually very important. But it becomes crucial at precisely those moments that represent turning points in the evolution of policy. At such moments innovation, not coping, is the order of the day.[4]

Croly, we now know, was right about the promise of American life, but his prescription for making it come true, however well suited to his time, needs to be replaced today. Yet we can learn a valuable lesson from his boldness and his willingness to dispense with the status quo. In education, more than in most domains, we confront a situation today that resembles the paradox with which Croly opened his book. Many features of the status quo have become dysfunctional. As long as we let custom constrain our actions, we will make little progress. We must gird ourselves, once again, to sacrifice the ways of the past so that the new promise can be realized. That is going to be as difficult an undertaking as any we can imagine. But it is hard to think of one that will do more good for our children and our country.

Notes

1. Harold L. Hodgkinson, "All One System: Demographics of Education, Kindergarten through Graduate School," Institute for Educational Leadership, Inc., Washington, D.C., 1985, 7.
2. National Alliance of Business press release, Washington, D.C., May 6, 1992.
3. Stanley M. Elan, Lowell C. Rose, Alec M. Gallup, "Twenty-third Annual Gallup Poll of the Public's Attitudes Toward the Public Schools," *Phi Delta Kappan* 73 (September 1991): 46.
4. Irving Kristol, "U.S. Foreign Policy Has Outlived Its Time," *Wall Street Journal,* January 21, 1988, 30.

Part VII

America in the World

Chapter Seventeen

America in the New World

Howard H. Baker, Jr.

When Herbert Croly wrote *The Promise of American Life* in 1909, the carnage and cold war that would plague much of the twentieth century were not yet in view.

William Howard Taft had just succeeded Theodore Roosevelt as president of the United States. Vladimir Lenin was in exile in Switzerland, the Russian Revolution of 1905 having failed. Great Britain was master of the seas, as it had been for two centuries. Adolf Hitler, aged twenty, was an obscure painter of postcards in Vienna.

But even then, there was much to presage the grim new age about to begin:

- Prince Ito, who had authored the Japanese constitution and built Japan into a world power, was assassinated in 1909 by a Korean nationalist.
- President Taft chose Pearl Harbor as the Pacific base for the U.S. Navy, believing it more defensible than the Philippines' Subic Bay. Taft called Congress into special session to lower tariffs and thus ease economic tensions in the world. Congress raised six hundred tariffs instead.

- And from the Balkans came this dispatch, dated February 24, 1909: "Now Serbia is arming itself and demanding that the Austro-Hungarians leave Bosnia and Herzegovina, an area they fully annexed just last year. Serbia has coveted the region since losing it six hundred years ago.

  "The Western European Powers are trying to prevent armed conflict in the Balkans by pressuring the Serbs to give up their territorial ambitions in return for economic compensation. But Serbia will have none of it."[1]

The point, of course, is that new world orders are difficult to predict, much less ordain. And old world orders—some centuries old, still burning with ethnic or even tribal rage—are more stubborn and enduring than presidents and diplomats suppose.

Nevertheless, we have witnessed an epochal event—the collapse of communism and with it the empire of the Soviet Union—exactly eighty years after Croly published his masterwork, and we shall have a new world order whether we want one or not.

Finding Our Way In a New World

The cold war, with its comforting certitude about the forces of good arrayed against the forces of evil, has given way to a new world in which there is much less certainty and in which discussions of good and evil seem suddenly quaint and often irrelevant.

There is not much order in this new world. Since the fall of Communism in 1989, the United States has found itself confronted with a wide range of international challenges:

- the arrest of the Panamanian dictator on drug trafficking charges;
- the suppression of prodemocracy student demonstrations in China;
- significant reductions in the nuclear arsenals of the former Soviet Union and the United States;
- the liberation of Kuwait from Saddam Hussein;
- the destruction of Yugoslavia by its own people;
- mounting trade frustrations with revolving-door governments in Japan;
- a frightening confrontation over the possible development of nuclear weapons in North Korea;
- the restoration of a democratically elected president in Haiti;
- the conclusion of the North American Free Trade Agreement and a new General Agreement on Tariffs and Trade (GATT) lowering trade barriers among 123 nations;
- a Cuban emigration crisis precipitated by the ever-wily Fidel Castro;

- entreaties from Eastern European countries, and from Russia itself, to be allowed to join NATO;
- the realization of an old dream of economic union in Europe;
- a peaceful revolution in South Africa, wrought by a former prisoner and his former prosecutor; and
- a tenuous but tremendous stride toward peace in the Middle East, leading Jordan and the Palestine Liberation Organization to end a state of war with Israel after nearly half a century.

This is quite a foreign policy agenda for a country that has been doing its best to turn inward for the past five years. And the variety of issues on this agenda suggests that the end of the cold war—far from being the "end of history," as Francis Fukuyama famously predicted—was in fact the beginning of the most intense season of history-making events in fifty years.[2]

Despite this rush of events, the United States has not yet decided how it wishes to deal with the post–cold war world. Weary of the burden we have borne as leader of the free world since the 1940s, believing that today's highest national priority is a restoration of our economic, political, and social structure here at home, most Americans have simply declined to focus on the insistent world beyond our borders.

Indeed, public-opinion surveys conducted in 1994 found that all foreign policy and defense issues *combined* ranked with poverty and homelessness for fifth place on the list of issues Americans are most concerned about— trailing crime, health care, jobs, and the decline of morals.[3]

And yet we know that we are increasingly interconnected with the rest of the world. Forty percent of America's jobs are tied directly to international trade. The energy crisis long behind us, we again import more than half the oil we consume, and the percentage is growing. Financial services, telecommunications, agriculture, and a host of other sectors of our economy are now truly global in scale. Advances in transportation shrink the planet a little more every day. Middle Eastern terrorists blew a gaping hole in New York's tallest building in 1993. The tragedies of the world are broadcast in our living rooms as they happen. And every nationality on earth has a second home in America, where more than a million new pilgrims join us every year in search of the promise of American life.

So even if we agree with William Wordsworth that "the world is too much with us" (and it is with us quite a bit more now than when he penned those words in 1807), it is not going away. As the world's only remaining superpower, we have special responsibilities we never sought but nevertheless must bear.

We may be consoled (and then again, we may not) by the fact that our tenure as the world's only superpower is likely to be a short one:

- "Greater China," comprising the mainland, Taiwan, and Hong Kong, now has a larger gross national product than all of Europe, and its ambitions are far from satisfied.
- Japan, already an economic giant second in size only to the U.S., now has the world's third largest defense budget as well.
- Germany, newly unified, is wending its cautious way back to the front ranks of political as well as economic power, and with wise and patient statesmanship it could lead a united Europe to economic, political, and military parity with the United States early in the next century.
- India, long known as the world's largest democracy, now boasts a middle class larger than our own, and superpower status for the colossus of the subcontinent seems now more a matter of will than means.
- Russia itself, shorn of its imperial burdens and its suffocating ideology, may very well reinvent itself as a market economy and restore itself to greatness on the foundation of its superb scientific and technological prowess, its vast natural resources, and its remarkable people.

These facts notwithstanding, the United States is likely to have at least a decade of political, economic, and military preeminence ahead. What should we do with it?

A Little History

Most of our history suggests that we will not want to do much. The most consistent principle of American foreign policy in the last two hundred years has been the intense desire to be left alone.

Our Founding Fathers despised the diplomatic intrigues that animated the courts of Europe in the eighteenth century; and the desire to avoid anything more than "temporary alliances for extraordinary emergencies," in President Washington's phrase, was the overriding imperative of early American governments. Thomas Jefferson's purchase of the Louisiana territories from France, for instance, was first conceived as a defensive measure to keep Napoleon from exporting European politics—and ever-shifting war alliances—to the American mainland. And the War of 1812 was declared by an upstart America against the greatest military power of the day—Great Britain—to secure neutral rights for American shipping and to get the British navy to stop taking sailors off American ships.

The Monroe Doctrine, first declared in 1823, was an enduring testament to American isolationism, committing us not to take sides in European wars and not to allow further European colonization of our hemisphere. This doctrine stood as the foundation of American foreign policy for more than a century. Even our brief flirtation with imperialism during the McKinley and

Theodore Roosevelt administrations was rooted at first—at least in the public imagination—in a desire to free the people of Cuba and the Philippines from the oppression of a foreign power.

Similarly, the Open Door policy toward China—promulgated in 1899 by John Hay, McKinley's secretary of state (and Lincoln's former White House assistant) and reinforced in 1900 by his terms for ending China's Boxer Rebellion—renounced any U.S. imperialist designs on China and discouraged such designs by other global powers. For decades, this policy was enshrined with the Monroe Doctrine as a fundamental tenet of American foreign policy.

Flawed, and sometimes fraudulent, as these policies of neutrality may have been in practice, they were in any event the basis for 150 years of peace with the world (broken only by wars with Libya in 1801, Britain in 1812 to 1814, Mexico in 1849, and Spain in 1898). Indeed, both the Monroe Doctrine and the Open Door policy were still inspiring isolationists to oppose America's entry into the world wars in 1917 and 1941.

Herbert Croly's own proposal for a "national foreign policy," espoused in *The Promise of American Life,* concentrated largely on binding the United States, Canada, and Latin America in a cohesive "international system." A man of his time, Croly defended American colonialism only in countries where "the people whose independence is thereby diminished are incapable of efficient national organization."

But he was prescient enough to see that Europe, the United States, China, and Japan "must all eventually take their respective places in a world system." He viewed Europe with traditional American suspicion, but even here he prophesied—nearly a decade before America entered World War I—that "at some future time the power of the United States might well be sufficient, when thrown into the balance, to tip the scales in favor of a comparatively pacific settlement of international complications." Under such conditions, he concluded, "a policy of neutrality would be a policy of irresponsibility and unwisdom."

America would, of course, be called upon to tip the scales in precisely this way in both World War I and World War II, and it was in the aftermath of these global conflicts that the old American tradition of live and let live first came into conflict with the responsibilities of a new global power to keep the peace, resolve conflicts by means short of war, and promote prosperity in the world.

President Wilson's dream of a League of Nations, organized and empowered under the Treaty of Versailles to accomplish exactly those goals, was shattered when his own countrymen rejected his ambitious plan. America yearned not for the exercise of world power but for a "return to normalcy," to the less complicated life it had known before the Great War. Thus enervated, the league was powerless to stop the march of totalitarianism in the 1930s, and war would engulf the world yet again within twenty years of Armistice Day.

America's vain effort to stay out of World War II—passing laws requiring neutrality, preferring lend-lease programs to military intervention, extending the military draft by a single vote six months after Hitler had invaded Poland, contenting ourselves with being the "arsenal of democracy" rather than defending it directly—would collapse with the Japanese attack on Pearl Harbor, and once again American soldiers and sailors would "tip the scales" against the aggressors.

The statesmen who guided America immediately after World War II were vastly more successful than Wilson had been in reconciling the country's fundamental pacifist and isolationist nature with its new global responsibilities.

While the American military demobilized with astonishing speed—at a rate of more than a million men a month by December 1945—American diplomats were building the postwar world according to a distinctly American design. Its pillars included the United Nations, the Marshall Plan, the World Bank and International Monetary Fund, GATT, and NATO.

At the heart of all these American proposals—economic, military, and political—lay a moral foundation rare, if not altogether unprecedented, in the history of diplomacy. Americans are uncomfortable with balances of power, spheres of influence, and other staples of the diplomatic trade. It is embedded deep within our national character that, if we have to engage with the wider world at all, we will do so only in the service of some higher calling: the expansion of human rights, the defense of freedom, the alleviation of suffering, and the promotion of prosperity.

America's allies and adversaries alike have always been suspicious and uncomprehending of our commitment to these ideals and moral imperatives. It does not help when we fall short of them ourselves, as we have inevitably done. Still, there is a remarkable consistency in America's historic approach to international affairs, and after more than two centuries of diplomatic history, both we and the world should be able by now to understand and define what is important to the United States, what is worth fighting for, working for, and waiting for, and what is not.

The Value and Danger of Ambiguity

Yet we have also learned that drawing these distinctions too finely can itself be a temptation to the international adventurism we seek to discourage. In a 1950 speech, Secretary of State Dean Acheson drew a widely publicized defense perimeter around the United States that included Japan but pointedly excluded South Korea. Five months later, South Korea was invaded by its belligerent neighbor to the north.

A little ambiguity is desirable to keep potential aggressors off guard, but not so much ambiguity that a Saddam Hussein can misinterpret our resolve to defend Kuwait or that the Serbs can overrun the Bosnians with no fear of intervention by the United Nations—or the United States.

Walking this tightrope requires exquisite diplomatic balance, even for a lone superpower. We must not be, or appear to be, arrogant or arbitrary in our use of power, but neither can we be a "pitiful, helpless giant," as President Nixon warned a quarter-century ago.

In the decade ahead, while our influence as the world's only superpower is at its peak, I believe we should concentrate our energies and resources on the following seven objectives: making America work, breaking down barriers to trade, resolving conflicts without war, limiting nuclear proliferation, restructuring the military, reforming international organizations, and choosing our commitments carefully.

Making America Work

Former secretary of state George Shultz once said that the single most important contribution to America's foreign policy success in the 1980s was President Reagan's decision to fire the air traffic controllers who illegally went on strike in 1981.

This act, said Secretary Shultz, showed the world in dramatic terms that Ronald Reagan was as good as his word, that he would do what he said he would do, that he had the courage of his convictions.

In the same way, if America expects to convince the world that democracy and free enterprise are the best way to organize societies and economies in the twenty-first century, we need to strengthen those institutions here at home and make America the "shining city on the hill" of which President Reagan often spoke.

The collapse of communism demonstrated conclusively the stultifying effects of centralized government planning and control. In the end, the center could not hold, and the Soviet empire disintegrated, laying bare a lethal legacy of near starvation, environmental degradation, worthless currency, and a brutal system in which all private and personal initiative was suppressed and the dictates of a rigid, regimented state were all-encompassing.

The American system should be the antithesis of the Soviet: it should localize rather than centralize, encourage private enterprise instead of government-mandated solutions, and invigorate the economy with lower taxes, less heavy-handed regulation, more competition in the marketplace, and a smaller government in Washington, D.C., that does a few things well and lets states, communities, and people do the rest.

Nelson Mandela recently wrote that he and his colleagues in the African National Congress were inspired to seek justice in their homeland by the Atlantic Charter propounded by President Roosevelt and Winston Churchill in 1941. The charter represented a pledge by the United States and Great Britain to defend freedom of speech, freedom of religion, freedom from want, and freedom from fear, as well as to renounce any territorial ambition, restore self-government where it had been crushed, and allow equal access to trade and raw materials. As other countries, newly free of Soviet domination, choose their political and economic fates in the years just ahead, we must provide similar inspiration to them, demonstrating that our system of government and our free market economy are the world's greatest engines of human and economic progress.

We must also demonstrate that we can work together, that Americans of many nationalities, religions, races, and political points of view can reconcile their differences for the greater good. In Washington, this is called bipartisanship, and we must have more of it in the years ahead. It would be tragic if, in the hour of our triumph over one-party statism, we should suggest to the world that multiparty governments are recipes for gridlock and pointless acrimony. But in a much larger sense, this reconciliation takes place on a grand scale every day, as millions of citizens of every background interact with one another. This is the true glory of America—a tolerant, productive society which derives strength rather than weakness from its diversity.

Making up only 5 percent of the world's population, this remarkable people produces 22 percent of the world's goods and services. Our economy is twice as large as that of our closest competitor, Japan. Our workers are the most productive in the world. Our science and technology are the world's best, and our natural resources remain the envy of the world.

We have the capacity to do anything we set out to do in this country, and if we bend our efforts toward the alleviation of suffering, the spreading of prosperity, and the safeguarding of individual freedom in the world, we will have distinguished ourselves indeed. We will be the only nation in history which had the sole power to destroy the earth and chose instead to serve it.

Breaking Down Barriers to Trade

Among the most important foreign policy triumphs for America in the immediate post–cold war era has been the ratification of four increasingly far-reaching free trade agreements—with Canada, Mexico, the Asia-Pacific nations, and the 123 nations participating in the Uruguay Round of GATT.

These agreements represent America at its best: diplomatically, politically, and economically. While none of them is without flaws, all have committed the United States and its trading partners to the freest systems of trade in history. Government-sponsored tariffs and subsidies are giving way to a global competitive market destined to add immensely to the wealth of the world.

Further free trade agreements with our neighbors in Latin America are next on the agenda, and when completed these will bear a striking resemblance to the "international system" that Croly envisioned for the Americas eighty-five years ago.

Expanding trade and prosperity will also enhance the stability and security of the world, binding nations closer to one another commercially, socially, and politically. Harvard professor Robert J. Barro has observed that "more political freedom does not have an important impact on growth, but improvements in the standard of living tend strongly to precede expansions of political freedoms," as recent experience has shown in Chile, South Korea, Taiwan, Spain, and Portugal.[4]

Professor Barro's analysis suggests that attempting to export democracy to less-developed countries without first trying to encourage a market economy in those countries is a design for failure and frustration, both for us and for the countries we seek to help. Democracy flourishes best—and most spontaneously—where the standard of living is most robust.

Free trade and free enterprise should thus be the outriders of American diplomacy, followed by political reforms sped along by prosperity. But in encouraging those reforms, we must not insist that other countries remake themselves in our image. A government featuring a strong president, a powerful Congress, and a watchful judiciary suits our national personality and meets our political needs. But we should not be disappointed if other countries decline to adopt this American model in all its particulars.

Great Britain has a system of parliamentary democracy—under a monarchy—which is so inconsistent with our political values that we fought two wars to escape its control. Yet Britain is today, and has long been, America's best friend in the world. We have worked successfully (though not without friction) with socialist governments in France and Spain, with conservative governments in Germany and Canada, with a royal family in Saudi Arabia, with a revolutionary government in the new Russia, and with governments of near-infinite variety across the planet.

China, which is a long way from democracy, has nevertheless traveled a considerable distance from classic communism in its successful quest for economic growth. Encouraging that trend toward free markets and free people is of paramount importance to our relationship with China, despite our lingering outrage at the brutality with which the 1989 prodemocracy demonstrations in Tiananmen Square (and subsequent protests for human rights) were suppressed.

Even in Russia, the citadel of communism for seven decades, the rush to a market economy has been nothing short of breathtaking. Seventy percent of

Russian industrial enterprises have been privatized in the last two years. Forty million Russians have become shareholders in the private economy. There are now nearly three hundred thousand private farms tilling Russian soil, producing more than a third of the country's agricultural products. Inflation, at an annual rate of 100 percent, remains an urgent problem, as does the influence of organized crime, but Russia is rapidly coming to the stage where it will trade a revolutionary agenda for an evolutionary one. It will be concerned less with the transformation from a command economy to a market economy than with more traditional issues of price stability, productivity, and job creation. The political leadership of the country reflects this incipient shift: Boris Yeltsin may be the boisterous politician at the center of attention, but Prime Minister Viktor Chernomyrdin, a low-key former engineer, has been quietly stabilizing the postimperial Russian economy.

While we applaud their moves toward market economies, we must not expect China or Russia—or any other country, for that matter—to do everything we would like them to do on the schedule we would prefer. But it is important that we recognize and encourage the profound changes going on in those countries. Patience is not a virtue Americans prize very highly, but patience is precisely the virtue we will need to lead the world toward greater political and economic freedom.

Much of the world already finds us a bit too arrogant, too sure of our virtues. Pressing too hard, too fast, too rigidly to reinvent the world according to our values will not yield the results we seek.

Resolving Conflicts Without War

Fervently as we may hope that a rising tide of prosperity will encourage comity among nations and dignity for their citizens, there is ample evidence that wishing for peace or working for prosperity will not always be sufficient to avert the scourge of national or civil conflict.

As this chapter is written, Bosnia is being torn apart by a Serbian faction bent on territorial conquest, political control, and "ethnic cleansing." We have seen Somalia and Rwanda fall into hellish states at the hands of their own leaders. We have seen Protestants and Catholics in Britain and Ireland locked in mortal combat for twenty-five years over who will govern Ulster. These tragedies, played out on our television screens, break our hearts and stir our national impulse to do something.

But what? Send a division of the U.S. Marines into the crossfire? Impose economic sanctions that punish the innocent along with the guilty? Send a check through our foreign aid program and hope for the best?

I believe we have an opportunity, during our season as the world's only superpower, to help resolve such conflicts more discreetly and effectively.

Nowhere on earth have the enmities between neighbors been more violent or intractable than in the Middle East. Yet it is here that American diplomacy has performed its greatest miracles.

All its Arab neighbors declared war on Israel on the day it was created in 1948. From that first day, the United States stood staunchly by Israel's side, taking her cause as our own in every regional dispute, anxious to defend the one democracy in the Middle East against either regional or Soviet-inspired threats.

But after the Yom Kippur War in 1973, the United States discovered that a more useful role for all parties involved was a more evenhanded approach to the continuing quarrels in the Middle East. We struggled against considerable odds to gain credibility and trust among the Arab states, and this confidence-building process went on for years before the frontline states began to consider seriously an American role in negotiating peace among old enemies.

President Carter, President Anwar Sadat of Egypt, and Prime Minister Menachem Begin of Israel took a giant step forward with the Camp David Accords in 1978. President Bush and Secretary of State James Baker took another when, in the aftermath of Operation Desert Storm in 1991, they arranged for the first-ever summit meeting of all the Middle Eastern states in Madrid.

From that meeting, from years of painstaking diplomatic preparation by a superb and undervalued American Foreign Service, from the embrace of the policy of evenhandedness by President Clinton—as well as from the courage and conscience of the principals themselves—have come agreements between Israel and the Palestine Liberation Organization, then between Israel and Jordan, with more surely on the way.

This is the service to which America's power and prestige should be applied all over the world. In Bosnia, for example, the local parties, the United Nations, and NATO stumbled over one another for two years with little credit in the exercise for anyone. Could the United States have played a more constructive and conciliating role acting unilaterally rather than through the UN and NATO? At the end of the tragedy, it is difficult to know, but it is a question I propose we ask more often of ourselves when major conflicts arise around the world.

President Clinton has commissioned George Mitchell, the former U.S. Senate majority leader, to see what the United States can do to encourage, through economic means, a reconciliation between Britain and Ireland. Are there other trouble spots where a $6 trillion economic partner could be helpful in smoothing the waters? Maybe so.

Limiting Nuclear Proliferation

The ability to deal with conflict effectively without constant resort to military force will be more and more important as additional nations gain the ability to become nuclear powers.

For most of the last half century, the world's nuclear powers have constituted an exclusive club. Only the United States, the Soviet Union, Great Britain, France, and China have acknowledged that their military arsenals include nuclear weapons. But rumors have abounded for years that other nations as well have unlocked—or bought—the secrets of nuclear weapons technology. Indeed, this technology—some of it fifty years old—is no longer particularly advanced, and many countries probably have the scientific ability to deploy nuclear weaponry. It is even possible that nuclear weapons may now be controlled by institutions other than governments.

Several former constituent states of the Soviet Union now have individual control over significant parts of the huge Soviet nuclear arsenal, and there is no longer a central military command in Moscow to manage, maintain, and safeguard these weapons. It is a hopeful sign that the Ukrainian government—which controls more than eighteen hundred nuclear warheads from the old Soviet arsenal—has become a signatory to the Nuclear Non-Proliferation Treaty. Less hopeful is the fact that, in Russia itself, a black market has developed in the traffic of weapons-grade plutonium and uranium—crucial components of nuclear weaponry. The prospect of fissionable materials being passed around on street corners to agents of unknown interests is nothing less than terrifying. So is the prospect of Iraq, Iran, and North Korea with uninspected nuclear facilities.

This is the environment in which the Nuclear Non-Proliferation Treaty is to be renewed in 1995. Other nations have never conceded that simply because the United States and a few other countries were first to build nuclear weapons, we were therefore entitled to a nuclear monopoly. Now that the technology is becoming ever more commonplace, we have a serious problem on our hands.

What should we do? Three things, to begin:

First, we should proceed with diligence to develop and deploy an effective missile defense system. With the dismantling of the former Soviet Union's enormous missile inventory, it is no longer necessary to provide for as comprehensive and extensive a Strategic Defense Initiative (SDI) as that first proposed by President Reagan in 1983. But in today's world, with the proliferation of nuclear weapons in the hands of an increasing number of nations large and small, we could be hard put to determine with certainty where an attack was coming from, let alone to retaliate.

Ten years of SDI research and development has surely made it possible for us to create a defensive system that is relevant to today's threat. The ability to detect, track, and destroy nuclear weapons launched from anywhere on earth is within our technological grasp, and I am sure that virtually every nation in the world would seek the protection of this nuclear shield. The nations that may balk at such protection are probably the ones we should worry about.

Second, we should make a condition of offering that protection full compliance with the terms of the Nuclear Non-Proliferation Treaty and the inspection schedules of the International Atomic Energy Administration.

Third, we should make clear to those nations that will not agree to these terms and inspections that economic and political sanctions may well be imposed on countries remaining outside the nonproliferation community.

The construction of even such a limited nuclear defense system is a feat probably within the reach of only the United States. Using that ability to protect the world against the greatest single threat to its survival is the most responsible service we could perform as the world's only superpower.

Restructuring the Military

Deploying the nuclear shield is only one of the fundamental changes we must make in the way we prepare for—and thus deter—armed conflict at every level of engagement.

Again making the most of our technological advantages, we should restructure our forces to rely more heavily on the "brilliant" weapons systems now in development: systems that can limit American casualties while inflicting increasingly exact punishment on aggressors. There is, of course, no substitute for the resourcefulness and bravery of American military men and women, but it would be folly to put these magnificent people in harm's way when there are other means of achieving the same military goals. The development and deployment of sophisticated electronic weaponry is the logical extension of the doctrine of overwhelming force that served us and our allies so well in Operation Desert Storm.

A sensible and careful reduction of the size of our traditional armed forces will be possible as these new systems are brought into service. But whatever the size of the force, we must maintain it at the highest possible state of readiness. This means investing the necessary sums to pay, train, equip, and enable rapid deployment of America's fighting forces. Recent trends in defense spending will not achieve this result—they move in the opposite direction—and must be reversed.

That does not mean the kind of money that was required to restore America's defenses in the early 1980s. We are, in fact, spending a lower percentage of our economic output on national defense today than at any time since Pearl Harbor. Defense spending now ranks below Social Security, Medicare/Medicaid, and interest on the national debt as the fourth largest line item in the federal budget. With the exception of a redesigned SDI, we need not invest heavily in the kinds of strategic armaments necessary to our defense during the cold war. But we must devote substantially more resources to developing new tactical and theater weaponry to support our combat forces on the ground, at sea, and in the air.

In addition to developing new national defense systems, the American military must focus on making itself strong, supple, and ready to deal with conflict at any level. David Abshire's concept of "agility" described in chapter 18 is helpful here. As we have seen many times in the past five years, conflict in the post–cold war world is local or regional. To be rendered muscle-bound by an overreliance on strategic weaponry is to be incapable of dealing with the most likely military challenges of the future.

The technological advances in weapons systems that are feasible in the next decade may make it possible to reduce even further the number of men and women in uniform. But we must not begin cutting the forces, or risking their readiness, before there are well-proven means of doing the jobs we ask men and women to do now.

More important than any of these issues is the credibility of the United States when it threatens the use of force. President Bush said the Iraqi invasion of Kuwait would not stand, and it did not. If we are as resolute in the future, and if we remain convincingly prepared to win on the battlefield, we should be able to influence the behavior of rogue states and deter aggression before it starts.

Reforming International Organizations

As Bosnia and Somalia have shown, the peacekeeping structure of the United Nations is ripe for review and reform, and it is increasingly evident that many of the structures erected five decades ago are no longer adequate for the new world of the twenty-first century. The UN Security Council, for example, had as part of its original permanent membership a state that no longer exists: the USSR. Russia has inherited the Soviet Union's seat at the Security Council table, but the world is much less Eurocentric now than it was in 1945, and countries like Japan can make persuasive claims for Security Council membership.

The UN has grown over the years to encompass dozens of specialized agencies and to employ many thousands of international civil servants. Just as the new United States Congress is reducing the number of its standing and special committees and interest caucuses—and cutting the size of the congressional staff by one-third—so should the United Nations endeavor to pare its structure and refocus its mission.

The United States has complained regularly and vigorously in the past about the spiraling costs, inefficiencies, and limited accountability of UN operations. We should insist on regular reviews of each UN enterprise to see if it is doing its job and if the job is still worth doing.

We should consider appropriate ways to address the fundamental deficiencies of the United Nations and its charter in today's world. The highly uncertain result of another San Francisco Conference (like the one in 1945 where fifty countries gathered to found the UN) probably makes a wholesale reorganization effort too risky. But it is not too early to ask member states to open the debate on how the UN charter could be improved and made more relevant to the world of the twenty-first century—a world that will be more Asian, more prosperous, more oriented toward private enterprise than toward government programs, and more diverse in its outlook and aspirations than the strictures of the cold war once allowed.

For all the criticism of the UN over the years (much of it justified), we cannot expect from it a consistent record of success when we lay at its door the most intractable problems in the world: famine, orphan conflicts, global warming, and the like. But the UN's chances of success in any endeavor will fall precipitously as long as its mission is muddled and its structure bloated.

NATO, too, must reexamine its mission as it prepares to meet the challenges of a new world. Created as an instrument of collective security at the dawn of the cold war, NATO performed its original mission splendidly, standing its ground until the Soviet empire disintegrated from within. But in the new world, NATO's mission must be redefined, establishing a new relationship between its current members and the rest of Europe.

NATO should quickly embrace at least some of the states and satellites of the former Soviet Union and bring them into the fold of the free world. Political way stations like the Partnership for Peace, which advocates a graduated approach to full NATO membership, can in fact be destabilizing distractions from the central mission of NATO: a free and secure Europe. Negotiating an Eastern European state's progression from Warsaw Pact member to NATO member (through the Partnership for Peace) could be a diplomat's life work. We do not have time for such gradualism, and there is no need for it.

An expansion of NATO to include as many Eastern European nations as are willing to abide by its membership terms should proceed as quickly as possible. Russia may be sensitive to the timing and scope of the conversion, but if we believe in the sovereignty of states and in the security and stability of Europe, a rapidly enlarged NATO should be our primary political goal on that continent.

The World Bank, the International Monetary Fund, the Inter-American Development Bank, and other international financial organizations, all of which have done extremely important if largely unsung work during the past half century, are also due for a mission review. Government-to-government lending and borrowing have been eclipsed, then dwarfed, in recent years by the investment of private capital in the developing world. Similarly, while traditional American foreign aid programs have been trimmed (from $20 billion five years ago to $14 billion this year), the Overseas Private Investment Corporation (OPIC) is already guaranteeing $2 billion annually in private financing for projects in the developing world, and OPIC is almost certain to grow rapidly in the next decade.

This shift of primacy from the world of public servants to the world of private markets represents not the failure but the success of the government programs organized and sponsored by the United States through the cold war years. At the end of World War II, no other country had any substantial capital to invest in reconstruction. It was our commitment to provide this reconstruction and development financing—even to our recent enemies—that created the world we live in now, a world more prosperous and democratic than we dared to dream of a few short years ago.

Choosing Our Commitments Carefully

America has been at its best on the world stage when it has made commitments it was willing to sustain for years, even decades if necessary, at substantial cost in lives or treasure or both. Where we have faltered is in making commitments we were not prepared to honor on the terms promised or to the degree required for success. Vietnam is the most obvious example of a half-hearted national commitment whose costs proved too high to sustain a political consensus but whose terms of engagement were too confining to allow a military victory. "No more Vietnams" is a phrase enshrined in our national psyche now, but it is critical that we understand and agree on what that phrase means.

What it does not—must not—mean is that the United States will forever forswear the use of military power. As we have seen with such tragic consequences in Bosnia, if the United States does not commit its troops in an international military engagement, our allies are not likely to bear a prolonged military burden alone. And in cases where our own national interests are at stake, the credible threat of military force is absolutely essential.

The Hungarian uprising against Communism in 1956, largely forgotten in this country but vividly remembered in Hungary, demonstrated the cruelty of raising expectations of American intervention and then dashing the hopes of courageous dissidents with the meager gift of moral support. Moral support may be a soothing balm to our national conscience, but such support alone can be worse than no support at all.

The fact is, we should not get involved in most of the world's military conflicts—and we must not expect that every conflict in which we engage will be as quick and easy as Operation Desert Storm. That massive military operation, a hundred-hour war in which American casualties were amazingly few, was without precedent in military history, and we must not assume that future American military engagements will be as swiftly and clearly decisive.

We are tempted, as a moral and compassionate people, to act and intervene when we see innocent people suffering at the hands of brutal aggressors. But the same compassionate impulse runs rapidly in the opposite direction as soon as we see flag-draped coffins being borne by honor guards to Arlington National Cemetery. Unless we are prepared to stay the course when casualties inevitably come—unless a cause is important enough to us to justify the shedding of American blood and repeated scenes of grieving American families—we must not commit our military men and women to the battlefield.

How do we decide which causes are worth risking American lives to defend? To a large extent, we know such a cause when we see it. Any large commitments of American troops in the future should, like Desert Storm, be the joint decision of the president and the Congress. This will ensure that there is sufficient political consensus to sustain a major military campaign against the evil day when coffins come home and the faint of heart counsel retreat.

I am not suggesting a literal compliance with the War Powers Resolution of 1973, which I continue to believe is an unconstitutional infringement on the president's prerogatives as commander in chief. That resolution's terms are so restrictive, its consultation requirements so cumbersome, and its legislative "negative veto" procedure so patently unconstitutional that its very existence tends to raise tensions on both ends of Pennsylvania Avenue at precisely the moment when solidarity and constructive consultation should prevail.

For all the attention we have given Bosnia and Somalia in the last two years, and for all the sympathy we feel for the victims of aggression in those sad countries, neither of these conflicts was susceptible to a purely American military solution. Neither, frankly, was that in Haiti, where our involvement was blessed with rare good luck and an extraordinarily successful appeal to military honor from America's most appealing soldier, General Colin Powell. Haiti had all the makings of a military and political disaster. The last time we occupied Haiti, we were there for seventeen years. It is my fervent hope that this time our involvement will be measured not in years but in months.

As it was ill-advised of Dean Acheson to draw a precise American defense perimeter that excluded Korea, so it would be ill-advised for us to announce in advance—or even to decide in advance—which causes we will defend and which ones we will not. Such a list would risk aggression and terror everywhere else.

In any event, discussions of "vital national interests" almost always devolve quickly into recitations of important sea lanes, essential natural resources, and the like, and a challenge to our supply of bauxite is not likely to stir the martial passions of the American people.

The Expansion of Freedom

What stirs Americans, and has stirred us for more than two centuries, is the idea of freedom: personal, political, economic, religious, and every other kind.

The quest for freedom is the great engine of America's remarkable progress from a collection of seaboard colonies to a continental state to the most powerful nation in the history of the world.

Threats to freedom are what have incited this peaceful people to war five times in this century.

Defending freedom, and building economic, diplomatic and military structures to aid in that defense, have constituted the great American enterprise of the last half century.

Not for nothing did we call the West the "free world" during all those years at sword's point with totalitarianism. The Four Freedoms embodied in the Atlantic Charter—freedom of speech, freedom of religion, freedom from want, freedom from fear—have animated our hopes and steeled our resolve through decades of danger and sacrifice.

The free world has won the cold war, and that momentous achievement has been neglected in the rush to build a new world order. We should take some time to savor this victory of freedom, to enjoy its blessings, and to offer them as an inspiration to the nations still struggling to make their way in this challenging new world.

America's overriding policy toward this new world should be a simple one: the expansion of freedom. Our aims for the world should be free trade, free markets, free political institutions, free speech, the free exercise of religion, and a free press—as well as the freedom simply to be left alone.

We should always be prepared to defend freedom, but my hope is that we will be able to use our influence in more peaceful ways to incline the world toward security, stability, opportunity, prosperity, human dignity, and justice.

In the coldest days of the cold war, President Kennedy envisioned a world in which "the strong are just, and the weak secure, and the peace preserved." Because of the courage, skill, and sacrifice of the American people, we are nearer that world than I ever thought we would be in my lifetime.

The triumph of freedom—the ultimate promise of American life—has hastened the day. If the expansion of freedom in the world is America's legacy during our tenure as the world's only superpower, we will have used our power wisely and well.

Notes

1. "Turmoil Besets Balkans," February 24, 1909, in *Chronicle of the Twentieth Century,* ed. Clifton Daniel (Mount Kisco, N.Y.: Chronicle Publications, 1987), 121.
2. Francis Fukuyama, *The End of History and the Last Man* (London: Penguin Books, 1992).
3. Times Mirror Center for the People and the Press, *The People, The Press, and Politics: The New Political Landscape* (Los Angeles: Times Mirror, October 1994), 121–22.
4. Richard Barro, "Democracy: A Recipe for Growth?" *Wall Street Journal,* December 1, 1994, A18.

Chapter Eighteen

An Agile Strategy
for Power and Peace

David M. Abshire

The year 1909, when Herbert Croly published *The Promise of American Life,* was the year Admiral Robert E. Peary first reached the North Pole. It was the dawn of an era of dramatic discoveries and new technologies—the Model T, the airplane, and the Great White Fleet. It was the end of the era of realpolitik, and unbeknownst to Croly and his contemporaries, the end of America's Manifest Destiny, which knew no limits and feared no clear and present dangers.

Today, at the dawn of the post–cold war era, it is ironic that U.S. national security is confronted with a constellation of complex conditions more like those facing Croly at the end of the nineteenth century, and less like those familiar to the present generation, which has faced the unifying threats of communism and Soviet imperialism. The cold war required a simple strategy based on meeting the needs of one of two nuclear superpowers frozen in confrontation, with much of the world divided accordingly. Near the start of the cold war, George Kennan conceptualized a Western strategy of containment against further Soviet aggression, hoping that the walled-off empire would eventually mellow or erode. U.S. national security institutions, alliances, and doctrines were built on this essentially linear strategy. If rigidities developed in some of the cold war institutions used to implement this strategy, it was because they reflected the rigidities of confrontation, whether at the Berlin Wall or the thirty-eighth parallel in Korea.

Today, America faces a dramatic reversal of this picture. The United States no longer needs a linear strategy. It needs an agile strategy that can help it to pilot the rough seas of a "new world disorder." The global environment is not rigid and linear, but highly fluid and mobile—despite exceptions such as the northern borders of Kuwait and South Korea. It is as if a huge ice cap has broken up, and we must now try to make our way through the icebergs in uncharted waters. As Admiral Peary had to negotiate his way back from the Pole with as much skill and care as he used in getting there, we now must navigate the breakup of the cold war.

The challenges of such an environment are not new to history. Similar challenges in the eighteenth and nineteenth centuries led to shifting alliances, miscalculations, and misperceptions, which eventually culminated in World War I, World War II, and then the cold war. Croly's book never envisioned such horrors. To prevent a repetition, we must, in Abraham Lincoln's words, truly think anew and act anew, as we *have not been doing in recent years*. It is in this spirit that the following ten elements are offered as the building blocks of a new and agile strategy.

One: The Proper Use of Power

Yale historian Donald Kagan argues in his recent book, *On the Origins of War and the Preservation of Peace,* that "peace does not keep itself." A nation wishing to preserve peace must not only maintain the strength sufficient to make its deterrent power credible, but also "act realistically while there is time," as opposed to avoiding the burden "until there is no choice but war."[1]

The first requirement is to recognize the difference between power and force and to maximize the former to shape the strategic environment. We sometimes forget that the classical purpose of strategy in peace and in war is to influence the behavior of opponents and allies alike, and of others as well. Strategy is not something that is necessary only during wartime (when deterrence and diplomacy have failed); it requires a pervasive and ongoing integration of foreign and domestic capabilities that can be used to achieve deterrence to prevent war in the first place, or "compellence," to use a more recent term, to influence in advance the actions of an opponent.

Strategy connotes a keen appreciation of the difference between the use of *power* and the use of *force*. Admiral Arleigh Burke, in a 1962 lecture entitled "Power and Peace," noted the tendency of many would-be strategists to overlook the larger purpose of power in the first instance, that is, "the capacity to induce others to behave according to the patterns in one's own mind."[2] Edward Luttwak, the well-known military historian, argues in his 1976 *Grand Strategy of the Roman Empire* that power works very differently from force:

> [Power] works not by causing effects directly, but by eliciting responses—if all goes well, the *desired* responses. The powerful issue an order, and those subject to their power obey. But in obeying, the latter are not passive objects of the power relations (as are objects of force). They are actors, since those who obey carry out the required action themselves.[3]

If the admonitions of Burke and Luttwak were needed in the 1960s and 1970s, they are needed all the more now as we work to respond to the fluidity of today's environment. Understanding the distinction between power and force is important because many of the debates and crisis responses of the post–cold war era have centered simply on whether or not to use force. This is usually the wrong way to formulate the problem and dooms us to a *reactive* rather than a *proactive* stance. Indeed, it reflects the absence of strategy. Historically, even at the strictly military level, brilliant commanders knew their purpose was to influence the action of the opponent, as at Ulm in 1805, where Napoleon compelled his opponent to surrender without fighting a real battle.

Indeed, Sun-tzu's "perfect victory" was to win without fighting. This we did successfully in the cold war. We deterred the USSR from its threatened attack on Europe without firing a shot. We did this through power—an orchestration of various means, of which the potential use of force was only one. A calculus of risk was set up for a would-be aggressor. The key to Soviet strategy was to divide the Western Alliance. The daily discipline of the North Atlantic Council of NATO foiled this strategy time and again. Such steadiness of strategic purpose gave NATO credibility then. As a former ambassador to NATO, I believe it is an open question whether NATO would actually have used its nuclear weapons (once faced with parity and, in certain areas, Soviet superiority). But we effectively affirmed for the Soviets the risk that we would do so, and thereby deterred them. Thus the NATO alliance and structure are arguably the most dramatic examples in history of the concerted use of power because they not only deterred a major military opponent, but they also prevented the very real possibility of World War III.

This writer believes Prime Minister Slobodan Milosevic of Serbia could have been deterred in 1992 without firing a shot if NATO, with its panoply of power, had been charged at the outset with the management of the Yugoslav crisis. If the West successfully deterred Stalin, it stands to reason that with daily consultation and the discipline of the council to keep the allies in step (and they have been constantly out of step in Yugoslavia), the West could have deterred Milosevic and others from the very beginning.

Instead, Germany broke ranks at the outset, Milosevic later played off one ally against another, and, after prolonged political wrangling, NATO was drawn in incrementally and piecemeal under UN control. NATO forces were often hampered by procedural disagreements with the UN and suffered from a disunity of command. The lessons of that other incremental war, Vietnam, were ignored. The West's lack of unity and tendency to act incrementally, in short, constituted the antithesis of the effective use of power, which requires consistency of strategic purpose, unity in execution, and the creation of a calculus of risk and punishments for would-be aggressors.

Two: Defining National Interests

If the United States is going to use its power effectively to influence the behavior of others, it must first establish a hierarchy of national interests. Presidents Harry Truman and Dwight D. Eisenhower, both of whom were globalists, knew how to do this while avoiding the distraction of lesser challenges. Truman knew that if the United States was to meet the Soviet threat, it had to exercise decisive leadership in Europe. Eisenhower maintained the European priority but also had a keen sense of strategic proportionality elsewhere in the world.

When there is a direct threat to the United States, everyone concludes that strong defense is in our vital interest. Many now say, however, that with the end of the cold war there are no foreseeable direct threats to the United States. But this is not true. Weapons of mass destruction—nuclear missiles and chemical and biological weapons, some in the hands of terrorist or renegade states—are now or soon will be a threat. Given the questionable status of the roughly 10,100 nuclear warheads possessed by the former Soviet Union (including Russia, Ukraine, Belarus, and Kazakhstan), a dozen or more nuclear powers could easily emerge in the next ten to fifteen years, creating what some think could be a state of nuclear anarchy.[4] Among other results, this would add further urgency to the question of missile defense. NATO in fact may soon be threatened from the south and the east in this regard.

But there is a host of other "what ifs" and significant contingencies that can affect U.S. national interests. As an example, what if the reformers lose, and Russia moves to reestablish its former hegemony? What if an economically dynamic China, potentially the largest economy in the world, continues its already substantial military buildup? What if Japan rearms in reaction? What if a unified Korea launches its own arms buildup, and Congress pulls U.S. troops out of the Pacific, thereby creating a dangerous security void?

What if Algeria and the rest of North Africa succumb to militant fundamentalism? Or what if a class B or C power—say Iraq or Iran—attempts nuclear, chemical, or biological blackmail against the United States?

Although these contingencies may seem unlikely at present, each could emerge rapidly. Without a carefully prepared agile strategy, the United States could easily wind up colliding with events rather than controlling them. If Americans think the geopolitical environment cannot change radically in the next twenty years, we should recall that in 1920 the Weimar Republic was disarmed, devastated, and flat on its back, posing no conceivable threat to the United States, and that the United States was about to enter into a naval treaty with Japan. To avoid such complacency, the United States must continually be on guard against weaknesses in its regional alliances. An agile strategy does demand certain anchors to U.S. national interests, and the United States must firmly anchor its power in the Atlantic, the Middle East, and the Pacific.

Three: The European Anchor

The Atlantic commitment as manifested in the North Atlantic Treaty Organization had its roots in the cold war. In addition to deterring the Soviet Union, NATO also provided stability in Western Europe, chiefly by anchoring West Germany to the west and reconciling it with former adversaries. Prior to the creation of NATO, European wars had been almost a constant since Charlemagne's children divided his empire. Thus, with its two missions, the alliance ended the kinds of ambiguities and chances for miscalculations by aggressors that led to the world wars.

The United States must remain in Europe, not only in the air and on the sea, but on the ground, where our unfailing commitment is symbolized. This fundamental requirement of our grand strategy and our national interest has not changed with the end of the cold war. We must remain a strong shareholder in Europe if stability is to be maintained. The disgraceful performance of the United States and its European allies in the former Yugoslavia must not cloud our judgment on this matter. It is almost unthinkable that there are voices distorting the lessons of the Yugoslavian debacle and arguing that we should no longer anchor our power in Europe, that we should abandon NATO and withdraw completely, thus insanely inviting history to repeat itself.

Maintaining political stability is particularly important because there exists a zone of potentially unstable countries in Eastern Europe. To resolve this situation, it is important that the alliance move forward with a strategy and timetable for accepting Poland, the Czech Republic, Hungary, and possibly Slovakia as full alliance members, once they meet NATO's strict membership requirements. This is nothing but a continuation of the same process that over time added Greece, Turkey, and Spain to the alliance. Both France and Spain are members of the North Atlantic Council, but not the Defense Planning Committee and integrated commands. The eastern countries could be similarly positioned until such time as they are capable of full military integration, and such integration is politically desirable.

NATO should, however, devise a second-circle formula for Russia and Eastern European countries in order to avoid any provocative actions that could needlessly raise tensions. In recent articles, both former secretary of state Henry Kissinger and former national security adviser Zbigniew Brzezinski have stated that Russia's legitimate security concerns should be guaranteed in a formal treaty with NATO, and that a new mechanism should be developed to give Russia its proper place in consultations on European security.[5]

Such a mechanism already exists, to some extent, within the framework of the Conference on Security and Cooperation in Europe (CSCE). On a more substantial level, all former Warsaw Pact countries (including all republics of the former Soviet Union) are already members of the often overlooked North Atlantic Cooperation Council (NACC), a body that has been in existence since 1991. NACC meets twice annually and brings together both diplomatic and military officials from member nations. In addition to its semiannual meetings, the NACC sponsors military staff exchanges to foster further security coordination. The cooperative structures of NATO and NACC have been further enhanced by the Partnership for Peace, which has been reaching out to non-NACC European nations.

Granting all the former Soviet republics full NATO membership (with veto power) would rob NATO of agility and make it too reminiscent of collective security schemes that have failed in the past. NATO must not become a mini-UN or a CSCE. We should, however, take the position that a NATO enlarged by Poland, the Czech Republic, and Hungary will actually help the moderates in Russia over the long term by adding to European stability. It could also help deter extremists who might be tempted to renew Russian hegemony over parts of Eastern Europe.

We should recall that firmness by the Bush administration, in the face of strong objections by Moscow, led to incorporation of a united Germany into NATO. If we lack resolve and prolong indecision through a series of annual NATO meetings, we will simply provoke corresponding outbursts by the Russian president (such as occurred in December 1994 at the meeting in Hungary) and stir Russian emotions unduly. Russia should not be made to feel isolated, for the West is, after all, doing its best to restore Russia's economy. Indeed, this second-circle formula would treat Russia as the Congress of Vienna treated post-Napoleonic France. At the congress, the four victorious powers formed the Quadruple Alliance, which was linked to the larger Concert of Europe, and into which defeated France was brought as a leading member. Peace was preserved for many decades. Today, it is essential that we re-create conditions of deterrence and stability; the lessons of 1914 and the 1930s remind us how unstable conditions leading to miscalculation and mis-perception produced two world wars.

Four: A Middle East Balance

Zbigniew Brzezinski refers to an "arc of instability" that, among other areas, includes the Middle East. The Middle East today extends through Central Asia into Europe, through the influence of Islam. The Persian Gulf remains especially unstable, with such uncertain factors as Iran and Iraq. Yet politically and economically, this region remains vital to the industrial democracies. We should foster the growth of the Gulf Cooperation Council and increase the prepositioning of equipment and strategic mobility of our forces. Above all, we must seek to secure the Arab-Israeli peace process; and U.S. forces in Europe and at home must be made more agile if we are to project power and deter aggression in the Middle East.

To develop greater agility, we should break out of the compartmentalized cold war command structure of two distinct U.S. military commands. During the cold war, our allies were always worried the Soviets might feign an attack on the Middle East to draw NATO troops from Europe, and then launch their blitzkrieg at undermanned NATO defenses. To guard against that possibility, we set up another distinct command headquartered in Tampa, Florida, called the Central Command, which controlled U.S. forces deployed in the Middle East. We now need to restructure and consider combining these commands in order to synergize our forces. Doing so would increase the agility of our forces and enhance our effectiveness in Europe, Africa, and the Middle East.

Our European allies, especially Germany, have outdated ideas on the role of U.S. troops in Europe. Germany (for internal reasons) often asserts that American forces are there exclusively to defend Germany and Europe. Our allies need to be told in no uncertain terms that U.S. troops in Europe are for *both* European and Middle Eastern security. They should be made to understand that Middle Eastern security is more important for them than it is for us, given their far greater dependence on Middle Eastern oil.

Consistent with this theme, NATO command post exercises targeted at Middle Eastern contingencies should be conducted annually and designed for maximum political flexibility; varying the flag—whether that of NATO, the Western European Union, or some ad hoc combination—under which such deployments operate would achieve the latter end. New logistical require-ments should be instituted. We must be positioned to prevent, compel, and deter, not simply react. We must meet future mobilizations by Iraq on the Kuwaiti border with severe and decisive punitive measures, and the intention to do so must be conveyed in advance, not after Iraqi forces begin to move.

Indeed, NATO and its assets should be looked upon as an extraordinary logistic and planning pool to be tasked "out of area" (to use the cold war terminology for the original treaty area) as necessary. This, in reality, is exactly what happened in the Gulf War, when the U.S. Seventh Corps from NATO carried out General Norman Schwarzkopf's "Hail Mary" play around the Iraqi right flank. By openly planning with NATO forces, the West can enhance both deterrence and defense by helping to underwrite the Arab-Israeli settlement and foster Gulf security.

Five: The Pacific Anchor

The world's dynamo in terms of economic growth is the Asia-Pacific region, which has no alliance comparable to NATO. The United States, which has strong bilateral alliances with Japan and South Korea and maintains ground troops in both countries, should attempt to strengthen ties between Japan and South Korea in order to ease historical tension between these two countries and effectively trilateralize our alliance structure. There are also some nongovernmental initiatives that should be supported, such as the Pacific/CSIS [Center for Strategic and International Studies] Council on Security Cooperation in the Asia-Pacific.

Over the next thirty years, the Pacific region will be an area rife with insecurities and power struggles that could even lead to war, especially if the United States pulls back now. We should attempt to anchor our relationship not only with Japan and Korea but with China as well. In this regard, CINC-PAC (the U.S. Commander in Chief Pacific forces) in Hawaii plays a unique role not just militarily but also diplomatically, through visits and exchanges throughout the region.

China's extraordinary economic growth might one day make it the world's largest economy. Its massive population, huge land mass, inevitable surge into high technology, and substantial nuclear capability, combined with its ongoing military buildup, give it an awesome position in the Pacific and, indeed, in the world. On the level of geoeconomics, the United States must attempt to bind China to the industrial democracies through increased trade and investment, improved business practices, and membership in international economic institutions such as the World Trade Organization. In terms of geopolitics, the United States must attempt to incorporate China into a broad security network of Pacific Rim nations as we seek to maintain an effective balance of power. The United States must recognize that this emerging China is clearly a real security concern, and plan for a range of contingencies as we shape our agile strategy.

The Taipei-Beijing relationship also deserves watching. The People's Republic of China has said openly that a unilateral declaration of independence by the opposition party coming to power in Taiwan could lead to conflict. The United States has specific, legal obligations to aid Taiwan with its defense under the Taiwan Relations Act of 1979, so it holds the key to deterrence and defense in this region. Questions concerning the role of the U.S. in defending Taiwan, however, arise at a time of growing bilateral military relations between Beijing and Washington. Similarly, the U.S. has an interest in preserving rule of law in Hong Kong prior to and following its July 1, 1997, reversion to Chinese sovereignty.

The potentially oil-rich Spratly Islands and the gas reserves of the South China Sea are another point of contention among no fewer than six countries. Such conflicting territorial claims raise further security concerns for Vietnam and the other rapidly developing nations of South and Southeast Asia, including an increasingly powerful India. If there are any doubts about the need for a strategy of agility and flexibility, conditions throughout Asia should dispel them.

As we complete this global survey of our defense needs, it is clear that the United States must have the capability to handle more than a single contingency at a time. The 1994 Iraqi advance to the Kuwaiti border at a time of instability in North Korea and concurrent with our move into Haiti illustrates this point. Freedom of action is a key principle of strategy, and historically such freedom has, time and again, been inhibited by the demands of competing crises. The League of Nations, which hoped that Mussolini could be used to counter Hitler, broke down as a result of its unwillingness to invoke full sanctions against Mussolini when he invaded Ethiopia. For the United States, a fundamental condition for maintaining an agile strategy is that we retain freedom of action even in simultaneous crises. Lack of such freedom restricts our use of power and can encourage miscalculation and aggression.

The United States should seek the return to a strategy of deterrence and should maintain a balance of power in these crucial areas of continuing confrontation. Deterrence is a word that has almost dropped from the official dialogue since the end of the cold war, as if deterrence could be practiced only in a nuclear standoff. Deterrence is not a use of force, but a use of power with the potential use of force. World War I, World War II, the Korean War, the Falklands War, and even the Gulf War could all have been avoided with the proper mix of commitment and power. Too often in recent years, we have merely been reactive to crises, and often our uncertain trumpet has made them worse. An important exception to our recent record occurred in the 1994 Gulf crisis, when the Clinton administration's resolute and swift deployment of forces sent a signal to Saddam Hussein that any renewed aggression or attempt at blackmail would be met with determined resistance.

Six: Clear Criteria for Intervention

Considerations of when and how to intervene inevitably lead us to the subjects of peacekeeping, peacemaking, and humanitarian assistance. We must distinguish between interests that are vital and those that are important but nonvital. Maintaining the trans-Atlantic and trans-Pacific alliances, as well as maintaining the stability of the Middle East, is in our vital interest. The Caribbean region has also historically been an area of vital interest for us. If we are to intervene in this region, as we did in Croly's day and as we have done three times recently, then responsibility on the ground should be primarily ours, as it was in Grenada, Panama, and Haiti.

But in most cases elsewhere, especially where the United States does not have alliance commitments or geographic proximity, we can selectively offer a comparative military advantage—strategic mobility and logistics—but require others with closer historic and strategic ties to the area in question to secure the ground. The United States can also offer to help train these intervention forces at our bases. But we should now develop a general doctrine, as Nixon did in the Pacific during our withdrawal from Vietnam, which puts the responsibility of providing ground forces on others.

In defining what our interests are in areas of uncertainty, the calculus should be a *dynamic,* not a static, equation. President Eisenhower understood this in 1954, when he developed five criteria that had to be fulfilled before the United States would commit its forces to Indochina. Eisenhower insisted that before any intervention was ordered there had to be indigenous support; allied support; congressional support; a workable plan for quick, decisive action; and a plan for withdrawal.

Although the U.S. was at its peak of cold war power in 1954, Eisenhower decided not to intervene in Indochina, despite the recommendation of the chairman of the Joint Chiefs of Staff, because his clear criteria were not met. Without such clear criteria and conditions, the next two administrations backed incrementally into a war of attrition in Vietnam.

In 1984, Secretary of Defense Caspar Weinberger laid down criteria for U.S. intervention in general.[6] Ten years later, in the absence of the overarching Soviet menace, Weinberger's criteria are still valid insofar as they go, but they relate exclusively to the application of military force, and do not address the use of power. This writer would draw upon Weinberger's criteria but go beyond them. The decision to intervene with actual force must first be placed in the context of options available for projecting our nation's power to influence another country or to deter an aggressor. In cases where we have clearly defined political and military objectives, any intervention should be carried out according to a disciplined formula akin to that used by Eisenhower in the 1950s.

An agile strategy would suggest U.S. military intervention only in situations fulfilling the following criteria:

1) we first have presented an opponent with a calculus of risk and punishment to include combinations of proactive diplomacy, economic sanctions, and the psychological impact of possible military intervention;
2) clearly defined alliance interests in Western Europe, Japan, and South Korea are threatened;
3) there exist threats to our important interests outside of alliance obligations, and there is a capacity and a will to win swiftly; or if victory is delayed, there are agreed-upon cutoff points where costs begin to outweigh potential gains;
4) there is a reasonable assurance of indigenous support in the area of intervention;
5) every attempt has been made for allied support and burden sharing;
6) we have evaluated the country's postintervention capacity to move toward some form of representative government and market economy;[7] and
7) we have a reasonable assurance of support from the American people and have consulted with leaders of the Congress.

Another form of force is retaliatory punishment, which is often confused in public debate with intervention on the ground. There are some unique situations in which stand-alone, retaliatory actions by air and sea can serve a very important role in influencing an aggressor. The Israeli strategy of immediate retaliation following terrorist attacks has had some effect against its foes. U.S. naval and aerial retaliatory strikes against Libya in 1986 completely quieted Qaddafi's rampant terrorism. Early in the Yugoslav crisis, punitive strikes as the centerpiece of a coercive strategy against Milosevic might have caused him to abandon the objective of a Greater Serbia.

If retaliatory punishment does not work, then policymakers have to accept that fact, and to realize that there are not and will not be forces on the ground that can become embattled or taken hostage. Our agility is thereby maintained.

There was something lost, however, in the U.S. debate over whether to use force in the former Yugoslavia. The black-and-white alternatives presented missed what is at the heart of strategy: the orchestration of power with force to create a calculus of risk and compel an aggressor to change his mind. In confronting such a calculus, the aggressor cannot be sure that any particular action will take place; however, if we establish a history of *decisive* actions, any aggressor will be compelled to fear us. This is different from bluff, where a specific act is threatened but not carried out. This calculus of risk for the potential aggressor was the heart of NATO deterrence; it was what Richard Nixon tried to create in Vietnam as he set out to withdraw U.S. forces without losing all strategic initiative or giving the appearance of a rout. Power, combined with the potential use of force, is a part of the strategic equation, and an agile strategy incorporates a broad range of options.

As for our forces serving under UN command, the United States has operated successfully in peacekeeping as a part of a multinational observation force in the Sinai desert, and as an "able sentry" in Macedonia. These are examples of classic peacekeeping under chapter 6 of the UN Charter, which defines such operations as taking place with the consent of both parties and performing an umpire role, often between antagonists, in order to create transparency, to observe, and to report. When we take part in humanitarian operations, a circumscribed role such as we played in the final stages of the Rwandan tragedy should be the model, not an operation like that in Somalia, where so-called mission creep and excessive intra-UN politics greatly limited U.S. effectiveness. The mission creep moved the UN from peacekeeping to attempted peace enforcement, and that involved taking sides. Whenever the U.S. commits itself to peace enforcement—acting against an aggressor—it should be wary of serving under UN commands unless we are in charge, as we were in Korea and in the Gulf. A UN sanction of authority is one thing; a UN military command in execution is quite another. Because of lingering cold war politics, moreover, most peacekeeping efforts would at times be best served by having neither U.S. nor Russian troops on the ground.

But above all, the United States needs to avoid exhausting itself in extraneous and difficult engagements that drain limited resources and immobilize us like Jonathan Swift's Gulliver. Unless we preserve our resources and allow for mobility, the United States will lack the long-term power and freedom of action to defend its national interests. We should be mindful of Frederick the Great's warning: "He who tries to defend everywhere will end up defending nowhere." In short, we must choose carefully where we commit our power, lest we squander it.

Seven: A Defense Investment Strategy

An agile strategy requires a new approach to defense investment. Such an approach centers on the classical military concept of economy of effort, which involves, in modern-day parlance, cost effectiveness, multiplier effects, comparative advantage, and, above all, the elimination of needless overlapping, layering, and compartmentalizing in our defense and intelligence structures.

We must confront the prospect of a defense budget dominated by today's readiness needs and operational requirements, which also allows for response to humanitarian and civil crises. If the United States does not have readiness today, it can cost lives today; if the United States doesn't modernize for tomorrow, that too will cost lives. The danger is that today's needs are being met at the expense of tomorrow's, that we are failing to invest in new technologies that could help shape tomorrow's defense environment, restore effective deterrence, and ward off major catastrophes that directly affect our national interests. Today's crises may be minor compared to those we may face tomorrow.

We need an overall defense investment strategy as we prepare for the possibility of conflict, just as we must have a defense operational strategy when we fight. The investment strategy obviously must deal with readiness, force structure, and modernization—the mix of short- and long-term concerns.

In all of these endeavors, especially at a time of military downsizing, U.S. leaders should also turn for examples and know-how to our greatest success story: a leaner, tougher, more competitive American business sector. Profitable businesses such as Procter & Gamble, Ford, and Johnson & Johnson have worked with outside management firms as well as task forces of their own employees to reduce layering, eliminate faulty work through quality approaches, and maximize competitive advantage.

Professor Michael Porter of Harvard University first wrote on "competitive strategies" in business, and some military reformers have tried, with little success, to incorporate his work into the Defense Department. A blue ribbon advisory panel, composed of successful defense and nondefense corporate leaders, should be formed to ask the challenging questions: how can our entire defense structure and its methodologies be reshaped, and how we can define and multiply our industrially competitive advantages in the military? Unlike the defense establishment, which is tested only infrequently on the battlefield, those fighting the diaper wars, the cola wars, and the generic-versus-brand-label wars compete head-to-head every day all over the world. Hence corporations, especially good ones, are flexible and agile because they constantly deal with the challenge of change in technology and in the marketplace. The advisory panel would address what Norm Augustine, president of Lockheed Martin, noted several years ago:

> The defense procurement process is government by 30,000 pages of regulations issued by 79 different officers with direction provided by 29 congressional committees and 55 subcommittees— all monitored by a force of overseers the size of an army division.[8]

The panel, however, should go far beyond procurement issues and help place the Department of Defense in a more competitive posture through a new defense investment strategy. It is interesting that military leaders talk so much of being good strategists in war—with clear objectives and priorities, economy of effort, multiplier effects, freedom and agility—yet these leaders don't think in terms of a similar strategy of investment in peace.

The secretary of defense's Bottom Up Review (BUR) called for a force structure with the ability to engage in two near-simultaneous regional conflicts while also advancing its capabilities—an ability necessary for a great power. A CSIS study calculates that the BUR force requires approximately 4.5 percent of gross domestic product (GDP) per year in order to remain fully modernized at its planned size. This figure translates into a defense budget of at least $311 billion for FY 1996.[9]

The Clinton administration admitted a $40 billion defense shortfall in meeting BUR targets during 1994. Furthermore, its FY 1996 defense blueprint falls $64 billion short of the CSIS estimate of the full cost of the BUR force.[10] The administration's planning allocates about 3.2 percent of GDP to defense through FY 2001. According to the General Accounting Office, there could be a shortfall in future U.S. defense programs of up to $150 billion by FY 2001.[11] By maintaining the force structure without sufficiently funding research and development and modernization programs, the administration is living off of earlier investments in defense.

What this means is that we are putting off the cost of replacing an obsolescent force structure, even though this cost will be much higher if we wait until the turn of the century. It would appear that near-term force reductions below the BUR plan are warranted in order to finance the needed research and development for future high-tech capabilities that will be necessary after the turn of the century.

While we should spend more on defense, we especially need to spend *better*, because of the near- and long-term defense requirements. Spending better must be the essence of an agile strategy. The United States cannot be agile without a somewhat smaller, but more technologically advanced, force structure beyond the turn of the century. We must give priority to those investments that will help us answer the spectrum of transcentury risks and threats described earlier.

These considerations must all be a part of a new rationalized defense investment strategy. Such a strategy must begin with the defense industrial base. Between fiscal years 1987 and 1993, 940,000 defense workforce jobs were eliminated.[12] There is still vast overcapacity, yet critical technologies are at risk in a harum-scarum reduction. As has been said, "Three full plants are cheaper to operate than six half-empty ones." The government, without inhibiting competition, should encourage mergers and strategic alliances as a way of preserving our defense industrial base.

A second element of a rationalized defense investment strategy is reform of the procurement-acquisition process. With many companies leaving the defense business for the commercial sector, the Defense Department must alter its rigid acquisition practices to allow and encourage access to dual-use technologies. Current archaic regulations require companies to wall off their defense from their nondefense businesses. This cold war rigidity hinders full exploitation of our competitiveness, and it blocks desirable technology flow from the nondefense to the defense side. The Pentagon thus misses out on state-of-the-art dual-use technologies.

A third element of a rationalized defense investment strategy is synergizing the defense industrial capabilities of our prime alliance partners. Greater commonality among defense systems is critical. More cooperation in research and development and production is essential. These are the only ways to ensure that modernization programs are possible for both us and our allies. Otherwise, we will each price ourselves out of the defense market with too many new systems—be they fighter aircraft, tanks, or warships—for too few contracts, thus foregoing the economies of scale essential for cost-effective operations. Such cooperation involves reduction of export control barriers and foreign investment restrictions that impede collaboration. U.S. reform of acquisition regulations and military specifications and standards should include establishing common specifications, standards, and buying practices with our allies.

In fact, given the greatly reduced spending for defense and the current excess industrial capacity in all Western democracies, the political pressure will be in the opposite direction, towards renationalizing defense production. The revolution in military affairs may, however, offer new opportunities for international cooperation among those firms doing high-level systems engineering—work characterized by software applications and interfaces to enable high-tech weaponry to be integrated among allies.

A U.S. defense investment strategy is possible, but only if we have cooperation between the executive and legislative branches, and encourage cooperation with our alliance partners. Otherwise, we will continue to spend more and get less—violating the principle of economy of effort and hindering an overall strategy of agility.

Indeed, it is impossible to develop a truly agile strategy without congressional reform in which we streamline the cumbersome system that demands duplicate hearings, other redundancies, compartmentalization, and micromanagement. Better budget reviews, an integration of committees, and some new mechanism, possibly a joint steering committee on emergency response, are necessary. The proposed committee could cut across Intelligence, State, Defense, and Commerce committees in emergency situations. The executive branch should likewise form a version of such a committee to increase its own ability to respond to crises. (It took six months or more of fumbling for the government to decide how to pay for removing nuclear material from

Kazakhstan.) We cannot afford to have the executive and legislative branches remain as notoriously lacking in agility as they are today.

Eight: Capitalizing on the Technological Revolution

In seeking to enhance a strategy of agility, we should look at relevant lessons from the past. For example, the 1920s was a time of far greater downsizing of military forces than today. It was also a tragic time, when the democracies failed to capitalize on a military-technological revolution. In the immediate post-World War I period, the United States perceived no major threats. Germany had been soundly defeated, Japan had been an ally, and we had just signed a naval limitation treaty with Britain and Japan. In the United States, military innovation ceased, and both the United States and Britain eliminated their tank corps. (Tanks had first been employed successfully by the innovative British colonel and military historian, J. F. C. Fuller, at the Battle of Cambrai in November 1917.) The U.S. told tank experts Colonel George Patton and Colonel Fuller to go back to the horse cavalry and polo playing.

Germany, in accordance with the Versailles Treaty, was forced to downsize its army to one hundred thousand men, and was not permitted to possess an air force. In the Weimar Republic, General von Seekt turned to quality, mobility, and combined arms. By the mid-1930s, Hitler's Reich had married air power with armor, and in May 1940, with forces generally inferior to the French, the German blitzkrieg knifed through the French defenses in the Ardennes and reached the channel in ten days. The generals of the blitzkrieg had wrought a military revolution while the Americans, French, and British slept. A military revolution, therefore, usually involves not just a single new technology, but a new way of military thinking and combat organization as well. The United States needs to organize a military revolution in planning and in operations to exploit our technological advantages, and we need creative military reformers like Fuller and Patton to lead this revolution.

With the end of World War II, atomic weapons were perceived as the key element of the new military revolution, but today, missiles and "smart" weapons have, to some extent, rendered nuclear weapons obsolete. Precision-guided munitions are both more accurate and more practical. They also offer great potential deterrent capability. In Europe, for example, two military features key to the NATO triumph over the Soviets were attributable to a technological revolution but were driven largely by an information revolution. One feature was the Strategic Defense Initiative (SDI), which was strategic in fact as well as in name, because the Soviets could not have matched it technologically, and because, once deployed, it would have worked to nullify their nuclear striking power. Whether or not SDI was deployable is now beside the point because of the effect it had on our opponent in creating a calculus of risk.

The second feature was tactical, involving the planned or actual deployment of U.S. conventional battlefield information technologies such as infrared vision, stealth capability, and overhead platforms—such as the space-based Global Positioning System (GPS) and the Joint Strategic Airborne Reconnaissance System (J-STARS)—along with a range of precision-guided munitions. The combination of these information technologies would have reversed the Warsaw Pact's conventional superiority in Europe had it maintained its position, but as the Soviet marshals began to recognize the imminence of a precision information revolution in which they could not compete, they grew more willing to accept Gorbachev's grand turnabout. Our new systems led to a triumph of power, not force, because Gorbachev was persuaded to change course without a shot fired on either side.

One irony is that the weapons developed for NATO to confront the Warsaw Pact were the very weapons that facilitated the triumph over the Iraqis in the Gulf War. Secretary of Defense William Perry, who was in on the ground floor of this information revolution in the late 1970s but who lacks the funds to activate it fully today, argues that a major part of our technological thrust in this next decade is going to lie in applications of the dramatic developments in information technology, because the power of the microprocessor is not only driving civilian industries in our country; it has the potential to drive developments in the Defense Department as well. I say potential not because we are not using information technology, but because we are not using it to anywhere near its full capabilities. I believe that the scientists and the engineers, who were the heroes of the cold war, will again have the opportunity to be heroes in this new era.[13]

Potentially, robotics can have as profound an effect on the art of war as did the tank. Unfortunately, the same conservatism that hindered the adoption of the tank could likewise slow the utilization of robotics and other promising information technologies. Information systems hold great promise, but without fortified safeguards they are also vulnerable to penetration and manipulation by an adversary. Furthermore, too much reliance on these systems (removing the human element) could paralyze our strategic response. On the political level, it is important, and indeed possible, to develop strong bipartisan support for such advances and safeguards if we are to achieve our agile strategy.

Nine: Countering Ballistic Missiles

In our defense investment strategy today, we have failed to give priority to countering the coming nuclear-tipped ballistic missile threat, because it is considered too expensive and because of treaty restraints. Our new antiballistic missile (ABM) strategy should encompass several elements: 1) continuing efforts at nonproliferation through the ABM Treaty and its inspection process, while recognizing the obstacles to full success; 2) investing in better capabilities for preemptive actions; and 3) interpreting and renegotiating the cold war ABM Treaty as it applies to theater (localized) missile defense programs (adherence to this treaty was responsible for the lower accuracies of Patriot missiles in the Gulf War). We should upgrade Patriot, go ahead with the Theater High Altitude Area Defense system, and allow the navy to develop the Aegis combat system into an antiballistic missile system.

Unfortunately, some of the cold war debate on SDI, or "star wars," and its bearing on nuclear deterrence has diverted too many people's attention from the dangers of less sophisticated nuclear devices, as well as from biological and chemical weapons, in the hands of irrational rulers. These are weapons that could threaten our troops worldwide as well as within the continental United States. To counter the latter threat, clearly at some point we should work towards deploying a light area defense of the United States, although we must also bear in mind that no ABM or area defense system can approach being airtight when a Piper Cub or a suitcase can easily get through.

As for our larger strategy, were twelve to seventeen countries to obtain nuclear weapons, with four to six possessing long-range delivery capability, it would be essential to have a global system to detect launch, as well as a defense capability that could knock out these weapons over the launcher's area before they reached the target area. A rigid interpretation of the ABM Treaty is in the interest of neither the United States nor Russia. Here is an excellent opportunity for our defense investment strategy to develop counter-proliferation capabilities, including the all-important strategic overhead, jointly with our allies in NATO and Asia.

We must stress that the lifeblood of the present technological and military revolution is *information*—the commerce of the future. The age-old infantry mission of "find 'em and fix 'em" is today more and more information intensive. What has become most vital is to deny information to the adversary by using nearly unbreakable codes and ciphers (there are no unbreakable codes and ciphers) and enhanced communications capabilities such as fiber optics, secure satellite links, and electronic countermeasures. The ability of the new technology to blind or deceive the enemy is substantial indeed. Our stealth technology is a case in point, and we need to put more effort into this new component, which is ideally suited to an agile strategy.

Defense intelligence can be the greatest beneficiary of the information revolution, but it will need to be restructured if it is to take advantage of both civil and military information advances. The better we are able to collect, process, analyze, and disseminate intelligence, the greater will be our strategic and tactical advantage.

If the United States wants to do more with less—developing true economy of effort while maintaining an effective competitive advantage industrially—it must invest more in research and development. Between fiscal years 1995 and 1999, the Defense Department's research and development funding will undergo a cut of 25.3 percent, making it the most heavily cut segment of the defense budget.[14] Clearly, we are not adequately investing in many areas of advanced research and development, although the information revolution beckons us to do so.

Ten: Leadership, Character, and Education

We have spoken of the use of power—the power to persuade and influence—as compared to the simple use of force. When Napoleon said that the moral is to the physical as three is to one, it showed a keen understanding of this component, one that is psychological but nevertheless real, and, in fact, often decisive.

To create an agile strategy that can address these future contingencies, we must begin with the president. There is no substitute for a president's power, leadership, and capacity to command respect, because, as plainspoken Harry Truman said, it is with the president that the buck stops. In a sense, there is greater demand today for presidential leadership than during the cold war. As the cold war progressed, the strategy and rules of nuclear deterrence became accepted by both sides. The Kremlin and the White House fully understood the potential use of nuclear forces as a deterrent, as well as the catastrophic consequences of nuclear war. Now that we are much more dependent on conventional power, it has become easier, for example, for a Saddam Hussein to misperceive U.S. intentions and military capability. Furthermore, the consequences of conventional war have always been harder to anticipate than those of a nuclear exchange. This is why a more comprehensive doctrine on the use of U.S. power in crisis situations is needed. Yet such a doctrine depends upon presidential articulation and leadership. For example, the full panoply of U.S. power must be magnified wherever possible, with alliance and coalition solidarity brought to bear, as President Bush accomplished so brilliantly in the Gulf War.

Presidential leadership must involve both the accumulation of power and the creation of the necessary organization for its use. Truman was not an intellectual, but he had the right instincts, a keen sense of history, and skilled advisers. The Kremlin knew where he stood. Faced with the threat from our former wartime ally, the Soviet Union, Truman knew he had to organize. At home, the National Security Council (NSC), the CIA, the Defense Department, and the long-range Policy Planning Staff at the State Department were his creations, as were the Marshall Plan and NATO. We must learn from Truman the importance of consistency and the art of institution building—and how to link that art with strategic direction and with the proper orchestration of power and influence.

Truman's successor, General Dwight Eisenhower, the supreme commander of allied forces in Europe during World War II, was the master of process, of how to separate the immediate from the longer term. No other president after him has duplicated his skill in this regard. Eisenhower divided his National Security Council into two parts, an operations section and a planning section, that is, a short-range and long-range section. Each section had an able head and both always met with the president as a team. Eisenhower successfully avoided the tendency to allow immediate crises to overtake long-range strategic interests, and we must learn from him how to achieve this ongoing balance. No subsequent president followed this organizational formula—one that might have prevented our mistakes in Vietnam.

The Eisenhower approach suggests how to organize ourselves for an agile strategy. We need a new defense operations structure that can employ our resources with maximum flexibility and efficiency. We need to acknowledge that we do indeed face a "new world disorder," and that to date we have done a poor job of conceptualizing and organizing to meet the immediate challenges of today's fluid environment. Regrettably, we have stumbled from one intervention to another: Bosnia, Somalia, and Haiti. But these peacemaking and peacekeeping episodes, while distracting, are minor compared to the possible major challenges outlined earlier. We must face the present, but we must also address the needs of the next century. Hence, the classic dilemma mentioned above of balancing the immediate with the long term. It is similar to the current need to confront the elimination of budget deficits and to ensure Social Security solvency after the turn of the century. If we fail to think seriously in terms of decades, in both foreign and domestic areas, our children will reap the whirlwind.

The first institutional change must occur in the NSC machinery, which should be restructured to resemble the Eisenhower model, with the addition of a presidential counselor on long-range strategy. The State, Defense, Treasury, and Commerce Departments should be included in the long-range analysis and planning component of this model, with special side channels reporting to this presidential counselor. The new counselor should work on a post–cold war conceptual framework, addressing our national interests in addition to those common interests we share with like-minded nations. This does not mean constructing some elaborate, rigid architecture for a rapidly changing environment. What it does mean is becoming good at strategy in a classical sense, constantly measuring ends, means, and contingencies while avoiding being surprised, and seeking to shape rather than react to the strategic environment. It means developing criteria for intervention, as Eisenhower did in 1954. It means producing the types of comprehensive annual national security reports that Henry Kissinger produced as national security advisor at a time when global politics had to be reconceptualized. These are all jobs for the counselor, who would be free to think beyond the crises of the day to prevent the crises of tomorrow.

New long-range planning machinery within the NSC must facilitate the building and orchestration of power and influence, with potential force only one of a range of elements at its disposal. It must devise ways for presidential communication of our new strategy and doctrine, which would build our influence worldwide. Yet the machinery must go beyond the traditional dimensions of power by seeking out our comparative advantages. For example, an agile strategy must take into consideration the new world of finance. One trillion dollars circulates through the world's financial markets every twenty-four hours, outside the control of central bankers. It is a clear strategic challenge for senior U.S. policymakers to analyze and incorporate such revolutionary financial dimensions because, in a crisis, these can be defining national security considerations. Perhaps our greatest nonmilitary deterrent capability vis-à-vis attempts by Russia to reestablish its East European hegemony is our financial leverage. The bankrupt Russian state is largely dependent on continued Western financial support, without which Russia might descend into economic chaos.

Organizational changes, however, are finally not paramount. Before Pearl Harbor, the United States had information it failed to use; before Midway, the United States had information it did use. The different outcomes of the two battles illustrate the overriding importance of the human factor, of that which cannot be automated, in national security. Organization alone is no substitute.

The human factor involves competence, leadership, and character. Our military institutions, long the finest in the world, try to teach all three. This chapter has discussed power. In our democracy, power relates to all three. Virtually the only thing the United States did right in the disarmament years of the 1920s and 1930s was to maintain and even enhance its military educational institutions. As superintendent of West Point in the early 1920s, Douglas MacArthur reformed the academy by introducing not only the humanities, but also the formal honor code. The Industrial War College, established in 1924, was the first joint service college that included business leaders. Pearl Harbor was war-gamed at the intellectually thriving Naval War College in 1931, which housed the ghost of the great Alfred Thayer Mahan. Colonel George Marshall innovated tactics at the Infantry School at Fort Benning, where he mentored future top generals. These teachers and students were the inspired men of character who were later involved in the greatest mobilization in human history, and who led the United States and its allies to victory in World War II.

Today, some argue that Officer Candidate School (OCS) and the Reserve Officers' Training Corps (ROTC) can be substituted for the academies and that the advanced institutions can be eliminated. Eliminating the finest military educational system in the world would be shortsighted in the extreme and would jeopardize our future as a nation. Our military education system needs to be reformed and enriched, not reduced or abolished. If we are to keep the standards of OCS and ROTC (the latter having contributed so significantly to the success of our active forces, reserves, and National Guard), then we must have the professional base of education and training that only the service academies provide. At a time when there is such serious discussion of the crisis in the American education system—a system that seeks to impart character in addition to knowledge—it would be folly to weaken or abandon the academies.

Can leadership and character really be taught? Can values be instilled? Plato was convinced that they could. He set up his academy, which endured for centuries, not only to teach philosophy—that is, the love of wisdom—but also to build values and leadership. Our service academies have attempted for more than one hundred years to teach leadership and character.

To be sure, Plato's academy did not always succeed, nor have our modern-day military academies always succeeded. But we also know of Periclean leaders such as West Point–trained General Robert E. Lee, whose impeccable character and military virtue made him the model for generations of military officers. Some may look upon Lee as a purely Southern hero, but actually, he is a national hero. After the Civil War, Lee used his position and his role as a progressive educator at Washington College to help reconcile the nation. Two West Point graduates, Lee and Ulysses S. Grant, began the healing of a nation at Appomattox Courthouse.

In today's armed services, General Edward C. Meyer's concern about a "hollowing out" of military forces involves more than just readiness. It can involve a hollow spirit, a hollow quality of life, and, perhaps most dangerously, hollow leadership. Military history repeatedly teaches us that it is better to have a small force that is well led than a force strong in numbers but weak in leadership. Furthermore, we cannot allow our recent peacekeeping, peacemaking, and humanitarian missions to divert military education and training from their primary mission: producing officers who will fight and win when national interests are at stake. We must neither mute nor dilute the profession of arms.

This returns us to the promise of American life. Competence, leadership, and character are essential, and if these qualities are not instilled in soldiers and civilians alike, there will be little promise for the American way of life. Croly was correct on this score. But now these qualities must be developed to an unprecedented degree because of the speed and complexity of changes that will confront our leaders in the age of agile strategy.

An Agile Strategy

To achieve the new promise of American life in the post–cold war world, the United States needs an agile strategy built on the wise use of power and anchored to our national interests in Europe, the Middle East, and Asia, with clear criteria for any interventions or retaliations abroad. We need to make better use of our defense resources through an investment strategy that capitalizes on the information revolution and aids in missile defense. We must recognize that leadership, competence, and character—in everyone from the commander in chief down through the ranks—are of utmost importance, and that we must nurture those educational institutions that breed such precious attributes.

We must remember that there is simply no country capable of assuming global leadership on the scale of the United States. Frequently, even foreign critics tacitly acknowledge the critical need for American leadership in maintaining world stability and an effective balance of power. Our values—those of the Declaration of Independence and of the Constitution, those of Washington and Lincoln, are admired and imitated worldwide.

If the United States is destined to lead, rather than merely exist in a world of chaos, its national interest and the global interest must come together. Both require that the United States, as the leader, maintain a sense of priority and an economy of effort in addressing any future challenges. When there is no nation to take the United States' place, it is in both the nation's and the world's interest that the United States not squander its power, but retain its ability to construct a strategy for a more peaceful and humane world. If the United States does not, no nation will, and we will bequeath to our children a world of chaos. Lincoln was right: "We are the last, best hope." That is truly the promise of American life, a promise we must uphold and a promise we must be prepared to defend.

Notes

1. Donald Kagan, *On the Origins of War and the Preservation of Peace* (New York: Doubleday, 1994), 567, 573.
2. Arleigh Burke, "Power and Peace," a Walter E. Ledge lecture at Princeton University, 1962, quoted in James Allen Smith, *Strategic Calling: The Center for Strategic and International Studies, 1962–1992* (Washington, D.C.: The Center for Strategic and International Studies, 1993), 11.

3. Edward Luttwak, *The Grand Strategy of the Roman Empire* (Baltimore: Johns Hopkins University Press, 1976), 196–97.

4. United States Congress, Office of Technology Assessment, *Proliferation in the Former USSR* (Washington, D.C.: U.S. Government Printing Office, September 1994).

5. Zbigniew Brzezinski, "A Plan for Europe," *Foreign Affairs* 74 (January/February 1995). Henry Kissinger, "Expand NATO Now," *Washington Post*, December 19, 1994, A27.

6. Weinberger said that the United States should commit combat forces overseas only 1) in support of vital interests; 2) if the commitment is wholehearted and reflects an intention to win; 3) where we have clearly defined political and military objectives; 4) if we are willing to reassess continually the relationship between our objective and our involved forces; 5) when we have a reasonable assurance of support from the Congress and the American people; and 6) as a last resort ("The Uses of Military Power," remarks at National Press Club, Washington, D.C., November 28, 1984).

7. Without this, our interventions will merely prop up countries that will collapse following our withdrawal.

8. Norman Augustine, "High Noon," remarks at National Press Club, Washington, D.C., June 7, 1994.

9. Stephen Cambone, Daniel Gouré, and Don Snider, *Defense in the Late 1990s: Avoiding the Train Wreck* (Washington, D.C.: The Center for Strategic and International Studies, 1995), 18.

10. Ibid., ii.

11. U.S. General Accounting Office, *Future Years Defense Program: Optimistic Estimates Lead to Billions in Overprogramming* (Washington, D.C.: U.S. Government Printing Office, July 1994).

12. Norman Saunders, "Employment Effects of the Rise and Fall in Defense Spending," *Monthly Labor Review* 10 (April 1993).

13. William Perry, remarks at Global Air and Space 1994 International Forum, Crystal City, Virginia, May 5, 1994.

14. This information is from a Department of Defense FY 1995 budget briefing, Washington, D.C., February 2, 1994.

Index

About the Authors

David M. Abshire cofounded the Center for Strategic and International Studies and currently serves as its president. He is a graduate of West Point and was decorated for service as a front-line commander in the Korean War. He served as assistant U.S. secretary of state, was the first chairman of the U.S. Board for International Broadcasting, and was a member of the president's Foreign Intelligence Advisory Board. He was ambassador to NATO and received the Presidential Citizen's Medal as well as the highest Defense Department civilian award, the Distinguished Public Service Medal. In 1987, Dr. Abshire served as special counsel to President Reagan. He is the author of four books, including *Preventing World War III: A Realistic Grand Strategy* and *Foreign Policy Makers: President vs. Congress.*

Lamar Alexander has been governor of Tennessee, president of the University of Tennessee, and U.S. secretary of education. He is a senior fellow and chairman of "The New Promise of American Life" project at Hudson Institute. He was codirector of Empower America and cofounder of The Republican Neighborhood Meeting, a satellite television network that connects Republican gatherings across the country each month. He is the author of three books and numerous articles. Mr. Alexander lives in Nashville, where he is counsel to the Baker, Donelson, Bearman, and Caldwell law firm.

Howard H. Baker, Jr., has been a U.S. senator (the first Republican ever popularly elected to the U.S. Senate from Tennessee), President Reagan's chief of staff, and vice chairman of the Senate Watergate Committee. He has been the keynote speaker at the Republican National Convention and a presidential candidate. Senator Baker also served three years in the U.S. Navy during World War II. He was a delegate to the United Nations and served on the president's Foreign Intelligence Board. He has received the Presidential Medal of Freedom and the Jefferson Award for Greatest Public Service Performed by an Elected or Appointed Official. He is also a noted photographer and author of three books: *No Margin for Error, Howard Baker's Washington,* and *Big South Fork Country.*

Philip M. Burgess is president of the Center for the New West, an independent, market-oriented, nonprofit think tank in Denver, Colorado. Dr. Burgess taught public policy and management at Ohio State University, where he was Mershon Professor of Policy Sciences, and the University of Colorado; he also served as executive director of the Federation of Rocky Mountain States and president of the Western Governors' Policy Office. He is the author or coauthor of numerous books and articles, including *New Choices in a Changing America* and *Profile of Western North America.* He writes a weekly column on political and economic issues for the *Rocky Mountain News* and Scripps Howard News Service.

John J. DiIulio, Jr., is a professor of politics and public affairs at Princeton University, nonresident senior fellow in the Governmental Studies Program at the Brookings Institution, and director of the Brookings Center for Public Management. He has authored, coauthored, and edited several books, including *No Escape: The Future of American Corrections* and *Governing Prisons: A Comparative Study of Correctional Management.* Dr. DiIulio is a member of the National Commission on the State and Local Public Service and has served as a consultant to federal, state, and local governments on public management and criminal justice issues.

Chester E. Finn, Jr., is John M. Olin Fellow at Hudson Institute, where he directs "The New Promise of American Life" project and cochairs the Educational Excellence Network. He is also professor of education and public policy at Vanderbilt University (on leave). He served as assistant U.S. secretary of education from 1985 to 1988. Dr. Finn is the author of nine books, including *We Must Take Charge: Our Schools and Our Future* and *What Do Our Seventeen-Year-Olds Know?* (with Diane Ravitch), and numerous articles and essays on education.

Francis Fukuyama is a senior researcher at the RAND Corporation and has recently completed a book titled *Trust: The Art of Association in the Creation of Economic Prosperity,* to be published by Free Press in 1995. He is also a consultant to the Policy Planning Staff of the U.S. State Department. In 1992, he won the *Los Angeles Times'* Book Critics Award for *The End of History and the Last Man.* His articles on foreign affairs, democracy, immigration, and other topics have appeared in *Commentary,* the *New Republic,* the *National Interest,* the *American Spectator,* and a number of national newspapers. [Note: The views expressed in this book are the author's own and do not reflect those of the RAND Corporation or its sponsors.]

Michael S. Joyce is president and chief executive officer of the Lynde and Harry Bradley Foundation in Milwaukee, Wisconsin. Prior to his association with the Bradley Foundation, Dr. Joyce was for seven years executive director and trustee of the John M. Olin Foundation in New York City. He has been a teacher of history and political science at the secondary school and college levels, and is contributing editor to a textbook series in the social sciences and is the author of numerous research studies and articles. He is chairman of the Philanthropy Roundtable and serves on the boards of a variety of civic and charitable organizations.

William Kristol is chairman of the Project for the Republican Future. He served as chief of staff to the vice president of the United States from 1989 to 1993, and was chief of staff to U.S. Education Secretary William Bennett from 1985 to 1988. Before moving to Washington, Dr. Kristol taught at Harvard University's John F. Kennedy School of Government and the University of Pennsylvania.

Frank I. Luntz is president of the Luntz Research Companies, Inc., and an adviser to Congressman Newt Gingrich. *Time* magazine recently named Dr. Luntz "a rising star" in America. Some of Dr. Luntz's clients have included Mayor Rudy Giuliani of New York, Ross Perot, Governor Pedro Rossello of Puerto Rico, the Reform Party of Canada, the British Broadcasting Company, the *New York Post*, the *Wall Street Journal*, *Newsweek*, ABC News, and PBS. He is an adjunct assistant professor at the University of Pennsylvania.

James Nuechterlein is editor of *First Things: A Monthly Journal of Religion and Public Life* and associate director of the Institute on Religion and Public Life in New York. He has also served as professor of American studies at Valparaiso University. His articles on American history, political thought, and culture have appeared in the *American Scholar, Commentary, National Review,* and many other journals.

Diane Ravitch is a senior research scholar and adjunct professor of education at New York University and nonresident senior fellow at the Brookings Institution. From 1991 to 1993, she served as assistant U.S. secretary of education for research and improvement, and counselor to the secretary at the U.S. Department of Education. She is the author of six books, including *National Standards in American Education,* and has edited eight books, including *The American Reader* and *The Democracy Reader* (with Abigail Thernstrom).

Carolynn Reid-Wallace is senior vice president for education at the Corporation for Public Broadcasting. Previously, she served as assistant secretary of education for postsecondary education at the U.S. Department of Education. Dr. Reid-Wallace also served as vice chancellor for academic affairs at the City University of New York. She has been a Rockefeller scholar, Ford fellow, Fulbright lecturer, and professor of English and dean of the college at Bowie State College in Maryland.

Alan Reynolds is director of economic research and senior fellow at Hudson Institute. He was formerly chief economist with Polyconomics in New Jersey and vice president of the First National Bank of Chicago. Mr. Reynolds is a frequent contributor to the *Wall Street Journal, Forbes, National Review,* and the *Washington Times,* as well as the semiannual *Wall Street Journal* survey of economic forecasts. Mr. Reynolds's research at Hudson Institute has covered topics such as the conditions attached to IMF loans to Third World countries, the politics and economics of NAFTA, and U.S. tax and budget policies.

William A. Schambra is director of general programs at the Lynde and Harry Bradley Foundation in Milwaukee, Wisconsin. Previously, Dr. Schambra held senior positions at the U.S. Department of Health and Human Services and the U.S. Department of Justice. He was codirector of constitutional studies and director of social policy studies at the American Enterprise Institute. He is the editor or coeditor of seven volumes, and is the author of dozens of articles and essays on political theory, constitutional law, and public opinion, among other subjects.

William A. Schreyer is chairman emeritus of Merrill Lynch & Co., Inc., and has previously been chairman of the board and chief executive officer. He has also served as vice chairman of the board of the New York Stock Exchange and was a leader of stock exchange delegations to the former Soviet Union and to the People's Republic of China. Currently, Mr. Schreyer is a director of Callaway Golf Company, Deere & Company, True North Communications Inc., Schering-Plough Corporation, and Willis Corroon Group. He is chairman of the board of trustees of his alma mater, Pennsylvania State University. He served as an officer in the U.S. Air Force from 1955 to 1956.

Robert A. Sirico is the president and founder of the Acton Institute for the Study of Religion and Liberty. His pastoral ministry has included a chaplaincy to AIDS patients at the National Institutes of Health in addition to his current position as minister of reconciliation at the Catholic Information Center. Father Sirico's writings have been published in numerous journals, including the *Wall Street Journal, Forbes,* the *London Financial Times,* and the *Washington Times.* He has also contributed to five books. In 1990 he was inducted into the Mont Pelerin Society. He was recently appointed to the Michigan Civil Rights Commission by Governor John Engler.

Abigail Thernstrom is a senior fellow at the Manhattan Institute and an adjunct professor at the School of Education, Boston University. Her book, *Whose Votes Count? Affirmative Action and Minority Voting Rights ,* won four awards, including the Anisfield-Wolf Book Award for the best book on race and ethnicity in 1987. She is a member of the Aspen Institute's Domestic Strategy Group and serves on the boards of the Manhattan Institute's Center for the New American Community, the Institute for Justice, and the Women's Freedom Network. She has been a stringer for the *Economist* and writes frequently for a variety of journals and newspapers.

Stephan Thernstrom is the Winthrop Professor of History at Harvard University. He has also taught at Brandeis University, UCLA, Cambridge University, and Trinity College. He has held fellowships from the Guggenheim Foundation, the American Council of Learned Societies, and the Olin Foundation. He is the author of four books, including *A History of the American People* and *Poverty and Progress: Social Mobility in the Nineteenth Century City,* and the editor of one. His books have been awarded various prizes and awards. He and his wife, Abigail, are currently writing a book on race relations in the United States since World War II.

Paul Weyrich is president of the Free Congress Foundation and founder and chief executive officer of National Empowerment Television, a twenty-four-hour public affairs network seen across the country on local cable and broadcast stations and via satellite. Mr. Weyrich also served as the founding president of the Heritage Foundation and founded the American Legislative Exchange Council. The current publisher of the *Political Report* and *Empowerment,* he served as a columnist, senior editor, and copublisher of the *Conservative Digest* in the 1980s.

About Hudson Institute

Hudson Institute is a private, not-for-profit research organization founded in 1961 by the late Herman Kahn. Hudson analyzes and makes recommendations about public policy for business and government executives, as well as for the public at large. The institute does not advocate an express ideology or political position. However, more than thirty years of work on the most important issues of the day has forged a viewpoint that embodies skepticism about the conventional wisdom, optimism about solving problems, a commitment to free institutions and individual responsibility, an appreciation of the crucial role of technology in achieving progress, and an abiding respect for the importance of values, culture, and religion in human affairs.

Since 1984, Hudson has been headquartered in Indianapolis, Indiana. It also maintains offices in Washington, D.C.; Madison, Wisconsin; Montreal, Canada; and Brussels, Belgium.